KANT'S POLITICAL THOUGHT

HANS SANER

Kant's Political Thought

Its Origins and Development

Translated by E. B. Ashton

The University of Chicago Press

CHICAGO AND LONDON

TO GERTRUD AND KARL JASPERS

Originally published in German as *Kants Weg vom Krieg zum Frieden,*
vol. 1: *Widerstreit und Einheit: Wege zu Kants politischem Denken,*
© R. Piper & Co. Verlag, München 1967 ·

The University of Chicago Press, Chicago 60637
The University of Chicago Press, Ltd., London
© 1973 by The University of Chicago
All rights reserved. Published 1973
Printed in the United States of America
International Standard Book Number: 0–226–73475–7
Library of Congress Catalog Card Number: 73–77627

CONTENTS

NOTE ON SOURCES

In this translation, as in the German original, Kant's works (except for *Critique of Pure Reason,* see below) are cited from the Akademie edition (Berlin, 1900 —). The first figure refers to the work (see Register of Kant's Works, pp. 357–63), followed by volume and page number. If the page number is followed by a semicolon and another number, this indicates the respective "reflection" in the Kantian fragments collected in 71–73, 75, 78, 79, 81, and 83–85 of the Akademie edition.

Critique of Pure Reason is cited (with A indicating the first printing, B the second) from the edition in Philosophische Bibliothek, vol. 37a (Hamburg, 1956).

Kant's correspondence (L) is cited from the second edition, by number, date, and correspondent, without volume number.

The sources of lecture texts cited from transcriptions not yet included in the Akademie edition appear in the respective notes.

In the Register of Kant's Works the main English versions now in print are listed following the German titles, but the translations of Kantian texts in this volume are mine. Dr. Saner seldom quotes Kant's lengthy sentences in their entirety; he usually lifts phrases or clauses out of the original prose and works them in quotation marks into his own, making any consistent use of existing translations impossible. The principal ones have been taken into consideration insofar as they were reconcilable with Dr. Saner's text. Readers familiar with them should have no trouble finding any passage cited, and if the English renderings differ from mine, the very difference may further the comprehension of what Kant's own wordings mean.

E. B. A.

PREFACE

Politics is based on reason. It begins with the use of reason, not with the political act. What we think, and how, has political consequences. It was this insight of the Greeks which Kant recaptured originally, and which he expressed, as Plato and Aristotle had before him, in the unity of politics, education, and metaphysics. His political thinking is part of the great tradition of Western political philosophy; it is one of the peaks of that tradition.

To understand it, we have to go to the roots of Kant's philosophizing. The substance of his political philosophy stems from his basic metaphysical posture. Its thought forms move in the categories he had long been using to unlock the world's phenomenal existence. From the outset, his philosophy as a whole is also a political philosophy.

To demonstrate this takes documentation. I offer it in two volumes. The first is a book of preparation for Kant's political thought; the presentation and exegesis of that thought will be reserved for the second.

The present volume might seem to be a sort of introduction to Kant. It makes no such claim, although its themes are indeed comprehensive. In the first part the early works are searched for thought forms which later came to be filled with political contents. In the second, the forms and functions of literary struggle (polemics) in the history of Kantian thought are analyzed and linked with the forms and functions of political struggle in the history of mankind. The third part shows a basic feature of Kantian metaphysics: the thesis that all things in the world come from struggle and turn toward peace. The vinculum of these three different paths to Kant's politics is the common tension of contrariety and unity.

Every step on these paths is demonstrable by Kantian thoughts. Contexts of which Kant himself was not fully aware are pointed out now and then, but always on the ground of Kantian rudiments. This book seeks to lay the foundation for an exegesis of Kant's political thought that can dispense with preconceived guidelines from elsewhere.

Particular thanks are due to Professor H. A. Salmony for the patient sympathy with which he followed the gradual progress of my work, and for the help he gave wherever required. His seminars, in which large parts of it were discussed, helped to create the space in which the work could come into being.

Basel, 22 April 1967   Hans Saner

INTRODUCTION

In some respects, Kant's political ideas are located at the periphery of his work. It was not until late in the seventh and chiefly in the eighth decade of his life that they were put into cohesively written form,[1] and the space they occupy in his writings is infinitesimal: between 1½ and 5 percent, depending upon the scope accorded to the word "political."[2] Except for a few references and two short expositions,[3] hardly any of Kant's political thinking got into the three Critiques; he scattered it in installments, as it were, through occasional philosophical writings[4] to which he liked to give an air of accidental play. His *Idea for a Universal History, Cosmopolitan in Intent,* for example, was called an "elucidation" exacted by a brief, all but unintelligible, news item. Of *Reply to the Question, What is Enlightenment?* he said that as Mendelssohn had already spoken on the theme, he was publishing it only to "try to see . . . whether chance might lead to an accord of thoughts";[5] of *Presumable Beginnings of Human History,* that he was venturing "on a pure pleasure trip . . . for the recreation and health of the mind"; and of *The End of All Things,* that he was playing with ideas "partly pitiful, partly cheerful to read."[6] His most important political treatise, perhaps, and the only one whose title is political in the strict sense of the word, the "tract" *Perpetual Peace,* was presented as "reveries,"[7] a collection of "views hazarded at random."[8] Contrary to his strong systematic leanings, Kant had always shrunk from systematizing these seemingly casual thoughts. In 1801, when an unknown professor named Andreas Richter asked permission to disseminate his philosophy "also in the parts on which we have nothing from you as yet—namely, politics as an entire system,"[9] Kant gladly granted the request, pleased to be rid of a task which he himself could no longer have discharged.[10] And as much as eight years earlier he had hoped that outside help would relieve him of the toil on *Doctrine of Law,* the only systematic part of his

I

political philosophy. At the time, Fichte had written to say that his soul was "aglow with a great idea" for solving the problem posed in the *Critique of Pure Reason:* "A constitution of the greatest human freedom under laws"[11] (30: A 316/B 373). As if he had only been waiting to shed this burden, Kant wished Fichte luck: "I should be happy if you were to beat me to this business or, rather, to make my part in it dispensable."[12]

Lack of a system; scant space; late writing (at a time of senility, as some have said);[13] placement outside the main works; non-committal tone—all these moments have resulted in the very modest place assigned to political thought in the history of Kant interpretation.

Other reasons may have contributed. Kant was never active in politics, as Locke, Hume, and Montesquieu had been before him.[14] And after the death of Frederick the Great, when the political authorities began to curtail his literary freedom, Kant let it pass, not without reservations, but in a wholly unheroic posture: "When the world's strong men are in a state of intoxication, a pygmy who values his skin is well advised to stay clear of their quarrels."[15]

For the specific realm of politics in the sense of Gentz and Machiavelli, the arena of the *raison d'état,* Kant had only ridicule and regret. He never worked out a political program which any political movement to date might have justifiably cited. In fact, when the leaders of the French Revolution seemed for a while to be putting critical philosophy to ideological use, Kant, despite several invitations, did nothing to further their purpose.[16] No wonder, then, that history was not too much affected by his political ideas. While Hegel's had virtually directive force for all subsequent thinkers, and those of Marx changed the world, Kant's remained on the sidelines, their originality and topicality always perceived by a few men only.

As we said, this situation is characteristic of the literature on Kant. Serious research into his political thinking took a long time to get underway at all; when at last it did begin, it was as an effort to explain his ideas historically, by the ideas of others. Their many fathers were found,[17] but Kant himself was lost.

By now, of course, we have many publications on the subject, but with few exceptions they are minor works of the "Kant's thoughts about . . ." variety—works based on the tacit premise that their topic is, after all, a peripheral area of critical philosophy. In their metaphysical horizon (not in the horizon of philosophical history) even such major studies as the one by Borries[18] are simply more detailed elaborations within the same limits. The comprehensive Kant interpreters mostly discuss the political ideas only marginally, often on just a few pages.[19] The great exception is Karl Jaspers.[20] Besides granting relatively hyperdimensional space to those ideas (about one-fourth of his Kant exegesis), he crucially stressed their significance by weighing them against the whole of Kantian metaphysics. For the first time, justice was done to their metaphysical rank.

Our own approach to Kant's political thought rests on the view that in a sense it is the heart of his philosophizing. In principle, proof of this view can be offered from two sides. We can look at the material contents of the thought, or we can look at the formal thought structures. In this book we have chosen the second procedure, because it seemed to us that formal inquiry takes precedence over material inquiry and must define the fundamentals of material exegesis. We are aware, of course, that in a discussion of formal aspects the material ones cannot be excluded, and that an elaboration of the form always presupposes an understanding of the contents.

Our interpretation was guided by the following reflections. The circle of problems central to political thought can be circumscribed in Kant's phrase "the way to peace." He starts politics moving, advances it, and sets its goal. We look for his originality, not in a first statement of political thoughts and opinions, but in the homogenous relation of these thoughts to his thinking as a whole. We therefore cannot approach them from outside, as happens in the history of ideas, for example. We have to reach them from within. By "from within" we mean from the Kantian system and from the thought form, from within the thoughts.

We have tried to pursue these reflections in the following manner. "Way to peace" is a figure of speech that encompasses the "war/peace" dualism, which in turn points to such other dualisms as repulsion/attraction, motion/rest, chaos/order, diversity/unity, difference/identity. For a start, these take us to Kant's early natural-scientific and metaphysical writings. In their area, we shall in part I find the thought forms, the concept formations, the evolutionary processes which later acquire material contents of a political nature, and we shall arrange them so as to draw attention to the typical course of Kantian metaphysics. Here it can already be seen that antagonism has the predominant function of impelling to a unity which is completely attainable only in the idea.

In part 2 we shall inquire into the significance of struggle in the development of Kantian thought. Kant will emerge as a polemicist, a fighter for metaphysical goals—though not yet for political goals. The discussion will be partly historical, but it will serve the formal inquiry proper by making it clear that struggle was the motor of advancement even in the history of Kantian thought.

In part 3, the forms of antagonism in critical metaphysics and the ways of bringing them to unity will be investigated in the fields of speculative reason, of practical reason, and of judgment; we shall contemplate their common features and point out the recurrence of these features in political philosophy. This part will uncover the transcendental reasons for struggle and will indicate at the same time in how profound a sense Kant is a peacemaker in metaphysics.

We hope to show in this first volume that Kant's political thinking is suggested throughout his work, that it is an organic outgrowth of that work. As the basic problem of Kantian thought proves time and again to be the turn from diversity to unity, we may see its most concrete unfoldment in political thinking. In this sense we regard the political thinking as original and central.

While in some respects, as we said at the beginning, Kant's political ideas occupy the periphery of his work, this does not mean that they are peripheral ideas.[21]

PART ONE

ORIGINS OF
POLITICAL THOUGHT FORMS

I note in passing that the great contrariety among
things of the world—considering the frequent occasion they give for similarities, analogies, parallels,
or whatever else we want to call them—does not
deserve to be so very casually overlooked (17: II,
132).

The purpose of the first part of this book is not to prove that all
of Kant's political ideas are somehow implicit in his early writings. Such an absolutizing statement would be untrue. But it can
be demonstrated that the forms of certain basic political concepts
or thoughts are discoverable in his very first works, and it is these
forms we should like to point out. We shall do so from the points
of view of diversity, of the road to unity, and of unity. Initially
this arrangement may be regarded as a mere ordering schema.
As the work progresses, it will turn out to be typical of the
course of Kantian metaphysics.

I. DIVERSITY

*Antagonism in the Concept of Monads and
in the Concept of Unsociable Sociality*

In his second dissertation, *Monadologia physica*,[1] Kant develops for the first time the theory of a dynamic concept of matter. The fulfillment of space, according to that theory, lies not in a purely static simultaneous presence of atoms but in the continuous conflict of spatially active monads. This was not demonstrable for an empiricist, a natural scientist; it could be proved only by a metaphysician, a philosopher of nature. Obliged to accept confrontation with the maxim of all natural scientists, *"Hypotheses non fingo,"* he could counter with a line of his own: *"Ex hac sane via leges naturae exponere profecto possumus, legum originem et causas non possumus"* (10: 1, 475; in this way we can indeed expound the laws of nature, but not the origins and causes of these laws).

Kant conceives the monads as simple substances not composed of multiple parts that might exist individually and separately.[2] They are interrelated, and together they constitute matter.[3] But this does not mean that they themselves are material. Their inner being is nonspatial; it is by their effects that they replenish space. They are nonspatial centers of forces whose sphere of action lies in space. That is to say: they are not spatial in themselves; they are spatial only for each other. Space is the form of their coexistence and coefficiency.

The single monad, in the realm in which it is effective, keeps others from penetrating it.[4] This power of resistance is a repelling energy which Kant (not without some hesitation) calls "impermeability."[5] By itself, that energy would not be able to provide bodies with a clearly delimited space. A counterforce, attraction, must work against the action of impermeability. In their conflict, the two basic forces establish the limits of expansion.[6]

This means that the purely passive repletion of space with inert matter *(materia iners)* is abandoned. Taking its place is a twofold conflict of forces: the conflict of the opposing active modes of *one* energy center, and the conflict of different energy centers acting upon each other. Every physical thing, the way it appears in space, at rest and devoid of tension, is purely accidental and already a subjective human product. The substantial side of matter lies behind materiality; it is made up of the energy centers which generate the incessant conflict *within* matter. Everything material is thus in contention and in motion.

What matters to us is the conception of the monad as a unit in which two basic forces counteract one another and achieve the right effect only in union—and achieve it not just for the single monad, but for the coexistence of multiple monads. For we believe that we find this conception again, almost thirty years later, in a central political concept of Kant's: in that of "unsociable sociality."

In *Idea for a Universal History,* published in 1784, Kant attributes to society a structure very similar to that of matter. He endows man—the social monad, so to speak—with an "unsociable sociality" (43: VIII, 20), a seemingly paradoxical disposition in which two basic drives collide: one toward association, and the other toward individualization. The tendency to associate is man's natural political component. Thanks to it, man attracts his fellow men and feels attracted to them. Counteracting this drive toward socialization is the equally natural egotistic drive toward self-preservation, aimed at isolation in particularity. If man had nothing but the social drive in him, he would dissolve in the mass, abandoning all his individuality and activity; if he had nothing but the individual drive in him, his barbarian isolation could not but make the formation of any society impossible. The interplay of forces, their antagonism, has a useful effect: the individual wants to be associated, but so as not to give up the individuality of which he will first assure himself by crude means; and he wants to be himself, but so as to hold himself available for association at the same time.

The cultural significance of this interplay of proximity and distance will be discussed later. At this point it is enough to find the concept of unsociable sociality, which is the motor of politics, clearly outlined in the thirty-year-old concept of the monad. Kant borrowed it from Kant, and from nobody else.[7]

Subsequently, by the way, the antagonism of the physical monad proved fruitful in pure practical philosophy as well. If we are asked to consider the relations of rational beings in the intelligible world, we can do it only by analogies to the physical world. We therefore think of these relations as the effects, so to speak, of attraction and repulsion—in other words, of mutual love, which seeks union, and of respect, which commands distance. Only in their interplay will the two forces jointly create a proximity which nonetheless grants freedom, and a distance which nonetheless permits participation. (The concept that would unify both forces is lacking here, of course, and the analogy is thus not wholly conclusive.[8])

How do we justify our assumption that this parallel formation of two concepts did not happen by mere chance—that after thirty years and a complete aboutface in his philosophizing, Kant knew very well what he was doing? The systematic arguments supporting the assumption, and the Kantian utterances that strengthen it to the point of certainty, will be discussed in detail at the end of this chapter. Here we mention only two pieces of historical evidence.

In the course of his academic career Kant probably taught twenty-one four-hour classes on theoretical physics,[9] fifteen as an assistant and six as a full professor. We know from Gerhard Lehmann's published edition of the lectures,[10] and previously from Erich Adickes,[11] that they were couched in the most elementary terms. Kant introduced his students to the simple, basic physical relations without presupposing a thing, but in universally appealing fashion. He gave these lectures also in the summer terms of 1781, 1783, and 1785—during the period, that is, when his *Idea for a Universal History* was written and published. He no longer mentioned the physical monads in the lectures, but he did discuss his dynamic concept of matter.[12] The concept was definitely on his mind in 1784.

We find additional confirmation in his *Metaphysical Foundations of Natural Science*. Kant published this in 1786, but he had been working on it for some length of time. *Idea for a Universal History* was written while he was intensively engaged in studying the concept of matter, a concept which had meanwhile undergone material changes without a dent being made in its formal structure.

After the fourth dissertation[13] Kant parts with the theory of monads. Henceforth, matter is inertly phenomenal. It cannot be reduced to a simple absolute, no more than any phenomenon;

like space itself, it is infinitely divisible.[14] But the dynamic concept of matter as such is maintained by Kant throughout the critical period.

In *Metaphysical Foundations* we find matter defined, for dynamism's sake, as "that which is mobile insofar as it fills a space" (33: IV, 496). To "fill a space" means here to resist any other mobile thing whose own motion would cause it to invade the mobile matter. The resistance of matter is offered, not to a mechanical motion that would dislodge it, but to an outside attempt to diminish its own proper space.

Matter does not fill space by just being there, devoid of force and tension, but "by a special moving force" (33: IV, 497). But we can conceive only two original moving forces of matter: one that "can cause others to approach it (or, which is the same, can resist when others move away from it)," and a second force, "whereby a piece of matter can cause others to move away from it (or, which is the same, can resist when others approach it)" (33: IV, 498). The first is the power of attraction; the second is the power of repulsion. Kant also calls them the pulling and driving forces.

Neither force is able to limit itself. If there were the driving force only, matter could not but disperse in infinity; space would become all but empty. And the pulling force, working alone, would be bound to contract matter in a mathematical point, and there to cause an unimaginable process of self-permeation. Space would become a complete void. Each force necessitates the counterforce. Their conflict is the premise of the inner possibility of matter as such (cf. 33: IV, 498 ff.).[15]

Inevitably, the critical concept of matter is without recourse to absolute unity; but antagonism continues to be the proper core of matter. The analogy to unsociable sociality is unmistakable.

The last question that remains unanswered is how to interpret this analogy.

The parallel between the early physical concept and the political one of a later date does not permit the rash conclusion that Kantian politics rests on a natural-scientific base.[16] The concept of matter as such was no scientific feat as yet. It was neither found by direct research nor subject to scientific testing. Instead, it was a metaphysical hypothesis whose fertility for cosmogony gave it a scientific vindication. It had to be systematically fertilized before it could show Kant's essentially scientific way of thinking.

The parallelism will therefore be circumscribed with due caution, as follows: a metaphysical basic concept of the philosophy
of nature rests upon a conceptual structure that was later filled
with the contents of a metaphysical politics. The concept of
unsociable sociality was formed in analogy to the early concept
of monads.

The Function of Antagonism in Nature and History

In his *Universal Natural History and Theory of the Heavens,* the
youthful Kant drafts a picture of the Creation considerably at
variance with the biblical myth. He too assumes a creator,[17] for
without an act of some sort it is downright incomprehensible
how something should come out of nothingness. The "natural
substance" (4: 1, 310) or, as it is called elsewhere, the "elementary
basic substance" (4: 1, 263) had to be "created" (4: 1, 310). But
the passage from nothingness to a state "that can follow upon
nothingness" (4: 1, 263) must not be too substantially conceived as
a divine act. Kant phrases it warily: the basic substance is "a
direct consequence of divine existence" (4: 1, 310), and its nature
is a consequence of "the eternal idea of the divine intellect" (4: 1,
263). The basic substance, its character, and the first state of the
world are thus directly related to God without the necessity of
feigning a tangible knowledge about the source of creation.[18]

There is no explaining how the existence of God makes possible the existence of matter and its immanent basic laws; but it is
in this creation of the possibility that the direct act of God
consists. Thereafter, all his works are indirect. Matter is now
active due to the antagonism of its basic forces, and God works
through these forces insofar as he enables them to exist. Any
direct intervention of God in the law of those forces is unthinkable. It would be a divine act against the divine intellect—a
monstrosity.[19]

While matter and its basic forces of attraction and repulsion
may thus be presupposed, everything else in cosmogony must be
explicable by mechanical laws. The process of creation is turned
over to the workings of the dynamic principles inherent in matter.
It will last as long as there is matter. But since the existence of
matter is the result of the existence of God, it must be considered

imperishable. This is why creation is "never finished" (4: 1, 314). The antagonistic energies of matter are ceaselessly at work, building worlds out of the "boundless space of chaos" (4: 1, 235) and letting other worlds fall back into their central suns.

In what may be the most audacious pages Kant ever wrote,[20] he described this gigantic struggle of infinite space with chaos roughly as follows:

Destruction starts out from the mundane bodies nearest to the center of the universe. From there it spreads "gradually farther, so that by the slow decay of motion all of the world that has run its course will in the end be buried in a single chaos" (4: 1, 319). During the process of decay, the scattered elements "at the opposite boundary of the developed world" (4: 1, 319) are condensing, forming new suns, with every developed world thus "confined midway between the ruins of destroyed nature and the chaos of unformed nature" (4: 1, 319).

In smaller cadences, the solar systems contract by loss of motion; in immensely large ones—though still small in view of infinity—the same happens to stellar systems (4: 1, 320 ff.). If we could survey the universe and at the same time see the aeons correspondingly accelerated, the process of creation would be visible in direct motion everywhere; we would see it at work in the decay of the worlds as well as in their new formation. "This is the essence of the structure of the world as a whole: it is eternally becoming" (94: XXI, 138).[21]

The universal struggle that appears in inorganic nature as the conflict of matter and the process of creation can be seen again, in different fashion, in the organic and creatural realms.

Nature shows no mercy to its products. A single cold snap destroys "countless multitudes of flowers and insects" (4: 1, 318). A drop of water is settled by hostile animal species, by "rapacious varieties armed with tools of perdition, which even as they assiduously hunt down others are in turn destroyed by mightier tyrants of this water world" (17: II, 117). Natural disasters will "extirpate whole nations from the earth" (4: 1, 318). There seems to be no peace in nature.

Kant sees something majestic in the idea that all natural things are locked in universal combat: "If I look at the rancor, at the violence, at the riotous scenes in a drop of matter and then lift up my eyes to behold the vastness of space, teeming with worlds as with grains of dust—no human language can express the feelings which this thought evokes in me, and the subtlest metaphysical analysis must yield to the peculiar majesty and dignity of such a view" (17: II, 117 note).

Struggle as such is therefore viewed as no tragedy. For all its cruelty, it is the means of renewal, the creative process. The downfall of a world does not inflict an irreplaceable loss on nature; it is by this sort of waste, rather, that nature demonstrates its surplus of creative vigor. Man "seems to be the masterpiece of creation" (4: I, 318), yet even he cannot escape the natural law. From a cosmological point of view, his destruction is nothing but "a necessary shading in the diversity of its suns" by which nature "adorns" its eternity. This is as true of an individual's death as of the extinction of a species.

Kant adds that it is therefore the part of wisdom to accustom one's eye to all the upheavals of nature, from the end of worlds to the death of individual persons. For all those upheavals are "the ordinary ways of Providence" (4: I, 319). If we consider that what destruction makes so overwhelmingly manifest is the infinity of creation—an infinity so vast it can deal with galaxies as if they were flowers or insects—we may even take "a kind of pleasure" in seeing things perish. Their roles have been played out. It is time for their exits. They are finite, paying their tribute to finiteness. Better things will replace them. Nature wills it so; it is "its rule of proceeding" which applies to great and small alike.

The following observations are important in this context. The warfare we see in nature is the consequence of the antagonism outlined in the dynamic concept of matter. Its proper end is not to destroy but infinitely to expand creation. If we take it for an end in itself, that warfare is destructive; but its function as a means to the ultimate end of creation always involves the destruction of destruction—a creative process. This is its justification. The teleological view of nature projects an element of theodicy into the struggles in nature.

There is an analogy to this in Kant's philosophy of history. In history, the material that must be given is man with his natural endowments. The sort and manner of his endowments is not un-equivocally determinable, but that they are destined to be fully and efficiently developed is certain. Insofar as they are cultural endowments, gifts for civilization and morality, their development is tantamount, so to speak, to the creation of humanity. This creation, unlike the mythical one of man, is conceived not as a singular divine act but as a continuing process in human history. It is the self-creation of mankind, understood as an infinite challenge. The real motivating force to meet the challenge is antagonism, that twofold disposition of unsociable sociality. "The means employed by nature to bring all its gifts to unfoldment is their antagonism in society, provided that this too will eventually turn into a cause of social order under law" (43: VIII, 20).

The first effect of the employment of this means is the war of all against all, with relations between men apparently governed by their passions alone. Then, after necessity has forced individuals to coalesce in civil societies, there will be war between those societies. Viewed in isolation, both types of struggle constitute the truly incriminating evidence against man. Reason forbids their acceptance as ends in themselves, but both of them are rationally understandable as means of nature: the first type as the instinctual spur to action, the stimulus without which progress would not even be a possibility, and the second type as impelling mankind to create itself where the free will to do so is lacking. Thus struggle and war are sublimated in the creative process of intelligible mankind. They are necessary insofar as man is not yet free; they are salutary insofar as humanity would have to decay in sheeplike, stupid bliss or else perish miserably in a violent global despotism; they are justified, finally, insofar as they exist for the sake of lawful accord and general external freedom. Struggle and war are thus not absolutely reprehensible, and not reprehensible in every sense. We can look at the horrors they have caused in human history and still find room for their justification. But since it is a matter of mankind creating itself, this vindication is essentially anthropodicy. It does not rest upon empirical history but on the intelligible destiny of man. This is why it will not let us despair even where the depravity of man is most clearly visible: in war.

We do not go so far at this point as to say that Kant saw nothing but a parallel to natural history in the evolution of intelligible mankind. To find out where he draws the analogy closely and where he breaches it, we would have to trace the two evolutions in exact detail. For the moment, therefore, we are interpreting this particular analogy as a mere analogous *function* of similar concepts in related processes. Antagonism in general expands the natural creative process and advances the human one. The idea of political struggle is thus subject to the same determination by laws as the idea of cosmological struggle in natural philosophy. From the viewpoint of philosophical history this may mean that, to Kant, the great lines of natural history became road signs to the history of freedom. Philosophically, it means that the two distinct realms, united in the same determination by laws, spring from one unknown ground that is more encompassing than either one of them. The analogies point to this ground, but they give us neither its name nor a closer definition.

Here, too, the relation to natural science is unmistakable but must not be overrated. We said before that the formation of the dynamic concept of matter is not a properly scientific achievement, that it belongs to the realm of natural philosophy. We would have to say the same about the function of antagonism. It is a speculative conception, not a scientific discovery; but it is conceived in such a way that it may turn into a guideline for discoveries. It is in those alone that it must prove its scientific character.

In the pursuit of such analogies it is instructive to see not only where they are closely drawn but also where they are breached. If we do not want to regard the breaches as mere arbitrary acts, if we find a consistency in them, they indicate that political thinking evidently feeds also on sources that are, or were, not at work in the thinking of natural science. We look for the breaches in order to get to these sources wherever we can; our aim is not just to find breaches of form. In our set of problems we see two breaches, though neither one concerns the function of antagonism as such.

Kant depicts struggle in nature as a chain of giant upheavals in whose constancy evolution is caught up. Revolution and evolution are not things apart; they are interrelated in such a way that revolution is an evolutionary link and evolution is the permanence of revolution.

In passages of historical philosophy we come upon analogous thoughts now and then—as when Kant says, for example, that as far as intent is concerned, past history constitutes a series of attempts to set up a universal monarchy, but nature, in a sense, will not permit this: once such world empires have grown to a certain size, they will be broken up again by revolutions (36: VI, 34 note). This game, he adds, may go on until chance distributes the world so as to bring it into a certain inner balance, which may serve as a transient basis for a law of nations. Here the revolutions are still part of evolution. They are conceived from the point of view of nature—of nature in the sense not of the totality of phenomena but of an all-directing will that manifests itself in the appearance of nature—and on the hypothesis that this will is rational. The revolutions take their bearings from the laws of nature. The analogy is maintained.

Besides, we encounter it in other fields of Kantian metaphysics —in education, for instance. In the second essay on *Philanthropin*, Kant says that real progress in educational matters is not to be expected of gradual reform, only of a rapid "revolution" (29: II, 449). Similarly, he maintains of mathematics (30: B x f.), of physics, and of the natural sciences (30: B xiii f.) that they became sciences by revolution, and that metaphysics would likewise have to be set on the path of science by "a total revolution" (30: B xxii). Parallel to this turnabout in the way of theoretical thinking is a turnabout in practical thinking for which he calls later. In the first part of *Religion within the Limits of Reason Alone* he asks himself how the perversion of the mutual qualification of duty and tendency might be rescinded. This is downright unintelligible; only one thing is certain: it must be brought about "not by gradual reform . . . but . . . by a revolution in mentality" (36: VI, 47) that will reverse the state of mind radically, "once for all" (38: VII, 57). In all these cases, revolution proves to be an inescapable condition of progress.

Only in the politics of law is the analogy breached. In the state the development of legal relations must not be advanced by revolutions, for these always break the law, and the law cannot be improved by being broken. The legal evolution of the state must do without revolution even if revolution would serve its ends. Kant prefers tyranny to anarchy, for the injustice of a tyrant's reign will not be total, any more than justice will be total in a republic; but anarchy knows no law at all, neither just nor unjust. In revolution the rule of law rebounds into anarchy, a condition destructive of civic existence as such. Revolution is not just a relapse into injustice; it is a relapse into the state of nature[22]—

although in a successful revolution that primitive state will re-
bound once again into a civic condition. From the point of view
of the law, Kant sees but one way of thinking: absolute rejection
of future revolution as a means of political progress, and absolute
protection of the revolution that has succeeded.

But is he not reducing his own thought to absurdity? Is it not
too easy a way out of the dilemma to legitimize victorious revolutions of the past and to brand future ones illegitimate under all
circumstances? Is this not a case of "Jesuitic casuistry" (59: VIII,
344), with the additional drawback of actually serving always the
powers that be?

Appearances may suggest such questions and interpretations.
Viewed in depth, things look different. The analogy is breached,
in this case, by the idea of law. Resting directly on morality, this
idea commands respect beyond all empirical human conditions.
It lives only where it is realized in definite historic states of law.
There is no natural law without positive law. Any man who
cherishes the idea must want the real human community of a
state of law. To attack that state is thus to attack the idea; it is
for the sake of the idea that revolutions to come must be rejected
while successful ones are justifiable by their reproduction of the
state of law in which the idea can spread. The paradoxical stand
on revolution results from an insolubly paradoxical basic datum
of philosophy: that something which is above time (the idea of
law) comes alive for man only *in* time (in positive law).

If temporality, as used by Kant, is interpreted solely from our
own point of view, we shall run into frequent contradictions that
can perhaps be rationally glossed over, but only at the cost of a
violent curtailment of the supratemporal relation. But if we view
the temporal in a supratemporal perspective—in our case: if we
consider revolution under the aspect of the idea of law—we come
to understand the insolubility of the paradoxes, and yet we
come to know, without reducing the distance between their
poles, that in a wider horizon they will be voided.

Still, one objection remains to be raised. We said that the
reason why the analogy is breached is the idea of law, an idea
rooted in morality. But in fact, the close connection of natural
and positive law greatly restricts the political individual's freedom, in the name of law. The absolute ban on revolution compels
the individual to bow to whichever power happens to rule at the

time—yet freedom is morality's reason for being. What is asked here, in the name of law and morality, jeopardizes the very root of morality.

We cannot ignore this objection. Kant takes no explicit stand on it, but there is one indication that it gave him pause: the breach in the analogy—the ban on revolution—is breached in turn. In the treatise *Perpetual Peace* Kant says that political wisdom will not suppress a revolution "when it happens naturally" (59: VIII, 373 note), but will accept it as "nature's plea" that the desired legal conditions at last be realized.

This is one of Kant's typical revocations. In the name of freedom, the political revolution which no positive system of law can approve ahead of time is nonetheless, ahead of time, given a chance to transform itself into a legal revolution. Kant's basic position that a future revolution is unlawful in principle is potentially called into doubt, without being voided.

Exempting politics is one way to breach its analogy to nature; but there is also the breach by way of its complete inclusion in nature.

A distinct manifestation of cosmic struggle is the struggle between creatures. Living things are destroyed either by other living things or by acts of nature. This is part of the grand order and ultimately not tragic; nature is always about to make use of destruction, or already using it, as the constituent factor of a new order. The cosmos, the neat order, remains undisturbed—not in spite of, but essentially by way of, all the struggles that occur in it.

In the philosophy of nature we look on man, so to speak, as a mere point in the cosmos. We subject him to natural laws and do not grant him an exceptional position. We interpret his perdition cosmologically, not morally or cosmopolitically. We regard war as the natural conduct of natural beings, the conduct to be seen everywhere, and at the same time as nature's shrewd device for the regeneration of mankind. The philosophy of nature speaks of man, and of human things in general, as if their direction were out of man's hands.

It is not rare for Kant, the lover of grand perspectives, to adopt this cosmological vista in political thinking. He speaks of war, then, as he speaks of the plague (cf. 78: XV, 971; 1550),[23] and of a man's death as of the wilting of a flower. He means to survey the whole course of mankind's history from the a priori intelligible course of natural history. What man seems in this course to be doing arbitrarily is subject to natural mechanisms; what he freely creates is a free fulfillment of natural laws. Man thinks of himself as planning in one way or another, but nature has always included him in its design already; it steers him systematically and, if need be, by force (cf. 59: VIII, 360 ff.).

What guides Kant in this way of thinking is no longer a regulative analogy of nature and politics. In a sense, it is a new breach laid into the analogy, in the direction of materially including all things in the natural realm. Here the unifying element is not a lasting likeness of conditions, but a passing sameness of the ways of looking at different things. The consequences of this breach are somewhat troublesome. It calls human freedom into question and seems to simulate a knowledge it cannot provide. In interpreting politics we shall have to ask, in principle, how to understand that breach.

That nature and politics are viewed in the same manner is a passing phenomenon that can be canceled at any time. This means that different ways of looking at the two are possible, and that Kant evaluates differently from different points of view. Political concepts as well as all discussions of them are thus moved into a realm of many layers, a realm in which the definitions of the concepts come to be, and in which relative statements about them must remain in flux. To visualize this cogitative posture, we can use the model of the theory of motion.

The Relativity of Motion and of Philosophical Concepts[24]

The relativity of all motion is a thought which Kant unfolded in two treatises almost thirty years apart: in his *New Didactic Concept of Motion and Rest* (13) and in *Metaphysical Foundations of Natural Science* (33). By tacitly excluding the possibility of absolute space, the first, a short piece in which Kant announced his lectures for the summer term of 1758, already radicalized Newton's theory of relativity.[25] But not till *Metaphysical Foundations* did Kant dispose of a conceptual language that enabled him to let absolute space stand as a regulative idea while exposing its objectification in a "physical generality" (33: IV, 482) as a common methodological lapse.

He aims at the relativity of space from two points of departure: from the relation of the moving agent, and from the condition of the moved object. Assumed as a basic axiom, both times, is that motion is a purely empirical concept.

Motion is a change in location.[26] An object's location is determined "by its external relation to others which are about it" (13: II, 16). Motion is thus a change in these relations (33: IV, 482) or, as Kant puts it in *Metaphysical Foundations,* "a change of the relation in space" (33: IV, 554).

To begin with, we can relate a thing to its immediate surroundings. A successively expanding view involves new correlates and makes new relations possible. Potentially, their sphere extends as far as space, and their number is infinite.

A state of absolute rest would mean that all relations are immutable; a state of absolute motion, that all of them are changeable in relation to something ultimate.[27] Both states lie outside experience, for they presuppose the synthesis of all diversity in a numerical unity.

Motion and rest are relative when some relations change and others simultaneously remain the same. In experience this happens all the time. We can make it clear to ourselves by imagining the spaces that surround us, as follows:

Motion is given in appearance only (33: IV, 554). Its possibility presupposes empirical space, the material space which on its part is mobile and qualified. We can perceive its motion against the background of a wider material space. The condition of motion itself is thus infinitely conditioned. The regression of empirical spaces remains interminable.

And yet, in the idea, our reason terminates the regression by means of an absolute space. Behind every space that moves into experience, this absolute one is projected as the sort of dematerialized space on whose ground the empirical one can be conceived as moving. It is the mere "logical universality" (33: IV, 482) of a space encompassing all other spaces. It is "the idea of a space" (33: IV, 563) that permits us to view every space as moving, and thus all motion as mutual and relative—as mutual because the mobility of space allows us to conceive the motion of an object either as its shift in space or as an opposite shift of space itself;[28] and as relative because in the infinite encompassment of mobile spaces each encompassed one is taken into the motions of the encompassing space.

An example from the early Kantian treatise we mentioned gives an impressive demonstration of the relativity of motion.

Suppose a ship lies at anchor in a river flowing from east to west. Resting on the cabin table is a ball. The ship weighs anchor and starts drifting downstream. In relation to the ship, the ball remains at rest; in relation to the river bank it moves in a westerly direction. But the earth turns around its axis in an easterly direction, moving the ball along with it. Even faster in the same direction, the earth circles the sun—another motion in which the ball participates. At the same time, however, the sun with all its planets moves around the center of the galaxy, and perhaps the galaxy itself is moving about in the universe.

"I ask: which way, and how fast? No answer is forthcoming. And now I get dizzy; I no longer know whether my ball is resting or moving, whither and at what speed. Now I begin to see a shortcoming in the expressions I use for motion and rest. They never should be used in an absolute sense, but always respectively. I never ought to say, 'A body is at rest,' without adding the things with respect to which it is resting; and I never ought to say it moves, without naming at the same time the objects to which its relation changes."[29]

This doctrine of the relativity of motion gives us an important pointer. What is mobile comes to appear in relation to something else, and any statement about it includes its current relation. Hence the predicate of the statement applies relatively. It must change with the relation. An absolute definition always misses the point, because there is no absolutely fixed point in space. As the horizon expands, the contradictions in the relativity come to appear as complementary rather than as contradictory.

It is true that at no place in Kant's writings are there explicit methodological indications of any kind of analogy between his treatment of political concepts and the theory of motion; and yet the analogy seems clear. The statements about empirical political concepts, about war and peace in particular,[30] are so divergent that a thinking that fails to relativize can only leave us helpless.

Take war, for instance. At one time it is a way to enforce one's right, a *"modus ius suum persequendi,"*[31] a substitute for law, a "means in need" (59: VIII, 346): it is thus "rightful"[32] and compatible with "holding civil rights sacred" (35: V, 263), and in the legal sense, in any case, not criminal from the start (84: XIX, 546; 7892). At the same time, however, we read that war destroys every constitution (38: VII, 87 f.) and would accordingly have to be the transgression par excellence. Kant calls it an "indispensable" cultural instrument (49: VIII, 121), a "mechanism of Providence" (39: VII, 330), as well as "the worst evil that can befall the human race" (84: XIX, 611; 8077) and the instrument of human self-destruction (39: VII, 276). He says that war improves the mind (35: V, 263), preserves virtue (86: XX, 102 f.), promotes courage and equality (86: XX, 105 f.), and above all, secures freedom, the premise of morality.[33] But at the same time it is "the destroyer of all that is good" (38: VII, 91), "the greatest barrier to morality" (38: VII, 93) which "always revokes" the purposes of mankind (38: VII, 89), a "portent of Judgment Day" (58: VII, 331)—in short, the socially manifested ruin of mankind, against which reason casts its "irresistible veto: There should not be any war" (37: VI, 354).

It would be rather naïve to meet all these qualifications simply on the ground of the theorem of contradiction—as if one could do what we have just done: juxtapose them on a single plane like pieces of a mosaic. The conditions and concepts to which the subject relates here are different each time. With every change in the relation, he enters, so to speak, into a new thinking space in which the predicates are also changed. The predicate is codetermined by the relation of the subject.

To put it in concrete terms, it makes a difference to the predicate whether we speak of war in regard to the laws of nature, to social institutions, to the idea of the right, or to the laws of reason. Relative to natural laws, war can be understood as harmony, as mirroring the cosmic order in empirical society; relative to social institutions, it can be understood at one time as a destructive factor, at another time as a constructive element. Only from an absolutely fixed point of view would the predicate become absolute. We do not find such a point in the sensible world; in the intelligible world it is the point of contact between the being and the ought. This is the point from which war and peace will get their only possible absolute qualifications. To carry those into historically determined situations, as constitutive principles of judgment, is methodically impermissible.

The consequence is clear: to understand the predicates, we must, each time, consider the relations also. If they are included, contradictory predicates may prove to be complementary.

So much for this analogy. It means that philosophical concepts are not absolutely definable because, in fact, they do not occur in isolation; they occur in the conceptual world, in which they enter into an indefinite number of relations. What would be absolutely true is the totality of infinite reflection, not the statement excerpted from that reflection. Hence the dynamic character of Kantian thought. To capture some of its unschematical mobility, let us transcend the analogy in two points.

Philosophical concepts would not be definable even in isolation. To define means "to represent originally the full concept of a thing within its limits" (30: A 727/B 755). This requires clear and adequate characteristics of the concepts (they must be "full"). Their number must be assertively stated (they must be "defined within their limits") and not merely obtained by derivation (they must be "originally represented"). "In line with such a requirement, an *empirical* concept is not capable of definition at all, only of *explication*" (30: A 727/B 755). By concept, which covers a type of objects, we mean now more, now fewer of the characteristics of that type, depending on the requirements of the distinctive criteria we are asking about at the moment. The empirical concept "is thus never assured of its limits" (30: A 728/B 756).[34]

In another sense this is true also of such a priori concepts as "substance," "cause," or "right." Since no clear visuality is given along with these concepts, they may contain many dark notions that will be ignored in an analysis of the concept, though always considered in its use. No analysis can give more than presumable assurance. Hence Kant's advice to prefer "exposition"—a more cautious term, which leaves the critic a margin for assent with reservations (30: A 729/B 757)—to the word "definition."

The only concepts fit for exact definition are the ones that have been conceived arbitrarily. Those are definable, for one must be able to say what one means by them. Yet even here Kant adds a limitation: perhaps this original definition is no more than the declaration of a project without any corresponding reality. Perhaps it is contrived nonsense. Ultimately, Kant regards as fit for definition only those arbitrary concepts which can be represented a priori at the same time: "Mathematics alone has definitions" (30: A 729/B 757). In mathematics, an object is conceived as it is a priori represented in visuality. It is the only case in which concept and representation are congruent, because the concept is originally given by the representation.

The line between philosophical and mathematical definition is thus to be strictly drawn. Philosophical definitions are mere expositions of given concepts, expositions that can be explicated in analyses without ever being apodictically certain of completeness. As a matter of principle, they leave a margin for error. Mathematical definitions are constructions of concepts accomplished by a volitive synthesis. Their completeness is apodictically certain. They leave no margin for error.

The difference allows Kant to draw important conclusions. Mathematics begins with a complete definition, which is also the genesis of the concept; in philosophy, the concept always precedes the definition. Here the definition *comes to be,* in an exposition which gradually grows more and more complete without ever becoming assuredly whole. This is why in philosophy the definition must conclude the work rather than open it. Philosophy is a road to definition, not a road that starts out from definition. Along this road there are several stages of exposition, all of which may claim to be correct, but on given premises only. Their differences do not permit the swift conclusion that they are due to errors and contradictions. So-called discrepancies may have a thoroughly positive significance. This is why concepts are much more intractable in philosophy than in mathematics. Philosophy requires us to keep an open mind for the marginal conceptualities, and yet this openness must be balanced by critical delimitation. It takes a kind of "conceptual musicality."[35] Without this, a supposedly scientific rigor will keep us in a state of permanent outrage at philosophers' inconsistencies.[36]

There is a further difficulty to be considered. Two shifts in the use of reason may occur when we are dealing with concepts: first, a shift within the natural concepts, and then a shift from the natural concept to the rational one.

Our judgment, which always conceives the particular as covered by the universal, has two ways to proceed in regard to natural data. If the universal, the concept, is given, definition and knowledge will enable us to put the single thing in its place. But if only the single thing is given, if the universal is what we are looking for, our judgment has yet to design the universal and will subsume the particular under it later, as under a regulative principle which allows man to create an effective unity without defining the particular. In the first case, the statements are made in consciousness at large and are universally valid; in the second case, they are made in the mind and are parts of elucidative projects that teach man to understand nature in relation to himself, without regarding that which he has understood as known.

It is concretely possible to talk of war in a defining sense, for instance, when we try to subsume it under the concept of law, as a substitute for law; but at the same time we can talk of it in teleological projects, in ways that are merely elucidative, never defining. Both statements will sound apodictic, the way definite statements do. The point is to know, each time, which mode of holding something for true applies. Without this knowledge, Kant's philosophy of history, for instance, could not but paralyze reason.

Besides this change in rational usage within natural concepts, there is the shift from the intellectual concept to the rational one. It is one thing to discuss intellectual concepts, which can be explicated for the sake of a cognition because they always have a visuality corresponding to them; it is quite a different thing to talk about rational concepts, to which no statement applies as definitely knowable because nothing visual can be compared with what we mean. Intellectual concepts do cause the troubles we mentioned—they are not conclusively definable, and in using them we must consider their relations of the moment—but they can lead us to particular knowledge. Dealing with rational concepts is infinitely more complex. They are concepts that transcend all possible experience. Language as such, insofar as it defines, is inadequate to them. What we say about them is always what we do not mean. Thought has found no words for them, so to speak. All statements about them are therefore laden with negations that take back what has been said, yet without stating it more validly in the reversal. An intentional theoretical approach to the substance of these concepts is impossible. Kant therefore seeks access to them via the ought. He asks what they mean to us, and what we ought to do to realize their substance in humanity.

This means—to give an example from the realm of political thinking—that when Kant speaks of peace it may be an empirical concept about which he ventures to state particular cognitions. When he speaks of "eternal peace," however, something basically different is going on. A shift has occurred in the use of reason. Cognition is no longer sought for definition's sake. Peace as an idea is considered, not under the aspect of what it is, but under the aspect of human freedom. The goal is no longer to comprehend a datum, but to meet a challenge. The fundament is no longer a knowledge, but a faith.

Behind Kant's politics, as behind his entire metaphysics, lies a way of thinking we might circumscribe as follows:

It seeks to define what is definable, without regarding the definition as final or conclusive. Rather, that way of thinking unlocks cogitative realms beyond the definition and ceaselessly places it in new relations, aware that this makes relative cognition endless, and absolute cognition impossible. Beyond this defining usage, such thinking puts the object into meaningful drafts that run through the whole, helping us to illuminate the object rather than to know it, and it eventually anchors the object in the One that sounds the call to his freedom heard by man.

Within these spaces of knowledge, understanding, and faith— of consciousness at large, the mind, and reason—Kant's thinking moves without schemata, without drawing special attention to each transition. To get any idea of how complex a process occurs each time, we must develop a sensibility for that peculiarly mobile thinking.

2. THE ROAD TO UNITY

The cardinal problem of all politics is the establishment of civic unity, whether among many individuals or many states, and whether in a firmly delimited area (a state, a union of states) or in an unlimited area ("the world"). Here we draw upon the field of natural philosophy for a few thought models that came to point the way for Kant's approach to the problem.

The Community of Substances and of Citizens

In the third section of his habilitation thesis of 1755 (6: I, 410ff.) Kant states two new metaphysical principles which he himself regards as "*consectariorum feracissima*,"[1] as "highly fruitful in their consequences." They are the principle of succession and the principle of coexistence. The first means that substances can change only insofar as they are linked with each other;[2] the second, that finite substances are not yet in community by their mere existence, that community as *commercium* (not as *coexistentia*) must be established, rather, by the divine intellect, the common primal ground of their existence.[3] To Kant, this second principle especially remained important. In the Fourth Dissertation (26: II, 406ff.) we find it discussed once more, and then again in *Critique of Pure Reason* (30: A 211ff./B 256ff.)—although there, of course, without reference to a divine founder.

A change in substances can occur only insofar as they are linked with others. A simple substance, free of any external conjunction, is immutable and timeless. This is true only of God, the infinite substance. Finite substances are not independent, for their diversity is not reducible to unity. Their conglomerate would be a stabilized chaos. Nature would remain without an *influxus physicus*. Hence, finite substances must be connected.

This is not enough, however, for connection would still be conceivable without change. Its consequence would be a congealed order. This is why the connection must be dynamic, why finite substances interact.

Yet irregular interaction could do no more than bring forth a dynamic chaos. If the principle of interaction is to engender an orderly community, not mere coexistence or accumulation, it must be established by the divine intellect, the common primal ground of the existence of substances. This is the establishing and preserving force of dynamic community. The establishment has occurred in the antagonistic disposition of matter[4] and in the laws of nature. The community lives as long as there is substance. Its existence is guaranteed by the existence of God.

There were consequences of these principles that mattered to
Kant about 1755: the reality of bodies; the rejection of dualism;
the acquisition of a uniform world principle and of a uniform
space governed throughout by Newton's gravity. But with those
we cannot deal here. What has to be stressed for our purposes is
the analogy in the law of the state—an analogy with fatal consequences—and its successful breaching in the law of nations.

Man, the substance of mankind, does not live in isolation. His
mere existence always relates him to other men. But in a state of
nature this relation is chaotic. The community has yet to be
founded. It is founded by nature and man at the same time—by
nature insofar as it invests man with the antagonism that is his
spur to unity; by man insofar as he establishes the law, without
which no general external freedom would be possible. Not just
anyone is capable of this intentional establishment; it is the exclusive province of the *omnipotens,* the sovereign, the sole "font of
the laws" (37: VI, 321 note), to whom Kant accords quasi-divine
powers. He is the "creator" and "preserver" (56: VII, 291) of
order. The existence of civil society is both assured and jeopar-
dized by the sovereign's existence.

How are we to interpret this analogy? The conditions of the
possibility of civil community pose a transcendental question of
public law, to which Kant's formal answer is the same he gave
thirty years earlier to the question, What ultimately makes it
possible for substances to coexist? The relation of God's will to
the community of substances is identical with the relation of the
legislator's will to the community of citizens.

In the intelligible world, incidentally, we find this structure
once again: in the ethical state Kant conceives a supreme legislative being, with respect to which all moral duties are commandments—a being that rules and preserves this world and, as its
"founder" (36: VI, 152), is the reason why there can be a community of rational men at all. We can therefore extend our
equation: the will of God as the world's creator is to the community of substances what the sovereign's will is to the community
of citizens, and what the will of God as a moral person is to the
community of rational men.

The possible dangerous consequences of this analogy will have
to be discussed later. It moves the legislator—perhaps the people,
perhaps a group, perhaps only an individual—into a fatal prox-

imity to God. By exalting him above every law it subjects those
over whom he wields power to his license. It is important to see
this equality of relations if we do not want to shut our eyes to
the absolutist features present in Kant's *Doctrine of Law* (37)—
never as a fundament, nor as a tendency proper, but still, at
times, in the consequences—or to excuse these features by a
passing reference to the Age of Absolutism. Kant did not simply
take them over from outside. He found their rudiments in his
thinking, and in *Doctrine of Law* he strengthened them involuntarily, so to speak, by his love of formality. His failure to breach
the analogy here is not without significance.

For in the field of international law[5] Kant did breach the analogy. States, he held, interact simply by coexisting. If their constitution does not correspond to the popular will, which reason
alone can determine, they impair and injure each other by their
mere presence. Their mutual relation to one another is war—
with interruptions, but always a state of war. To turn this into a
state of reciprocal legality, international law must be established.
In line with the analogy there would have to be some universal
omnipotens by whom this law is originally established and com-
pliance with it made obligatory. But here Kant breaches the
analogy. There can be no such *omnipotens,* he argues. For no
man is a citizen of all states, and no state is called to mastery over
other states. This is why the establishment of law rests upon free,
gradually spreading entrance into a universal federation that does
not void the sovereignty of states. Kant calls it a "league of nations." Unlike a "nation of nations," the league has no coercive
power; it always rests on the free will of moral persons.

The breach in the analogy is neither self-evident nor arbitrary.
It is not self-evident because there had been drafts of unity before
Kant, with the universal or, at least, the European *omnipotens*
seen either in an individual potentate (the emperor, the pope), in
a single nation, or in an exclusive group of states. And it is not
arbitrary because it has an important function: it prevents unity
which in itself is the goal, from turning into universal monarchy,
which would extinguish all freedom. The breach rests upon the
will to political freedom, without which the will to unity leads to
perversions.

It may seem odd that Kant maintains the analogy in national
law while breaching it in international law. To put it in simplified

terms: in the first case, the law goes before freedom; in the second, freedom goes before the law. The reason is plausible: if freedom outweighed the law of an individual state, the result would be anarchy. The individual's freedom would enable him to claim exemption from the law as such. A state that rates freedom above the law is renouncing its coercive power. It manifests its readiness for anarchy and thus, in principle, voids itself. It is not possible to place freedom above the law of a state.

International law is another matter. There it is not a physical person but a moral person, a state, which is claiming freedom. With other states it lives in conditions of nature, but internally it remains a system of law. Its freedom poses no threat to the law's existence, but the law might pose one to the existence of freedom. Kant's seemingly contradictory combination allows him to safeguard the law while granting freedom, as much as remains possible, on a cosmopolitical level.

Physical Reciprocity and Legal Equality

A further analogy appears in the problems of physical reciprocity and legal equality. It is not difficult to uncover, because Kant himself has variously pointed it out.

In his lectures on physics we come upon several discussions of the reciprocity of physical forces. Matter—in its appearance, not in its basic structure—is an inert substance[6] occupying space. In connected shape it forms bodies; matter is "the body's fabric."[7] Bodies are reciprocally related to one another, with action equal to reaction. "The quantity of force which one body imparts to another is the quantity with which the other resists. . . . The quantity of motion is equal in two bodies working upon each other."[8] Applying in both cases, although in different respects, is the fundamental law of mechanics: *actio est aequalis reactioni.*

This law of reciprocity, presented and demonstrated in detail in *Metaphysical Foundations* (33: IV, 544 ff), has an analogy in the reciprocity of legal obligations. The state can place no citizen under an obligation that is not equally and mutually obligatory for all. No one has the right to compel others and at the same time to evade compulsion. All are subject to one law and considered equal before it. "The rules of law . . . are reciprocal" (83:

XIX, 199; 6393). The state of law is a state of "equal action and reaction" (56: VII, 292).

How far does this analogy extend? It extends as far as laws do, as far as the relations between citizens can be brought into the form of laws. We can imagine laws that permit inequality, but even those put all citizens under the same formally reciprocal obligations. Reciprocity may prevail in their substance, but it must prevail in their form. This is Kant's approach, for example, to laws governing material goods and property as a whole.[9] In those, mutuality lies not in assuring all citizens of an equal share of goods but in guaranteeing that all are free to own property. Kant is aware that in fact the inequality of possessions results in unequal power to command and rule. He does not mind this, for the form of reciprocity, and thus of equality, has been preserved. Those who would make Kant a socialist because of his proclamation of equality are mistaking that formal reciprocity for a material one. The law—to Kant a mere reduction of license to a liberty that does not conflict with the liberty of others—would then become a partial or total reduction of everyone's freedom to a common level. To keep from bringing about this perverted equality, Kant puts up with inequality, whose consequences may be dreadful, and he calls for the equality that remains possible: the assurance of an equal chance for all. This is why many laws intervene only where this equal chance is blocked: there must be no hereditary nobility, no serfdom by birth, and no condemnation to poverty by laws withholding opportunities for advancement; but there may be a nobility of freedom, a nobility of merit, as well as the serfdom of those who lack independence, and the poverty of the indolent. Laws are reciprocal when the same possibilities are open to the freedom of all subjects of the state.

Kant's tremendous rigor in clinging to the principle of reciprocity, and thus to the analogy shown here, is most evident where formal mutuality always joins with a material one: in the law of retribution.

Retributive law belongs to the penal law, which in Kant's *Theory of Law* is considered part of public law. By penal law he means "the governor's right to inflict pain upon the governed because of their crimes" (37: VI, 331). To Kant, as a matter of principle, legal punishment is not a corrective. It is imposed not to better a man but to expiate a crime. There is punishment because a crime has been committed. According to Kant, this is the only basis for punishment that accepts even the criminal as a subject, without making him a thing in the plans (perhaps only in the educational plans) of another person. It is the criminal subject's own personality—in which morality always stays alive as a potential—that calls for radical punishment, and the penalty must not be abated or remitted at any price, not even if clemency should make the citizenry as a whole more perfect. "The penal law is a categorical imperative, and woe unto him who snakes his way through the convolutions of the theory of happiness to dig up something whose promised advantage would relieve him of punishment or even of a degree of it, according to the pharisaical slogan 'It is better for one man to die than for all the people to perish.' For when justice perishes, it is not worth men's while to live on earth" (37: VI, 331–32).

The only question is the principle on which punishment may be imposed. To Kant, it can only be based on the principle of retribution before the bar of justice. This alone makes the punishment fit the crime both quantitatively and qualitatively and does not ultimately leave it to the subjective pleasure of judges. The penal law, therefore, rests on the principle of reciprocity. "What you do unto another you do unto yourself," is its main tenet. "When you insult him you are insulting yourself; when you rob him you are robbing yourself; when you assault him you are assaulting yourself; when you kill him you are killing yourself" (37: VI, 332). Substitutes may be found to punish libel, theft, and battery; the point is that the substitute must have the same effect as the crime. If, for example, a rich citizen publicly insults a poor and lowly one, letting him pay a fine will not suffice; instead, Kant suggests making him kiss the poor man's hand in public, perhaps, for he should be humiliated because he has humiliated another.

But in one case there is no conceivable substitute: in the case of murder. There is no equating "life, however wretched, with death" (37: VI, 333). The principle of mutuality, which in the final analysis is the principle of justice, ranks infinitely above each human existence. Kant cannot conceive of a case in which a murderer's life might be spared. "Even if civil society were to dissolve with the consent of all its members . . . the last murderer held in prison at the time would have to be executed first, so that everyone would have done unto him what his deeds merit" (37: VI, 333). Execution, as the "categorical imperative of penal justice" (37: VI, 336), is here "the best equalizer" (37: VI, 334) on behalf of public equality. "Sentimentality" and "humanitarian affectations" (37: VI, 334–35) that would avoid the death penalty are nothing but "sophistry and perversion of justice" (37: VI, 335).

Reading such lines in *Doctrine of Law,* we do not quite know what is greater, our outrage at the barbaric judicial practice for which a trail is blazed here or our admiration for a thinker with the courage of his consistency. One thing is certain in any case: the lines must shatter the image of Kant as a philanthropist whose cozy humanitarianism always makes him think promptly of the individual's welfare in the world. To use his own words, this image itself is one of the humanitarian affectations. The ground of Kant's character is far more inexorably molded by the rigor of natural laws, so to speak. Having absorbed the formalism of those laws, he spreads it all over his thinking and does not shrink from its consistency.

In the context of our theme it is important to see that Kant's principle of legal equality does not go back to the achievements of the French Revolution, nor does it go back to Rousseau. It does indeed appear for the first time in 1763, directly after Kant began studying Rousseau—when he calls it man's "only natural necessary good" (86: XX, 165). But we must interpret these words correctly: "necessary" means free of chance, as those laws are. Even at that time the egalitarian background had nothing to do with revolutionary pathos; it had to do with the stringency of a mechanical law fertilized in the intelligible world by analogy.

If we ask with Kant what underlies this law, we note that its ultimate basis is not science. In *Metaphysical Foundations,* he says that the thesis of mutual interaction is borrowed "from general metaphysics" (33: IV, 544); even what seems to be the purely mechanical law of equal counteraction is said to rest upon the "metaphysical law of community" (33: IV, 545). Again, therefore, we find a condition we know. A metaphysical idea that proved fertile for natural science is projected by analogy upon the metaphysics of law.

Despite this rigor, the analogy is breached in two points: upward in the citizens' relation to the chief of state, and downward in their relation to the dependent.

We have already pointed out that God as the world's creator is to the community of substances what God as a moral person is to the community of rational beings, and what the sovereign is to the community of citizens. At the time we mentioned the sovereign's dangerous proximity to God and suggested its possibly fatal consequences. In the question of equality under law, these consequences are now clearly apparent.

As God, the obligating subject, is flatly the person with "only rights and no duties"[10] in the intelligible world, so the sovereign is in the state the person "solely entitled to compel, and not subject to any legal compulsion" (56: VIII, 291). He is an *omnipotens* who can never be punished (37: VI, 331), and whom Kant therefore calls "irresistible" (84: XIX, 518; 7792), "irreprehensible" 84: XIX, 518; 7792), and even "sacred" (84: XIX, 516; 7781). Because there is no power superior to him, "everything must be expected of his mercy" (84: XIX, 520; 7800). It is wrong of him, the lawmaker, to exercise executive and judicial powers at the same time, but the wrong he commits is a human wrong, not a legislative wrong. In every case, even as a tyrant who deprives men of their freedom, he as the lawmaker remains the apex of justice and the epitome of law as such, the one who cannot do wrong. In a word, the sovereign is above the law as God is above duty.

This may not be dangerous as long as the people are sovereign and the monarch merely represents them. Kant's position on the sovereign would then mean only that the monarch has no authority to coerce the people; all that he has is supreme power among equals. The paramount power, not subject to coercion, is the people's. There can be no doubt that in his idea of the republic Kant ultimately aims at this relationship (56: VII, 294–95), but the way he does it blocks the road of progress at the same time: where the people are not sovereign, where the monarch is not just their representative but the absolute lawmaker himself—whether by historic tradition or by arbitrary usurpation—there Kant regards the de facto sovereign as inviolate and unassailable. One man is in possession of all power, then, and all the people are at his mercy, for good or ill, no matter what he may do.

Every right the people may claim to have against this overlord is to Kant presumptuousness and an assault upon justice. It is high treason, duly atoned for by death alone. If many are implicated in the plot, their punishment may—lest the state be depopulated, and to avoid the public "spectacle of a charnelhouse" (37: VI, 334)—be commuted to deportation by a legal act of majesty. But where the people, in the name of law, dethrone or even execute the monarch, Kant views the event as a "total reversal of all concepts of law," as the "external crime that can never be extinguished" (37: VI, 321 note) and whose irreparability can be compared only to that of mortal sin.

The consequences are clear. Kant does not wish to deliver subjects to tyranny; he would really like to hand them a tool for their protection; but he does it in a manner that invites abuse. Expecting better times to come, he accepts the abuse along with violence and despotism. The permanent aim is freedom, but passing violence must be suffered. Kant's formal legal thought shows no way out of this dilemma.

He has no better luck with his downward breach in the analogy. The law, he says, puts all citizens of the state as subjects under a reciprocal obligation. But now comes the reservation: not every member of the state is a citizen in the legal sense. To Kant, being a citizen means being a "colegislator" (56: VIII, 294). What makes one a colegislator is the capacity to vote. To have this, it is not enough for a man to be of age and of sound judgment; he must also be independent. Kant's term for this is that every citizen must be "his own master," that he must be *sui iuris* (56: VIII, 294). To be his own master he must have something to live on, whether property or a skill that enables him to acquire property. A citizen should not have to serve anyone but the state. Anyone constrained to subsist by holding himself at the disposal of others (Kant lists servants, journeymen, artisans of the lower sort, handymen, tenant farmers, tutors, and all those who make their living in their master's household) lacks a civil personality. In the legal sense he does not share in state citizenship, only in state protection. He is under the protection, but also under the compulsion, of laws in the making of which he cannot take part. He is a passive member of the state, not an active one. Although he may always lay claim to human equality, he can no longer claim civil equality.

It has been pointed out, and rightly, that this inequality has historic grounds, that Kant was at least as progressive as the most progressive of the revolutionary constitutions.[11] But if one looks at things, as we do here, first of all from the point of view of the analogy alone, such extenuations do not count. What remains is the question why the equality of civil rights and duties is less universal than the equality of interaction in the realm of bodies. A purely historical reminiscence is not an adequate answer, with Kant himself citing a legality that is not equally historical. There remains the offensive fact that in one respect the disadvantaged, the unpropertied, are disfranchised to boot—and this in the name of law.

Real Repugnancy and the Effect of Evil

In a publication from the year 1763, *An Attempt to Introduce the Concept of Negative Quantities into Mundane Wisdom*, Kant distinguishes two kinds of conceptual opposition. An opposition can be either logical by contradiction, or real without contradiction. In contradiction, the logical opposition, a predicate is simultaneously affirmed and denied of the same thing. In the total voiding of both statements, this erroneous concatenation yields an unconceivable "nothing at all," a *nihil negativum irrepresentabile* (18: II, 171). In real opposition, in antagonism, two predicates of one thing are opposed to each other. This opposition too results in a sort of voiding; but the voiding leaves either a thinkable something or a nothingness that can be conceived as an outcome, a *nihil privativum representabile* (18: II, 172), which Kant calls "zero = o."

An example: if we say of a motion that at the same time, and in the same relation to things, it is and it is not, this is logically repugnant and can mean absolutely nothing. But it is logically possible to say that a motion is composed of two forces, one of which drives forward with a power of ten while the other pushes backward with a power of eight. The result of this real repugnancy is a forward motion with the power of two. If the two opposing forces were equal, the result would not be absolutely nothing; it would be the merely relative nothing we call rest. "Here there is rest, not because of a lack of moving forces, but because they counteract each other" (18: II, 199).

Real repugnancy is a conflict of forces that are positive in themselves, and of which one is called positive and the other negative only for the sake of indicating their relation to each other. In an absolute sense the mere relational signs + or − do not mean anything yet. We may call falling a negative rising, just as we may call rising a negative falling. Each relates negatively to the other. This is why every opposing factor that is a positive ground of opposition is called a negative by Kant. "For example, the negative of going up is going down, by which I do not mean a negation of the other, but something in real opposition to the other" (18: II, 175).

Negatives always occur in twos, at least. They are really repugnant to each other if one of them partly or wholly voids the effects of the other. Real repugnancy is a reality if the two negatives are linked in the same subject; it is a possibility if the negatives arise in different subjects and their effects can void each other just the same.[12]

Wherever there is a positive cause at work and the effect is still nothing, the cause must be linked with another positive but opposing cause. The voiding of the effect of a positive cause permits us to infer a positive cause of opposition.

Just as there are two nothings, one of which is a thinkable result while the other is unthinkable nonsense, there are two modes of ineffectiveness and two kinds of evil. One comes from a real opposition. Its schema is called $A - A =$ zero $=$ o. It is ineffectiveness by privation; indeed, Kant calls it privation. The other ensues from mere absence, from the lack of a cause; and Kant calls it lack. Whether a given negation is privation or lack we can tell only by reflecting on the individual case; and sometimes, for lack of cognition, we cannot tell. To Kant, what matters is to see that the two possibilities exist. He says that scholastic metaphysics, for example, knew only one form of negation, the negation due to lack—that its great mistake was to take all privation for a mere absence rather than for a consequence of real repugnancy. Those metaphysicians regarded negation in every sense as due to a lack of being. This deprived them of thought possibilities and distinguishing criteria, and at the same time it made everything negative seem innocuous.

Kant's efforts to make the thought model of real repugnancy bear metaphysical fruit began in the precritical period. He thought this model would enable us to understand that pleasure is not just a lack of displeasure, and displeasure not just a lack of pleasure; that like virtue and vice, love and hatred, coming to be and passing away, the two are negatives to one another. To him these problems of detail mattered less than the newly gained cosmological propositions: that the sum of everything positive in the world is constant,[13] and that the sum of real causes in the universe totals zero—propositions "of extreme importance" because they are the premise of the world's perfection (18: II, 198), but not of equally extreme transparency. After all, Kant himself says that they are "not lucid enough" for him (18: II, 197).

The zero that comes out of real repugnancy—a net result on which "perfection of the world as such very largely depends" (18: II, 198)—later plays an important role in the idea of political progress.

Mankind's "greatest" (43: VIII, 22) and "most difficult" (43: VIII, 22) problem is to make the republican type of government work in a worldwide league of free peoples barring war as a political means. This task will be solved "last of all" (43: VIII, 23) and not without grievous straying; the reality of history, the fact that it is a history of wars, seems to show, rather, that the whole task is unrealistic. But the question is whether the thought that mankind might incessantly approach that final goal is also unrealistic. It is unrealistic as long as the evil in man as a political animal is not considered; it is unrealistic, at least, as long as this evil is not turned into the truly political factor.

The idea of progress must start from the worst of cases we can think of. We may hope for the good will of men, and we should appeal to it, but we must reckon with their ill will. The worst case we can think of is that ill will simply holds a general lien on political action, and that politicians, as far as their actions are concerned, are "a nation of devils" (59: VIII, 366)—but human devils who possess an intellect and at least a rudiment, although perhaps an ineffective rudiment, of good. In other words, thoughts of progress are utopian and tautological as long as we base them solely on an increase in morality due to good will, instead of on an increase in legality due to egotism. The idea of progress by good will must always remain as a postulate; but the idea that progress exists in spite of, and thanks to, ill will is the sober and eventually the only hopeful basis of an anticipatory design.

That good can take effect despite, and thanks to, evil is a Kantian conception modeled after real repugnancy. The forces of good gather in one direction. What this means in the language of "negative quantities" is that the forces of good have no negatives among them, that good is without real repugnancy. Thus we read previously of the good as such that "in the supreme being there can be no grounds of privation or real opposition" (18: II, 200). God is the being without real repugnancy.[14]

The forces of evil, on the other hand, are "not unanimous" (84: XIX, 491; 7687) but "opposed and contrary to one another" (75: XV, 632; 1448). License is lawless and counteracts itself. In the language of "negative quantities": the forces of evil do have negatives among them; in evil lies real repugnancy and the possibility of real repugnancy. The result is changeable, depending on the direction of individual forces. In the ideal case it can be zero. This would not mean that there is no evil; it would mean only that evil, although at work everywhere, would remain ineffective as a whole. To fight against the effectiveness of evil, if not against its root, is always possible; it is a task which skill can solve without morality: by directing—which can be done—the effects of the evil basic forces against each other so as to form a self-voiding force field of evil effects, with the net result equal to the nonbeing of evil.

> But now nature comes to the aid of the rationally founded common will that is revered but impotent in practice, and its aid is rendered by those very selfish leanings, so that it takes only a good organization of the state (which men are capable of) to direct those forces of nature against each other in such a way that one will hamper or void the destructive effects of the other—until the outcome, from the point of view of reason, is as if both forces did not exist, and as if man, though not a morally good human being, were nonetheless compelled to be a good citizen [59: VIII, 366].

The problem of state institutions can thus be solved even among bad men. From the viewpoint of real repugnancy it can be stated as follows: "How a mass of rational creatures—all of whom want general laws for their preservation, but each of whom secretly tends to except himself from these laws—may be so ordered and given such a constitution that their private mentalities, even though conflicting, will still block each other so that the outcome of their public conduct will be the same as if they were not so evil-minded. Such a problem must be soluble" (59: VIII, 366). It must be soluble because the forces of good, however feeble, have no opposition. They can break through the force field that has become ineffective.

It is important to see this way of thinking, which has come from mathematics and rational mechanics. It may keep us from understanding Kant's thoughts about progress exclusively from the side of practical reason. Their true tension lies in the fact that they combine the suspended thinking of the theory of ideas with the solidly constructed thinking of mathematics and rational mechanics. To expect progress from a mechanism alone would be philosophically as naïve and disastrous as it would be politically naïve to expect it from morality alone. Not all of progress evolves on the restricting condition that we might hope for it only if we do what we ought to do. Removing obstacles to progress is already progress of a sort, and these obstacles first of all are merely the effects of evil, not evil as such. The thesis that skill can remove them is the element of *Realpolitik* in Kantian thinking about progress; but the other thesis, that the removal must be anchored in morality, points to the metaphysical foundation which that skill requires in order to make sense.

Thanks to this twofold ground, progress need not begin with the most difficult part: with the moral turnabout in which the decisive progress is always presupposed, and the thought of which will always be a (necessary) circle. Instead, we begin with what is easy, with a mere aptitude that can succeed even without morality, but can be justified only by its all but imperceptible opening of a field of activity for freedom. In the order of the sensible realm—but only in that order—skill outweighs morality. Kant's hope, therefore, is not that the moral turnabout will produce a good order of the state, but that a good state order will lead to moral improvement. We can, he says, "see in the really given and quite imperfectly organized states that their outward conduct already approaches the precepts of the idea of law, although this is surely not caused by inner morality (just as it is not to morality that we can look for a good constitution of the state, but the other way around: it is from such a constitution that a people's good moral education can primarily be expected)" (59: VIII, 366). Here too morality is presupposed, but as no more than a rudiment, a potential. The premise of the turnabout, on the other hand, is always a supremely real morality. Kant's thoughts of progress are morally patient and politically possible.

Only one thing remains unclear: Who coordinates the antagonal forces of evil so that, in effect, they will void each other? Kant gives several answers. He calls the intellect the necessary premise—which would mean that the coordinator is a human being whose intellect must will the state and at the same time see through evil, so as to steer its forces. Nature does it, says another answer; nature, by the law of natural antagonism, constrains political man to will the state. Reason, says a third answer—for the use it makes of man's selfish impulses is to "make room for its own end, for the legal precept, and thus, insofar as it is up to the state, to promote and safeguard peace, both foreign and domestic" (59: VII, 367).

A nature that guides the human will and a reason that uses it stealthily, so to speak, and imperceptibly for its own ends remind us of Hegel's "cunning of the idea." But our sense of methodology forbids us to identify that concept with Kant. His thoughts are not dialectical advances to an absolute knowledge that is Being itself; they are drafts of a reflecting judgment, drafts which on principle can never congeal into knowledge. They teach us to understand—not in order to know, but in order to act according to what we have understood, at the risk of having misunderstood it.

This is no place to go farther in interpreting these thoughts, however. In our context it is enough to point out one of their aspects: their analogy with an earlier treatise.

How may we interpret this analogy? Perhaps as follows: about 1795, in his tract *Perpetual Peace,* Kant asks himself how it is possible, despite the antagonistic forces of the passions that always work in politics, to unify the state-building will so as to enable it to set up a republic. His answer formally follows the schema of real repugnancy which he had developed more than thirty years earlier, in his mathematical, natural-scientific, and simultaneously metaphysical *Attempt to Introduce Negative Quantities into Mundane Wisdom.* In general, the analogy concerns the arrangement of variously directed forces so that they will void each other, whether the arrangement is accomplished by nature, by prudence, or—stealthily, as it were—by reason. Once again, thought forms employed by Kant, the metaphysical scientist, are rediscovered in Kant, the political thinker.

The Formation of the Epicycloid and of Civic Order

At times Kant likes to have human advance to a worldwide civic order guaranteed by nature, so to speak. At those times he speaks of history's possible course to such an order as if it were sublimated in the course of nature. The premise of this parallelism is that nature and history are jointly encompassed by a broader space, from which both derive their concurring legality. These ideas too are analogies of thoughts which the early writings base upon very precise conceptions.

Things are subject to the natural order—according to Kant's principal dogmatic treatise of 1773, *The Only Possible Proof to Demonstrate God's Existence*—insofar as "the forces of nature provide sufficient grounds" for their existence and change (17: II, 103). The power of nature must be recognizable as the effective cause, and the effect itself must be produced in line with the rules of natural effectiveness. Kant's term for whatever these definitions cover is "natural mundane occurrences" (17: II, 103). If the effective cause lies outside nature, or if the effect is produced by natural forces but not in ways of natural effectiveness, we might talk of supernatural occurrences. Lying outside nature is the sufficient ground of free acts. In arbitrary action there are "no natural grounds" (17: II, 104). This seems to mean that there is no conjunction of freedom and nature.

This sharp division is not the last word, however. Nature and freedom combine in manifold ways. There are forces of nature capable of ruining individuals or whole states, for instance, and their connection with free acts is not that they appear in punishment of those acts. They strike the guilty and the innocent alike. What makes these arbitrary acts of nature akin to free human acts might be, rather, that their seemingly irregular occurrence depends on secret natural laws that work only at large intervals.

Statistics also seem to indicate such undiscovered laws governing acts of freedom.

More clearly visible is the connection between arbitrary acts and certain "punishments and rewards according to the natural order" (17: II, 105). Excessive intemperance, for example, will be followed by illness. Moreover, freely acting creatures exist in nature and are always linked with laws of nature. Although not subject to compelling causes, they are subject to causes that limit arbitrariness by secret rules. "It accords with experience that even the freest of acts are thus dependent upon a great natural rule" (17: II, 111).

Man has no way of knowing just where a single free act stands in the parallelism to this great rule. He can never survey the whole because he is always in the whole. This is why he sees every free act outside nature. But in the infinite series of acts the parallelism with the course of the natural rule must become visible. The rule can be visualized in many natural objects, in the origin of river beds and mountains, for example, or in that of the system of the universe. The road is always one from chaos to cosmos, from disorder to lawful order by way of antagonism. In the language of mechanics the road to order can be phrased as follows: "The forces of motion and resistance continue to interact until they are least impeding to one another" (17: II, 129).

In its purest form, this road is observable in the formation of the epicycloid. As the meshing cogwheels in a gearbox turn, they put up resistance to each other, due to the failure of the cogs of one wheel to fit perfectly into the slots of the other. In turning, they are gradually ground down until they have assumed the form of an algebraic curve called epicycloid. This brings them into the ideal form that permits meshing with a minimum of resistance. It would be possible, with great technical difficulties, to produce this algebraic curve from the beginning; instead, we let nature do the job of working out the perfect order by means of friction and resistance alone. The process is observable, and once we have understood the rules followed by nature in this case, we may be able also to understand its secret procedure in the infinite series of free acts, without regarding those as mere "mechanical side effects" (17: II, 114).

Three decades later, when he wrote his most important political treatises, Kant had developed a new dialectics of freedom. It recalls his precritical one in several points. Events in the world and free acts are constituted from different sources: the mundane event is the necessary consequence of a causal chain endlessly qualified in the course of time: the free act is spontaneous testimony to the freedom to do things, cutting across time and originating in reason. All political events originate either in the sequence of causal relations or in rational good will. They are accordingly either occurrences mechanically propelled by laws of nature or acts of original production under laws of freedom. The two kinds of action are completely separate, not in their consequences but in their origins. But in similar fashion as in the precritical period, this radical separation too is breached in various, rationally not always unimpeachable ways to an unknown unity.

To encompass the alternative "freedom or nature," Kant resorts to an "as well as." According to him, actions do not have to result exclusively from freedom or exclusively from necessity. They can be tied to both, rather, in different respects. An effect can be taken as free regarding its intelligible cause, and as necessary as far as phenomena are concerned. A parallelism of two different causalities with respect to one action is possible. A political act can, in a parallel view, be free as the original doing of men and at the same time necessary as a historic happening.

According to Kant, the course of history as an infinite series of acts can be conceived threefold. We can think of it as a steady rise to a goal of humanity, as the continuous decay of an originally happy humanity, and lastly as a senseless to and fro in the same place. The ascent by an infinite advance that has become a challenge is what Kant calls "eudaemonism" or "chiliasm"; the perpetual decline from bad to worse is called "moral terrorism"; and the alternating rise and fall in moral standstill is called the "abderitism" (38: VII, 81) of historical contemplation.

The chiliastic view is romantic if human progress is conceived in it as moral growth beyond man's natural disposition. After all, where should the increment in morality come from? We could expect it only from human freedom, but since effects do not exceed the capacity of the effective causes, the increase can never go beyond the natural disposition of men. The "sanguine hope" (38: VII, 82) for a better and better mankind has, accordingly, nothing to it.

Chiliasm is not romantic, however, if progress is understood simply as the ever-increasing unfoldment of the moral disposition in mankind. This unfoldment is possible to human freedom, and it must be achieved by that freedom.

Kant regards the terroristic view as unacceptable because the constant decline from bad to worse would have to bring the human race to the point of "self-extirpation" (38: VII, 81). The terminal point of this evolution would be the global suicide of mankind, an idea which Kant conceives now and then but never weighs in full earnest. To him the idea is always a sign that his thinking has gone astray.

Likewise, reason shrinks from the hypothesis of abderitism. This would reduce all of humanity's endeavor to no more than a "farce" (38: VII, 82) and, at best, a bad tragedy" (56: VIII, 308)— to a stage play in any event, with moral and amoral forces constantly exchanging roles and neutralizing each other. What would be played there—with the consent of some of the actors, perhaps, "because they are fools"—would end up as "eternally one and the same" (56: VIII, 308), a thought incompatible with that of a supreme morality working in the idea as the first cause of the world.

With which of these drafts does Kant himself agree? In his empirical contemplation of history he says of abderitism: "This opinion may well have a majority of votes on its side" (38: VII, 82). It reflects what history shows us: an absurd sameness, planless as a whole. But the point is not this empirical contemplation, but an aprioristic one. Its intent is not to impart knowledge by "prophesying" but by "predicting" (38: VII, 79) so as to make future action possible and to unify it. For the sake of this practical purpose, Kant is obliged to look upon progress as possible, at least, and thus to call for it—for progress not as an increment of morality but as the constant worldwide unfoldment of the moral disposition of men, for which increasing legality creates favorable conditions. The Kantian patterns of the course of history are thus aligned with an aprioristic eudaemonism that is understood as an idea, not as a prognosis. In the following we schematize its presentation so as to make the analogy with the course of history visible in two ways.

Kant's conception of the hypothetical course of history is twofold: from the worst of possibilities, and from the best. These two ideal constructions delimit the range of the variations in which—ultimately never quite reliably—human action originates now in liberty, now in license. While this action will never take the straight course of the mapped-out possibilities, it will have to move within their bounds. Yet if both series of acts, free ones as well as arbitrary ones, show an analogy with the course of nature, we may assume that the steps between them, whether sprung from license or from liberty, also remain somehow linked with nature. This gives us a certain assurance regarding all things to come. That assurance never allows us to venture prognoses—for from ideal constructions, from drafts of the whole, we do not get to know reality, only the bounds of possibilities—but we always know that it rests on what encompasses freedom and nature.

We draft the eudaemonistic course of history along the lines of *Idea for a Universal History* and *Perpetual Peace,* starting with the worst possibility in the motivation of individual historic acts. The sole effective impulses to political action, then, are ambition, greed, and selfishness. They guide rulers' arbitrary determination of political events, in such a way that each one, driven by his own passion, seeks a certain form of global unity. These forms are mutually exclusive. Where one touches another, conflict is the natural result—at first a clash of arguments, perhaps, but finally one of arms. The concord variously pursued by license recoils into discord: "Man wants concord; but nature knows better what is good for his species: it wants discord" (43: VIII, 21). Discord ties the rulers to antagonism, which is a natural mechanism and thus comprehensible in natural concepts. Following its dictate, history is a chain of conflicts and wars which disperse mankind over the globe; reconcentrate it, of necessity, in states; become more violent, due to that concentration; and finally, at the point of greatest peril, compel the establishment of international law. In this case it is a mistake to consider history a product of human freedom. As a whole it remains subject to natural laws, because the concepts of arbitrariness are concepts of nature,[15] not of freedom. The infinite sequence of historical acts is comparable to the mechanical law of the epicycloid; like that law, it has to bring about concord by means of discord. It is precisely with reference to the maddest acts of human license, therefore, that Kant speaks of "the great artist Nature" (59: VIII,

360) who will not impose laws of duty but will establish its desired order by commanding and, if need be, coercing man against his will. The worst possible eudaemonistic course of history is thus sublimated in the natural law and can, in analogy to the course of nature, be sketched in ideas as ideal types.

The design of the best possible course of history—sketched approximately, at least, in Kant's *Debate of Departments* and called for, in principle, in all his political writings—starts with the assumption that political acts originate in the good will anchored in the law of reason. Until now, of course, history provides no illustrations of political action proceeding consistently toward a morally based order. But it does give us a *signum*, a "historic sign" (38: VII, 84) in which morality is manifested as a cause. Kant thought he could see this sign in the worldwide approval bestowed on the French Revolution. Because this approval was hazardous everywhere, he felt it must have sprung from a morality newly awakened in mankind; and thus experience itself seemed to him to attest the reality of the best possible design—a design in which man freely founds the republican order, first in the different states and then, by their free federation, in the world as a whole. He thus creates the political condition in which war is freely abolished and its suspension guaranteed by human ethics.

The infinite series of these free acts also remains tied to nature. The intelligible origin in freedom takes effect in phenomenality, and it does so by starting a new causal chain but simultaneously, without a break, joining it to the phenomenon that has resulted from natural causality. The effect of freedom fits thus into the effect of natural necessity, with freedom essentially proving to be the capacity to combine the intelligible realm with nature and to do this by law. Freedom is the boundary concept between the two realms, wholly rooted in the one but always working toward the other also.

It cannot concern us here whether this conjunction of nature and freedom is tenable in detail. What matters to us is to see that even the best of political possibilities—invariably to act on the intelligible ground of reason—will produce effects not running counter to the effects of nature but imperceptibly meshing with the natural ones, although originating elsewhere. The whole spectrum of political effectiveness can thus be considered secured, as it were, by the course of nature. This course aims always at the creation of the cosmos out of chaos, which is why history's entire course, whether the initial driving force was license or liberty, is anticipatorily drafted in analogy to the natural process of creation. History is the infinite creative process of freedom, a process which, like everything that occurs, can be understood in a parallel view: as a natural process (in analogy to the self-created order of the epicycloid) and as a challenge for freedom.

Does this securing by nature entitle us to make prophesying prognoses? It could do so only if the two ideal constructions were purely realized. In one case nature would repeat, according to laws of mechanics, what it universally accomplishes already; in the other, it would be good will itself that fulfills its prophetic prediction.

What comes between, in both cases, is man, who can find the "turning point" (38: VII, 83) everywhere within the disclosed range of variations—man who acts now freely, now arbitrarily, and keeps bringing new sides of his indeterminable disposition to the fore. In regard to particular historic acts it is therefore flatly impossible to venture any theoretical prognosis. Without relinquishing its dignity, however, reason cannot conceive the infinite series of acts as an eternal to and fro. A rational man can never knowingly assume the "standpoint of Providence" (38: VII, 83), and yet, in pure reflection, he seems premonitorily to survey, in analogy to the series of natural acts, what would have to happen if men or nature were to make reason effective. He always keeps hoping to be en route to the grand order: to the conjunction of nature and freedom according to inner principles of the law in mankind. The terminal point of this hope is not the moral law, but a unity not to be seen through by the *intellectus ectypus*—a unity that is "neither nature nor freedom, but is linked with the ground of freedom, with the supersensory" (35: V, 353; cf. 341). It was at this unity that Kant aimed his thoughts in the period of critical metaphysics as well as in that of *The Only Possible Proof.* For this unity's sake he construed all his dubious links between things that the human intellect cannot help separating; for its sake, he fell into paradoxes he did not always recognize as such, and for its sake, perhaps, he sometimes passed the bounds that continue to delimit critical reason.

In summary, we have uncovered not merely one analogy, but several. We found the first, in an early treatise, in the relation between a naturally formed order and the infinite series of free acts—a relation we find again, twofold, in the drafts of history. What this means for the lines on nature as the guarantor of peace is that those lines, on their part, are conceived in analogy to the formation of a natural order in the epicycloid. Here, too, thought forms of the early natural philosopher are unmistakable.

3. THE ANCHORING IN THE ONE

The analogy we have just seen, between the course of nature and the infinite series of free acts, drew our attention to something that is neither freedom nor nature but encompasses both. We call it "the One." It is a kind of anchor, pointed out time and again by the trend to unity that we sense throughout Kant's work. But when we try to get hold of it in the analysis of critical philosophy, it fades away. Remaining tangible are dualities and trinities or a multiplicity of unities we can name: unity of consciousness, unity of experience, unity of nature, unity of purpose, and so forth. All of them are mere reflections of what they refer to. The One remains incomprehensible. It remains in the background, so that it will not infrequently be overlooked or passed by. Kant's philosophy may seem, then, to be dualistic.

In the early writings, the anchoring in the One is still clearly visible. Here we try to show that it remained a determining factor in the late works also, and thus for Kant's political thinking.

The One Ground of Every Possibility

In none of the other precritical writings is the One that underlies everything pursued with the intensity of *The Only Possible Proof.* There the One is equally the basis of all reality and all possibility, with something real ultimately guaranteeing the possibility of the possible, while the possible points to the existence of the real. How are we to understand this?

The difference between reality and possibility is not a matter of their logical conjunction. What is real is not more essential than what is possible. *In* the real thing, "not more is posited than in a merely possible thing" (17: II, 75). But *by* the real, more *is* posited than by the possible: posited along with all the predicates of the possible thing is existence, which "cannot itself be a predicate" (17: II, 74). This is why a definite possibility (though presupposing reality at large) gives us no definite reality as yet, while a reality gives us its possibility and, furthermore, the absolute position of existence.

Possibility is either formal or material. A thing is formally possible if its predicates are linked without contradiction, both among themselves and with the subject; it is materially possible if it contains any material for thought at all. An elliptical square is formally impossible; materially it is possible, since ellipse and square are both thinkable, if not in this conjunction. Because of the conjunction that makes it inwardly impossible, the elliptical square will never be called a possibility; but in principle, material possibility is given as long as "there is a cogitative datum" (17: II, 78). Not until all existence is voided will the material possibility disappear. The negation of all existence is not formally impossible—because existence by itself contains no predicate at all and is not a predicate—but neither can it be said to be formally possible, for it always takes something material to show formal possibility. Without any existence there is no possibility at all. Since there is possibility, however, it is "downright impossible that nothing exists at all" (17: II, 79). Conversely put, in the form of a thesis: reality is a condition of possibility.

This invariably presupposed reality is the first real ground "wherein and whereby every cogitative thing is given" (17: II, 83). Without it, there would be nothing. Since there is possibility, the first real ground is absolutely necessary. As the necessary being, it is unitary, uniform, immutable, and eternal. In a word: the invariably presupposed reality is God. Thus *The Only Possible Proof* already answers the question which Kant explicitly raised only in the prize treatise, *Inquiry into the Clarity of the Principles of Natural Theology and of Ethics,* which he published a year later, in 1764. It is the question that came to be fundamental in Schelling's[1] philosophizing: "Whether it is possible that absolutely nothing exists at all" (21: II, 297). And the answer has an audible ring of Descartes and Leibniz: There is not nothing, because there is God. The fact that makes me conscious of God's existence is that my thinking cannot do away with possibility as such. For the fact that I am thinking demonstrates that there are cogitative data, and that accordingly there is material possibility—which in turn necessarily presupposes a unitary Something.

Thus everything real and cogitative goes back to, and indicates, a primal ground. The primal ground is the transcendental reason why there are any possible and real things. In it, all things are linked, whether they belong to the realm of nature or to that of morals. Kant cannot prove the existence of this ground, of course, because he recognizes "that all our cognition ultimately terminates in insoluble concepts" (17: II, 73); but he is not only confident but sure of his ability to indicate the proof, at least, and to elucidate in it what the ultimate One might be.

It is questionable whether this analytically attained and dogmatically maintained One as a supporting ground can continue to play any part in Kant's critical philosophizing. Since this is characterized by a turn away from ontology and toward the self-contemplation of reason, we initially tend to look for the One in reason. But human reason itself cannot be the One. Reason is multifarious and limited. It is multifarious because it really includes three different faculties—working with concepts, conceiving ideas, and passing judgments—and because in the fields that go with these faculties, in speculative cognition, the design of unifying ideas, and the playful view of beauty, it must exercise irreconcilable functions. And our reason is limited because in cognition it can always grasp only in the particular what is reality for us; it can never grasp reality in itself, or the totality of reality; and it is limited further because, while constituting reality by our free acts, it must promptly leave the effects of this reality to the law of natural causality. Other expressions of the limitations of reason are the many gaps and holes in its system, which Kant himself sees and considers unavoidable. Why can the intellect think in categories only? Why are there exactly twelve categories? Why do we know only two forms of visuality? Why is our faculty of judgment tied to precisely these functions? How could the conditional relationships of duty and inclination ever come to be reversed in man? How is it possible for man to change? What is the substrate of appearance? What is the unity of the world as a whole?

All these questions, and we might list many more, indicate data which reason does not give to itself, but in which reason finds the field of its activities in predesigned forms. Solely in the contemplation of beauty does reason seem to gain access to the whole of being, but this occurs only in play and ultimately indicating something else, of which beauty is a symbol.

Reason is not the One. Hence it is not sufficient unto itself. Yet its very lack of self-sufficiency spurs it toward the One—which it does not know, but to which it can point by the construction of an infinite intellect, its counterimage. This counterimage is the *intellectus archetypus*. Of that we have "not the slightest conception" (31: IV, 316 note); but we draft its structure in ideas, to different ends: to show on this counterconstruction to the human intellect what the merely thinking intellect is not; to point beyond all dichotomies at the unity of a possible primal ground, and thus at the focus of all relative unities; to make us feel the intelligible ground of reason, the fact that it is not independent.

Our intellect must look to our senses for a visuality that always rests upon some given existence, in order to bring it under concepts by discursive thinking. But the *intellectus archetypus* can produce things intuitively by original visuality (cf. 30: B 72, 135). It constitutes reality by its self-consciousness. To the archetypical intellect, the possible is always real already; it does not need any synthesis to reduce diversity to the unity of consciousness (30: B 138–39). The infinite intellect itself constitutes absolute unity.

Our intellect always proceeds from "the analytically universal ... to the particular," which must be given to it by visuality and is subsumed by it under the universal, thanks to accidental concordances. The *intellectus archetypus*, on the other hand, proceeds without concepts from the "synthetically universal," from the view of a whole as such, to a particular. No part of the process is accidental; each is sublimated in the necessity of the one organic whole (35: V, 407). The *intellectus archetypus* knows no split between the particular and the whole, because the whole is always pre-created by its self-consciousness. It knows no split between possibility and reality, because its own view creates existence; no split between chance and necessity, because everything equally springs from the one self-consciousness; no split between mechanism and teleology, because the archetypical intellect establishes both purposive and mechanical unity. While we can always look at organisms only as if nature had intentionally joined them to unified ends, "independent reason" (30: A 678/B 706) creates the infinite lawful accord on its own. In a word: wherever our finite intellect cannot transcend the dichotomy, the all-encompassing One would always be transparent to the *intellectus archetypus,* because it already is that One.

The idea of this perfect intellect becomes important to our reason. Since the unity of our use of reason is the condition on which we have it at all, reason always takes its bearings from the idea of the archetypical intellect—not only so as to find in it "the school, and the very basis of the possibility, of the greatest use of human reason" (30: A 694–95/B 722–23), but also to have the "protection of such a primal ground" (30: A 678/B 706) for conceiving the systematic unity of the cosmos in ideas and recognizing all cosmic dualities as provisional. Based upon independent reason, its "feeble image" (30: A 678/B 706), human reason, dares to conceive the One itself.

Critical reason conceives this One, the intelligible substrate, as an idea. It advances to this idea by various ways, in various reflective contexts, and then calls it by various names, trying to designate something unknown in itself. From the viewpoint of nature as the totality of internal and external phenomena it is "the intelligible substrate of nature without and within ourselves" (35: V, 345). Viewed from the single phenomenon, it is the thing in itself, or the being in itself, which somehow—but in a manner not transparent to us, "for about the causal relation of the intelligible to the sensible there is no theory" (37: VI, 439 note)—qualifies the phenomenon. From the viewpoint of freedom, it is "the supersensory substrate of humanity" (35: V, 340) in the subject with which freedom is linked; from the viewpoint of beauty, the unknown ground in which freedom and the law are "joined as one, in a common and unknown manner" (35: V, 353); from the viewpoint of the cognitive faculty, the "supersensory substrate" (35: V, 344) that harmonizes all our cognitive faculties. Viewed from the modes of contemplating nature, it is the unknown ground on which teleology and mechanics meet (35: V, 422), and viewed from thinking, it is the substrate which simultaneously underlies nature and "our capacity to think" (35: V, 255).

What thus assumes different functions and takes different names in different contexts of reflection is always the One, the unknown. Kant indicates this by his way of making connections. The intelligible is the substrate within and without ourselves, the common root of thought and nature; it unites nature and freedom. It is the unknown that encompasses all Kantian metaphysics to the extent of its being *docta ignorantia*. To sidetrack it in one of its reflective functions (in the thing in itself, for example) is equally un-Kantian as to want to see it exclusively in another (in the substrate of mankind, for instance). Primarily, Kant is neither an epistemologist nor an ethicist. He is an encompassing metaphysician who will, in some respects, grant primacy in his cogitative universe to practical reason.

How is this intelligible substrate to be analogous to God in *The Only Possible Proof?*

The early treatise said of God that he is the ultimate ground of all real, possible, and conceivable things—in other words, the reality which transcendentally underlies everything pure and simple. In critical philosophy, only boundary concepts remain as such a ground. They are designations for the intelligible substrate, and in the context of our reflections we attach to them an absolute necessity. For in the language of transcendental philosophy we might put the question of Kant's prize treatise in the following terms: Why do experience and appearance exist at all? Why are there not only delusions? Kant answers that there is appearance because, beyond all subjective conditions that make it possible for things to appear, there is the objective condition which in a manner unknown to us makes appearance possible and confines it. The intelligible substrate is the "ground on which the faculty of conception can be defined in line with its sensory character" (54: VIII, 215).

Yet why is this intelligible substrate? We can answer only κατ' ἄνθρωπον, in a circle: So that there will not be delusion alone. It might be denied, perhaps, that the mutual basing of phenomenon and substrate on each other is a circle. Appearance is the *ratio cognoscendi*, or better, the *ratio indicandi* of the substrate; but the substrate is the *ratio essendi* of appearance. This, in turn, would mean that there is not delusion only, because there is the intelligible substrate—of whose being I come to be cogitatively conscious, for one thing, as I perceive reality, a common world.

Insofar as this unknown thing is also the substrate of freedom and thought, we must take it for the *ratio essendi* of everything real and thinkable. We may say, therefore, that the intelligible substrate, the One, assumes in *Critique of Judgment* (35) the function of that which *The Only Possible Proof* called God.

If the question why there should be an intelligible substrate is to be answered κατ᾽ ἀλήθειαν, however, what will occur—and therein lies the difference from the answer in the early treatise— is a collapse of the fundament. "The absolute necessity which is so indispensable to us, as ultimately underlying all things, is the true abyss for human reason. . . . It is an inescapable thought, but an unbearable one as well, that what we imagine as supreme among all possible beings should say to itself, as it were: 'I am from eternity to eternity; besides myself there is nothing but what I willed to be—yet *whence am I?*' Here everything sinks beneath us; the most perfect as well as the least hang in an unsettled balance before mere speculative reason, which can make either one vanish without the slightest hindrance and at no cost to itself" (30: A 613/B 641).[2]

The analogy we think we are seeing extends only to the transcendental function of the One in relation to everything else. It does not extend to the definitions of the One; not to the way it is held to be true, the way we speak of it; not to the freedom that gives us access to it. The analogy will say no more than that in both the critical and the precritical period everything rests transcendentally upon the One.

How does this affect politics? In general, we might say, in the measure in which it affects all metaphysics. Political thinking also aims at this One, as shown in our speculation about the parallelism of the course of nature and the infinite series of free acts. Like parallels, both lines intersect in infinity. In another sense, the One shows up in politics as a postulate. If politics is to be the way of freely realizing the one human order, each political act rests upon the intelligible substrate precisely because of the witness it bears to freedom. Morality is the faculty of directly basing political acts on the One. In the end, therefore, only one kind of politics aims at the goal in each act, beyond any short-range purpose—a politics based upon ethics.

But does this not contradict all that we have been saying about politics as a task of prudence? After all, even this kind of politics finally rests on the One, though not by human action. But Kant is not thinking of action's being based upon the One directly; he thinks of an indirect basing that extends over the infinite series of acts. The difficulty is that no man can survey the infinite series as governed by natural causality. No man has the eye of Providence; none can tell where his acts stand in the infinite series and how his next act will fit into the series. His purely arbitrary act, even if directly calculated to a purpose, is therefore "subject to fate" (59: VIII, 370). Whoever thinks that with mechanical prudence he might use natural causality for his own ends is surrendering his ends to powers he cannot control. He would be surrendering himself. Our previous speculation on nature as a guarantor of peace cannot be brought into this calculation. It is a mere draft of reflective judgment; human reason is not "enlightened enough" (59: VIII, 370) to handle its determination. Politics as a purely "artistic assignment" (59: VIII, 377) is bound to fail.

For this very reason we need the law which holds political action in bounds, and we need morality, on which law can be established. Here our reason is lucid enough: it knows what it ought to do. It is not asking too much of reason to look upon politics as a "moral challenge" (59: VIII, 377). Hence the inalienable proposition: "True politics cannot take a step without having paid previous homage to morality. . ." (59: VIII, 380). This does not mean that it might dispense with prudence. Politics is the use of legality to extend the law that founds community; it takes prudence, cunning, force, an insight into real historic situations, and the positive right which is always wrong at the same time. But none of these is the last hinge of political action. For our reason, the positive law that is given is not yet the law that binds. This law lies in the idea alone, in the source from which morality derives the lawmaking power that gradually brings right into the world. It is in the idea that prudence, cunning, and force must find their limits. Then only, politics may "hope, however slowly, to advance to its persistently radiant stage" (59: VIII, 380).

The call to politics from freedom has its full urgency regardless of the speculation from the course of nature to peace. Although it is true that both arbitrary and free acts are ultimately founded on the One—the first directly, and the second indirectly—it is also true that qualitatively there is a "worldwide difference" (59: VIII, 377) between the two modes of foundation. The first will not attain its goal until the end of all things; the other always attains it in time, but cutting across time. The call to freedom in politics is a challenge to proceed toward world order so that the way will rest upon this One, not just in the goal, but everywhere en route. It is a call for that which alone is worthy of reason: the conscious concentration of political acts in the One.

4. CRITIQUE AND DEFENSE OF OUR UNDERTAKING

In part 1 we have sought to indicate the origins of some forms of political thought, and to fit these indications into the course of Kantian metaphysics. We thought we could see:

· that the early concept of monads provided the schema for the concept of unsociable sociality;

that these two concepts have analogous functions in the story of Creation as a history of an all-encompassing struggle in nature, and in the course of history as the history of the creation of mankind;

that the doctrine of the relativity of motion enables us better to understand the ambiguity of political concepts, and of philosophical concepts as a whole;

that Kant's thoughts about coexistence and community of substances came to point his way to thoughts about the founding of civil society and its relation to the founder;

that basic legal relations are considered in analogy to the basic mechanical relations between bodies;

that the historical functions of war and of evil are predesigned in the doctrine of repugnancies;

that the natural origin of the epicycloid in a gearbox is the observational and cogitative model for the origin, in line with concepts of nature and freedom, of a perfect social order;

that the concept of the intelligible substrate in *Critique of Judgment* assumes the same function of a transcendental ground of all things as the early concept of God in *The Only Possible Proof;* and that all in all, therefore, Kant's early natural-scientific and metaphysical writings are of fundamental significance to the structure of important political concepts and forms of political thought. Pointed out time and again in our presentation were the numerous breaches in the analogies, to show their relativity and to forestall the misconception that they alone might let us understand Kant's political thinking.

All these observations were brought into a schema of order. The analogies that aim at division were brought under the aspect of "diversity"; the analogies in which diversity is organized in the direction of unity were combined under the title "road to unity"; the analogy that refers to unity and to the One itself was given the motto "unity." In the process, this schema of order gradually proved to be typical of the course of Kantian metaphysics, a course clearly demonstrable even in the early writings. Starting out from diversity but anchored in the idea of the One, this metaphysics always moves along the road to unity.

Our presentation is open to grave doubts. They will help us clarify our premises.

Critique of the Presupposed Monism

The allegedly demonstrable course from diversity to unity—it may be said—projects into critical philosophy a monism which in fact it does not contain. Rather, what might be shown in this philosophy is a consistent dualism. Kant's metaphysics is a "two-worlds metaphysics."[1] It guarantees the existence of both the phenomenal and the noumenal world; it secures knowledge and experience as much as it facilitates faith. Man's twofold rational faculty corresponds to this duality, providing categories for the phenomenal world and drafting ideas for the noumenal one. Both are types of concepts designed for man, who is himself a twofold being, a naturally constituted creature of the senses and a rational creature that constitutes reality. Kant's entire system bears the stamp of this dualism, clearly shown in the division of his metaphysics into one of nature and one of morals, as well as in the many dichotomies. Kant himself regarded dualism as unbridgeable, pointing to his inability, for instance, to unite the two roots of cognition, the senses and the intellect of man, or to bring about a unity of duty and inclination.[2]

We may be told that the whole one-sidedness of our presentation shows even more clearly in what we sometimes call "a will to unity," sometimes "a will to the One." Kant calls this transcendental idea the "law of homogeneity" (30: A 659/B 687). It is a regulative principle which our reason is indeed immensely concerned with, but which alone would not enable us to think. For distinction's sake we need the contrary idea, "a transcendental law of specification" (30: A 656ff./B 684ff.). The principle of homogeneity is the condition of rising from lower to higher concepts; the principle of certification is the condition of descending from higher to lower concepts. Both equally lie in the interest of reason. We may be more concerned with unity at one time and more with diversity at another; but to grant precedence to either as a matter of principle would be absurd. Both are mere regulatives. A dispute about them would impede truth more than promote it.[3]

Whoever stresses merely the idea of the One will be suspected of having succumbed to the dialectical perversion of the regulative principle into a constitutive one. He is rationalizing. This is why everything said here about the course of Kantian metaphysics may spring from an exegesis of critical thought which has itself ceased to be critical. To ignore dualism has devastating effects: metaphysically it leads to dogmatism; logically, to a failure to differentiate; and politically, to violence.

We might respond as follows:

Our critics have spoken of dualism, of monism, and of a two-world metaphysics. Without exact restrictions, all these terms go past Kant. Dualism, according to Schelling, is every doctrine that starts out "from two absolutely different and mutually independent principles."[4] As monism, on the other hand, we can designate every doctrine that assumes a single substantial or effective principle alone. But where in Kant do we find the two different independent principles? How do we get hold of the one that stands alone?

Since there can be but one totality, the phenomenal world and its substrate are one and the same world, viewed through two media of cognition. The *intellectus archetypus* leaves this totality unsevered. The *intellectus ectypus* severs it, but becomes conscious of this severance only in reflection from conditioned phenomenality to the unconditional "that." It seeks a more profound knowledge about the irremovable dichotomy, but it is precisely in striving beyond conditionality that it seems to achieve the opposite of what it seeks. Ectypically intellectual reflections founder on the unity that is their goal. But the unconditional direction of thought remains and puts Kant's metaphysics on its peculiar course.

We can, therefore, talk of a Kantian dualism only insofar as man, a severing *intellectus ectypus,* finds himself in the world. Yet this means that there is no dualism in the proper sense. There are not two independent and intrinsically heterogeneous principles; there is only the humanly irrevocable disjunction of the one unknown principle by its unalterable medium of cognition.

For monism, on the other hand, this means that while the one principle is always sought, it never comes to be determinable. In each individual experience, the one principle is as if it were not. Its reality is purely transcendental.

As for the term "two-worlds metaphysics," this might be acceptable if it designated nothing but the split of the one world into its two aspects, a world in itself and a world for us. Since the term suggests more, however, it is as much a font of false associations as Nietzsche's "background world." Dualism, monism, and two-worlds metaphysics all fit a truth and suggest a falsehood. It is better to dispense with them and, instead of merely naming a thing, to visualize it in reflection; this alone will keep our thoughts unfalsified.

Kant himself referred occasionally to the problem of dualism. In the third section of *Nova dilucidatio* he mentioned the *insana opinio*[5] of the Manicheans, who attribute the governance of the world to two equally original and independent principles, although it must follow from the theorem of coexistence ("Finite substances are in community only insofar as they are formed in mutual relations by the common primal ground of their existence, the divine intellect"—6: 1, 412–13) that a substance cannot have anything to do with things of the world unless it is their common cause or has arisen with them from a common cause. If we exalt one of these principles into the cause of *all* substances, the other can have no way to determine anything about them; and if we conceive the one principle as merely the cause of *some* substances, there is no community between those and the rest. We would have to assume that one of the two principles depends upon the other, or that both are encompassed by a common cause. But this would contradict the premise of dualism. From the metaphysical point of view, dualism is unthinkable.

In the first edition of *Critique of Pure Reason* Kant accords a limited validity to the term. In the chapter on paralogisms, he calls the theory of the uncertainty of all external sense objects an "idealism," the theory of the possible certainty of these objects a "dualism" (30: A 367). The dualist, as distinct from the materialist and the spiritualist, is said to take matter and thinking creatures into his doctrinal concept "as things existing for themselves" (30: A 380). But he does so only "in the empirical sense" (30: A 379), the only sense in which there can be matter at all; in a transcendental sense there cannot be any dualism. "The transcendental object which underlies the external phenomena, and likewise that which underlies the inner visuality, is neither matter nor a thinking being in itself; it is a ground, unknown to us, of the phenomena that give us the empirical concepts of the first sort as well as of the second" (30: A 379–80).

Hence the formula for monism and dualism that might perhaps be acceptable: empirical dualism, but transcendental monism. In this formula we understand the duality of the principles as something that is definitive in phenomenality but ultimately not definitive, while the unity of the principle is ultimately definitive but can never be definitively attained.

From this point of view there are two possible forms of dogmatic Kant interpretation. One establishes an empirical monism, the other a transcendental dualism. By the latter, evil may be wrought in speculation only; the former carries evil into politics. The result of empirical monism would be the utmost violence. Our presentation was an attempt to avoid both forms of dogmatism.[6]

The charge that we made dogmatic use of the regulative principle of homogeneity is unwarranted. The will to unity shows as much in the principle of specification as it does in that of homogeneity. According to Kant, both are "principles of systematic unity" (30: A 662/B 690). Above them there must, therefore, be a higher concept of the One, encompassing both. Kant points to this concept when he says that the principles of homogeneity and specification are so linked by the principle of affinity that a differentiating contemplation of all things is made possible by the three together, "since they have all sprung from one stem" (30: A 660/B 688). It is at this root—which lies behind the dualism of homogeneity and specification and is not merely the affinity principle—that Kantian metaphysics aims. Our presentation is thus not absolutizing a regulative, which always needs a complement.

But as for the One we are speaking of here, this is indeed not logically thinkable any more—which would be a valid objection against a system that would settle the One in the realm of logic and conceive it as a determinant. It would be a system logically based on an illusion. Kant never goes that far. He indicates the One, aware that he will never have it. In this attitude, the logical undefinability of the One does not obscure the lucidity of that which is logically definable in diversity.

Critique of the Intent of Our Undertaking

With respect to the intent of our undertaking, that is, our attempt to show that thought forms of Kant's early writings are at work in his political thinking, it might be objected that all these analogies are questionable, since they start with the assumption that equal relations prevail in the natural and the moral realms. For this is the premise of analogy: relations in both cases must be equal. How can we know that they are? And if we cannot know, why assume it? Are we not simply leveling basic distinctions and thus eventually jeopardizing the autonomy and the supremacy of ethics? Here, too, the secret motor is an uncritical premise: the thought of a continuous ascent from physics to metaphysics. But in reality there is a leap between these realms, a leap which in the interest of ethics should not be glossed over.

To this criticism we might respond as follows:

In the precritical period Kant actually tried to ascend from physics to metaphysics. We have an example in the treatise on "negative quantities," in which the forms of repugnancy, worked out in numerical relations, are transferred to metaphysics. There we read that the method of this transfer is generally commendable—that, for example, "from the mathematical view of motion, combined with cognition of space . . . a great many data come to hand in order to obtain the metaphysical view of time in the channels of truth" (18: II, 168).

In the prize treatise of 1763, Newton's method is adopted as the proper method also of metaphysics.[7] It is said to consist in tracking down the legalities in things that are easily observable and transferring them to "complex natural occurrences" (21: II, 286) whose legality is not transparent.

The point is clearer yet in *The Only Possible Proof*, a metaphysical treatise into which Kant wove a summary of the cosmogony that he had worked out in strict accordance with natural laws. The inserts, he says apologetically, might seem to threaten the unity of the contemplated object—"yet as my intent in these cases aims primarily at the method of using natural science to ascend to a cognition of God, I could not well achieve this purpose without such examples" (17: II, 68). The axiom of this ascent is an old, unquestioned heritage of academic philosophy: conceptual cognition applies beyond the realm of visuality.

Critical philosophy did away with this axiom. Without visuality, whether empirical or pure, no cognition is possible any longer. The noumenal world, the world of ideas, is severed from the phenomenal world. We know nothing about it. Kant does not conceive this severance as a leap, however, but as a boundary on which a junction occurs. Here, too, he may be guided by an old metaphysical regulative of the contemplation of nature: *In mundo non datur abyssus, saltus, casus, fatum.*[8] The leap which overthrows the systematics of a doctrine "cannot be suffered in a philosophy" (94: XXI, 407) unless we want to give up making connections between concepts.

Kant's view of the way in which the noumenal might possibly be related to the phenomenal is about as follows. The intellect is limited. It occupies a full realm of experience, surrounded by an empty realm of the noumena. Regulative ideas take it to the bounds of knowability. "Here is a real conjunction of the known with something wholly unknown" (31: IV, 354) to which reason "points" (31: IV, 355). In this conjunction we must take care at the same time to avoid transcendent judgments by an uncritical use of categories, and yet, by means of categories, to connect concepts that lie outside immanence. We can reconcile both demands only "on the boundary of all permissible use of reason" (31: IV, 356; cf. IV, 357). We are staying on that boundary when we limit our judgments strictly to the relation of the noumenal to the character of our reason or to our world in general. We are not attributing qualities to the noumenal itself, then, only to its relation to the phenomenal. The words we use still have a thing-

like character, but it is no longer transferred to the object we
mean (31: IV, 357).[9]

Cognition is assured only if the reality of concepts can be
shown. The reality of empirical concepts is guaranteed by examples, that of intellectual concepts, by a pure view of the schema.
Rational concepts alone are left without an objective means of
representation. So reason resorts to a "makeshift" (81: XVIII, 567;
6301): subjective representation in the realm of objectivity. What
is represented here is not the unknown as such but its relation to
us. The thing represented is the reproduction of this relation on
the basis of concepts of immanence. It makes the relation thinkable. The representing agent serves as a thought model for the
represented thing—not really as its symbol, as Kant calls it. What
links the two is the analogy, which Kant defines as "a perfect
likeness of two relations."[10]

Analogies, he says in *Universal Natural History,* must guide
us "wherever the intellect lacks the thread of infallible proof"
(4: I, 315). Later, they are the guidelines of our reason wherever,
as a matter of principle, there cannot be cognition any more, only
elucidation. We owe it to the analogy that rational concepts,
though objectively empty, do not remain definitively empty for
us. It is with their help, for example, that God's relation to the
world of the senses becomes conceivable for us in terms of man's
relation to one of God's products (81: XVIII, 554 f.; 6286). What
reason does for us can in the conjunction of force and effect be
conceived in analogy to causality; what immortality means to us,
in analogy to the conjunction of a very long time and all time
(81: XVIII, 221; 5552).

One question remains unclarified: What entitles Kant to assume that relations are equal? His metaphor of a boundary location suggests the false notion that I might at least look across the
boundary, might see the unknown country and determine how
things over there look from my point of view. Yet if nothing but
a dark void lies beyond my place on the boundary, all determination ceases, including the determination of relations. I have first
to populate this void with ideas of reason, and to posit my relation to the objects of the ideas. Why does Kant posit these
relations in analogy to the physical world? Why not, as in the
contrary construction of the *intellectus archetypus,* so as to complement other known relations? Presumably, the maxim of "the

universal unity of reason" (81: XVIII, 97; 5119) leads him to assume that the legality of phenomenal things rests upon the legality of intelligible things. It is on this premise only that we might understand the passage: "The intelligible world has laws to fit me for every world, . . . whatever natural or social constitution, my own or external, I may come into" (81: XVIII, 221; 5552).

To the objection that these analogies blur the distinction between the realms of nature and of ethics, between the phenomenal and the noumenal world, we might reply that on Kantian premises it is not up to me whether or not I want to think in analogies, only whether or not I want to consider the intelligible realm at all. If I want to consider it—and I am urged to do so by a rational need, so that perhaps I am not free in this respect either—my only means of representing what is unknown in itself is the analogy. It does not confuse things; it conjoins, and it conjoins relational concepts only. To be able to assume a relational equality at all, however, we must indeed conceive a transcendental monism beyond empirical dualism—a primal, unattainable ground of all thinkability and legality. This monism does not jeopardize the autonomy of ethics, but it is a premise of my ability to will the utmost generalization of the principle of my free acts in laws of nature.

Critique of the Method of Our Undertaking

Even if one should accept what has been said, two objections can still be made to the method of this part of our book.

(a) Time and again, inferences in the field of transcendental politics have been drawn here—now from mechanics, now from mathematics, now from cosmogony or from dogmatic metaphysics. Each of these inferences is a μετάβασις εἰς ἄλλο γένος, a step into an alien field. Coming out of this are falsely defined concepts. The whole of part 1 seems therefore like a chain of logical transgressions. If Kant himself should be responsible, he would have to be told: *Caesar non est supra grammaticos.*

(b) When Kant was reflecting on analogies, he was doing so either with respect to the concept of God or with respect to freedom and immortality. Here, statements on the principle of these object-bound analogies were used to broaden the principle of analogizing at will, and to set up relational equations that are questionable in themselves. Such equations must be justified not only formally but historically; it must be proved that they were performed by Kant himself, and that he was aware of his method. Otherwise they may remain of interest as exegeses, perhaps, but nothing will be clearly, unequivocally proven about Kant's actual procedure.

Kant himself has answered both of these charges.

Ad (*a*) In logic it is impermissible to transfer cognitions from kind to kind. Definite criteria of cognition and distinction are obtained on definite objects; they are objectively valid only for those objects or what is to be subsumed under the objects, not for anything alien in kind. But the step from the field of knowing into that of not knowing is not only permissible but necessary. In this step we do not claim to convey objective cognitions or even probabilities; we draft subjectively necessary hypotheses and ideas, in analogy to known things. The passage into a completely new field takes us simultaneously into another use of reason and into another mode of holding things to be true. What is transferred loses its concrete reality and gains a *"realitas noumenon"* (81: XVIII, 554; 6286). He who takes the step transforms objective cognition into a guideline of subjective elucidation. No "inference" on an alien field is drawn at all; an alien field is merely made accessible to elucidation.

This use of analogy cannot lead to falsely defined concepts, because no concepts as such are defined at all; only their relation to us is considered. Combined with this methodological consciousness, analogy is not an impermissible metabasis. It always links only κατ᾽ ἄνθρωπον; κατ᾽ ἀλήθειαν; it leaves the gap unclosed. The thinker's task, therefore, is not to avoid analogies because they are, allegedly, impermissible transgressions; his task is to keep analogies from turning into such transgressions. In Kantian politics, as everywhere in critical philosophy, the task can only be performed by a sense of methodology. This must make it transparent that the same basic thoughts can have a wholly different weight and meaning in precritical and critical writings. In the course of this first part we had to speak predominantly of the same thought forms, which may have allowed the impression to arise that the thoughts themselves had the same degree of certainty attributed to them each time. To make clearly evident that this is not the case would require an interpretation of Kant's politics in their entirety, which is not our task here. What is said in this chapter should thus not be taken as such an interpretation; it should be taken as a demonstration of equal thought forms, from which—and really against our basic intention—we open interpretive vistas that are possible, but never exclusively possible.[11]

Ad (*b*) That in thinking politically, along the lines we have shown, Kant was consciously analogizing is a fact that can be proved. We find the first indication as early as 1765, in the important and informative *Remarks on Observations on the Feeling of the Beautiful and Sublime*. Kant says here that a man's only natural and necessary property in relation to the will of others is equality and freedom; in relation to the whole, it is unity. "Analogy: by repulsion a body fills its own space, as every man fills his. By attraction, all parts join into one" (86: xx, 165).

Some five years later he writes: "The relations of law can be compared with those of bodies."[12] In both cases the reciprocity of relations applies according to the theorem *actio est aequalis reactioni*.

This thought is then taken up again in *Prolegomena*: "There is thus an analogy between the legal relations of human action and the mechanical relations of moving forces: I can never do something against another without giving him the right, under the same conditions, to do the very same thing against me; just as a body cannot act with its moving force upon another without thereby causing the other to counteract it as much. Here the right and the moving force are quite dissimilar things, and yet there is complete similarity in their relations" (31: IV, 357–58 note). And after six more years the same thought is clarified further, in *Critique of Judgment*: "So I can, by analogy with the law of equal action and reaction in the mutual attraction and repulsion of bodies, conceive the relations of the members of a community under rules of law; but I cannot transfer those specific definitions (material attraction or repulsion) to the community and ascribe them to the citizens, to make up a system called the state" (35: V, 464–65).

About 1773 we find the analogy between the formation of society and the origin of the world: "Small societies are formed by inclination, civil ones by need, and states by war. We cannot see to the end of this evolution, but it is pernicious for itself and for mankind. What is the ultimate consequence? That the state is a body of free civil societies, which in turn, with still larger ones, makes up a corps, as do the systems of stars" (75: XV, 607; 1394). In *Anthropology*, the historic function of war is compared with an "engine of Providence . . . where the forces striving against each other are indeed impairing one another by friction, but are still kept running regularly for long times by the push or pull of other mainsprings" (39: VII, 330).

Finally, in *Doctrine of Virtue*, Kant puts antagonism to use for the intelligible world in analogy to the physical world: "When we are talking of laws of duty (not laws of nature) in man's external relation to each other, we think of ourselves in a moral (intelligible) world in which the connection of rational beings (on earth) is used in analogy with the physical world, by attraction and repulsion. By the principle of mutual love they are directed constantly to approach one another; by the respect they owe each other, to keep their distance from each other. And if one of these great moral forces were to decline, 'the void (of immorality) would with its gaping maw gulp down the entire realm of (moral) creatures like a drop of water' (if I may use Haller's words here, only in a different respect)" (37: VI, 449).

All of this seems to me to permit the conclusion that one may speak of conscious analogizing where Kant, often after an interval of decades and without methodological reflections, clearly lets himself be guided by an analogy as a "very important aid to our cognition."[13]

Let us summarize the conclusions reached in part 1: A comparison of Kant's early writings with his political thought —which is materially unfolded only in his late writings— shows this thought guided not infrequently, and at decisive points, by analogies that go back to the early natural-scientific and metaphysical treatises. We can demonstrate such analogies in concept formations, in trains of thought, in evolutionary processes. Cogitative structures that had long been formed would acquire political contents later, most of them three decades later. As forms they had been cast from the beginning.

If only because of this inception, Kant's political thinking will not be regarded as unoriginal, let alone as the epiphenomenon of a philosopher's waning strength.

PART TWO

KANT AS A POLEMICIST
The Struggle for Metaphysics

> In every debate about truth we have a common
> interest as between friends (man and wife) and
> should therefore be sympathetic rather than exclu-
> sive, selfish, and egotistical. I must begin by noting
> where the other is right (79: XVI, 273; 2213).

In our discussion, in part 1, of the analogies between Kant's
early natural-philosophical and metaphysical writings and his
late political ones, the motif of antagonism and conflict kept
reappearing in concept formations, thought forms, and evolutionary processes. This motif may be presumed to have special
relevance in critical philosophy, a relevance which our previous
findings let us understand as the impulse to unity. We look for
that unity, first, in the history of Kantian thought, and there,
broadly put, we see conflict as contention with ideas, whether
the ideas came from great philosophers, from contemporaries,
or from Kant himself. As an overall term for the manifold forms
of this conflict we choose the concept "polemics." In part 2 we
talk about Kant as a polemicist, and about the significance of
polemics in the history of his thinking.

Philosophical polemics can be discussed in two perspectives
that differ in principle. In one of these, the word means a mode
of the controversy that reason throughout its history carries on
with itself. This controversy runs anonymously, as it were,
through the entire history of thought, from era to era and from
system to system. Individual thinkers are viewed as mere organs
of reason in its incessant polemical monologue. The weight of
their individuality pales before the historic function of their utterances. In part 3 this function will be discussed under another
name.

In the other perspective, polemics means a mode of the contention between one thinking existenz and the claims of another.

This controversy is waged from thinker to thinker, either as a dialogue or as several monologues concerning each other. It is this sort of polemics that we discuss in part 2.

As an aid in distinguishing the types, we employ the terms "major" and "minor" polemics. By major polemics we mean the struggle of historically evolved reason against its own claims insofar as they have arisen from uncritical self-understanding; by minor polemics we mean the struggle of any historic existenz against opposing claims. Minor and major polemics do not designate different kinds of polemicizing; they refer to different aspects of the same phenomenon. What is major polemics must find its language in the ever-particular contention of specific individuals. The struggle of reason is an abstraction that makes its concrete appearance in the struggles of thinkers. Concretely there is only minor polemics. All major polemics must be comprehensible as minor polemics.

But not all minor polemics are major ones at the same time. We may ask about their importance to the history of reason. Faced with this question, any concrete polemic will appear either as an insignificant quarrel of two individuals who are confusing the essence, or as a fight between one historic existenz and another—a fight that may be subjectively momentous and yet objectively trivial—or, finally, as the outflow of major polemics, as the use which reason makes of a historic voice, so to speak. If a philosophy believes not only in possible forward steps taken by rational men but in the real progress of reason (albeit only by forward steps of rational men), the third meaning of polemics has particular relevance.

Kant himself did not make this terminological distinction. In his reflections on metaphysical debate he almost always meant major polemics. Where he himself was drafting methods of debate, he could not help thinking of minor polemics, insofar as they are at the service of major polemics. And where he was finally polemicizing himself, it was done with a sense of responsibility to the progress launched by his critique. His overriding interest seems to have been in the side of polemics that concerns the history of reason.

Despite all this, we stick to our proposed terminological distinction. In this distinction we look at factual polemics in the framework of Kantian philosophizing as a whole. We need not abandon the insights gained from an analysis of such polemics. Here we mean not only, and not primarily, those insights into specific problems taken up in a polemic; we mean the ultimate insight in the name of whose authority the fight is waged at all. This tells us not only about a thinker's views and personal peculiarities; it gives us a glimpse of the roots of his philosophizing. The analysis of factual polemics will come to have its own philosophical substance.

5. KANTIAN DRAFTS OF THE MODES OF CONTENTION

Designs of the modes of philosophical combat can be found at various points in Kant's work, dating from altogether different periods. In a sense, they frame his work. The first draft, bold in its claims but hardly conscious yet of the fight's significance in principle, appears in the preface to the very first essay; the last, more reserved in its claims, but aware by now of the weight of the themes, in *The Debate of Departments* (38). In between, we find drafts in *Critique of Pure Reason* and in *Critique of Judgment*. Brief references are scattered throughout Kant's creative activity.

In our presentation of these modes of combat we choose to start with a chronological procedure.

Dispute and Controversy in the Early Writings

Kant has no uniform terminology for the various modes of philosophical contention. To our knowledge, the word "polemics" does not occur in the precritical writings, but the adjective "polemical"[1] does occur several times. It is used in those days for a specific manner of instruction, opposed to the "doctrinal" (79: XVI, 783; 3332) or to the "didactic" (79: XVI, 839; 3442). The type of instruction is polemical if the material is not deductively unveiled in a structure of proof but acquired and elucidated in contention. Since every type of this disputatious instruction is called polemical in the early writings—the central type, the critical (accompanied then by the skeptical), was not added until later[2]—we may, without doing violence to Kantian usage, employ "polemics" as a cover concept for all modes of philosophical contention.

On one occasion Kant himself dissected this cover concept and thus specified the polemical modes: "To controvert for truth's sake; to dispute for the sake of being right, i.e., superior in debate (eristically, quarreling)" (79: XVI, 857; 3473).

Hence a polemic carried on for truth's sake would be a controversy, while a dispute would be a quarrel sought in order to strengthen one's ego. The aim of the first is cognition; the aim of the second, victory. Only the first can be truly philosophical; the second is but a collective term for philosophical perversions. The distinction as such aims primarily at the authority in whose name the struggle is waged. In our sketch of its modes we shall therefore try to separate combatants, combat, and combat methods along the lines of their governing authority, so that insofar as the early writings provide material at all, we may draft two polemical borderline forms that are mutually exclusive, in other words, in conflict with one another.

Every polemic begins with one combatant automatically claiming either to catch the other in an error or to be able to show him the truth more clearly. The claim appears the more immodest the more eminent the victim's name and the more insignificant the name of the attacker. And if, like the twenty-two-year-old Kant in his first publication, one has the temerity to challenge almost all important living experts in a field along with such great dead ones as Descartes and Leibniz, the claim seems virtually brazen. Kant knew this, and yet he did not give up the claim. "There is a good deal of presumptuousness in saying that a truth wooed in vain by the greatest masters of human cognition has shown itself first to my mind. I dare not justify this notion, yet neither did I wish to renounce it" (1: 1, 10).

The refusal to renounce was justified because the claim as such says nothing yet about the authority in whose name it is ventured. We may think about it like Lessing,

> Kant starts a serious business:
> Mankind to educate.
> He rates all living forces,
> Only his own he does not rate,[3]

and thus dismiss the claim as vain, indeed as laughable. But we also can, and in retrospect we really must, think as follows: Kant was never vain. What he expresses here is the fact that great experts can err, the courage to use one's own intellect, and a readiness to dare to know and—usually resented even more—to communicate this knowledge.

There may be an external criterion that will make it clear when a claim is justified. This is the will to publicity. Any claim, however large, must be permissible on two conditions: if it goes against thinkers who can still reply unless they are too vain, and if the man who makes the claim does want an answer. It is not the text that decides whether a claim is vain; if it were, everything new would have a strike against it. The crux is in the name of which authority the claim is ventured. Our only possible assurance that this authority is the pursuit of truth lies in the will to publicity. Where this is given, the charge of vanity becomes an irrelevant and discriminating argument *ad personam*. It is not rare for the charge of vanity to be more vain than the seemingly vain claim itself.

Of the polemical claims in Kant's early writings it might thus be said that claims as such are inevitable; the question is by what authority they are made. In the pursuit of truth, as manifested in the will to publicity, no claim can be barred, because in the public forum no claim is definitive; all are set forth in order to be argued and corrected. The challenge, then, is nothing but a more effective bid for a discourse. Its very brusqueness may hide a will to communicate.

A polemic that freely dares to challenge the partner presupposes freedom in two ways. As "freedom from" it means not to be bound by "laws of reputation" (13: II, 15), nor by past "philosophers' teachings" (21: II, 275) or seemingly infallible definitions. In this freedom, the reputation "of the Newtons and Leibnizes" counts for naught "if it should set itself against the discovery of truth" (1: I, 7). The thesis "of however famed a man" (1: I, 9) counts for naught if the intellect cannot follow. Such freedom liberates from reputation, admiration, and awe to the extent to which they cripple intellect and reason.

This indicates already that such "freedom from" is at the same time a "freedom for"—namely, for truth and reason. As such it is freedom to test all things anew, since truth has not yet been definitively discovered (cf. 6: I, 387); and it is freedom to find one's guide to truth in reason (cf. 13: II, 16). In the end, as freedom "to obey no other persuasion than the intellect's train of thought" (1: I, 7), it comes to be the freedom to be oneself.

Freedom to be oneself involves "rather hateful consequences" (1: I, 9). But it is legitimized by the cause, by the great men under attack, and finally by the authority cited for the attack: even a "dwarf-sized scholar" (1: I, 9)—and that is what the young Kant considered himself—may surpass a great one in a certain point, without being superior to him in the whole domain of scholarship. In the field of accuracy it is possible, in specifics, to know better than one's intellectual superior.

The great victims themselves became great by making use of freedom. The use of freedom, without which there is no insight, must matter more to them than individual insights. What makes little men possible partners of great men is love of freedom, not agreement on views (1: I, 8). The ultimate justifications of this freedom are reason and truth, for they assure that it is more than license.

Free scholars alone are suitable polemical opponents. But we find love of freedom and veracity only where we find true merit and true scholarship. To the young Kant, truly free scholars are those upon whom no higher praise can be heaped "than that all views, not excepting their own, may be unhesitantly criticized before them" (1: I, 7). Such men speak "the cautious language of reason" (24: II, 333). In their hands "all things become precise, intelligible, and agreeable" (18: II, 170). Their minds are always open to new things. Not only does their honor remain safe in contention (1: I, 138); it is an honor to have them as adversaries (1: I, 13). To make adversaries of them is an expression of gratitude, for without their work one might have been incapable of accomplishing anything.

Aside from these true scholars, the young Kant spurns many opponents because they cannot be true adversaries. With those one must not bother, because they do not count. They are the many who judge without reading or listening. They criticize what they have only heard about, what they do not know, what their prejudices will not let them see. "They are the ones who dwell at the foot of Parnassus, as the saying goes . . . and have no voice in the choosing" (1: I, 8).

This sounds presumptuous; but one must know whom Kant numbers with this multitude. It includes the metaphysical intellectuals "whose pretended insight does not know any bounds" (18: II, 204); the sophisticates who act as if human happiness depended upon finesses (17: II, 65); the know-it-alls who find "no basic truths that cannot be demonstrated" (16: II, 61); the "thorough philosophers" who look so deeply into things "that to them nothing remains hidden, inexplicable, and incomprehensible" (18: II, 201); and, finally, the professional experts whose academic tone "relieves the author as well as the reader of reflection" (24: II, 333) and whose "methodical prattle" has banished the Socratic word "I do not know" from the academies (24: II, 319). It is always the thinkers along academic and professional lines, the notables in the "school sects" (21: II, 275), whom the young Kant settles at the foot of Parnassus, at the place where he does not care to tarry in discussion.

The polemicist whose authority is the quest of truth will adapt his methods to that quest. He will "therefore make his investigations as simple and easy as possible" (1: I, 13), so that accuracy may be found in them along with illumination. He will not "stray across the sidewalks of philosophical contemplation" (1: I, 13), not even by way of courtesy and "ceremony" (1: I, 12). He may dispense with the outward signs of respect, with good manners, skillful toning down, mild language, because his fight itself is a form of respect. To him, error is error, falsehood is falsehood, and benightment is benightment, for he wants nothing but "to confess the truth without circumlocution" (1: I, 12). Bulk judgments are alien to him. He will show "how much truth there is in his opponent's assertions" (79: XVI, 845; 3455); he will bare the delusion that has led the other into error, and will eradicate its cause. "Rebuttal ought to be a step on the way to reunion, and that by way of correcting the cognitions on both sides" (79: XVI, 845; 3455). Thus the "cause of contention is removed" (79: XVI, 845; 3455). One argues "in order to agree" (79: XVI, 847; 3458). Polemics is "the method of participating in the general cause of human reason" (81: XVIII, 53; 4992). Mistakes are viewed as trivial; their correction offers the partner "a helping hand" (81: XVIII, 54; 4992), so that finally, with both cooperating even though embattled, truth may be served. Polemics comes to be the *"methodus Socratica"* (79: XVI, 850; 3465), the art of being midwife to the truth.

Next to this Socratic method, the practices of the multitude seem like poor attempts to serve personal vanity by stealth. Many resort to complicated and obscure proofs and save themselves "with the aid of night" (1: I, 15) from embarrassments they would have to admit in daylight. They add to the number of proofs as if their multiplicity could substitute for the cogency of a single one. They retreat to metaphysical hypotheses of "such immense flexibility" (24: II, 341) that all things can be covered with them. Conviction is put forth as insight, with a belief offered in the garb of science. Finally, help is sought in tricks: in the *argumentum ad verecundiam* (79: XVI, 850; 3464) that leaves the verdict up to reputation rather than to reason; in the *argumentum ab odio* (79: XVI, 857; 3472) that would allow strong affections to make up for the weakness of the intellect; or in the slick lawyer's proof (79: XVI, 858; 3474) that builds the triumph of one merely on the weakness of the other.

What the difference between the methods comes down to is that one of them looks for the partner's intrinsicality, for his strong side, and for clarification by means of that side, while the other besets him as a nonentity, points out that nonentity, and thereby covers his own.

He who polemicizes in the Socratic manner will approach the discussion in a certain basic posture, which Kant circumscribes as follows.

Such a polemicist wants truth. For truth's sake he must take the liberty to reexamine all past thought with factual arguments. To do this, he must "place a certain noble confidence in his own powers" (1: I, 10), and in that confidence, aware of the possibility that he may be in error, he must dare to leave "the beaten path" (1: I, 10). Such self-confidence will not prevent him from recognizing flaws in his cognition, flaws which he himself cannot correct. He makes no secret of these flaws; he makes them public, so they will be clarified. He checks the plaudits that are always ready for his own achievement, and he mistrusts them as long as the achievement is not equally prized by others. He sacrifices the "charm" (1: I, 31) of extensive cognition to a more thorough cognition, and he refrains from demonstrating his powers by means of "subtle error" (14: II, 29). Calling for "limitless assent" to his thoughts is alien to him. He knows that letting himself be convinced takes as much merit as convincing others; for to allow oneself to be convinced may well presuppose a superior measure of renunciation and self-examination. Involuntarily, of course, he will claim to be right; but he will not say so with the assurance of one who deems himself above instruction. "The claim to be right, so confidently voiced at the beginning, when one was stating one's reasons, is difficult to give up—but not quite so difficult if it was mild, uncertain, and modest" (17: II, 68).

The absence of vanity, of "partisan zeal" (1: I, 181), and of prejudice brings such a man to a "balance of emotional leanings"

(1: 1, 181) that will open his mind to the truth wherever it appears. Kant himself acquired this posture in his youthful writings. His literary self-portrait from the 1760s is also the best portrait of a Socratic polemicist:

> I have cleansed my soul of prejudices; I have expunged every blind devotion that ever stole inside me, to open doors for some imaginary knowledge. There is now nothing I care for, nothing I revere, but what occurs by way of sincerity in a calm mind accessible to all reasons; it may confirm or confound my previous judgments, may convince me or may leave me undecided. Wherever I meet something instructive, I make it my own. The judgment of one who refutes my reasons is my judgment—after I have weighed it first against the scale of my self-love, and then *in* that scale against my supposed reasons, and have found in it a greater substance [24: II, 349].

We thus find two modes of polemics in the writings of Kant's youth: the Socratic and the eristical. They have separate origins, and in *The Debate of Departments* we shall see the old Kant return to the distinction in an altered form, and see him regard it as the truly essential distinction. To the Kant of the three *Critiques,* however, it could not suffice.

The Polemical Use of Reason
in Critique of Pure Reason

In *Critique of Pure Reason,* aftereffects of the distinction between controversy and dispute are noticeable in a new pair of antitheses, "critique" and "polemics."[4] But these are not the modes of contention that Kant is unfolding. He is asking about a third, rather, which on the basis of the first two can be conceived as the critic's struggle against the polemicist. Kant calls this third form of combat the "polemical use of reason": "By polemical use of reason I mean the defense of its theses against their dogmatic negations" (30: A 739/B 767).

Three things are worth noting in this explication: (1) it fails to clarify the term "polemics"; (2) the "polemical use of reason" is a defensive discipline; (3) Kant views his polemical antagonist purely as an exponent of dogmatic negation.

What does this tell us about the new character of contention?

Ad 1. Kant does not speak of the polemics of pure reason. The term "polemics" is not explained at all. Kant evidently takes polemics for a mode of combat in which a critical thinker will not engage. To him, therefore, it is clear from the start that "there really need not be any polemics of pure reason" (30: A 750/B 778). Thanks to this negative statement, we may, in contradistinction to critique, venture to draft a counterimage of Kant's understanding of polemics, so as to clarify what a polemical use of reason is.

Critique, as rational self-knowledge, always has to do with claims of reason; in polemics, as uncritical contention, we deal with the more or less elucidated claims of a "fellow citizen" (30: A 739/B 767).

What we do in object-related critique is to peel off, and to transfer to objects, the rational norms we have obtained in self-knowledge. Polemics is a combative establishment of norms without previous critique.

In critique we recognize that its fundament lies in philosophical faith, and we therefore resign ourselves to remaining at the bounds of not knowing. In polemics we take this fundament itself for a knowledge, and the misconception leads us to exorbitant claims.

Critique is a mode of contention in which we seek not to confirm subjective maxims but solely to extend and elucidate reason; polemics is a mode of precritical contention which positively or negatively passes the bounds of reason, in quest of a knowledge that cannot exist. In polemics we want to validate this knowledge by force, by way of subjective principles. A man who is primarily and offensively polemicizing must not "be regarded as a critic" (30: A 742/B 770). Polemics, as a fight for the subjective claims of thinkers, is thus degraded in comparison with critique, the fight for the objective claims of reason.

Ad 2. We can now understand also why the polemical use which critical thinkers make of reason must be a defensive discipline. Critically elucidated reason makes no uncritical claims; it has only to ward off such claims. At the same time we see why that use of reason cannot be anything but defensive: against uncritical claims, any reasoning, neutrally testing examination is out of place. The passing of bounds annuls such a claim from the start. There cannot be any point in allowing oneself to be critically questioned by its proponents. The defense is therefore confined to "merely thwarting our opponent's spurious insights, which are to impair the proposition we assert" (30: A 776/B 804).

Ad 3. After that, it can no longer surprise us to find Kant regarding his polemical antagonist purely as an exponent of dogmatic negation. Failing to see through his claims right to their fundament, the polemicist insists on them dogmatically. As dogmatic claims they are exclusive, and thus always aimed at the destruction of others. They are negative in principle. They therefore force us to use reason polemically and, since they are inaccessible to critical argument, to defend ourselves by counterattack.

Foreshadowed in the relationship of critique, polemics, and the polemical use of reason is the dialectical relationship of thesis, antithesis, and synthesis, which encompasses the modes of contention in *Critique of Judgment*. Insofar as critique may be understood as contention, it is the everlasting common struggle of critical thinkers for objective rational claims; polemics is the contention of subjects about the validity of their uncritical claims; and the polemical use of reason is the critical thinker's defensive battle against the exorbitant claims made by a subject. Inherent in this characterization is a qualification of the three. Critique is the intrinsic, ultimately unpolemical contention of reason with itself; polemics is the unintrinsic, irrational quarrel about trivia; the polemical use of reason is its forcible involvement in a fight on which the attacker has put the stamp of unintrinsicality. Critique occurs in freedom, polemics in license, the polemical use of reason in the defense of freedom against the challenge of license.

Where is the proper place to make polemical use of reason? In principle, it is wherever a polemic requires reason to react. Its place, therefore, is in *metaphysica specialis,* but not in all of that either. In *metaphysica specialis* we advance to a knowledge of not knowing, and to Kant this makes it a science of not knowing. Up to that point, the polemicist would still have to accept cogent instruction from the critical thinker. But then, in regard to the *meaning* of not knowing, the thinker's arguments cease to be generally valid. Where they are the issue, uncritical claims can only be rejected or destroyed, not confronted with correct claims. There even rational men speak only "the language—justified before the most acute reason—of a solid *faith*" (30: A 744–45/B 772–73).

If we can find an arena in this fashion, we can still find no issue. "For how can two persons debate an issue the reality of which neither of them can represent in any real experience, or even in a merely possible experience?" (30: A 750/B 778).

Ending in a similar split is the question about possible partners in the polemical use of reason. I have a partner, and yet I have none. In colloquy, three combinations are conceivable: there might be two critical thinkers confronting each other, two dogmatic ones, or a critical and a dogmatic one. The discussion of the first pair rests on a sound basis leading to the unanimous knowledge that they either know or do not know. The debate of the two dogmatics would be mere "grandiloquence" and senseless "child's play" (30: A 743/B 771) in which there can be no definitive victory; it may be amusing for us to watch their antics "from the safe seat of criticism" (30: A 747/B 775). Only the talk between unequal partners seems to suit a polemical struggle. When Kant speaks of the polemical use of reason, he is thinking of this combination; but he thinks of it from the critical thinker's standpoint. Wherever the two partners meet, reason has already made its choice, and always in the critical thinker's favor. His opponent is not rated a free adversary, not one to be taken seriously. Objectively it is already established that he is in the wrong. The discussion is simply a means to validate the existing "prejudgment" against him, and to show him that, where he believes he can fight, he would do better to keep quiet. We are dispatching a partner who cannot be a true adversary.

Like the partners themselves, their starting positions in the struggle are unequal. Considered with a speculative interest, both do indeed share an "equal chance" (30: A 776/B 804). They have "no documented truth" (30: A 751/B 779). But as Kant views his dogmatic antagonist exclusively as an exponent of negation and does not say anywhere that critical negation might be conceivable also, the two do not share the same chance when they are considered with a practical interest. Before that interest, reason speaks out for the rational faith that permits postulating immortality and the idea of God, because the thought of compensatory justice is sacred to reason, and the idea of a "teller of hearts" is indispensable. According to Kant, only the man who advances the postulates on grounds of rational faith can justify his faith κατ’ ἄνθρωπον, at least. His faith gives him "title to a property" (30: A 739/B 767) that protects him from all impairments. The applicable rule is *melior est conditio possidentis* (30: A 777/B 805). It is thus clear from the start that a denial of the postulates cannot rest on any practical interest. The exponent of negation is denied even the right to cite practical principles for his vindication.

The methods employed in the polemical use of reason are defensive methods. They are subject to the principle governing all methods: "No just cause may be defended by unjust means." The fight is waged "with weapons of reason" only (30: A 744/B 772); but in the questions of God and immortality reason is not compelling.

One such method is "skeptical polemicizing" (30: A 763/B 791). Without conveying any meaning, we stick to the one cogent insight left to us: here one cannot know. This will not satisfy the critical thinker himself, but it will scare the dogmatic one out of the stately course of his supposed certainty and will upset his conceptions. He will be at a loss, and for moments, perhaps, he will feel the doubts that make him listen to skepsis. This alone would not make a critical thinker of him, but such "preliminary training" (30: A 769/B 797) would serve to give his mind a turn toward criticism.

In "hypothetical polemicizing" we go a step farther. We use hypotheses to sustain the argument for the postulates which we are making on grounds of rational faith.

Hypotheses in the field of not knowing are opinions or poetic fictions under the supervision of reason. They are supported by what possible certainty is left: by the insight that the controversial concept as such is not made impossible by inner contradictions. This ground of certainty gives them the predicate of adequacy. Adequate hypotheses alone are permitted as means of polemical combat. They do not, therefore, give us a license to substitute hyperphysical reasons for missing physical ones; they merely permit us, on grounds of possible certainty and with the intention to make practical sense, to take a step into not knowing. They are subjective maxims for the achievement of meaning, "permitted as weapons of war, not to base rights upon them, only to defend rights" (30: A 777/B 805). Hypotheses are concepts devised for defensive purposes, instruments of defense with the finite function of withdrawing critical thought from the grasp of dogmatic thought and simultaneously dispatching the dogmatic thinker's "self-conceit" (30: A 781/B 809) with the delimiting verdict *non liquet* (30: A 742/B 770). Having served this function, they are given up again.

In extremity, a critical thinker must be allowed to do what seems uncritical and to adopt a dogmatic way of polemicizing. He may do so because he will not succumb to dogmatic thinking but will use it as a means to fight dogmatism. This utilization may be forced upon him, for "after all, there really is no remedy we can think of, except to counter the grandiloquence of one side with another grandiloquence, based on the very same right" (30: A 757/B 785). The purpose is not to be grandiloquent oneself, but by big claims to stir the opponent to doubts that may make him lend an ear to critique.

Whether in skeptical, hypothetical, or dogmatic polemicizing, the polemical use of reason always has an immediate goal and a distant goal. The immediate goal is to rebut the dogmatic claims and to defend one's own critical claims. What must be prevented is that the opposite of the critical meaning we have set forth "can ever be stated with apodictical certainty, or even with the appearance of a greater certainty" (30: A 739–40/B 767–68) by our opponent; and at the same time we must see to it that our own meaning is not self-contradictory. This is the way to annihilate our opponent's claims and to make our own impregnable and thus withdraw them from the struggle.

The distant goal would be the dogmatic thinker's awakening to criticism. A polemic serving that goal would tend to get the opponent to reconsider the fundament of his theories. But the achievement of the distant goal is always hampered by the fact that the fight is waged directly for the immediate goal—for this always tends to have the fight broken off by an impregnable defense in which the struggle for critique must also cease.

If we want to criticize the Kantian draft of a critical thinker's fight against a dogmatic one, we cannot fail to see that Kant hardly notices the possibilities of contention. We are bound to be struck by the ever-recurring negative characteristics: the critical thinker resorts to the polemical use of reason only in self-defense, and his opponent is dogmatic—a word which Kant does not use in the neutral sense of someone thinking on other grounds. There is a value judgment here: the other's thinking springs from a perversion. His dogmatic claims deny the postulates of the ideas of God and immortality; they do something with which men of reason cannot concern themselves. The reasonable course, therefore, is to ward off those claims or to withdraw from the fight by rendering oneself impregnable. It is not that the critical thinker might not dare to fight; but the fight is really senseless, since it occurs in a realm in which there can be no victories.

This is why the combat methods are designed for breaking off the struggle. The one thing that would be worth fighting for— the critical elucidation of reason—is always presupposed in one of the partners already, and thus objectively secured. There is no possibility of open combat at the risk of casting doubts upon oneself. The principle of criticism has been established and is undoubtedly correct. It is the principle which restored reason to unity with itself and thereby ultimately banishes polemics from its domain: "There is accordingly no polemics proper in the field of pure reason" (30: A 756/B 784).

This reckoning with the fight for the subjective claims of thinkers rests upon definite, not generally valid premises.

The fight makes sense where it can lead to unanimity: in the fields of knowledge and of recognized not knowing. Unanimity shows in common, cogently attainable results; what leads to it is a philosophy that is itself scientific. Transcendental philosophy has to be scientific, because all it does is to draw the metes and bounds of the one reason that has been united in itself by self-knowledge. Hence its proper struggle must be scientific also.

Where these objectifying premises may lead can be observed in the young Hegel, who consistently absolutized them into objective ones and used them to design the essence and the sense of philosophical contention. We go into this briefly, because Hegel's manner of going beyond Kant plainly shows the dangers which the Kantian premises pose to discussion, and at the same time shows where Kant called a halt.

In his essay "On the Nature of Philosophical Critique in General and Its Relation to the Present State of Philosophy in Particular,"[5] Hegel says that all critique requires a standard independent of each individual phenomenon. The standard must be taken "from the eternal and immutable archetype of the thing itself"[6]—a thing that is either concrete or capable of being concretized as an idea. Philosophical critique does not differ in essence from any other kind of criticizing; it differs only with respect to its object, which is philosophy. The premise of its possibility lies in the idea of an objective philosophy, and the premise of its possible meaning lies in the possible concretion of that philosophy. The principle of philosophical critique says: There is *one* philosophy, and that has to be made real.

According to Hegel, anyone who denies the objectivity of philosophical critique would have to "assert the possibility of philosophies that are essentially different and yet equally true— a notion which, however great the solace it may offer, need really not be taken into consideration."[7] Instead, the true philosophy is unique simply because reason is unique. There cannot be several different and equally true philosophies any more than there can be different kinds of reason. Only the man who acknowledges these premises can be a meaningful critic. Hence Hegel's statements that philosophical critique "makes sense only to those in whom the idea of the one and same philosophy exists,"[8] that it can refer only to works "in which this idea is recognizable as more or less distinctly uttered,"[9] and that wherever the idea of absolute philosophy is lacking, the "business of critique . . . is thoroughly lost."[10]

On these premises he circumscribes the nature of philosophical critique. It is the struggle of the absolute against the limited in the field of philosophy. What knows that it is absolute will hold alien claims to be as nothing. It cannot possibly accept the limited as "something" (as a party), for by so doing it would put an end to its own absoluteness. It would itself subside into the party, and before the idea of philosophy it would be as nothing. To relinquish a claim to exclusiveness is self-destruction. To avoid that, objective philosophy must insist on its uniqueness. To that philosophy, all other philosophies fall into the category of unphilosophy. Objective philosophy annihilates their claims. Its struggle, as a battle of annihilation, is "the growing manifestation of nothingness"[11]—which is its counterpart.

We do not mean to equate Kant's fundament of polemics with that of Hegel. It does make a difference whether a philosophy is viewed as the concretized absolute or—merely in the matter, never in the manner—as the only possible unfoldment of human reason, which is subjective in principle. Kant dispenses with ultimate claims before the absolute. He does not think "God's thoughts before the Creation." But in colloquy this difference need not show. Kant's subjectivity is not individual; it is general and claims to encompass all of mankind, at least. In colloquy, therefore, the philosophy that springs from it is defensive, indeed exclusive, wherever it meets a philosophy that differs in principle. Its polemics, though conceived purely as a defense, will in extreme cases also turn destructive—though a period of rest is all it can hope to get out of destroying its opponent.

The possibility of a different basic attitude toward a partner who thinks differently arises only when a philosophy gives up its claim to be right and to objectify the truth, when it differentiates itself from science and theology and does not look upon all individual subjectivity as license. As far as we can see, the polemical consequences of such a philosophy have been thought through and broadly outlined only by Karl Jaspers. We briefly take up his draft[12] in order to show how polemics may possibly be freed from objectivity.

Since philosophy, to Jaspers, is not science, there can be no philosophy pure and simple as a concrete phenomenon; but there can be many embattled historic unfoldments of the idea of a *philosophia perennis*. Their contents are neither absolutely, cogently intelligible nor universally binding. Philosophy speaks out of the thinker's possible existenz, and its truth is evidenced by his uplifting to existenz. It is therefore essentially historic and essentially subjective—which does not mean that it is at the mercy of the subjects' unbounded license. Its performance in the individual is based on reason. It can link reasonable men. Still, its bond is neither demonstrably intersubjective nor objective; it is the solidarity of individuals resting each upon his own existenz.

If mere accuracy is not yet intrinsically philosophical, it cannot be the point of philosophical polemics to put over *one* philosophy as binding. Unlike any factual critique, this polemics is not an effort to win the fight and thus to void it. Instead, what we try to do in philosophical polemics is to get down to the essence of the struggle, so that its seriousness will make us feel the seriousness of philosophizing. We want not only to explore and influence the partner's views; we want to bring him to unreserved self-revelation. In his candor we hope to meet "the underlying, truly philosophical power" in him, the power which "either we feel . . . or we do not feel" but "cannot be forced to know by the intellect," the power that is "the appealing, truly effective ingredient in gifts of the mind."[13] To get close to this power in the partner, "to come face to face with it, as it were,"[14] and thus not only to perceive *what* he says, but to hear *on what grounds* he is speaking—this is the task of philosophical polemics. Beyond the thought contents, it asks for contents of essence: for the truth content of a manifested thinking and for the weight of a discovered existenz. It cannot, therefore, halt at any subject matter, not even if the subject matter is a thought. In such polemics, the speaker's person is the vessel of those contents and the representative of that power. His person is a way for both to make their appearance. Historic man does not stand outside philosophical polemics.

This polemics is a means of self-knowledge. The combatant seeks the uncovered opponent, so that in the struggle that sets them apart he may grow aware of himself. If he conquered the opponent, he would lose a medium of his own self-elucidation; if he did not fight him, he would stay obscure to himself. He therefore wants a partner who can be a real adversary. He seeks him in the realm of his essentiality, to clarify this essentiality in combat and to be clarified by it. Understood in this manner, philosophical polemics is both a challenge and a risk: a challenge to the partner, to allow other origins to move him in unreserved candor, and a risk of exposing oneself to the other and letting the shock consolidate one's own ground. Here the diversity of philosophizing is not a bar to polemics but the premise of its possibility. Because there are many philosophies, the single one has a chance to become transparent unto itself; but it has this chance only in the separation that occurs in struggle. Struggle is its unavoidable cathartic. It comes to an end only in total elucidation of thinkers as well as thoughts.

The reason why Kant, in reflecting on the struggle against someone who thinks altogether differently, missed this possibility of rational self-elucidation and self-knowledge may lie in the premises we mentioned earlier, premises which for centuries were part of philosophical tradition. For where he came to be conscious of the fact that contention cannot rest on any fixed conceptuality, Kant did develop a different mode of combat, one that remains open for interminable elucidation in the partners' struggle.

Debate in Critique of Judgment

In *Critique of Judgment,* Kant distinguishes three forms of contention, "dispute," "debate," and "quarrel," of which two —dispute and debate—are held to be philosophical. Both seek to bring about "unanimity of judgments by mutual resistance" (35: v, 338). But they do it in different ways, and with differing degrees of success.

A dispute rests upon objective grounds of judgment which can be stated in concepts. Its arguments lead to conclusions that have probative force. Unanimity is thus achieved by a process which is compelling and can be universally reenacted. The opponents are united in a common knowledge of things. Dispute bears the marks of scientific combat.

What makes *Critique of Judgment* important to polemics is that in "debate" it explicitly designs a second form of struggle— one that is not scientific but is nonetheless not only tolerated but regarded, within certain limits, as the only possible form.

Although the opponents in a debate will sometimes claim objectivity for their stated reasons, they can never state them in concepts. Accordingly, their judgments lack probative force. They have only one voice in their favor. Unanimity can thus no longer be compelled; we can only hope that it will arise from the partners' common sympathetic insight. There can be no talk of views being correct or incorrect where the determining reasons cannot be reduced to concepts; hence there are no absolute truth criteria in debate. A correction of views, and eventual achievement of an accord, can only be expected of the discussion itself. This is why, toward the opponent, a debate is not exclusive. It is a ceaseless invitation to him to engage in dialogue, to make comparisons, and not to tire of considering reasons that cannot be firmly laid down.

Where should debate be placed in philosophy? Kant puts it in the realm of the judgment of taste, and beyond that, generally, in the realm of reflective judgment. But what does this mean?

The faculty of judgment subsumes each particular under the universal. Kant calls it "definitory" when the universal is conceptually given, and "reflective" when it has still to be looked for in a mental motion that is free but critical. In this motion, judgment detaches itself from the particular, without losing sight of it, and it assigns the particular to a conceptually undetermined whole that requires subsumption to qualify as a universal. Named by Kant as the proper fields of judgment are the contemplation of beauty and the design of legalities for a view of nature.

Debate would thus be the only kind of contention possible in talking about beauty, and about the legalities which the human mind has drafted in looking at nature. In the field of beauty, debate cannot result in cogent unanimity because aesthetic judgments are subjective individual judgments; they rest not upon concepts but on the sensation of harmony between the intellect and the imagination. They have to be tried out. Since their determining grounds are not objective concepts, their predicates do not convey cognition; they merely convey reflective statements about the object, statements by which the free play of cognitive faculties is aroused in a manner we can feel. In aesthetic judgments we may hope for unanimity, at any rate. The transcendental point of their sensation exists in all humans, and the sensation itself is communicable thanks to a *sensus communis*— taste—which Kant ultimately anchors in morality.

In the second field there can be no compelling unanimity because objective concepts cannot be imposed on nature by reflection on the legalities of the view of nature; all that such reflection can do is to attribute subjective utilitarian principles to nature. Reflection invests nature with a systematics whose ultimate grounds are the subject and his cognitive faculties. Yet at the same time, reflection holds out hope for unanimity because its subjective principle is common to mankind, and because in the legalities of its view of nature it grasps the sensible natural laws as if they were the logical specification of that view.

In the realm of aesthetically reflecting judgment the final determining ground of all judgments is feeling; in the realm of teleologically reflecting judgment, the merely reflecting principles of the view of nature are judged by the intellect and by reason. According to Kant, the latter realm belongs "to the theoretical part of philosophy" (35: V, 194), and debate has both an aesthetic significance and an epistemological one. If this is true, debate should really be found in *Critique of Pure Reason* also. We therefore rephrase our question: Where are the limits of debate in philosophy? Or, to put it more precisely: (1) Is debate not already legitimized as philosophical contention in *Critique of Pure Reason*? (2) In what sense is debate (rather than dispute) the philosophical contention pure and simple?

One might be tempted to connect the modes of struggle given in *Critique of Judgment* with the modes of holding things to be true in *Critique of Pure Reason* (30: A 820ff./B 848ff.). Kant distinguishes three: knowledge, faith, and opinion. Knowledge is the objectively and subjectively adequate form of holding things to be true; faith, the form that is only subjectively adequate; opinion, the one that suffices neither objectively nor subjectively. One might say now that dispute, in which we can cite objective reasons for our judgments, is the mode of contention corresponding to knowledge; that debate, in which the grounds of our judgments are subjectively warranted but not objectively reducible to concepts, has its place as contention in the realm of faith; and that a third and last mode of contention that can be based neither on subjectively adequate nor on objectively adequate grounds—Kant suggests its possibility without naming it—belongs in the realm of mere opinions. We have called this third mode "quarrel." The consequence of the arrangement would be that in *metaphysica generalis* we can dispute; in *metaphysica specialis* we can debate wherever we are sustained by a faith—as we are, at least, in the doctrine of postulates; and wherever philosophy is no more than philodoxy, we can neither debate nor dispute any more; we can only quarrel. The arrangement would mean, furthermore, that where faith sustains a *metaphysica specialis,* the use we make in it of reason is a merely reflecting one. Implicitly, the faculty of reflective judgment is indeed already contained in *Critique of Pure Reason.*

Or one might build another bridge and say, perhaps, that three modes of philosophical contention are given in *Critique of Pure Reason*: critique, polemics, and the polemical use of reason. The three relate to each other like thesis, antithesis, and synthesis. But *Critique of Judgment* also names three equally interrelated modes of struggle: dispute, quarrel, and debate. Critique and dispute are modes of scientific controversy; polemics and quarrel are uncritical modes of combat. This suggests equating debate with the polemical use of reason. But the very progress made in the third *Critique* lies in the fact that, unlike the polemical use of reason, debate does not presuppose a dogmatic adversary—that debate, like dispute, is contention between critical thinkers.

Kant himself never made these assignations. While one may take them, the first in particular, for more than mere notions, they still followed the line of accidental characteristics only. They do not give us reason enough to locate debate in *Critique of Pure Reason*. We need a way to make the *principle* of debate, the faculty of reflective judgment, visible in the first *Critique*—and, as it happens, such a way has long been pointed out by August Stadler.[15]

In *Critique of Pure Reason*, Kant defines reason, in one passage, as the faculty "to deduce the particular from the universal" (30: A 646/B 674). This recalls his definition of the faculty of judgment in the third *Critique*: "Judgment as such is the faculty of conceiving the particular as covered by the universal" (35: v, 179). He says next, in *Critique of Pure Reason,* that if, presuming reason to be this assigning faculty, "the universal is already given and certain in itself, its subsumption calls for judgment only, and the particular is thereby necessarily defined" (30: A 646/B 674). The judgment referred is named more precisely in the third *Critique*: "If the universal is given, the faculty of judgment which subsumes the particular thereunder is definitory" (35: v, 179). In *Critique of Pure Reason* he lays down his term: "This I will call the apodictical use of reason." And he closes: "Or else the universal is only problematically assumed and is a mere idea, while the particular is certain; but the universality of the rule for that sequence remains a problem" (30: A 646/B 675).

In keeping with the analogy, Kant would now have to say what the problem requires. He leaves it out. We might replace it from the third *Critique*: "Yet if only the particular is given and the faculty of judgment is to find the universal to it, that faculty is merely reflecting" (35: v, 179). But Kant, in *Critique of Pure Reason,* goes on to say instead that "several particular cases are thus tried out on the rule, and when it seems that all particular cases we can name follow from it, we conclude that the rule is universal. This I will call the hypothetical use of reason" (30: A 646–47/B 674–75). Instead of naming the faculty of reflective judgment, he describes its activity. We cannot even infer from this that the term "faculty of reflective judgment" was still lacking, for in the lectures on logic (67: IX, 131f.) it was presumably already at his disposal. That the thing itself was not lacking is certain in any event. What corresponds, in *Critique of Pure Reason,* to the faculty of reflective judgment is reason in its hypothetical use.

That this correspondence is not just given in words but is set into the thing—into the function which reflective judgment serves in drafting general natural laws, and into the function which the hypothetical use of reason serves in directing the intellect—has been so clearly shown by Stadler that we may consider it assured. Instead of repeating his demonstration, we proceed directly to the question that is important for our purpose here: What does the demonstrated correspondence mean to philosophical contention?

Explicitly, debate as a mode of combat in which the grounds of judgment cannot be reduced to objective concepts is indeed not mentioned previous to *Critique of Judgment*; but as subject matter it is already implied in *Critique of Pure Reason.* In the third *Critique,* dispute and debate can be assigned to the uses, respectively, of definitory and reflective judgment. In the first, dispute would have to be assigned to the apodictical use of reason, debate to its hypothetical (regulative) use, and a third and last mode of contention, one that cannot be either dispute or debate, to the transcendent (constitutive) use of reason. That in his methodology Kant fails to keep these modes of contention clearly apart may be due to a wish to give only a training manual for the fight against an exponent of dogmatic negation, not a typology of the modes of combat.

Since the third *Critique* remained without a methodology, and since the methodology of the first does not take debate as philosophical contention into consideration at all, we are in the quandary of finding in Kant's writings only a very few clues to his views on debate. What we can know must largely be inferred by ourselves.

In debate we may hope for unanimity. The anchor of this hope in judgments of taste is the constant increase of moral culture;

in the hypothetical use of reason and in the faculty of reflective judgment it is the never slumbering sense of methodology. This sense allows us to see through the subjectivity of maxims. Where it has grown lucid, differences are clarified by recognition of the guiding rational interest which differs from case to case, and thus of the relativity of the maxims. But the accord that can be reached in each case is not a unanimity for all time. In this accord we do not nail down which maxims can be objectively valid, and which universalities are downright valid. The use of guiding concepts and ideas is clarified for the moment, in a clarification that must be performed anew wherever men are thinking. Each individual debate can thus be elucidated as a case at issue; but the debatable issue is not removed from the world. It remains a reality because subjective maxims are inevitable in the doctrine of ideas and in teleology.

Yet how does this mode of debate go with Kant's claim that his metaphysics is a science? Was he not, by the back door, admitting a mode of polemics that is justified only where there can be no science? He undoubtedly was. That Kant postulated and claimed a scientific character for his metaphysics is as much a fact as that in this metaphysics, and without clearly recognizing it himself, he opened the door to an unscientific mode of contention, and thus, in wide areas, threw its possible objective ground back into question. Both the claim and the hidden revocation are demonstrable. How are we to explain their exclusive simultaneity? No one will wish to accuse Kant of cleverly voiding in dialectics what he had posited in the claim; it would not conform to his thinking style. Rather, the contradiction results from his failure to draw a clear line between philosophy and science. To him, philosophy was a science—how exclusively so, will be seen in our next chapter. This claim of philosophy came to him as a legacy of tradition. He would ask whether and how metaphysics could be scientific, but never whether it ought to be scientific. The basis of his questioning was always the inherited disjunctive judgment that philosophy was either scientific or not entitled to exist. Whenever Kant disturbed this philosophical claim, he did so with the intention of confirming it. But the lasting effect—superior to the claim, in the long run—was exerted by the fact that he disturbed it.

Once we go so far as to remove some fields of Kantian metaphysics from this claim and to make them matters of debate, the radical question arises whether philosophy as such is debatable at all.

We are inclined to answer in the affirmative. There is room for debate wherever there can be no accuracy; and since it is precisely in transcending mere accuracies that philosophy comes into being, debate is the intrinsic mode of contention in philosophy at large. But answering in the affirmative on Kantian grounds as well would mean turning the faculty of reflective judgment into the intrinsic medium of philosophical thought. The antinomies of aesthetic judgment, which Kant regards as applicable to the judgment of taste, would have to be extended to the realm of philosophy as a whole.

The antinomies of taste (35: v, 338 ff.), which are to each other as thesis, antithesis, and synthesis, read as follows:

1. Taste is neither disputable nor debatable. What Kent indicates here is the third mode of contention, the quarrel. Everyone has his own taste. Nothing, not even the idea of a *sensus communis,* can create unanimity. Anarchy reigns in the field of taste.

2. Taste is disputable. There is one taste, based upon objective grounds of judgment. Unanimity can be achieved cogently, in conclusions that have probative force.

3. Taste is debatable, though not disputable. Contention brings an accord into view, although there is no compelling it.

A transposition of these antinomies to philosophy at large would yield the following theses:

1. Philosophy is neither disputable nor debatable. Every man has his philosophy. Philosophy is a private affair and as such a realm of anarchy.

2. Philosophy is disputable. There is only one philosophy. It is a science.

3. Philosophy is debatable, though not disputable. There is not just one philosophy; there are philosophies. They are irreconcilable; but the idea of the solidarity of rational men permits us to hope that, coming from different points of departure and proceeding by different ways, we may meet at the same goal.

There are no Kantian utterances that would justify this transposition. In words, Kant probably would have professed agreement with the antithesis, and in history this was indeed the first to take effect. The idealists understood themselves to be the philosophers of this antithesis. To them—with the exception of

Schelling in his old age—philosophy was either a science or nothing. At the same time, however, Kant had in fact partially surmounted the antithesis by way of the synthesis, by carrying the idea of the synthesis into metaphysics. This idea kept working slowly; it was not until our time that it came really, clearly to the fore, thanks to the systematic separation of philosophy and science.

Summing up, we have to stress the decisive character of the third *Critique* for our themes. What is designed in *Critique of Judgment*—next to the two previously known forms of scientific and irrational contention (dispute and quarrel)—is a third (debate). Kant does not regard this as a possible product of objective reasons, but he does consider it a product of critical reason. In fact he had already located it in *Critique of Pure Reason,* but not until *Critique of Judgment* was he methodically conscious of it. It was the third *Critique* that opened the way for a kind of controversy that defies cogent termination in the realm of accuracies, a controversy that is an interminable process of elucidating what transcends mere accuracies. Neither partner in this struggle can depend upon assured objectivities; both must dare to expose their principles—which are no more than subjective maxims— to the hazards of debate. No absolute document of truth confirms these maxims, only the test of battle. Truth exists before the start of a debate, but for the subjects it is the debate that brings it into existence.

Lawful and Unlawful Debate in The Debate of Departments

In *The Debate of Departments* Kant no longer speaks of three modes of contention, but of two. Both are called "debate," but he characterizes them by distinguishing adjectives, as "unlawful" and "lawful" debate.

The novelty is that this debate is carried on not among philosophers, but between philosophers and representatives of academic disciplines. As far as the respective interests are concerned, it is a debate *inter dispares.* Kant presents it in the interrelation of the traditional "faculties" or university departments. The three higher ones, the schools of divinity, law, and medicine, confront the lower, the department of philosophy. The crucial aspect of their confrontation, the true criterion of the debate, is not the difference between the sciences and their external doctrines; it is the fact that the authority by which members of the higher departments disseminate their doctrines differs from the authority cited by the lower one. This makes for the partners' inequality. To demonstrate it, we first have to deal briefly with the concepts of the higher and lower departments.

According to Kant, the three higher ones do not primarily train pure scholars. They chiefly turn out practitioners, "businessmen or technicians of learning" (38: VII, 18). In practicing what they were taught at the university, these men, whether clergymen, physicians, or officers of courts of justice, exert a threefold influence upon the populace. As clergymen they act upon the thinking and the mentality of the faithful and thus influence the ultimate source of the formation of their will; as members of the judiciary they keep the common people in check by safeguarding property; and as physicians they use their art to make the population physically strong. In the performance of their duties, all of them engage involuntarily in political action, and the government, recognizing this, endeavors to use them as instruments of its policy.

The government starts doing this at the university, by authorizing what is taught in the higher departments. It does not directly intervene in research—such action would expose it to fallibility—but it does choose among the research results that can be taught, and it sanctions what it has chosen. The choice is made from unscientific points of view. Rather than the expansion of truth, its criterion is the assurance and enhancement of political influence, "may the truth be what it will" (38: VII, 19).

This is how the teachings of the higher departments are molded. What they teach is not the truth and nothing but the truth; it is a politically advantageous, sanctioned truth. The teachings of the higher departments are "doctrines emanating from the arbitrary will of a superior" (38: VII, 22). In their research activities, of course, the teachers may and must always refer to reason; but in teaching they refer to "scripture" (38: VII, 22), to written texts containing, as the valid norm, that which the government imposes.

Thus the pure theologian cites not reason but the Bible; the teacher of law, not natural law but his country's; the pure physician, not biology but medical regulations. As the seat of the

higher departments, the university degenerates into a special interest agency which outwardly can still be justified as a professional
school—although an odd sort, with the ultimate aim of spreading
authorized doctrines so thoroughly among the people that they
will stay loyal and obey the government. That a university including only the three higher departments would be bound to
miss its real destiny is obvious. It needs another, one that will
serve truth alone.

The lower department, the philosophical faculty, is the true
seat of reason at the university. "Independent of governmental
orders" (38: VII, 19), it faces the free, open field of its own
judgment in which its spirit makes it search for truth alone. It
has the "unpretentiousness to be nothing but free, but to leave
others free also" (38: VII, 28). It is subject solely "to the legislation
of reason" (38: VII, 27), within which all doctrines are judged
"according to the principles of thought in general" (38: VII, 27).
It accepts nothing on grounds of authority. It recognizes no
crede, only the free *credo* that is always a confession of reason.
Oriented toward reason and freedom, it will publicly present the
truth, or what seems to it to be the truth, because without publicity "truth would not see the light of day" (38: VII, 20). It is
thus the organ of truth that will not propagate definite doctrines
but will test the truth content of all docrines, and will make them
its own only up to the limits of their truth.

The university is the place where the higher departments
come to converse with the lower one. They take as the truth
what authorized scripture bids them; the lower departments,
nothing but that which can stand the test of reason. Thus the
discussion springs from different fonts of truth, and any quick
accord across the chasm would be a "misalliance" (38: VII, 23).
The question is which font has primacy. Since reason alone may
claim it—nothing else having any qualifications whatever for
universality—the lower department presumes to judge the higher
ones. It places truth, "the first and essential condition of learning
as such" (38: VII, 28), above all utility. From its opponents it
demands no advance belief or acceptance; all it asks is that the
negative conditions of the search for truth not be spurned. The
opponents should "only not hamper the progress of insights and
sciences" (38: VII, 20 note). In discussion, they should not dig
themselves in behind subjective privilege but dare to fight openly,

rather, "on a free and equal footing" (38: VII, 23). By this, however, the lower department asks the higher ones to accept the primacy of its own font of truth. Equality puts the department of philosophy into the position of being really the higher one and as such controlling the other three.

The philosophical faculty exercises this control in an everlasting debate than can be lawful or unlawful.

A debate is unlawful either in matter or in form. It is materially unlawful if the issue comes to be something which should not be publicly debatable; it is formally unlawful if the grounds of judgment are taken not from reason but from the realm of individual-subjective inclinations. When Kant speaks of unlawful debate, he means the formally unlawful one that might come about in ways such as the following:

The debate aims at the departments' influence upon the people. The lower, which "adheres to the principle of freedom" (38: VII, 30), would like to gain influence solely by reason, freedom, and truth. But it is not to freedom that people look primarily for their salvation. They look to natural goals: to a long, pleasurable life, to the security of property, and to the guarantee of eternal bliss. The people, therefore, have a preference for practical men and immediate confidence in those men. They trust the doctor, the lawyer, and, on the threshold of death, even the priest. They willingly submit to their teachings, and that submission in turn obliges the practioners to give the populace the kind of precepts it will be glad to grant priority to. The government's executive organs come into a state of dependency upon the people—not, however, upon the clear will of all, but upon the leanings of many. With these leanings they align their practice. But as practical men they in turn work on the university departments, calling for doctrines in line with the popular leanings. Decisions on government sanction will no longer be made from the point of view of learning but from that of popular favor. The effortless compatibility of duty and inclination comes to be a principle of authorized doctrines. The consequence is a slovenliness fostered by the state. The university serves the welfare state, whose popular principles—a pleasurable life, safeguards for property, a pledge of eternal salvation—give to arbitrary government a semblance of being free, just, and God-pleasing.

"Here we have an essentially unlawful debate than can never be settled, between the higher departments and the lower one" (38: VII, 31–32). It is unlawful because in defending their doctrines the higher departments follow a principle unfit for any law; what they go by is "authorized lawlessness" (38: VII, 32), which makes them a menace to the lawful rational state. Involuntarily, their fight for their theories becomes a fight against reason. As such it "cannot at all be tolerated" (38: VII, 32), since the hope of winning it rests secretly on the annihilation of reason.

A debate, in short, is formally unlawful if it seeks to lend general validity to doctrines whose principles do not have the qualifications for unity, and if its aim is thus the annihilation of reason. The hidden intent is revealed not only in the citing of authorities which are not final authorities; it is also revealed in the recourse to practices which validate by force (threats, violence), by stealth (trickery, persuasion), or by bribery (complaisance). Even if only one partner has this intent as a matter of principle, the character of the debate is settled. We may also phrase it as follows: A debate is unlawful if, as a matter of principle, it is one partner's way to destroy the existence of reason.

This suggests already that the very goal will change if the debate is lawful. The goal, then, is no longer to achieve the greatest possible influence upon the people; it is to see all departments of the university make steady progress to more perfect doctrines. Their joint, encompassing goal is to liberate reason, to free the rational doctrines from "all restrictions placed upon the public judgment by arbitrary governmental action" (38: VII, 35). This common end unites both parties. Their fight is a *"concordia discors"* or a *"discordia concors"* (38: VII, 35)—not a war, "not the discord flowing from opposed final intentions" (38: VII, 35), but a debate, a, controversy with the one final intention to make truth and reason public, by means of freedom. The concept of lawful debate can thus be more closely circumscribed: in Kant's eyes a debate is lawful if the partners—on different premises, perhaps, but united in the will behind their one intention—act to disseminate reason and truth in freedom, following principles that do not run counter to reason and rational legality.

To make this lawful debate possible, the higher departments have to accept reason as an arbiter even though they teach only what is authorized—even though they teach it only because it is authorized. In fact, nothing but reason is called to sit in judgment. If the authorized teachings flow from a historical source, reason is "entitled, indeed obliged, to track down that source with critical deliberation" (38: VII, 32–33); if the source is rational, it is not subject to appraisal by anything but reason anyway; and if it is "purely aesthetic" (as a sense of sanctity, for instance), it must be reexamined "with cold reason" (38: VII, 33). No motivation can be spared the test of reason.

There are guidelines that apply to any such lawful debate. First, it "cannot and should not be settled by peaceful accord *(amicabilis compositio)*" (38: VII, 33). It must not be ended by amiability, only by the verdict of reason. Where amiability turns the scales, concealment, cunning, persuasion, and fraud are possible, if not inevitable. A premature will to make peace would deceptively create a superficial unity across the separate principles. It would be a peace contrary to reason, which aims at public presentation of the truth. A learned debate, though always seeking unanimity, is not sustained by a merely pacifist will. Pacifism in philosophy is a temptation to improbity.

Second, the debate "can never cease, and the department of philosophy is the one that must be prepared for it at all times" (38: VII, 33). The higher departments will always receive their doctrines from authority; for authorized doctrines are needed as long as freedom may be abused. A more general way of putting this is that there will always be other effective fonts of truth as well. The debated issue can be illuminated and perhaps even solved, but its debatability cannot be eliminated.

Third, a learned debate is only indirectly a political debate. At stake in it is not the privilege of sanctioning—not power, in other words—but the truth content of sanctioned teachings. The gulf between the representatives of reason and the representatives of power must remain. The former ought not to play government, for that would be insubordination; the latter ought not to play scholars, for that would be "pedantry" (38: VII, 19). Scholars in the seats of power would be corrupting their reason; incorruptibility seems to go only with impotence. On the other hand, if the powerful were to teach, their power would run the risk of fallibility. The realms are separated, but so that each will still be at work in the other: governments may rescind any doctrine that proves to be absurd, and reason can lay the ground for authorized teachings if they are rational. The debate is always one between scholars.

A political comparison might be made with a parliamentary chamber: the higher departments, as the government party, make up the Right, the defender of existing doctrines; the philosophical faculty is the Left, setting forth all rational objections to those doctrines. Or we might use the system of a state in comparison. With respect to sanctioned teachings, the government is then the legislative branch; the higher departments as a whole form the executive branch; and the lower department functions as the judicial branch. There is separation of powers, with the judiciary reexamining what the executive does, not what the legislature commands. In this metaphor too, the lower department carries more weight than the three higher ones, for all their outward possession of executive powers. The metaphor does not revoke the secret reversal in the departmental order of rank.

Fourth and finally, what is pursued in a debate by way of separate parties is the common goal to spread reason and truth in freedom.

These general principles governing lawful debate would really have to be specified for each of the three possible instances of contention between the lower and the higher departments. Kant does it in one case only, in the philosopher's discussion with the theologian. He does not seem to regard the debates with the jurist and the physician as equally significant. There are objective reasons for such a view: the physician stands on medical regulations, and the jurist, on statutes containing the law of the land—both, in other words, on legally valid writings—but the theologian alone claims that the text he stands on is not only sanctioned but sacrosanct. He regards it as "forever conclusive" (38: VII, 25). To the jurist's mind it is already clear that he will not find the *ius certum;* although creating absolute respect for valid laws, he knows that their temporal versions are not absolutely valid for all time. His book is open to arguments and exceptions. More widely open yet is the physician's book of rules for medical practice—for science is not at an end. It keeps submitting new material for authorization, and it is in the government's own interest to be prepared for new and better things. The theologian alone can expect no change. This makes him the most stubborn opponent. What takes place between him and the philosopher is the ideal case of debate, so to speak; there can be no sharper clash of opposites, for no one but the theologian will consciously teach that men have something higher than reason. We can say in Kant's defense that when he specified the general principles in this one case only he was—as often in *The Debate of Departments*—using the method of ideal construction to make the contrarieties as radically clear as possible.

And yet, why not the other specifications also? Perhaps they were simply forgotten. A close look at Kant's last treatise shows that it was not really constructed; it was compiled, rather, and then provided with a connecting introduction. It is an aggregate, not a system. Even so, since it names the issue and gives us the points of departure and the principles followed by the debaters, the debating methods also should be specifiable at any time.

What we get out of *The Debate of Departments* is not a new mode of contention; instead, the known modes are arranged according to their principles and divided into two types with varying methods and goals. How these types relate to the forms mentioned earlier will be clarified in the final section of this chapter.

The Modes of Polemical Combat

A tally of the modes of philosophical contention of which Kant himself was aware and on whose methods he reflected seems to be yielding ten forms: controversy and dispute; critique, polemics, and polemical use of reason; dispute, debate, and quarrel; lawful and unlawful debate. The relatively large number is due to varying principles of arrangement, and in part to synonymity; there really are not ten heterogeneous forms, only four. Twice the arrangement is dichotomical; twice it is trichotomical. The dichotomies, both in the early writings and in *The Debate of Departments*, take their bearings from the will that sets off the debate. There is a correspondence in principle, if not in all characteristics, between controversy and lawful debate and between dispute and unlawful debate. Common to the first pair is the principle of solidarity in the will to truth and reason, while the principle common to the second pair is the exclusive will to a triumph of subjectivity.

Correspondences are also to be found in the trichotomical arrangements. If by "critique" we may mean a mode of contention between critically thinking partners, Kant's intention is to have it correspond to what is called "dispute" in *Critique of Judgment*. Having shown, however, that "debate" also belongs in the first *Critique*—because Kant has located the faculty of reflective judgment in that work, under another name—we may say that what he means by critique *qua* contention is more concisely put in the antithesis of "dispute" and "debate." We then called "quarrel," in the third *Critique,* what in the first is called "polemics"—a term with which we dispense for clarity's sake—and the polemical use of reason, finally, has no correspondent in *Critique of Judgment*. The two trichotomies accordingly allow us to list four heterogeneous types of polemics: dispute, debate, polemical use of reason, and quarrel.

We can integrate these four into the two basic dichotomical types. Dispute and debate are unequivocally lawful modes of polemics; the polemical use of reason can be a lawless debate and a lawful one, depending on the partner who conducts it; a quarrel is an unequivocally unlawful debate. We can close, therefore, with a characterization of four types of polemics.

1. A quarrel is an uncritical mode of polemics that flares up wherever subjective maxims are to be rendered absolutely valid by perversion into objective principles. The man who gets them respected will unfailingly become a foe of reason, the annihilation of which is to permit subjectivity to triumph. Quarrel is the struggle that is exclusive in principle and always aims at the destruction of the partner or his claims. Parties to a quarrel do not know themselves united in the same final goal. Reason protests against quarrels.

2. The polemical use of reason is the defensive struggle forced upon a critical thinker by the aggression of an uncritical one. It is an exclusive struggle, but one which on the rational partner's side is directed against the exclusiveness of subjective claims. Although in extremity his methods are like the ones used by the uncritical thinker, they always spring from a radically different source and are intended to save reason from the grasp of unreason. This does not mean that the end justifies the means, for the polemical use of reason is subject to a restriction: it must not include employment of any method whose principle goes against

reason. Wherever its polemical use ignores this borderline, it becomes an unlawful debate.

3. Debate is that lawful form of contention between critical thinkers in which the grounds of judgment cannot be reduced to concepts. It is a struggle for the continuing elucidation of things that cannot be objectively determined, a struggle whose methods are marked by the will to reason and freedom.

4. Dispute is the properly scientific form of contention, the form whose judgmental grounds have probative force when they are reduced to concepts. This also is sustained by the partners' common will to truth and thus includes all men of reason.

Since the four modes do not have the same rational rank, all controversies are subject to the imperative to fight "sympathetically, not exclusively" (79: XVI, 273; 2213)—in other words, to shun quarrels, to make polemical use of reason only to defend its universal cause, but otherwise to spread reason by way of dispute and debate.

The four forms of struggle have their correspondences in political combat.

Comparable to a quarrel is the arbitrary war of aggression that is sustained purely by the idea of power, the war whose final form, the war of extermination, will in principle destroy the very possibility of peace.

Corresponding to the polemical use of reason is a war that is waged for the right, or for the republican order. The uncritical polemical opponent may be likened to a state that has not yet found the way to a republican form of government. Under certain circumstances, the republican neighbor of such a state may be forced to fight it.

Corresponding to dispute and debate is the political struggle for the expansion of reason and law. In politics, as in metaphysics, this struggle presupposes freedom, an honest state of mind, and the courage to be truthful. How closely politics and metaphysics are linked shows in the kinship of their combat methods, and even more evidently in the political significance of the several types of polemics.

In precritical polemics it is the attitude of those who polemicize —their unlimited will to truth on the basis of sincerity and freedom, combined with the courage to fight in public—that leads to the road to philosophical peace. We shall see later that this

attitude is at the same time the premise of the road to political
peace—a road which Kant understands in domestic affairs to be
the road to a republican order, and in foreign affairs, the road
to a free federation of republics. Socratic polemics would thus
be a republican discipline in what might outwardly, perhaps, be
still nonpolitical matters. By the way of thinking in which it is
conducted, this discipline can lend political relevance to every
discussion, no matter what its topic. That the young Kant already
knew of this connection shows in the preface to his very first
treatise, in which he points to Timoleon to justify his claimed
right to polemicize freely even against great men.

Timoleon, in the fourth century B.C., had freed the Syracusans
from the tyranny of Dionysius. Having defeated the aggressive
Carthaginians also and made peace with them, he gave the city
and the Greek portion of Sicily a new republican order. Then,
after barely eight years of activity, he relinquished his powers,
retiring to a serene, highly honored life among the citizenry. One
day he was taken to court. The judges themselves were shocked
by the temerity of his accusers. "But Timoleon"—so Kant tells
it, following Plutarch—"took a quite different view of the matter.
An undertaking of this sort could not displease a man whose
only delight was to see his country at the most perfect liberty. He
protected those who used their freedom even against him" (1:
1, 8).

The first political figure named in Kant's work is a republican
who becomes a paragon, not of political action only, but of the
whole thinking posture of philosophizing from which both cogitative controversy and political action arise. A political way of
thinking evidently starts earlier than political action, and it is
not just how the citizens act but how they think, and above all,
how they discuss matters, that has political relevance.

Political significance attaches also to the critical modes of
lawful combat, especially to debate. We find it already in the
hypothetical use of reason, in the faculty of reflective judgment,
and in the cultivation of taste. The first two have no absolute
guarantee of truth anywhere, but they do find relative confirmation in a systematics that is as unified as possible; and since such
a systematics cannot be won in confinement to oneself but must
be derived from a survey of all standpoints, both the hypothetical
use of reason and the faculty of reflective judgment take some of

their bearings from the thinking of others and include that thinking in their own. They need the public forum that turns private reflection into liberal and broadened thought. This is what qualifies publicity to be a carrier of truth. In expanding reason and truth it creates the premises of a republican political order.

Clearly seen and often mentioned by Kant was the political significance of taste. Here we can only suggest what would have to be further elaborated in any material presentation of Kantian politics: that human taste is educated only in public; that it is a way to civilization, just as sociality is such a way; that it is a means to promote culture and at the same time a product of culture; that it is finally a propaedeutic for developing morality, just as the development of morality is a school of taste. As a means of civilization, cultivation, and moralization, taste becomes a public propaedeutic of republican politics.

And as for debate, this is the real proof that the hypothetical use of reason (the faculty of reflective judgment) and the effort to clarify the judgment of taste have become public. What occurs in debate is the political awakening of which the hypothetical use of reason and reflective judgment are mere rudiments. From this viewpoint we can understand anew why a debate must not be exclusive. A tendency to be exclusive would be a negation of the political element in debate. It would be a departure from the principle of broadened and liberal thinking that has produced the debate.

This confirms once again what Kant's youthful writings have already told us: politics starts with the use of reason. Every discussion is a political performance. To have politics start only when political issues or power struggles are at stake means to refuse to understand it until it is a consequence, until it has become derivative. This would be tantamount to renouncing its comprehension. The Greeks, Plato and Aristotle above all, knew this long before Kant. To them, education and politics were organic growths on a fundament of metaphysics. Metaphysics, therefore, had to be constantly tested for consistency, and politics, for its metaphysical roots. Kant did not see this unity in the Greeks, and perhaps not even in himself; but he reestablished it in original fashion. Only his works, as distinct from those of Plato and Aristotle, show as yet no comprehensive recognition of that unity.

6. KANT'S POLEMICS AGAINST
HIS CONTEMPORARIES

In this chapter we analyze Kant's polemics against his contemporaries of the 1780s and '90s. The earlier controversies will be examined later, in a broader context. Our guide in structuring the material was the previously developed typology of combat forms.

Kant's Unpolemical Character

To his friends Kant appeared an unpolemical character. Their portrayals[1] show a cheerful, all but unshakable self-assurance, freedom from any narrowing arrogance, concentration on completing his work. The fertile hours—and they finally seem to have struck with the regularity of a natural order—were devoted to his work; the others, to good company and to reading. The thought of being nothing but a philosopher was alien to him.[2] He found little time to study his apologists and his serious opponents, two groups he regarded as deserving equally well of the Criticist cause;[3] for the customary jabs at differently-minded colleagues[4] and for arguments with the "vermin that's buzzing with squibs at the foot of Parnassus"[5] he found no time at all.

Age seemed to stiffen his "antipathy to squabbles."[6] It became virtually impossible for him to get his thoughts out of the tracks of the critical system in which they had circled for decades.[7] Grasping his opponents' writings, or understanding other systems, came to be an effort; if he wished to know a book now, he would ask a friend in whose judgment he trusted to read it and, translated into the Kantian language, to compare it with the main results of the *Critiques*. Replying was a task he liked to leave to others.[8]

His colleague Pörschke aptly characterized him in a letter to Fichte: "Nothing came as naturally to Kant as being a great sage. Of all human souls he is the last to feel his greatness, and he is surely the model of a modest writer. I often hear him judge his opponents generously, provided only that their attacks on him are not monkish and personal. That embitters him."[9] With this limitation we can accept Borowski's view—otherwise palliating—that even the replies to Eberhard and Schlosser would not have been written without Kant's being "goaded by others, and in part, too, being urged by men whose will he deemed himself duty-bound to comply with. . . . His unpolemical heart would truly not have inspired them."[10]

This unpolemical heart of Kant's strikes us also in his own few notes, which indicate what he was like.

"To me, as you know, profit and attention on a grand stage are not major impulses. All that I have wished for and received is a peaceful situation, exactly in line with my needs, alternately occupied with work, speculation, and social intercourse; a situation in which my mind, quickly affected but otherwise carefree, and my body—moodier yet, but never ill—can be kept busy without too much of an effort. Any change frightens me, however much it may seem to improve my situation, and I believe I must heed this instinct of my nature if I want somewhat to lengthen the thin and delicate thread being spun for me by the Fates."[11]

Worry about one's own measure and concern for one's work will often—in fear of failure, perhaps—be hidden behind a shield of magnificent calm, of apparent immunity to fear of attack. "In debate there is calm where there is superiority of reasons or strength" (75: XV, 505; 1140). In this posture, Kant would follow every search for truth with sympathy and interest. His enemy was not the man who thought differently, but the one who did not think at all; not the adversary, but the materially indifferent individual. Opponents who could be true adversaries were sought out by Kant; he even pleaded for such opposition, as long as the other was ready to attack the essence of divergent thinking frankly, chivalrously, and with the strength of his own thinking.[12] Kant, of course, knew all about the world of scholars. He knew that this world has "its wars, its alliances, its secret intrigues"[13] like any other world, and he knew that the game may be entertaining; but he did not like to play it. "Besides, to me an embittered learned debate is so unbearable, and the very state of mind in which one must wage it so unnatural, that I would undertake the most extensive explanation and vindication of my past writings against the keenest opponent who seeks insights only, rather than arouse and harbor an affect for which my soul never has room otherwise."[14]

His life as a man and as a thinker seems in tune with what he wrote to Garve, the first critic of his main work: "I am at peace with all the world."[15]

The Polemical Age

Against the background of contemporary biographical materials we can believe in Kant's willingness to live in peace with all the world. Alongside this willingness, however, stands the fact that never before had a philosopher arisen in Germany, or perhaps anywhere in the West, claiming, in so many words, to lay a new foundation for philosophizing.

This claim, combined with the insight that every creative philosopher is an intentional or unintentional ζῷον πολεμικόν, struck Kant's philosophizing contemporaries like a challenge, many indeed like a declaration of war. Since it was no empty claim, however, being based upon a philosophical revolution that gave rise to a new, life-sustaining philosophy, no thinker could remain indifferent to it. The claim was the more striking for being advanced at a time when, although philosophical discussion of details was in full swing, the ground of scientific metaphysics seemed to have been laid by Leibniz, expanded and popularized by Wolff, and consolidated by the reigning school in Germany. As Feder, one of the most renowned professors before the criticist breakthrough, put it in an argument with Kant: "This philosophy has now aroused so much attention, such concern among some, and so much hope and admiration in others, that no philosophy teacher has any more right to keep silent."[16] Feder's statement was at the same time a call to his colleagues to get into the discussion of the new philosophy.

This discussion had taken three full years to get started after *Critique of Pure Reason* appeared in 1781, with a baffled Kant interpreting the long silence now as an "affront,"[17] now as a sign of thorough studies.[18] Since about 1784, the year in which the first substantial work about *Critique* came out,[19] the discussion had been well underway, but the adherents of the old school were not easily shaken. Not until critical philosophy was propa-

gated (from 1785 on) by a reputable joural of its own—the
Allgemeine Literatur-Zeitung of Jena, founded by Schütz and
Hufeland—and not until Reinhold, a son-in-law of Wieland, had
published his readable and popularly intelligible "Letters on Kantian Philosophy" (1786–87)[20] in Wieland's *Der Teutsche Merkur*,
did talk about it assume larger dimensions. German thinkers
soon split into two camps variously named for particular interests
(criticists vs. skepticists, criticists vs. dogmatists, apriorists vs.
empiricists, rationalists vs. sensualists, Kantians vs. anti-Kantians,
and so forth), but of which one was always for critical philosophy
and the other against it. In more than a hundred periodicals they
spread their ideas—and thus, willy-nilly, Kant's ideas—far beyond the German frontiers. The *Allgemeine Literatur-Zeitung*,
for instance—probably the foremost German journal of the
century next to *Der Teutsche Merkur*, and the most zealous
protagonist of Criticism, along with *Berliner Monatsschrift*—
had in 1788, the third year of its existence, 2,000 subscribers,
which in effect meant some 40,000 readers. Outside the German
language area it had subscribers in Poland, Hungary, Italy,
France, England, Holland, Denmark, Sweden, and Russia.[21]

Thanks to the propaganda activities of Kant's adherents and
opponents, critical philosophy came into vogue. All possible
topics were talked and written about according to Kantian principles and by the deductive method. In the *Deutsche Monatsschrift* this trend was ridiculed in an article entitled "Kantian
Principles, a Literary Fashion Item."[22] The author preferred to
remain anonymous; writing against Kant often hurt a man's
prestige and obliged him to expect some trenchant responses.
People liked to show that they were Kantians, and in the long
run this was how they lowered the prestige of Criticism. There
is no denying that Kant's philosophy could not have spread so
quickly throughout Germany without the devoted, frequently
self-sacrificing help of his best adherents; but neither can we
deny that the mass of Kantians finally brought that philosophy
into disrepute. "The shame of our century," Fichte called these
Kantians;[23] Herder's disdainful word for them was "an unphilo-
sophical crew,"[24] and Pörschke's, "the most insolent gang . . . on
account of their stultifying parrotry and their intolerance."[25]
They were the usual excrescences of the "idolatrous worship of
a philosopher,"[26] as Nicolai put it.

The most untalented disciples practiced this worship by intro-
ducing scraps of critical terminology into the vernacular. Kant
himself, in the preface to *Theory of Law,* censured the "mischief"
of those "copycats" who would employ crucial technical terms
from *Critique of Pure Reason* for the mere "public communication of thoughts" (37: VI, 208).

The somewhat more gifted adepts' form of idolatry was to
swoop down like a horde of censors upon whatever in Germany
dared to attack Kant. A multitude of mediocre brains strove
overzealously to shield the real brain, which did not need their
protection.

The most gifted apologists, Fichte, Reinhold, and Beck among
them, worshiped by presuming to have a monopoly on understanding. Eventually each of them thought that nobody else
understood Kant.[27] Until then, the Kantians had closed ranks
against their enemies; now they carried the fight into their own
camp, involuntarily proving that Criticism's claim to be the
inner unification of metaphysics was immodest, indeed arrogant.
The Kantians' own obtuseness made it easy for the other side
to drive a wedge between Kant and them. In *Berlinisches Archiv
der Zeit und ihres Geschmacks* ("Berlin Archives of the Time
and Its Taste") one opponent offered "demonstrable proof that
Kant is not a Kantian."[28] More and more clearly, Kant was
made to feel the hard truth of the Italian proverb he quoted in
the reply to Eberhard and in his statement against Fichte: "God
preserve us from our friends; against our enemies we'll mount
our own guard."[29]

The groups included in the opposition made strange bed-
fellows. There were the old academic philosophers of the Wolffian school (Eberhard, Maass, Schwab, Flatt, Platner, and
others), who set up their own central literary organ in Eberhard's
Das Philosophische Magazin; the traditional scholasticists (Sat-
tler, Salat, and others), who disparaged the new philosophy from
their centers in Munich and Vienna; the skeptics headed by
Schulze, one of the most brilliant Kant critics of the time. There
were popular-philosophical and popular-scientific authors
(Garve, Feder, Nicolai) united mostly in the Berlin Academy of
Sciences, and romanticists tending to mysticism and revealed
faith (Hamann, Jacobi, Jung-Stilling, Schlettwein). There were
not a few satirists having fun at the Kantians' expense (Obereit,

Nicolai, and many anonymous ones). There were sensualists and intuitionalists (Herder, Schlosser, Wieland); a number of scholars with mathematical training, basically free, yet under the influence of Leibniz (Kästner, Klügel, Lichtenberg); and finally a few original philosophers (Fichte, Schelling, Hegel). Not all of these opponents lived in hostility to Kant and his thinking. Many, including the most important ones, felt indebted to him all their lives. Only the rigor of his claims and his consistency drove them into the enemy camp.

Quantitatively, the results of the debate are impressive. In the German language area alone, more than 400 publications on the new system in general had appeared by 1804, an equal number on its ethics, more than 200 on Kant's philosophy of religion, 130 on his philosophy of law, 70 on his logic, 60 each on his aesthetics and biblical exegesis, and so forth. All told, more than 2,000 essays and books pro and con, by some 700 authors, were printed in the last twenty years of Kant's life.[30] The trade fair catalogues were overflowing with books for, about, and against Kant. Everybody who philosophized in Germany felt obliged to take sides and did so to the best of his ability, whether in a simple document of thinking along Kantian lines, in an attempted popularization, in a supposed complementation, or in a critique.

Among the critical utterances we find all the variants of polemicizing: sober inquiries, acutely logical retorts, appeals to common sense, ironical jibes, sneering squibs, downright defamatory lampoons—a total picture that prompted Reinhold to ask uneasily, in a letter to Fichte, "Will our pursuit of science become, or remain, a *bellum omnium?*"[31] By the turn of the century all fields of transcendental philosophy had been dissected by critics. Many came to feel that the edifice Kant had erected in years of toil was being razed again. There seemed to be nothing left but the memory of an oft-praised, oft-mocked fundament with the systems of new philosophers rising on it to show that in his claims, at least, Kant had been mistaken. In learned circles—as Schelling put it crassly and Pörschke confirmed it in a milder vein—Kant was "philosophically dead."[32]

In those fifteen years of contention over the new philosophy, Kant often tried to nip occasions for a public quarrel in the bud.[33] But he did react to some attacks—first in 1783, in the appendix to *Prolegomena,* where he sharply challenged the first critic of his *magnum opus,* and for the last time in 1799, when he assailed Fichte's theory of science in a statement as ruthless as it was dogmatic in tone and language. In between, we find more than ten publications either replying to a challenge or initiating a debate. Once the great controversy had begun, Kant participated in it up to the very end of his publicistic activity. For all his readiness to live in peace with the world, he had no illusions about his ability to do so.

Polemical Use of Reason

Among Kant's polemics against his contemporaries, the ones against Feder, Eberhard, Schlosser, and Nicolai, as well as the public statements against Schlettwein and Fichte, can be characterized as defensive and exclusive.

The Challenges

Each of these authors laid down an unmistakable challenge to Kant. Feder's was the first review of *Critique of Pure Reason,* a review as ignorant as it was arrogant; Eberhard's, the thesis constantly reiterated in *Das Philosophische Magazin,* that a critique of reason—and a better one—had already been furnished by Leibniz; Fichte's, his claim to be the only man who understood Kant and the first to have purely presented Kant's intended system; Schlosser's, a belletristic intuitionism expounded in tones of genius, in aestheticizing language, and propagandistically combined with a critique of Kant's philosophy. Nicolai challenged in two ways: as a writer, by making fun of Criticism in humorous novels, and as a publisher, by bringing out philosophical literature hostile to Kant. Schlettwein, finally, did it in grotesquely lamenting letters about Kant's claim to be the first to teach a scientific metaphysics.

We use the first three examples, as more relevant, to illustrate Kant's fight against these men, and from each illustration we cast a brief glance at the rest.

Feder. Critique of Pure Reason appeared in 1781. Kant had been pondering the contents for twelve years, but then he had written the book in barely five months. This haste was due to

fear that "longer hesitation would finally make so extensive a
business burdensome to myself, and increasing age might perhaps
make it impossible in the end, whereas now I still have the whole
system in my head."[34] He knew that in this work he was placing
philosophy on a new foundation, and that in a literary form
requiring readers to do heavy mental labor. In his own view, "the
presentation of the materials . . . had not been sufficiently worked
out to conform with general comprehensibility."[35] To do so
would have taken him years more. He had forgone the effort,
hoping later to be helped by other people thinking along his
lines; for the moment he was not counting "on a prompt favorable reaction."[36] But he did expect people to see what was downright new in *Critique;* he expected them at least to understand
the basic metaphysical question as a question, to consider the
main points of its solution, and to respect the "praiseworthy
things which now and then may be found, after all."[37] Once his
thought came up against a thought in quest of understanding,
joint reflection on the new materials would in time illuminate
the presentation also.

What did come as the first critical reaction failed to live up
to these hopes.

On 19 January 1782, an anonymous review of a little over
eight pages appeared in section 3 of *Göttinger Gelehrte Anzeigen*.
The author (as Kant may have guessed) was Johann Georg Heinrich Feder, professor of philosophy in Göttingen and a contrib-
uting editor of the magazine, though the inspiration was not
his alone. In 1781 Christian Garve had visited Göttingen on a
journey. By way of thanks for many kindnesses shown him in
the *Anzeigen*, he offered to write a major review for the journal.
Having read Kant's early writings with pleasure, he asked for
the new work that had just appeared after so long a pause.
Distracted by travel and enfeebled by his chronic ailments, however, Garve soon realized that he "had made the wrong choice."[38]
He had the patience to read the work, but not the strength to
see it as a whole and compare it with past metaphysics. The
result was a long, not always exactly paraphrasing review that
did justice neither to the entirety nor to the novelty of *Critique
of Pure Reason*. Garve sent his manuscript to Göttingen, where
it got into Feder's hands and proved somewhat embarrassing.
The maximum space reserved for reviews in the *Anzeigen* was

one printed sheet (sixteen pages), and Garve's would have taken about a sheet and a half. Unwilling to break the rule and unable to ask Garve to write a shorter review, Feder "condensed," without asking Garve's permission. He made a digest of the review in his own peculiar style, "enriched" it in spots with reflections of his own, and closed with his own "overall judgment"—all without having gone through the formality of reading the book.

The product turned out accordingly. *Critique of Pure Reason*, it said, was a work in which the intellect was always exercised, "even if not always instructed"; a work "straining the reader's attention, often to the point of fatigue," though occasionally coming "to his aid with fortunate metaphors" or even rewarding him "with unexpected, commonly useful conclusions." As a whole, the introductory sentence concluded, the work was "a system of higher or . . . transcendental idealism," which "transforms the world and ourselves into conceptions and has all objects arise from phenomena by intellectual conjunction into one empirical series, and by the necessary—albeit futile—attempts of reason to extend and unite them in one whole and complete system of the world."[39]

This introductory sentence signals the perversion of the whole review. In passing, so to speak, the work is robbed of its uniqueness. It does not always instruct—and for Feder, this had consequences. Books that elaborate on what is known may be measured by existing stocks of knowledge. Measured thus, the new work will, as the conclusion indicates, have to be viewed as a futile undertaking. From this measurement Feder gets the self-assured tone of a man aware of his standards, one who may fearlessly issue qualifications because he knows about the topic. This measurement, finally, riveted his understanding to the basic errors so clearly apparent in his review of the "main theses."[40]

Because to Kant, we read there, space and time are not realities; his system of transcendental aesthetics rests on a fundament "upon which Berkeley also mainly built his idealism."[41] But what he, Feder, fails to understand is how reality can still be separated, then, from "fantasies and visions,"[42] and the world of dreamers from the world of those who are awake.

In logic, Kant is said to speak of laws of the intellect. "They are the generally known principles of logic and ontology, expressed according to the author's idealistic restrictions,"[43] and no attempt "further to clarify the entire task of the intellect"[44] is made.

Feder then drafts a pitiful picture of transcendental dialectics, concluding with this statement: "The only novelty the author adds here is that he summons the practical interest to his aid and lets moral ideas decide where speculation had left both scales equally weighted—or equally empty, rather."[45] But this very novelty "we prefer to disregard altogether, it being what we are least able to accept."[46]

There follows a report on methodology—an exhilarating one, for now it appears that "what pure reason must beware of is *discipline* . . . and what it must go by is the *canon* of pure reason. The contents of that cannot be more closely analyzed; a good part may be gathered from the aforesaid."[47]

And although Feder could not closely analyze the contents, he could pass judgment upon them, to wit:

The book might indeed serve "to acquaint the reader with the most notable difficulties of speculative philosophy,"[48] but the author did not seem to have found "the right, and calming, middle way between extravagant [!] skepticism"[49] and dogmatism. And yet, because that way "bears certain markers,"[50] he ought to have found it. "First of all, the right use of the intellect must correspond to the most general concept of proper conduct, to the basic law of our moral nature—that is to say, to the promotion of happiness."[51] If only one shunned contradictions and found the sufficient reasons, "common sense"[52] would lead him to the goal. Instead of taking this road, however, Kant was upsetting the "legality"[53] of now internal, now external sensations, inciting them against each other or confusing one with the other. Hence the inability of his idealism to adjust either to the concept of substance or to a natural "sort of conception and language."[54] Considering at the same time that his phenomena "are exactly that which we call objects and the world," one could only ask: "Why the argument against this commonly accepted language? What is the point, and what the source, of the idealistic distinction?"[55]

The ignorance of this first review may perhaps show even more in its silences than in its statements. Not a word about the fundamentally new science, the delimitation of reason by reason;

not a word about the Copernican turn; no hint at the distinction of analytical and synthetic judgments. The basic question of the new metaphysics, "How can there by synthetic judgments a priori?" is not even mentioned. The "heart of the matter," the transcendental deduction, and the vastly important chapter on schematism are ignored. There is no insight into the relationship of phenomenon and substrate, no notion of the science of not knowing. All in all, a review by a truly lazy mind that seems, at least, to use the principle that there is "nothing new under the sun, only worse," to relieve itself of toil.

And Feder was not just any odd reviewer. He had long made a name for himself throughout Germany. Called to the chair of philosophy in Göttingen at twenty-eight years of age, he had been welcomed by Lichtenberg, Kästner, and Heyne as their friend and equal. As one of the most famous professors, with the privilege of lecturing in the main auditorium, he managed to please everyone. His teaching style was "eirenical-eclectic,"[56] and his skill, to take from all authors the things that agreed with common sense, and to merge them into a pleasant, never over-taxing aggregate. Lockeans, Wolffians, and Crusians found him equally appealing, although he was not a member of any school and did not want to found a new one.[57] He thus seemed both instructive and loyal to all, superior and yet universally well-meaning. His books appeared in printings of a size not attained by Kant's works in his lifetime. In 1781, when he reviewed *Critique of Pure Reason,* Feder's textbooks were used "at almost all universities and many high schools"[58] in Germany; Kant, too, used them on occasion. Feder was one of the notables one visited on travels, or to whom one gave students a letter of recommendation. To be reviewed by him was an honor.

Kant did not appreciate the honor. Outraged by a piece whose levity bordered on malice, he hit back sharply.

Eberhard. Of all the assaults made on Criticism, Eberhard's was the most dangerous. As Schütz in Jena had founded the *Allgemeine Literatur-Zeitung* to disseminate Kantian philosophy, Eberhard, the occupant of Wolff's chair at the University of Halle, founded *Das Philosophische Magazin*[59] against that philosophy, in 1788. The *Magazin* was to be the central organ of all German thinkers who stood by Leibniz and Wolff. Against the advance of the new philosophy Eberhard was thus deliberately raising a shield inscribed with a name confessed by many eminent disciples —the name, in fact, of a whole school still strongly represented at the universities as the inheritor of the German Enlightenment.

Johann August Eberhard was the right man for this undertaking. Having studied theology at Halle and tutored for a while, he had gone to Berlin in 1763 as chaplain to a later Prussian minister of state, von der Horst. In Berlin he made friends with Moses Mendelssohn and Nicolai and in his spare time studied ecclesiastical history, the fathers of the Church, philosophy, and ancient and modern languages. The first fruit of these studies was a *New Apology of Socrates* (1772)[60] in which the state-employed preacher dared a vindication of the virtuous heathen, claiming to be able to judge him neither as a preacher nor as a scholar, only as a philosopher: "For the theories of the theological systems are nothing but philosophy, and therefore cannot be judged by anything but philosophy."[61] The courageous, elegantly written book provoked several retorts[62] and established Eberhard's reputation. Four years later, when the Berlin Academy of Sciences honored his *General Theory of Thought and Sensation*,[63] he moved to the forefront of contemporary professors. In 1778 he was called to Halle, to the chair of philosophy which von Zedlitz had repeatedly offered to Kant.[64] His social standing was thus at least equal to Kant's, but Halle gave him a larger sphere of action.

From his appointment on, Eberhard never stopped publishing. A multitude of compendia appeared under his name, all of them fittingly characterized by a line from the foreword to his *Metaphysics*: "It should contain nothing new, but should at times condense, at other times somewhat expand, the system in the natural and lucid order of its presentation by A. G. Baumgarten."[65] Besides these textbooks he published many works of varying size, including a four-volume *Manual of Aesthetics for Educated Readers of All Classes*,[66] a *Dictionary of German Synonyms*,[67] and *The Spirit of Primitive Christianity*[68] in three volumes. The real reason he remains unforgotten does not lie in this productivity, however, but exclusively in his opposition to Kant and in the periodicals spawned by it—in the four volumes of *Das Philosophische Magazin* and the two of *Philosophisches Archiv*.[69]

Quantitatively, Eberhard's achievement is impressive. By sheer hard work he familiarized himself with almost all the intellectual sciences, mastered seven foreign languages, and became an expert on the literature of those language areas. "He was incredibly well read in books of every description."[70] His foremost disciple, Schleiermacher, felt obliged to him throughout his life.

In his contacts with friends, Eberhard's personality must have been agreeable. Nicolai praised his "vivid imagination," his "encyclopedic memory," his "lucid intellect," his "acumen," also his "merry wit" and "unshakable veracity," his "tireless industry," capacity for friendship, and modesty.[71] One will not overestimate these clichés; even so, it is well to remember them in reading Kant's polemic.

Eberhard's comprehensive learning, his facile, quotable, and always courteous style, his large acquaintance, and his determination to mobilize against Kant whatever favored Wolff and Leibniz—all this made him an opponent Kant had to fear for a while.

Eberhard himself explained the purpose of his magazine as follows. A few friends, he said, had joined to inform each other of "the most recent occurrences in the philosophical world"[72] and to preserve those worthy of it in *Das Philosophische Magazin*. The time was auspicious, with large segments of the population suddenly interested in speculative philosophy. For, in a period of popularization, Kant had had the courage "to prepare a revolution in which philosophy would either win or lose everything."[73] "Its success surpassed all that the most sanguine hope could expect of the most fervid enthusiasm; the *Critique of Pure Reason* and the philosophy it contains caused a sensation the like of which had not been seen in the philosophical world for a long time."[74] The book had aroused enthusiasm, doubt, disappointment, and enchantment, with the philosophical public caught in the uncertainty of these conflicting emotions. "Since we begin our journal in this philosophical crisis, we shall frequently have to entertain our readers with the peculiarities of the Königsberg philosopher's philosophy."[75] Kant's own claim to lay the very first ground of metaphysics had "opened the field among us,"[76] and in the *Magazin* he, Eberhard, was accepting the challenge. "I feel that what moves me to do so is not a concern with ease, with any school, system, or predilection; it is not even fear of giving up a science to which I have sacrificed a large part of my life."[77] His only concern was "to inaugurate a calm and thorough joint investigation of the principles of Kant's critique of reason,"[78] far from the "vile spectacle of a learned gladiatorial contest."[79] The determinants of judgment should be "seriousness without bitterness, concern without heat, a strict but gentle and sincere appraisal, without glossing over one's own weaknesses or passing in silence over the strengths of the man one is appraising."[80] Daring to compare the old with the new in this posture, Eberhard would be able "more exactly to judge the necessity and the bounds of the philosophical reformation, more correctly to esteem the worth of both, and best to counter the wanton habit to reject one or the other without knowing both."[81] He would also "at times, before a qualified tribunal, undertake the defense of past metaphysics against its accusers who prefer a future one."[82] His hope was "now and then, before the judgment seat of an illumined impartiality, perhaps even to win mercy" for the old metaphysics.[83] His real goal, however, was not to make propaganda for one side, but "to facilitate a rational choice between the two."[84]

The very first essay, "On the Bounds of Human Cognition," clearly shows that Eberhard's intention was not as objective as his tone. "The principal service to metaphysics whereby Professor Kant sought to acquire merit consists in the more precise definition of the limits of the human intellect."[85] Whether or not he had shown these limits correctly deserved to be most exactly reexamined. Eberhard devoted a few pages to the reexamination and concluded that if "critique" meant an analysis of the laws under which each cognitive faculty brings forth its specific concepts, German philosophy had been made critical by Leibniz long ago. Kant, of course, deprived it of this character "by a mere fiat,"[86] but without offering "a semblance of proof"[87] for this fiat. Whatever was basic in Kant could be found in Leibniz, along with much that Kant spurned for no good reason. Kant was mired in the skepticism of Hume, whereas Leibniz, beyond any mere propaedeutic, had achieved a "rational psychology, cosmology, and theology."[88] The fact—as Eberhard wrote later and more lucidly—was "first: that the philosophy of Leibniz contains as much of a critique of reason as Kant's, for its dogmatism rests on an exact analysis of cognitive faculties that seeks to state exactly what is possible by means of each; only the results differ. If it is faithfully presented, therefore, this philosophy cannot be called uncritical. Second: that Leibniz's philosophy can contain, not only all that is true in Kant's, but more. What makes it capable of this 'more' is the reasoned expansion of the domain of the intellect to which its critical analysis of cognitive faculties entitles it."[89]

Thus the main thrust of *Das Philosophische Magazin* did not evaporate in idle laments about Kantian terminology, nor in sterile demonstrations of insufficient proof or hidden contradictions, nor in the rejection of specific philosophemes. It concentrated, rather, on the claim that was to legitimize Kantian philosophy as such. What Kant wanted to do was all right, but it had been done already—more thoroughly, more usefully, and with no noise about it. Kant might be conceded the merit of having raised important questions again, as a contemporary; but if the contemporaries were still familiar with Leibniz, they would have to acknowledge Kant's superfluity. This was the basic idea of Eberhard's critique. The task of all subsequent essays, issues, and volumes was to lend plausibility, relevance, and effectiveness to this idea.

Eberhard proceeded with skill. He took up the main points of *Critique of Pure Reason,* alternately showing them as contradicting Leibniz's critique of reason and as akin to it. He drew upon other collaborators, on Maass, Schwab, and Flatt, as well as on the two leading mathematicians of the time, Klügel and Kästner. Partly with their assistance, he "proved" that time and space rest upon things in themselves, that things in themselves are knowable in part, at least, and that Leibniz had already made the distinction between analytical and synthetic judgments. The insights obtained were tallied in striking juxtapositions of the "two" critiques of reason. The list of comparisons grew, with more and more items credited to Leibniz and debited against Kant.

Eberhard also knew just how to surround these inquiries with propagandistic bustle. He broke them up, continued them in subsequent issues, made deft connections, and referred back to previous installments. In between, he dealt with reviews, answered them, reprinted retorts that had appeared elsewhere; he slipped in a letter of thanks for the lucid comparison of Kant with

Leibniz and replied to it in a later issue. He inserted fables, entertaining news items, and poetry; he got important names to raise the magazine's prestige. But not for a moment, throughout this, did he forget his main purpose: to demonstrate that reason had been rendered critical before Kant, and that Kant, while deserving praise in details, was superfluous as a figure in philosophical history.

That Kant was enraged by this stubborn pretense to seek pure cognition while really bent upon the validation of a prejudice is understandable.

When a cry of alarm from Reinhold, in April 1789, described the reading public as "intimidated" by the *Magazin*—with indeed "a rather substantial and respectable part believing you to be refuted"[90] if Kant would not at least issue a public statement against Eberhard—Kant intervened in the quarrel. He took a hand, first, as the guiding spirit of a review by Reinhold, then as the author of a polemical treatise, finally as the organizer of a joint campaign that did not come wholly to rest until the collapse of Eberhard's publications.

Fichte. Fichte, the original thinker, has a mental stature so different from that of the two philosophy professors, Feder and Eberhard, that to classify him with the other assailants is really not permissible. His attack on Kant, too, was fundamentally different in nature. Fichte was not defending an old school from whose downfall he had something to fear; nor were his attacks made ultimately harmless by the fact that he had never understood the essence of critical philosophy. Originally as free a thinker as Kant, he had steeped himself in Kant's thinking and had experienced its depth existentially; it was from the core of that thinking, from its metaphysical tidal flow toward unity, that he had become Kant's opponent—and never with a will to fight him, only with the claim to understand him better and to put his intrinsic philosophizing on a scientific basis for the first time. To Fichte's mind, his very fight against Kant was a way of accepting and adopting Kantian contents.

If, just the same, we classify Fichte with the others, this is only because of our primary concern with Kant's combat methods, and because Kant—regrettably, it seems to us—gave Fichte, in principle, the same treatment he gave his other opponents.

Fichte read *Critique of Practical Reason* (34) in 1790. It made him feel like a changed man: "I live in a new world since reading the *Critique of Practical Reason*," he wrote to Weisshuhn.[91] The most beneficial effects seemed to him to spring from Kant's philosophy: it tamed his ever-active imagination, uplifted his spirit, and strengthened his mind.[92] It laid the ground for a character, "down to the wish to have a character,"[93] and thus caused an incomprehensible revolution in attitude that encompassed the whole of man.[94] Those days of his first Kant studies were "the happiest days I ever spent."[95] They filled him with the hope that philosophy might once more bring about "a new élan and a total rebirth" in mankind, and that then there would be nothing "which its effects will not cover."[96] Experience and hope instilled in him "the most wonderful reverence for the strangely unique man whom our age, after thousands of past years, had to engender."[97] Kant, "the pride of the human spirit,"[98] seemed to Fichte to have something "Godlike"[99] that evoked instant trust and lent wings to independent work. "I confess," he wrote to Kant, "that the thought of you will always be my genius, which impels me, as far as lies within my circle of activity, not to leave the arena without some benefit to mankind."[100]

At the same time, however, he soon came to feel a certain discontent. Not yet clear in his mind about its cause, he laid it to the fact that Kant's philosophy was "difficult beyond all conception."[101] "Nothing is more difficult than a clear presentation of Kantian ideas."[102] As his work progressed, Fichte thought he was seeing more clearly. He grasped the trend of Kant's philosophy, its flow toward unity, and simultaneously he noticed that its terminal point could not be grasped. Invariably, unity was pursued, but instead of attaining it, Kant often seemed to Fichte to come to a halt at superficial dualities and trinities without bothering to inquire beyond them. Not having reached the point of ultimate unity, he seemed to be passing off a multiplicity for unity. Fichte, to whose mind science could only be a whole system flowing from unity, took the final inconclusiveness of Kant's system to be unscientific. Perceiving at the same time, however, that for all its inconclusiveness everything would harmonize in unity as by a miracle, he concluded that Kant did know the entire system, even though he had never presented it yet. "I am convinced that Kant has not presented the system; but he has it in his possession."[103]

"Kant has the right philosophy, but only in its results, not in its grounds."[104] Fichte wondered about the reasons for this curious fact. Either Kant had "a genius that reveals truth to him without showing him the reasons,"[105] or he was miraculously guided by "a faculty of divining truth."[106] Or, Fichte went on reflecting, it might be that Kant had the reasons but did not sufficiently value the age he lived in to reveal the reasons to it; or he wished "purposely to leave the credit for their own research"[107] to his contemporaries; or he might have qualms about "reaping in his lifetime the superhuman worship which sooner or later must be his share anyway";[108] or all he wanted for himself was to be modestly credited with having shown the way.

However this might be, it was clear to Fichte—and confirmed by a perusal of Schulze's *Aenesidemus*[109] and of the writings of Maimon—that transcendental philosophy had "not yet been raised to the rank of an evident science."[110] But the way to raise it to this rank had already been shown to human reason, by Reinhold: "All philosophy must be reduced to a single principle."[111] The man who found that principle would "be presenting philosophy as a science,"[112] and this presentation was what Fichte considered his own proper task. In his view, the thing to be presented was Kantian; only the presentation itself would have to go beyond Kant, who had never given it yet. Of the principle, Fichte said at one time, cautiously, "I think I have found it,"[113] and at another time, with assurance, "I have discovered a new fundament, upon which all of philosophy is very easily developed."[114] The development would not take him beyond Kant's spirit—"but beyond the *letter* of Kant I hope to be able to go."[115]

Now that the system could for the first time be thought through all the way to rock bottom, Fichte wrote, "it seems more and more likely to me that Kant was deducing precisely from my principles,"[116] however often those principles seemed outwardly to contradict Kant. It was not until the transcendental system had been newly founded by Fichte that one could understand Kant at all: "Until now, Kant is . . . a sealed book, and what people have read into him is precisely what does not fit him, and what he wished to refute."[117] As Kant had been received so far, he was "the most outlandish monster ever begotten by human imagination,"[118] and Kant's own evident consent to this misconception could only be due to the fact that "he seems to have philosophized altogether too little about his philosophizing."[119] Kant himself did not understand Kant either. But Fichte did, because he knew the theory of science.

Fichte turned his new system into the premise of understanding Kant at all. Only his own philosophy was absolute; it could "be tested only by himself, not by the theses of any other philosophy."[120] Imperceptibly, step by little step, Kant's one-time servant had become Kant's master. His relation to Kant was that of a subordinate who is at once the qualifying factor. Kant was not the transcendental philosopher he thought he was; he was only the first step on the road to transcendental philosophy. In the final analysis, as Hegel once put it, Kant was "a good introduction to philosophy."[121] The true transcendental philosopher was he, Fichte.

This Fichtean claim attracted wide attention and carried an irreconcilable conflict into the transcendental philosophers' camp. When even Reinhold came out for Fichte, legitimizing his claim, Kant was variously urged to clarify his own position.[122] In 1799—not until the summer, perhaps—he read a solemn appeal by an unknown reviewer in the *Erlangische Literaturzeitung:* "Kant is the first teacher of transcendental philosophy, and Reinhold is the most excellent disseminator of the critical doctrine; but the first transcendental philosopher himself is indisputably Fichte. Fichte has realized the plan laid in the *Critiques,* and he has systematically carried out the transcendental idealism Kant suggested. How natural, therefore, is the public's desire to have the originator of the *Critiques* express himself publicly about the undertaking of his worthiest disciple, the originator of transcendental philosophy!"[123]

We do not know for certain whether Kant's statement was due to this public desire, to the continuing strife in the transcendental philosophers' camp, to Fichte's claim, to feelings of discomfort at Fichte's philosophy, or to an insight into the necessity of drawing a clear line between himself and Fichte. In any event, he did answer, and with plainness that left nothing to be desired in regard to Fichte either.

The others. Kant never had to fear his other challengers' capacity for thought, seldom their knowledge, but now and then their literary talent.

Friedrich Nicolai, tirelessly busy as a publisher, author, and letter writer, kept attacking Criticism and, above all, the activities around it throughout the 1790s. The attacks took varying forms, the most effective of which were Nicolai's humorous novels. His nimble imagination, receptive to all comic touches, fed upon a comprehensive knowledge of the world, of people, and of culture. He had the additional gift of conveying his criticisms to a large audience merrily and effectively, devoid of scholastical bombast. The irony, the wit, the occasional broad humor of his novels helped to undermine respect for critical philosophy and to implant an attachment to "healthy" empiricism. Kant presumably regarded this as a threat. In any case, he hit back hard and derisively.[124]

Johann Georg Schlosser, Goethe's brother-in-law, delivered his Kant critique in a courtly language saturated with clichés from antiquity and sprinkled with the modern metaphors of a would-be genius. He combined this style with a spirit sustained more and more by an aestheticizing Christianity. For his thinking, these were disastrous foundations.[125] With random analogies for guidelines, he engaged in visionary reflections on the most varied topics, presenting intuitions as certainties, synonyms as explanations, images as concepts, and escaping from every dilemma to the haven of revealed faith. "Orpheus and Christ" was his watchword. The tone he brought to philosophy alternated between pseudogenius and paternal wisdom. His critique, harmless from the point of view of knowledge, could be seductive because beyond the hard mental labor it seemed to show ways to an existence both pious and beautiful. Kant, therefore, would not leave it unanswered, attacking mainly the tone and the inwardly brittle foundations of Schlosser's thought.[126]

Finally, two exhortatory letters addressed to him by Johann August Schlettwein, the physiocrat, would have remained without any public significance if Kant himself had not published them with a reply.[127]

Kant's Replies
Kant responded to these six challenges. His replies were dictated by the insight that the attacks were presumptuously exclusionary in character, animated by impulses untouched by, or recreant to, Kant's reversal of the way of thinking. Their premise—unmentioned in the debate—could be reduced to a simple formula: Destroy Kant, or be destroyed by him.

The claim of exclusiveness as such was not what Kant rejected.

He too made that claim. But all depends on whether exclusiveness can be combined with the utmost universality—whether it will exclude only whatever does not qualify for universality. The point is the legitimacy of the exclusiveness one claims. A finding of exclusiveness is not enough to reject it; one must analyze the fundament from which it springs. In principle, this can be done in two ways: either by purely speculative penetration to the premises of the excluder and examination of their general validity, or by analysis of the tone and the practices used to advance the claim, looking through those at the basic intent of the subject. The first way takes us to the theoretical fundament of the exclusiveness claimed; the second, to its practical fundament. In the first instance we analyze a matter; in the second instance, a manner of polemicizing that speaks for the matter.

Kant's analyses follow the second course, without excluding the first. From the forms of address they proceed to the claim and its bases. An examination of the matter is added now and then, but it will only confirm what has already been shown by the analysis of tone and methods.

Analysis of exclusiveness. In each case of polemics, Kant would pay attention to the tone in which he was attacked; for to a man who can read, the tone unmistakably reflects some of the polemicist's basic attitude, which brings the animosity into the case.

In his public statement against Schlettwein, Kant distantly described this tone as "odd" and said it made the letter seem "peculiar" (70: XII, 367). He characterized the peculiarity more closely, as "bittersweet" (70: XII, 369 note). The duplicity of strict condemnation, brotherly helpfulness, and paternal discipline—this entire sanctimonious tone bespoke intentions one had better beware of.

A form of duplicity seemed to Kant to be audible in Fichte's tone as well, in the pathos of a mixture of respect, reverence, and condemnation that looked like a blend of friendship and hostility.

The contempt in Nicolai's basic mentality was evident to Kant in the other's "mockingly aping philosopher's" tone (64: VIII, 437).

Feder's whole review was written in the "lofty tone" (31: IV, 377) of a man "who must be conscious of important and superior insights, which thus far, however, he keeps to himself" (31: IV, 376). It is "so overweening a tone of disparagement and arrogance"[128] that its source could not possibly be a pure search for truth.

Likewise, according to Kant, Eberhard came on like a man "aware of the weight he carries with the philosophical public"[129] and therefore anxious to "parade his learning."[130] "I wish that this overweening charlatan's tone were held up to him just a little."[131]

In Schlosser's first attack, the tone struck Kant as the very crux of the polemic; his retort, in any case, was entitled "On a Newly Introduced Gentility of Tone in Philosophy." When gentlemen philosophize, he said, it does them honor, and their academic lapses may deserve indulgence. "But that would-be philosophers act gentlemanly can in no wise be indulged" (60: VII, 394). Their activity then can no longer be called philosophizing but merely "playing philosopher" (60: VIII, 394 note). It is a playful affectation with the hidden claim to stand above the philosophers and to suppress "the philosophers' inalienable right to be free and equal in matters of sheer reason" (60: VIII, 394). "The suppression occurs in the gentility of tone" (60: VIII, 394 note). Such a tone tends to attach itself to blind faith, and with that faith will, "by obscuring, end" philosophy (60: VIII, 394 note). Here too, the tone both covers and reveals the ultimate intent; though it may be civilized and, as in Schlosser's case, seemingly communicative by virtue of classic humane ideas, it still is philosophical only insofar as it is the undisguised "common tone" (62: VIII, 422) of truthfulness.

If the attacker's tone is an indication of his true intent, an analysis of his mode of combat will bring that intent into plain view. Kant's word for this mode is "practice" when the aim is "frank and honest dealing with a task"; the word is "practices" when the procedure follows the basic maxim of *mundus vult decipi, ergo decipiatur* (64: VIII, 437) and gains its end that way.

In Feder's review Kant felt he could see clearly through those practices. He gave a hint in the title of his reply: "A Sample of Judgment Passed upon *Critique* Previous to Examination" (31: IV, 372). The title points to the fundamental perversion: his "reviewer's rashness" (31: IV, 377) kept Feder from studying *Critique of Pure Reason,* but he judged it anyway, and that with vehemence and "wholesale, through and through" (31: IV, 375). Kant found his procedure "shrewd" (31: IV, 376). Feder knew he

did not know enough to judge the book; so he discussed it in a
manner that seemed to provide an orientation and led the reader
to a judgment without revealing the reviewer's "own knowledge
or ignorance" (31: IV, 376). He resorted to a "trick" (31: IV, 376),
enumerating isolated statements out of context and without an
insight into their premises, besetting "the reader's patience ad
nauseam" (31: IV, 376), scattering strictures, and giving himself
an appearance of superior expertise. He thus put himself in
position for announcing the verdict that all the novelty consisted
"in a mere linguistic renovation" (31: IV, 376). As a metaphysical
thinker he ought to admit that as yet there are no criteria for
judging metaphysics. He ought to declare himself ready, in principle, to be conciliatory in his judgment, because the discovery
of such criteria is "a common cause" (31: IV, 378). But this would
force him to confess that *he* does not yet have a metaphysics
either, and this confession he wants to avoid by deceiving himself
and others. "This man . . . I can guess by his manner."[132] He
must have feared "that such novelties might cost him some of
his own pretensions,"[133] namely, his so-called metaphysics. He
does not want to see, and this is why, "visibly wroth, he tramples
everything to the ground."[134] Against Kant, too, he employs an
"author's stratagem"[135] available to him in his role as contributor
to a learned journal: in the short time when Kant's reputation is
in his hands, he does his best to destroy Kant, in order to cover
his own failings. The only purpose left to him is to do harm. His
final motive is ill will, a desire not to know but to destroy, to
preserve the lie. In the name of science, Feder deals in vanity.

More cautiously phrased but just as radical in substance are
the judgments reached in analyzing the polemics of Schlosser,
Nicolai, Schlettwein, and Fichte.

While the distinction between the spirit and the letter is true
as such—Kant, after all, certainly legitimized it in his famous line
that one must understand an author better than he understands
himself—Fichte's use of it is illegitimate. What he puts into the
letter and presents as Kantian is a spirit that is no longer Kant's
spirit. The claim to be more Kantian than Kant (which causes
Fichte to call himself a transcendental idealist "more rigorous
than Kant was,"[136] and causes Kant to smile at Fichte as "a hyper-
critical friend"[137]) conceals a desire to use Kant for the propaga-
tion of one's own philosophy, to subordinate Kant's philosophy

to one's own, to make a means of it, and to annul its essence. Kant has seen through it all. He spoke of the spirit and the letter once before, in the reply to Schlettwein; it should have cautioned Fichte that once you start citing the spirit, you can put "whatever you please" into the words (70: XII, 368). He is alluding to that line now, two years later, in the statement against Fichte: "So I hereby declare *again* that the *Critique* should indeed be understood according to the letter" (70: XII, 371). The duplicity of Fichte's external relation to Kant merely reflects this double-tongued interpretation, this way of destroying the essence and acting as if one did not mean to destroy.

Schlettwein impressed Kant as lying in a different fashion. His letters, Kant says, are "plainly designed for publicity" (70: XII, 367), in other words, for a use that would be in keeping with the search for truth. Yet the eccentric character of those letters makes one feel that Schlettwein may be seeking another kind of publicity—the sensational and lucrative kind. The eccentricity is a sign of his intention. "For I have reason to suspect that Schlettwein wants only to make money by writing."[138] The point of the debate, to him, is to profit in the sphere of existence. To turn a profit, he turns two-faced even in his objections, charging a lack of integrity and yet proclaiming that the man he calls dishonest is dear to him: "But that one accuses another of lack of integrity and yet, in the same breath, addresses him as 'My Dear'—this is a bittersweet (dulcamara, a poisonous herb) that evokes suspicions of a murderous intent" (70: XII, 369 note).

Nicolai's practices struck Kant as not altogether dissimilar. As the "director of a factory" (64: VIII, 436)—his publishing house— Nicolai was quite simply pursuing his own interests. No man would blame him: "Self-interest is not a crime" (64: VIII, 437). And if he pursued his interests by "scurrility of wit," to give the public "something to ogle and laugh at" (64: VII, 436), that also was his business. But when this "publisher's acumen" was disguised as a fight for truth, when an ignoramus used contemptuous "distortions" (64: VIII, 437) to pose as an arbiter, when he twisted things for clownery's sake and clowned for his business's sake— in such a case one had to infer ill will. "But none are so blind as those who will not see; and here there is an interest behind the refusal: namely, by the oddity of the spectacle, of things being moved out of their natural position and stood upon their heads, to attract many curious, so that (for a short time, at least) a multitude of spectators will enliven the market and keep the literary business from falling asleep" (64: VIII, 438). If the clowning had any use, it was to make you turn away, sickened, and get to work. Judging as an ignoramus, and as a profitmaker advocating the truth one has twisted before, as a clown—this, to Kant's mind, was the sum of Nicolai's endeavors in behalf of critical philosophy.

The premise of Schlosser's practices—designed not for a school, but for a genius—was the citing of authorities that cannot be authorities for a philosopher: of feelings, premonitions, intuitions, and inspirations. "Of all principles, that of wanting to philosophize under the influence of higher feelings is most suitable for gentility of tone; for who would dispute my feelings?" (60: VIII, 395). The man who philosophizes in feelings is philosophizing without knowledge, but Schlosser acts as if he knew that this is how one should philosophize. "Acting as if" is the characteristic feature of his thinking. He likes to speak of practical philosophy as if he had studied its fundament, speculative philosophy; he talks as if a higher font of truth were open to him; he passes judgment on things—on the categorical imperative, for instance—as if he had seen through them. In the final analysis, all these practices of the gentlemanly "as if" are pretenses of searching for truth. Eventually Schlosser plays the game even with his beautiful reason: a beautiful game of acting as if it could really be reason. Unelucidated fictions have taken over, taken the place of the reality they would hold on to. But Criticism provides an insight into the character of fictions, compelling Schlosser to fight it. Kant plainly states Schlosser's intention: "All that matters to him is to get the *Critique of Pure Reason* out of the way, if possible" (62: VIII, 420). The way this is done—by sheer unacquaintance, by chicanery, by acting as if—permits us to infer, not just an evil bent, but philosophy's mortal enemy, the lie.

It is in answering Eberhard's attacks that Kant turns wholly relentless. What made him respond at all, he says, was not some particular cause: "This time, the only motive was to point out a certain behavior that has a characteristic side and seems to be peculiar to Herr Eberhard and to merit attention" (54: VIII, 246). To expose that behavior, to show it as a necessary consequence of the wrong attachment to the wrong cause, and thus to bare the thought structure of a dogmatism maliciously obdurate about its ends, but dangerously supple in its means—this is a major purpose of this polemic. It largely demonstrates the anatomy of a manner which stands for the unworthiness of its matter.

The ingenious disorder reigning in *Das Philosophische Magazin* was the first thing to make Kant suspicious. He regarded it as an insidious order, an artificial ὕστερον πρότερον (54: VIII, 188) designed to relegate the main task, the exploration of reason by reason, to the background. Cunning rather than insight had established this order, along with all the other practices. Eberhard used "a certain structural pomp" (54: VIII, 195) to keep his readers in suspenseful expectation; to outwit their judgment, he spun a web of references, citations, and hairsplittings—a web which he called "scientific" and Kant disdainfully called "chattering back and forth" (54: VIII, 189). These scientific trappings were then committed to battle against science. Eberhard would juggle, misquote, twist, insert ambiguities so as to get himself out of trouble in any event, "by a mere play on words" (54: VIII, 204); he would philosophize with "deliberate mirages."[139] Behind all this Kant meant to see an intent which Eberhard would rather have concealed from readers: "to destroy the *Critique* by a stroke of the pen, but at the same time to make room for a boundless dogmatism of pure reason" (54: VIII, 188). It was the effort of a man who can understand, but will not. The real evil, with which Kant would settle yet, was not the mistaken cause, but the ill will to mistake the cause.

Thus, to Kant, the tone and practices of all these opponents manifest the motivations and intentions behind their attacks. The ultimate motive is not love of truth, not serving science, not the endeavor to elucidate reason; the motive is ill will, the desire to have a subjective principle dominate in isolation. The opponents' intention is to preserve and expand their own philosophy, and—since that philosophy cannot stand beside the *Critique*—to destroy the *Critique*. In each instance, an analysis of the respective exclusiveness shows its foundation to be reprehensible from the viewpoint of practical reason, and untenable from that of speculative reason. Hence the response to the claim will attack both the person and the cause. Having to reckon with the oppo-

nent's destructive malevolence, the respondent may have to destroy on his part. Kant does it consistently and ruthlessly,
employing typical, ever-recurring methods, which we can analyze.

Methods of reply. The exposure of the tone, of the practices,
of the secret intentions and impulses of his opponents helps Kant
to force them to use methods that can stand up before the forum
of public reason. At the same time, he creates the conditions for
a fight *inter pares,* a struggle in which there is no incognito, no
guarantee by great names, and no security in "political" alliances.
Man to man, each personally responsible for the cause he is defending, each ready to acknowledge no arbitrament other than
that of reason—these are the combat terms. To assure them as far
as possible, Kant makes the struggle public.

He calls upon the first, anonymous reviewer "to step out of
his incognito" (31: IV, 379), so as "to end this onerous inequality
between an invisible assailant and one who defends himself exposed to the whole world."[140]

Eberhard's statements, even the ones citing Leibniz, are consistently taken for "his own statements" (54: VIII, 187), dragging
him out from under cover.

Schlettwein's letters, addressed to Kant privately, are made
public.

Schlosser is shown up as a "mystagogue" and "clubbist" (60:
VIII, 398) who philosophizes on principles that cannot claim universality and therefore cannot stand publicity either.

Nicolai, the anonymous author of *Gundibert,* is attacked personally and by name.

In a certain sense even the stress on "the letter" in the statement
against Fichte is a declaration in favor of publicity. The letter is
public; the spirit is hidden. One cannot refer to what is hidden by
evading what is public. Besides, the very publicity of Kant's
statement will oblige Fichte to clarify his two-faced relation to
Kant. His claims are no longer shielded by Kant's silence.

Corresponding to this will to fight in public is the way Kant,
in his replies, publicly follows up on the analysis of exclusiveness:
his mocking of the false claims, his indictment of the other's
person, and his demolition of the other's cause.

Kant fights the claims of his exclusionary opponents by making
them relative. The means employed is irony, in whose dosage he

is a master. Beyond the claim, his irony hits a cause and at the same time the man behind the cause, and it delivers all three to the smiles of their contemporaries.

Sometimes this irony flashes in the very titles of the replies, as in the ones to Schlosser and Feder and, above all, in the tract against Eberhard: *On a Discovery That Would Have All New Critique of Pure Reason Rendered Dispensable by an Older One.* There is irony in the word "discovery," skepticism in the phrase "would have . . . rendered," which suggests already that there is nothing to the new discovery, and finally a touch of mockery in the length of the title. It ridicules a story-telling mannerism of precritical philosophy, while at the same time precisely stating Eberhard's intention. Herr Eberhard, Kant goes on, made the discovery that a critique of reason—only a better one—was already contained in the philosophy of Leibniz. The claim is instantly stripped of the new and particular character of every true discovery; what happened to Eberhard is what usually happens: once something new is clearly visible, it can be seen in the old in which it was not seen before. What Eberhard views as his personal achievement is simply the consequence of a new, Kant-given possibility to see. The fighting author takes the credit for a deed, without knowing that he owes the means to his opponent. A "failure of the claim of novelty" (54: VIII, 187) is thus established; and Eberhard has no more luck with his material claim, for as far as results are concerned, the preexisting critique of reason is in all points "the exact opposite of the new one" (54: VIII, 187). Something new has been added indeed—not by Eberhard, but by *Critique of Pure Reason.*

No less sarcastically countered is Feder's tacit claim to be already in possession of a well-founded metaphysics: "It is very wrong of him, though, to withhold his discoveries from the world" (31: IV, 376). But then, presumably, he does so only because "a need of science may never have occurred to him" (31: IV, 376), in which case his malice would be somewhat extenuated by a blithely confident ignorance.

Schlettwein's efforts are commented on in the same tone. He wishes to overturn Kant's philosophy and found a new one—"an attempt every friend of philosophy will be happy and pleased to see made" (70: XII, 367).

Drenched with irony are the writings against Schlosser. He

is one of those philosophers "who have it *in* themselves, but can unfortunately not express and generally convey it in language" (60: VIII, 389). But this does not matter, for Herr Schlosser has found a philosophy "in which one does not need to work, only to hear and to enjoy the inner oracle" (60: VIII, 390), to be at one stroke in full possession of wisdom. "Long live philosophy by feelings, which leads us straight to the thing itself!" (60: VIII, 395).

Especially malicious is the irony in the statement against Fichte. Kant says he had advised Fichte in a letter to quit his "fruitless hairsplitting" and instead to "cultivate his gift for presentation . . . as it can profitably be applied to the *Critique of Pure Reason*" (70: XII, 370). In other words, the best thing Fichte could do would be to become a truthful interpreter of Kant's philosophy.

Enhancing the effect of Kantian irony is that at any moment it may turn into a seriousness none would dare doubt. It is never a matter of entertainment, always a road to judgment. And the judgment, on the person and the cause, may strike at any time.

In principle, an author has the right to be left alone as a person as long as he himself is committed to remain purely impersonal. Whether in philosophy such a commitment is at all possible is beside the point; Kant's view, at any rate, was that it was. But if a man's philosophizing is partly determined by some private will of his, by subjective principles and personal impulses, he cannot cite pure impersonality. He becomes answerable as a factual human being and, above all, as a moral person.

Kant does not relieve his opponents of this liability. He weighs them in the scales of their existential performance:

Nicolai may be astute as a businessman, but as an author he is "a fool" (64: VII, 437) and nauseating in the long run.

Schlosser, as a citizen, may be a gentleman; as a "philosopher" he is a mere *philosophus per inspirationem* (60: VIII, 398) whose "exaltation" (60: VIII, 398) is spurred to the attack by mendacity along with ignorance (cf. 62: VII, 421–22). Kant makes this charge into thin air, so to speak, as though to leave its understanding up to Schlosser. There can be no doubt that Schlosser understood.

Equally aimed at the void is the rebuke to Fichte. At times there are "fraudulent, deceitful so-called friends who aim to ruin us and yet speak a well-meaning language (*aliud lingua promp-*

tum, aliud pectore inclusum gerere). Of those, and of their carefully laid traps, one cannot be wary enough" (70: XII, 371).

The charge of moral failure against Schlettwein is not levied
in plain language either.

With Feder, Kant is more outspoken. Malevolent and simultaneously obtuse, Feder is the dazzler who will betray science for
his vanity's sake. Yet even here Kant holds back the most savage
words; he analyzes, rather, the activity, corresponding to the
words, as if to preserve the chance of resuming friendly relations.

Only in fighting Eberhard does he drop all reserve. Eberhard
is called "an artificial man" (54: VIII, 207), "a real falsarius,"[141]
a "metaphysical sleight-of-hand artist"[142] trained "by nature and
long habit"[143] in all sorts of tricks, a deceitful man "without a
bit of sincerity."[144] He is "made up of falsity,"[145] "attuned to
nothing but intrigue,"[146] and filled with invidious malice.[147] Here
the polemic is intended to destroy a person, not just a claim and
a cause. And, indeed, Kant's advice to his assistant Reinhold
was not to overdo "the delicacy"[148]—which he himself in this
case certainly did not.

Once the opposing combatant has been deprived of secret
weapons, stripped of respect as an authority, and ironically relativized regarding his claim, what remains to be done is the really
material work. It mostly ends with the opponent's cause left
undoubted, but with his claim either shattered or taken over by
Kant himself.

In Schlettwein's case Kant simply refuses to go into the matter,
namely, the challenge to a polemical discussion of critical philosophy. He tersely replies, "Nothing doing" (70: XII, 367). He
refuses battle, but appoints a substitute in Schultz, the mathematician, although promptly advising Schultz to "beware of any
obligation to correspond with him."[149]

Nicolai's claim to speak up in matters of philosophy is rejected
wholesale, as raised by an "uncritical ignoramus" (37: VI, 208)
and produced by total "ignorance and incompetence" (64: VIII,
437).

The result of Feder's material work gets about the same treatment. Only two points are taken up in Kant's reply. The reviewer,
he writes, was referring to a "higher" idealism—but "my place
is the fertile bathos of experience" (31: IV, 373 note). It used
to be the central thesis of idealism that cognition by sense ex-

perience is nothing but semblance, that the intellect and reason alone can assure truth. Now it is the other way round: the intellect and reason alone produce mere semblance; truth lies in experience only. It was therefore pointless to speak of idealism if one did not see at the same time that it was "a quite peculiar one," namely, a critical idealism which completely "overturns" (31: IV, 375) the past one and gives the first adequate guarantee for the reality of experience. But as for Feder's judgment on the categories and their deduction—that they are no more than the known principles of logic and ontology with an idealistic limitation—all that needs saying about this is "that no more miserable and even historically incorrect judgment could possibly be arrived at" (31: IV, 376 note). Materially the whole review is useless: it does not inform the reader and does not provide the author with an occasion to clarify things, or the reviewer with a way to understand them. It is an intrinsically senseless product of inferiority, employing prejudices to give itself an air of superiority.

Schlosser's attempt to ease the barbaric rigor of philosophizing by a philosophy of feelings and forebodings is dismissed with the remark that Schlosser accomplishes the very thing he would like to avoid. The "belletristic expression" of this "anticritical philosopher" (62: VIII, 420) brings barbarism into philosophy. It is the very disease he wants to cure. Critique alone can provide human reason with clarity about itself, and this clarity is the sole remedy for philosophy's barbaric side. Here, Kant is not merely refuting the charge but using it as a weapon to be turned against the enemy.

The procedure is similar in the polemic against Fichte. In his *Theory of Science* Fichte claimed to be establishing a total system of transcendental philosophy for the first time; Kant rebuffs the claim with the blunt statement "that I regard Fichte's theory of science as a wholly untenable system" (70: XII, 370). In fact, that theory is not a system of metaphysics at all; it is "neither more nor less than pure logic,"[150] which can never reach the point of material cognition. Fichte's assertion that Kant's philosophy is not the transcendental one as yet—that, at best, it is a propaedeutic containing the germ of the system—is turned around: Fichte's philosophy is propaedeutic. How his, Kant's, own system might be reduced to a propaedeutic is "incomprehensible to me" (70: XII, 371). "Regardless of that, however, critical philosophy's irresistible tendency to satisfy both theoretical and morally practical reason must convince us that no changes of view, no emendations or reshaped doctrinal structures await it; but that the system of the *Critique* is based upon a totally assured foundation, forever confirmed, and indispensable to mankind's highest ends for all times to come" (70: XII, 371). Kant rejects the charges radically, advances the opponent's claim on his own part, and tries to show that now it is legitimate.

This means of "retortion" (30: A 742/B 770) had helped him succeed once before, in the Eberhard battle. There he attacked Eberhard's crucial material points: his attempt to extend the causal category to everything conceivable, by deducing the theorem of cause from the theorem of contradiction; the effort to twist a final unity into objective reality in the objects; the tactic of rising from the sensory to the nonsensory at the cost of viewing the concept of sensoriness as just a vague way of conception; finally, Eberhard's statement—based on a misconception of the difference between analytical and synthetic judgments—that classic dogmatism had already solved the "principal task" (54: VIII, 228) of metaphysics. What appears from all these denouements and rebuttals is this: even had there been a pre-Kantian critique of reason, Eberhard was not given to see it, let alone to understand it. Next, Kant appropriates Eberhard's claim to speak for Leibniz. His own metaphysics, rather than a necrologue on Leibniz's, should be its true apology. For, in a sense, Leibniz can be understood only in retrospect, from the viewpoint of *Critique of Pure Reason,* which for the first time enables us to say clearly, in line with a guiding idea, what the old metaphysics implied but left unsaid. Thanks to that critique, the cornerstones of the old metaphysics—the theorem of sufficient reason, the doctrine of monads, and the preestablished harmony—prove to be pillars of a new edifice also.[151]

"Thus the *Critique of Pure Reason* may well be Leibniz's real apology even against his adherents, who exalt him with a praise that fails to honor" (54: VIII, 250)—just as it is the apology of great philosophers in general, though not the kind to get lost "in exploring words" (54: VIII, 251). It is an apology in which "all interpretations of what pure reason has produced from mere concepts" (54: VIII, 251) serve as the key to unlock the secret intentions that guided the great thinkers of all ages in elucidating

reason. To academic interpretation, Kant opposes the really liberating and productive exegesis that will risk understanding an
author better than he understood himself, and better than his
disciples want us to understand him.

Time and again, in similar fashion, Kant casts doubt on his
opponent's case. He denies the other's authority by exposing his
moral inferiority and material ignorance, and by an ironic relativization of his claims. Where there is no rejecting a claim as
such, however, Kant appropriates it and shows that he alone
satisfies it, and that his opponent wrongly makes the claim.

Kant does not use these elements of response in a fixed sequence. They are newly combined each time. Outwardly, the
effect of his polemics is due to their more or less skillful coordination. To illustrate his blending of the elements, we take up the
preface to the tract against Eberhard.

That foreword to *On a Discovery* . . . contains five paragraphs,
which altogether take two pages and a half.

In the first paragraph Kant tells the reader about Eberhard's
new discovery. His is no matter-of-fact account, however; it is
ironical already, from the outset relegating Eberhard's performance to the realm of things that happen every day. The opponent's
lack of authority is already intimated, the sense of personal and
factual superiority already visible; the reader's interest in a thesis
that might, after all, be unexpected is killed. All this takes two
sentences.

In the second paragraph, Eberhard is disarmed. No longer
will he be able to cite Leibniz. The disarming occurs in the
name of chivalry, of a battle that will be fought man to man,
on equal terms. Still, it cannot have escaped Kant that with this
blow he was decisively weakening his opponent, challenging
Eberhard to a fight in which he, Kant, knew he was the stronger.
The disarming is not carried out in an impersonal atmosphere:
Eberhard's references to Leibniz are already diagnosed as shrewd,
his arguments characterized as inadequate, his procedures
branded tricky and false. It is the disarming of a ridiculed,
factually and morally enfeebled foe.

After this "regulation" of the weapons, Kant devotes the third
paragraph to glancing, as he puts it, at the contest's formal side.
In fact, the whole paragraph serves a single purpose: now, after

the author and his cause have had the treatment, to make their organ, *Das Philosophische Magazin,* as consistently ridiculous. Kant draws on Eberhard's own characterization of the careless order reigning in the *Magazin,* and on that basis he plays with the ambiguity of the word "magazine," using it in the sense of a "storeroom" in which all possible things are deposited next to each other, or even in the sense of a "junk closet" where everything lies "upside down" (54: VIII, 188). This expression he promptly takes back, however—not to show any respect to Eberhard or the *Magazin,* but to unmask both of them systematically in the paragraphs that follow.

For the purposes of this unmasking, a formal analysis gets under way in the fourth paragraph. Cleverly hidden behind the liberal, seemingly artltess facade of the *Magazin* is a material perversion. By the suggestive methods of concealed propaganda, untested statements are raised to the rank of principles which will serve all subsequent thoughts as a canon. Things which at the close of a transcendental inquiry would still require a deduction to prove their claim are here posited dogmatically, "in good manner" (54: VIII, 188). "The last shall be first" is the principle of this procedure, and its consequences are the enthronement of dogmatism and the annihilation of critique. To this perversion Kant opposes the true order. It is the order of his *Critique.* It enables him eventually to nail down Eberhard's procedure, a procedure legitimized solely by justifying what has previously been posited illegitimately and dogmatically.

Kant is not content with the grasp he has on this perversion. In the last paragraph, its demonstration is directly followed by a reckoning—first with Eberhard's performance, then with his way of scientific philosophizing, finally with his moral personality. The account with the cause is settled indirectly, by a particular choice of words. Eberhard's "action" is said to be one "in two acts" and thus not only banished from the realm of philosophical thought to that of literary speech, but characterized as theater, as a farce. The theatrical performance calls for theatrical accoutrements, the so-called science—for references, citations, hairsplittings, all the pseudo-scientific patches and swatches whose ultimate ground is mendacity. Now Kant settles with the author: "It is bad enough to have to do with an author who does not know about order; but it is worse to have to do with one who creates disorder artificially, so that his shallow or false lines will pass unnoticed" (54: VIII, 189).

This ends the preface; the analyses of the subject matter can begin.

It is difficult to avoid the impression that this seemingly artless preface was itself "most planfully designed." The irony heaped on the opponent's cause, the disarming of the author, and the sneers at his journal are followed by a total, abrupt change of mood, with the cause analyzed as a deliberate perversion so that the perversion, its manner, and its protagonist can be damned—and all before the start of the real, factual analyses. The strength of this procedure is not, as in the case of Lessing's polemics, due to the lucidity of intelligence and style; it is due to the relentless consistency that seems propelled, so to speak, by the very architecture of reason, and to a denuding eye that permits no manner of untruthfulness to pass.

If a man combines factual response with an existential reckoning, as Kant does, if indeed he really condemns a cause because he recognizes the existential nonentity of its exponent, he must allow himself to be questioned about the legitimacy of his procedure—in other words, about his own absolute truthfulness in polemicizing. And on this point Kant's own contemporaries already raised some embarrassing questions. We make ourselves their advocate for a while, combining the questionable points so as to incriminate Kant, before we reverse our field, abandon this advocacy, and try to interpret the facts in the best possible light.

Dubiosities in Kant's Exclusionary Polemics

As dubious points in Kant's exclusionary polemics we regard, first, some which we neutrally call obscure; then the whole series of actions against *Das Philosophische Magazin,* and in that series, above all, the way Kant curried favor with the mathematicians; and finally his sometimes extraordinary ruthlessness, which his contemporaries (and not just the ones directly affected) were already deploring.

Obscurities. In volume 1 of the *Magazin,* while investigating transcendental aesthetics, Eberhard expressed the view that space and time must have "not only subjective but objective grounds" which are "not phenomena, but true, knowable things."[152]

"Their ultimate grounds are things in themselves."[153] Space and time—to Kant, mere forms of visualization—were thus to be understood as real things again. Kant took up these statements and added, in a subsidiary clause, this incomprehensible remark: ". . . all of which is literally and repeatedly asserted in *Critique* also" (54: VIII, 207). Eberhard did not allow this opportunity to pass: "If that is really asserted in *Crit. of Pure Reason,* literally and repeatedly, all differences between Leibniz's and Kant's critique of reason have come to an end, and complete peace reigns between them."[154] Kant made no further reply. His admission in this central question must have been either an error or a confusion. He never confessed to either one, not even after his opponents in this case had really taught him to know better.

The Leibniz interpretations mobilized against Eberhard also have a dubious touch. They would not be objectionable if Kant had used them as examples of an interpretive mode justified from the viewpoints of philosophy and of the history of reason, if not from a philological one. Two points make us skeptical, however,

1. The liberty which Kant took here as an interpreter is one he always denied to his apologists in practice, even if he granted it to them in theory. He did it to Beck, to Reinhold, and to Fichte. Fichte interpreted Kant the way Kant, in *On a Discovery,* had interpreted Leibniz; but after Kant had deemed himself entitled to ignore the literal text at times—because, "if taken in accordance with the letter" (54: VIII, 249), a system can become self-contradictory—he reminded Fichte of the letter. This twofold practice is dubious.

2. In *On a Discovery,* Kant seeks to justify his Leibniz interpretation not just by the history of reason but by Leibniz's will. He himself cannot have thought much of this justification, for at the beginning of 1793, drafting his entry in a contest which the Berlin Academy had first announced in 1788 and then, after several postponements, definitively included in the program for 1795 ("Quels sont les progrès réels de la Métaphysique en Allemagne depuis le temps de Leibnitz et de Wolf?"), he undertook another reinterpretation of the pillars of Leibniz's metaphysics: of the theorem of cause, of monadology, and of the preestablished harmony. Originally, this paper—which must be approached with some reserve, like all Kantian writings published by Rink—was presumably to be Kant's last word in the argument with Eberhard

and with academic philosophy at large, and here he is no longer taking Leibniz's crucial philosophemes for secret steps in the direction of *Critique of Pure Reason*. He calls them "instances of straying" (88: XX, 282) on the part of reason;[155] beyond doubt, he insists, they have neither advanced metaphysics nor initiated any such advance. Since both interpretations refer to Leibniz's will (and the first one certainly does so against Leibniz's intention), they seem to serve the ends of the particular polemic rather than those of an impersonal analysis. Eberhard had no trouble reducing these exegeses to absurdity[156] and telling Kant off, in a retortion of his own: "God save us from such apologists! Against our enemies we are well able to defend ourselves."[157]

Probably the ugliest quarrel raged between Eberhard, Reinhold, and Kant over a single word.

In *Critique of Pure Reason* Kant had created a new concept of sensibility. As defined there, sensibility is no longer a type of cognition as it had been to Leibniz, Wolff, and Baumgarten, but a root of cognition. It is as indispensable a part of cognition as the intellect, and it differs from the intellect not in degree but in essence. Sensibility is not a *cognitio obscura*. Baumgarten's line *"Cognitio clara major est quam obscura. Hinc obscuritas minor, claritas major cognitionis gradus est"*[158] has been invalidated insofar as it was supposed to say something about sensibility, the supposed *facultas cognoscitiva inferior*. To Kant the final consequence of that line would be that phenomena are obscure things in themselves, while things in themselves are intellectuated phenomena. In *Critique*, Kant frequently attacks this purely logical rather than transcendental distinction of sensibility and the intellect. On A 43 he sharply calls the distinction a "falsification" of the concept of sensibility—an unfortunately chosen word, since it seems to suggest malice.

Eberhard pounced on it. Having correctly defined the issue,[159] he tried to show that Leibniz had already known about a transcendental difference between sensibility and intellect—and yet, he wrote, on A 44 Kant was accusing Leibniz of a falsification of sensibility. "If one says this, considering the plain evidence to the contrary, can he be assumed to have closely and profoundly studied and maturely weighed the case? And if he then reaches so decisive and confident a verdict: 'Falsification!'—But let us stay within the bounds prescribed by our purpose."[160]

Eberhard had made a mistake about the page number. What Kant had said on A 44 was that the philosophy of Leibniz and Wolff had "assigned to all inquiries into the nature and source of our cognitions an entirely wrong point of view, regarding the difference between sensibility and the intellectual realm as merely logical, whereas it is manifestly transcendental." It was on the preceding page that he had called this a "falsification" and held Leibniz responsible for it, though not by name.[161]

Kant—who probably looked up only the passage on A 44 and did not find the disputed word there—got angry. A letter to Reinhold, containing material and directives for a review of the *Magazin* article, says that Eberhard's "forte is misquoting" and that in two places he had surpassed himself, "for there he turns into a real falsarius," completely misquoting A 44 and at the same time wrongly imputing an expression to Kant. "And then, as will happen to certain people who finally come to believe in their own oft-repeated lies, he gradually gets so excited about the immodest word alleged to have been used against Leibniz that this 'falsified' which exists merely in his own mind is charged to the author of *Critique* three times on one page (298)—What do you call a man who purposely falsifies a document in litigation?"[162]

Reinhold took up Eberhard's mistake in his review of the third issue of the *Magazin*. The chances are that he was aware of Kant's error; in any case he did tone down Kant's language, speaking neither of lies nor of falsifications, only of a "far from trivial writing and memory lapse"[163] that could not leave Kant indifferent. And then, cautiously: on Kant's page A 44, the word "falsified" could not be found, only the phrase "assigned an entirely wrong point of view." A reprimand for misquoting followed.

Eberhard quickly came back with a statement in the *Intelligenzblatt* of *Allgemeine Literatur-Zeitung*,[164] pointing out the disputed word on page A 43. Reinhold countered sophistically: the fact, he wrote, was that the word occurred on A 43, and on that page there was no mention yet of the philosophy of Leibniz. Eberhard could show easily that there was indeed such a mention on A 43, and he broadly described the whole argument several times in the *Magazin*.[165]

And Kant? He knew of the reverse his anonymous apologist had suffered. Still, having made his charge, he never dropped it.

In the very preface to his anti-Eberhard tract he accused the other of "twisting words" (54: VIII, 187), with special reference to the disputed passage. He came back to it later on, complained of having a "wrong expression" attributed to him, and mocked the "amusing manner" in which Eberhard would inveigh against his, Kant's, "temerity" (54: VIII, 218 note).

Eberhard promptly challenged him to specify the "wrong expression."[166] Kant kept silent. That he had read parts of volume 2 of the *Magazin* before the tract against Eberhard went to the printer is evident from letters he exchanged with his publisher, de la Garde.[167] The second printing of *On a Discovery* appeared in 1791; then, at the latest, Kant should have changed the accusing passages so as to conform with the facts as he knew them. He did not. The failure seems not so much to show mere obstinacy in the face of facts as to suggest approval and support of Reinhold's sophistical arguments.

The impression of duplicity in these three cases is not due to Kant's making an error—which is always possible—but to the fact that he left things obscure, publicly and, as it seems, intentionally. He who so often overturned his own nascent system, according to his own testimony; he who clarified so many other people's mistakes in the polemics about critical philosophy (and not in the exclusionary ones alone)—he never admitted a mistake of his own. We can scarcely assume that he did not see them. At times, perhaps, even Kant's will to clarity was limited by a certain weakness.[168]

The campaign against Das Philosophische Magazin, *and the wooing of the mathematicians.* The critical philosophers' entire struggle against Eberhard's journals can be divided into five phases. The first, in 1788, is marked by Rehberg's reviews of the first and second issue of the *Magazin*. Kant did not take a hand in this phase, but it must be regarded as a prelude to his actions. In the second phase it was Reinhold who fought in the front line, with anonymous reviews of the *Magazin*'s third and fourth issue; he received his ammunition from Kant, who remained the *spiritus rector* behind the scenes. In the third phase Kant himself appeared on stage with the anti-Eberhard tract. In the fourth, returning to the background, he courted the mathematicians' favor and sent his mathematician friend from Königsberg,

Schultz, into battle. There, too, he supplied the material, this time in a form almost ready for the printer. In the fifth phase, occasioned by the Berlin Academy contest mentioned before, he tried to settle accounts once for all, not merely with Eberhard and his journals but with academic philosophy at large. This paper remained a fragment and was not made public until 1804; it may be regarded as an epilogue to the fight against Eberhard.

The five phases cannot be neatly separated in time; the various writings often led to a long back-and-forth of replies extending far into the subsequent phases. They are definable, each time, by the combatants on the side of critical philosophy (Rehberg, Reinhold, Kant, Schultz, Kant) and by the roles played by Kant (none, *spiritus rector,* combatant, *spiritus rector,* would-be combatant). What matters to us is Kant's participation and conduct.

When the first two issues of *Das Philosophische Magazin* came out in 1788, Kant initially paid no attention. Rehberg reviewed them, but apparently not too convincingly; in any event, Jakob wrote not much later that most of the theses advanced in the third issue were "true and justifiable."[169] In April 1789, then, Kant received the letter from Reinhold[170] asking him to make a public statement against Eberhard. This was the cry of alarm which immediately set off the second phase.

Kant answered with two lengthy analyses of the *Magazin,* full of violent personal indictments designed "to make the man knowable in his entirety, both as to his insight and as to his character."[171] He wrote that he himself, especially at his age, had to devote himself to the completion of his work and to leave such quarrels to his friends—a hint for Reinhold, of course, which Kant proceeded to make unmistakably plain: "I would wish that you might help yourself to all of the above remarks as if they were your own property."[172] And if Reinhold did make use of them, it should be "in an emphatic way, if possible."[173] Besides, Kant gave him full freedom "to add my name as well, when and where it may please you."[174]

Reinhold now had a wealth of material, was authorized to act as Kant's interpreter, and had the right to refer to Kant himself. Small wonder that he took the hint and decided to use "the good sword you have so kindly lent me."[175] For his target he chose Eberhard's essay "On the Distinction of Judgments into Analytical and Synthetic Ones,"[176] which Kant in his first letter had

pointed out to him as particularly perfidious; the rest of the
material was held back "as a corps de reserve, in order, upon
the inevitable anticritique of Herr E., to move it forward and
thus to give his *Magazin* the coup de grace."[177] In the review,
which appeared in the *Allgemeine Literatur-Zeitung*,[178] Reinhold
cleverly inserted Kant's personal accusations and concluded by
citing Kant's judgment that Eberhard had "completely misunderstood" him.[179]

But Eberhard was too adroit an opponent. He took instant aim
at the error that was plain to see in the review—the confusion
of pages—and so, when Reinhold put himself further in the
wrong by a sophistical reply, he could conveniently be dispatched
by means of a detail. In any case, Reinhold's vaunted exposure
of Eberhard's knowledge and character could be summarily
turned back upon Reinhold himself, casting doubt upon both
his own knowledge and his own character. This lapse into sophistry weighs on the whole second phase and burdens even the
third. Reinhold was not the man to go on fighting. So, contrary
to his initial intention, Kant himself intervened—with arguments,
but principally with the weight of his moral personality.

Kant's treatise against Eberhard marks the third phase. We
have already described his mode of proceeding. The tract, like
everything Kant wrote, was widely noticed; a second edition appeared in 1791, a third in 1796. By this success it did great harm
to Eberhard, but its real purpose was not accomplished: the
Magazin was not destroyed, nor was Eberhard forced to give up
his comparisons. On the contrary, he received reinforcements.
Among his new contributors were the foremost mathematicians
of the time, Klügel and Kästner, later joined by Bendavid. Kant
may have feared that Lichtenberg too might side with them. He
suddenly found himself facing experts of renown, opponents he
really was afraid of. In the fourth phase, with an odd display of
bustle, he courted the mathematicians' favor.

Klügel, in volume 1 of the *Magazin*,[180] had begun a dissertation, "On the Principles of Pure Mechanics," which he concluded
at the beginning of volume 2.[181] It was neither directly pro-Eber-
hard nor directly anti-Kant; but it was based on Wolff and
Leibniz and thus anti-Kantian in effect, especially in Eberhard's
journal. The fourth issue of volume 2 contained three pieces by
Kästner: "The Meaning of 'Possible' in Euclidean Geometry,"[182]

"On the Mathematical Concept of Space,"[183] and "On the Geometrical Axioms."[184] Kästner also took care not to attack Kant openly, but one cannot fail to notice that his reservations in these essays—and in the subsequent fourth one, "On Neologisms, Notably in Mathematics,"[185] against the new "shallow teachers of geometry"[186]—are reservations against Kant as well. Kant too is meant when Kästner polemicizes against the false interpretation of the mathematical concept of infinity;[187] Kant too is censured when Kästner resents "the language mixers of today"[188] who can hardly be read without a "neological dictionary"[189] and whose perusal makes one yearn for Wolff, who was still writing German; Kant too is affected when Kästner simply confesses to "thinking still as Leibniz and Wolff have taught me."[190] At the same time, the beneficiary of all this was Eberhard, Leibniz's seeming defender.

This was clear to Kant also. The mathematicians' assistance worried him: "For I am concerned that Eberh., who has been recruiting mathematicians in order to have other pens lend a measure of credit to his scribbling, might find therein a pretext and occasion to incite them to impugn *Critique* from that side."[191] Even before *On a Discovery* was published, in August 1790, Kant collected objections to volume 2 of the *Magazin,* leaving them to the mathematician Schultz, this time, "to use at will."[192] Schultz's review was first to finish the job of forcing Eberhard, "as speedily as possible, to expose himself in his nakedness."[193] But then, after the Kästner essays had appeared, the review was to serve two more purposes: it was "to deny nutriment to the conceits which Herr Eberhard has developed from this seeming reinforcement of his party," and "to cure Herr Kästner himself of the idea that [Eberhard] said anything in line with his, i.e., the Wolffian, philosophy."[194] To this end Kant also put a cautiously worded reply to the Kästner articles at Schultz's disposal; if possible, this was to be inserted in the review "without abbreviation."[195] It contained the following summary: "In every point, reviewer finds Herr H. R. Kästner fully in accord with *Critique of Pure Reason*" (91: XX, 422).

The plan was clear. It was to isolate Eberhard by convincing Kästner, first, that critical philosophy was not at odds with the Wolffian one, and second, that Eberhard must not be taken for a representative of the latter. On Kästner's part, of course, both efforts presupposed a rather less than thorough knowledge of Wolff's philosophy.

Kant did most of the work required to put the plan into execution. He not only furnished the well-phrased but often insultingly personal material against the "mirage of the 'pictorial aspect' Eb[erhard] keeps prating about"[196] and the delicate, never insulting exceptions to Kästner's essays; he also took advantage of a trip then being taken by Jachmann to send a flattering letter "assuring the Nestor of all German philosophical mathematicians of my unlimited respect" and acquainting him with his concern: "At the same time, may I be permitted to explain that my endeavors, hitherto aimed at critique, are by no means, as it might seem, designed to counteract the Leibniz-Wolffian philosophy (which for some time past I have found to be neglected), but merely to lead by a detour . . . onto the same path of proper academic procedure and . . . to the very same goal."[197]

How are we to understand this? That Kant himself felt not too comfortable about his letter is suggested in a metaphor at the end of it. "In the above disputes" (the letter makes no mention of the disputes, but Kant was evidently thinking of them when he wrote it) he offered to accept Kästner as arbiter "if one might ask the olive tree to leave its fatness and go to be promoted over the trees."[198] Despite its biblical origin (Judges 9, 9), the line sounds stilted and spurious in Kantian prose. That neglect of the Wolffian philosophy never saddened Kant requires no elaboration; that he considered that philosophy passé and obsolete shows in the drafts for the prize treatise; and that he did not think so highly of "the Nestor of all German philosophical mathematicians" is demonstrable from *Opus postumum*. Kästner, we read there, was "a mathematician aged in the Wolffian philosophy, a philosophy voluminously modeled after the mathematical method and without a critique of reason" (94: XXI, 556). He was a man who "will turn poet also, for a change" (94: XXII, 486) and at times will even "play" the philosopher (94: XXI, 556), a man whose "poetic fancies filled with caustic wit" (94: XXI, 556) amuse the world, but who ultimately is "invidious, envious, and hostile" (94: XXII, 545) and therefore "immoral" (94: XXI, 98).

At the same time, Kant wrote a letter to Lichtenberg, presumably similar in content. That letter has been lost, but we know

Lichtenberg's answer, couched—as was Kästner's, by the way—in tones of profound respect. Kant in turn did not reply to either man until the spring of 1793,[199] at which time he is presumed to have been working on the prize treatise.

A few days after writing to Kästner and Lichtenberg, Kant sent Schultz "heartfelt thanks for the fortunate and masterly completion of a most laborious work"—work largely done by Kant himself, after all—and added this hint: ". . . in which it may be a consolation that occasion for a similar one might, if at all, arise only after a year."[200] He certainly had no intention of abandoning the fight against the *Magazin*. Rather, after a year he tried to enlist Beck, one of his most talented followers, who was originally a mathematician. Kant wrote him a letter suggesting that Beck carry out the plan of a publisher, Hartknoch, who wished a digest of the critical writings that would be exact while showing originality at the same time. Kant's idea was that this project would let Beck resolve "the contradictions in terms that I have been accused of," especially in *Das Philosophische Magazin*. To make this part of the job palatable to Beck, Kant added: "I have found the misconceptions in those criticisms so easily demonstrable that I would long have collected and refuted the lot of them if I had not forgotten to note and file each one that came to my attention."[201]

Beck did accept Hartknoch's offer (his digest appeared in three volumes, 1793–96)[202] but did not respond to Kant's hint.

Kästner, in spite of the friendly letter and of having said to Jachmann how much he regretted the quarrel with Eberhard,[203] wrote another article for *Das Philosophische Magazin*, coming out flatly for Leibniz. Besides, Bendavid, though not an opponent of Kant's, joined Eberhard as a contributor.

From Halle, where Klügel was teaching, Jakob sent word that the mathematicians were "the most inclined to misconceive the ideas of *Critique*, or even to regard them as dispensable."[204]

In fact, Kant lost the struggle for the mathematicians' favor. The *Magazin* did cease publication in 1792, but Eberhard promptly launched a new *Philosophisches Archiv* that kept up the fight until 1795. Kant too kept fighting. In a final phase he tried to prevail not only over his personal opponent but over academic philosophy.

This last phase is the "Prize Treatise on the Progress Made in

Metaphysics." There, Kant tried to do the impossible—to write a history of reason "mathematically," as it were (89: XX, 342), furnishing cogent, indisputable proof that in metaphysics Wolff and Leibniz were only two of "the numerous supposed conquerors" (88: XX, 318) while the crucial advance, the reestablishment of all philosophizing on a new foundation, had entered the world with *Critique of Pure Reason*. In all likelihood, the work was thus doomed to failure by its very goal.

One of the three prize winners, Schwab—the others were Reinhold and Abicht—was a close collaborator of Eberhard's. He judged the new period of metaphysics as follows: "In this new period we have not advanced in metaphysics, although we do have another famous metaphysicist."[205] To Kant, the last phase brought no cogent triumph over academic metaphysics either.

Looking over this whole campaign[206] against Eberhard, it is amazing to see how stubbornly and with how much political acumen Kant was fighting. As long as it seemed that the opponent, a good writer with bad arguments, might be handled by a good writer with good arguments, Kant picked Reinhold, the man with the greatest literary skill among his adherents, and supplied him with the argumentation. When Reinhold, in combat, laid himself open to suspicion, the man with the greatest moral weight stepped into the breach: Kant himself. When the mathematicians joined the fray, Kant sent a mathematician into battle against them, again supplying and—since Schultz was no Reinhold—more carefully phrasing the arguments. At the same time he sought to drive a wedge between Eberhard and the most dangerous foe: by turning into a temporary apologist for academic philosophy, he meant to isolate Eberhard and to crush him alone, by the demise of his journals. And when this plan foundered on the stubbornness of the mathematicians, Kant dropped all consideration for others who might be involved and set out to finish off academic philosophy as a whole.

It is not easy at times to rid oneself of the idea that this whole chain of actions was partly motivated by the same almost playful delight in shrewd strategy which caused the old Kant, when Napoleon invaded Africa, to draw up war plans for a secret detour which would lead to the conquest of Portugal and England.[207] But that for all of this playful element the enemy's destruction was not viewed as a mere game, that it was pursued with consistency—this is apparent from the ruthlessness with which Kant struck.

Kant's ruthlessness. Characteristic of this ruthlessness is the way Kant proceeded against Feder and Fichte. The first case indicates what devastating consequences it could have for a scholar to be attacked by Kant; the second, how Kant, in striking, could ignore the circumstances.

Previous to the review of *Critique of Pure Reason,* Feder had given Kant no occasion to suspect him of harboring ill will. Kant had seen examples of Feder's reviewing art as early as 1772, and the opinion he formed of it had not been high even then,[208] but over the years he had presumably been mollified by the general esteem Feder acquired. In 1779, in any case, Kant gave a student a letter of recommendation to Feder. The letter itself has been lost, but we can tell from the reply that it was evidently couched in very polite and even flattering language. Feder took it for a new "demonstration . . . that philosophy unites the hearts of its true devotees. . . . Be assured that I was full of reverence and love for you even before you knew anything about me. It is to you, in good part, that I owe my courage to philosophize on the platform just as one will philosophize in life, if at all. Do accept my thanks, then, along with eternal friendship."[209] As Feder put it later, these words were written "not only with due respect, but . . . with frank cordiality."[210] They were not mere flourishes. "For Kant," says Feder in a chapter of his autobiography entitled "Story of My Quarrels about Kantian Philosophy" and written about 1800, "I had the very highest regard ever since reading *Dreams of a Spiritualist*" (24). In the *Erlanger Gelehrte Zeitung* he had praised this book "in the strongest terms. . . . There were no other relations between the famed thinker and me when *Critique of Pure Reason* was published."[211]

Since Feder lacked both the temperament and the talent for polemics, since he revered Kant and surely did not mean to provoke him, we may ask ourselves where the review got its overweening tone and offhand manner. Feder himself gives a very candid explanation.

Soon after the appearance of *Critique,* he says, he had thumbed through the book and started reading a little. His first impression "was not favorable."[212] "To me it was no more conceivable how dogmatic metaphysics—which seemed to me to be sufficiently tempered and purified—could be so fiercely attacked than how in our time such a scholastical apparatus might be deemed necessary to the service of philosophy."[213] Before he had a chance to look at it thoroughly, Garve took the book along to review it. By then Feder had formed a conviction: "As I erroneously presumed," *Critique* was "a work not at all adequate to the genius of our time."[214] The premises of this prejudice were not quite clear to him later. He tried to find a psychological explanation in the fact that he himself had "in those days, by the excessive good luck that crowned my philosophical endeavors, been rendered careless and a little reckless."[215] "Hence some humiliation and shock could be needful and salutary for me."[216]

As it happened, the shock was severe. Once *Prolegomena* was published, the facts surrounding that review were soon bruited about[217] even though Kant had passed over them in silence. Feder, under cover of that silence, did not take up the challenge; it was not until a Kantian exhorted him publicly "to settle his matter with Kant"[218] that instead of confessing, he tried to prove his familiarity with Kant's work, and the seriousness of his own work on some basic philosophical questions. "To examine the Kantian philosophy," he published a book, *On Space and Causality*,[219] in 1788. He announced in it that he considered it his "duty to publish detailed inquiries into the human intellect, with the intention utterly to destroy, if possible, a faith of which, as shown by Kant's example, the least remnant can still do so much harm: the faith in concepts that are not of empirical origin."[220]

To Feder, this duty did a great deal of harm. Kant already had a few followers who knew more about his philosophy. They pounced on the book and virtually tore it to bits. Feder refused to admit defeat; when the *Göttinger Gelehrte Anzeigen* also turned its back on him, he founded "a *Philosophische Bibliothek* of his own," just as one might found "a standing army for political feuds."[221] There he could now place his articles; but in 1790 —when he published "An Attempt to Present the Kantian System as Briefly as Possible,"[222] trying to display his comprehensive knowledge and managing only to supply his critics with an entertaining collection of current errors—his "army" started shaking. The *Bibliothek* failed in the following year, and Feder dispensed with further German publications about Kant, if not with all forms of vengeance.

His literary fame waned after 1783, and more yet after 1788. When his journal failed in 1791, he "deeply felt this hitherto quite unaccustomed humiliation."[223] The students in Göttingen stayed away from his lectures. He lost the respect of "some eminently estimable colleagues."[224] Lichtenberg, for instance, who in the past had often been to his house, would now shrug him off with a smile. He was plagiarized everywhere. The "amputation which the critical upheavals in philosophy caused to be performed on my fame as an author and lecturer"[225] struck Feder, in his son's words, as a true "catastrophe."[226] He was "close to plunging into hypochondria."[227]

His only desire now was to resign his office and to withdraw from philosophical activities. But no one wanted him any more. He was through as a professor, and yet he had to remain one. At last, in 1796, he was named director of the Hamburg Gregorianum and given the chance to make a new start, albeit a step down the ladder.

While the direct cause of Feder's decline was the series of blows dealt to him by the Kantians rather than a second assault by Kant, their ruthlessness derived legitimacy from the ruthlessness of Kant's attack in *Prolegomena*. Having appeared not in a periodical but in a more and more widely read Kantian volume, and being left to stand there after outliving its functions, that attack grew in effect as the public became better able to absorb the basic ideas of *Critique*. It created an image of Feder which men made fun of and looked down upon, and it ruined a career. Later, Kant would hint that he might have too harshly judged Feder's character, if not his cognitive powers. We have a letter of his, to Reinhold, that amounts to a partial rehabilitation: "For all the narrowness of his mind, Feder is honest."[228] The public, of course, heard of this judgment only in 1825, when Feder had been four years in his grave.

No less ruthless was the blow at Fichte, which is so often minimized.

Fichte had opened volume 8 of *Das Philosophische Journal*, which he coedited with Niethammer, with two essays on the philosophy of religion, one written by himself, the other by Forberg. As Goethe cautiously phrased it, Fichte in particular "ventured to speak of God and divine matters in terms evidently contrary to the ones in which such mysteries are traditionally referred to."[229] An anonymous pamphlet against Fichte's alleged atheism promptly appeared[230] and soon gained wide circulation. Warning of Fichte's doctrines as a threat to political and ecclesiastic authority, it was noticed with displeasure at princely courts. The conflict came to a boil late in 1798, with the seizure of Fichte's journal at the universities of Leipzig and Wittenberg. A petition urging a reprimand for Fichte and Niethammer was sent to Weimar. Duke Karl August wanted to go easy in the matter, as we know from Schiller and Goethe, but Fichte insisted on a purely legal verdict. He defended himself provocatively, in vehement, threatening writings that were quite unacceptable for the court and turned Fichte's own friends against him. "For my person," Goethe wrote to Schlosser, "I readily admit that I should vote against my own son if he permitted himself such language against a government."[231] We cannot go into the details of the quarrel, but it climaxed in Fichte's dismissal from his professor's chair in Jena. He left Jena and tried to settle in Rudolstadt; the authorities turned him down. In summer 1799 he arrived in Berlin, then still a city without a university, hoping to be able to give private lectures, at least.

He had not been two months in Berlin and had only just gained a foothold when the *Allgemeine Literatur-Zeitung*[232] carried the statement in which Kant called Fichte's system untenable, disavowed "any share in that philosophy" (70: XII, 370), cast aspersions upon Fichte's character, and claimed to be laying the wholly assured foundation of the lasting system himself.

The factual basis of this judgment is questionable. Aside from a few pages of Fichte's first work, Kant had probably read only the "Second Introduction to *Theory of Science*." It could be said maliciously, therefore, that Kant's performance at the close of his polemicizing years was the very thing against which he had taken up arms at the outset: "a sample of judgment passed previous to examination" (31: IV, 372). The charge would be groundless, however, since Kant's own statement made it clear that he was not judging a cause, that all he was doing was to tell the public about a person's relation to a cause—that he was discussing not what Fichte's system was, but what he, Kant, took it to be (70: XII, 370). We might accept this if he had really done so.

But the ruthless part of Kant's statement is not his publication of a subjective opinion about a cause; it is his condemnation of

Fichte's person under the historic circumstances. There is no question that Kant knew of Fichte's difficulties. The fact that at the moment when Fichte was so sharply and perfidiously attacked, by opponents who were Kant's opponents also, disavowing a rival seemed more important to Kant than expressing solidarity with a thinker—this fact will always remain a stain on his record.

Complaints about Kant's exclusionary polemics. Several of Kant's opponents considered his exclusionary polemicizing undignified.

Schlettwein regretted his "depreciation and ridicule of meritorious men of our time" (70: XII, 362).

Nicolai felt obliged to "speak aloud about his ill-mannered treatment of me"[233] and to pillory "so utterly shallow and rude a piece of writing," in which Kant attacked by name rather than with arguments, declining "to the class of the most despicable scribblers."[234]

In Fichte's behalf it was Schelling who passionately took the prosecutor's role, chiding Kant for "obtuseness" in looking upon *Critique of Pure Reason* as "the cogitative pillars of Hercules" for all time, and in having nothing better to wish a man like Fichte than that he comment *Critique*.[235] Schelling—like Friedrich Schlegel, incidentally[236]—pointed to the situation in which Kant had published his statement; he thought he detected calculated malice behind it, and what he finally saw in "the whole story" was "a new character trait of the well-known sort: 'As Yr Majesty's most loyal subject' in the debate of departments."[237]

Fichte, who knew already that Schelling would publicly answer in his stead, reacted to the publicity about the statement with a pose of noble magnanimity, calm, and forgiveness. In private letters he expressed himself in his genuine intemperate manner, piling invectives on the timid, sophistical oldster,[238] who was "only a three-quarter brain," had "by his halfness acquired some reputation among contemporaries," and was now striving to perpetuate his "leaden mediocrity" and compelled to "end in vigorous self-prostitution."[239]

Compared with these indictments, the one drawn up by Eberhard is of special significance because it is the only attempt to analyze Kant's "method of disputing."[240] It cannot be said to cast a systematic light upon that method either; but it does recognize some of its elements, employs them in its own argumentation, and turns them back upon Kant.

No reader of Kant's *On a Discovery*, says Eberhard, can fail to "be struck by the tone of supercilious self-confidence that prevails throughout it"[241] and makes discussion impossible. According to Eberhard, Kant treats objections in a "tone of dismissal."[242] He likes to speak of other people's "practices" while lapsing into practices of his own: belittling another's strength as guile and resorting to guile himself;[243] attacking the order of the *Magazin* as "topsy-turvy"[244] and using it to twist and discredit before examining; mocking another's procedure, but only so as to feign superiority by "mockery."[245] "This ruse of war can therefore be regarded as the dominant character trait of Herr Kant's manner: to terrify the writer, and impress the reader, by showing contempt for opponents and simulating superiority."[246] The frightful example of *Prolegomena* was unforgotten. Kant's "insulting kind of debate" deserved "to become proverbial."[247] Its secret intent was clear: the reader must be prejudiced. "No other purpose can be served by the presumptuous way of looking down his nose to which Herr Kant has thus far treated all opponents."[248] This made clear also that the real basic will behind this polemicizing was not to elucidate reason. It was a subjective concern: "concern with his fame."[249] By this concern Kant was rigidly tied to his system and forced to "believe in the miracle" of its "unshakability."[250] This was why Kant resorted to "violent means"[251] and was sinking visibly deeper into a "literary despotism"[252] whose exclusive goal could now be nothing but "to destroy each attack with the attacker's own destruction."[253]

There is no denying that Kant's exclusionary polemics do contain material which anyone acting as counsel for his opponents might interpret the way Eberhard interpreted it. But we are now exchanging that advocate's role for the pursuit of a more impersonal interpretation of the facts shown here.

Another attempt to interpret the facts. We raised the question whether Kant's own absolute veracity entitled him to pass moral judgment on his opponents. And we found:

that in the controversy over the falsification of sensibility by Leibniz, Kant did not take back his charges and did not admit his mistake (any more than in some other cases);

that his interpretation of his relation to academic philosophy was ambivalent, and the two Leibniz interpretations he gave in the process were diametrically opposed to one another;

that he wooed Kästner in doubly ambiguous fashion, professing a personal esteem that is disproved by citations from *Opus postumum,* and attributing to his philosophizing a goal that was alien to it;

that in the campaign against *Das Philosophische Magazin* his political prudence sometimes bordered on guile;

and finally, that the collapse of Feder's career was partly his doing, that he sought to destroy Eberhard, and that in relation to Fichte he placed rivalry above solidarity.

A philosophical interpretation of these facts will not, in all fairness, be based upon psychological considerations, for that would permit the supposition of too many opinions and motives. We shall be guided, rather, by Kant's philosophical intent, and once this is seen clearly, we shall, to the limits of possibility, interpret the facts in the sense of his intent. It may well be, after all, that even in such an interpretation some facts cannot be understood as anything but lapses from a "practice" into the "practices" he fought in principle.

Kant's basic intention is this: what is exclusionary must be fought if its exclusiveness is incompatible with universality. He views his own exclusiveness as a bar to subjective exclusiveness, and as borne by a will to promote the common cause of reason. Since this battle must be waged against representatives of exclusionary philosophies—against those very contemporaries—he cannot do without prudence; but since it is a fight for reason, his prudence is subject to reason. "Sagacious, but never mendacious" —this is the principle of combat. On grounds of this principle, the several facts might be commented upon as follows.

Kant did fail to admit some defeats. But this does not mean he was incapable of such admission. Rather, he was acting upon a maxim which he himself had established for his opponent in the Feder case: "Silence is a confession" (31: IV, 378). It was not unfair to claim for himself a right that he accorded to his opponents: to make no public announcement of his own defeat.

In the controversy over the "falsification" of sensibility, Kant stood by his charge of misquoting. Outwardly this does look like support for the sophistical arguments advanced by Reinhold.

But we must remember that, as he wrote to Reinhold, Kant looked upon Eberhard's attack as "a document in litigation."[254] We shall see later how deeply this way of thinking was imbedded in Kant, and in a formally legal sense Eberhard's doubly imprecise rebuke had indeed put him in the wrong. Call it casuistical or not: this retreat to formal legalism is a way of thinking often encountered in Kant, and it was surely not based upon a leaning to sophistry.

Kant was ambivalent in interpreting his relation to academic philosophy. But this does not mean he interpreted it as needed. The relation actually was ambivalent. Kant tried hard to adopt the careful, thorough, academic method. He wanted its formal rigor passed on as a constant premise of philosophizing, although in the substance of philosophy he fought the mathematical method even as a youth. The ambivalence shows in his utterances about specific academic philosophers. It was not a product of guile; it was a true consequence of a type of thought that had emerged from academicism but had far transcended it later.

The wholly antithetical Leibniz interpretations cease being mutually exclusive if the first is seen as the product of Kant's original conception and the second as a reconstruction of the way Leibniz conceived himself. The only error is to regard the first as a declared intention of Leibniz's—an error which the second interpretation shows Kant to have overcome.

About the letter to Kästner it must be said that Kant's early writings prove his high regard for Kästner. The only full-fledged condemnation is the one in *Opus postmum,* written several years after the letter in question. In the interim Kant actually could have changed his view of Kästner, and there are various reasons to assume that he did. As for the statement on the intent of his philosophizing: this may be understood as a pedagogical measure, a means whereby a differently-minded individual was to be enlightened, on his own premises, about the sense of the new philosophizing.

And, indeed, Kant was "politically" prudent in dealing with his contemporaries. But why not? No one can ask that instead of judging the situation realistically, he should have let his many opponents destroy him as a contemporary. This astuteness would be objectionable only if it had lapsed into sophistry, as guile and cunning.

Concerning Kant's ruthlessness, however, one has first of all to bear in mind that an opponent who philosophizes in exclusionary fashion—due to the principles of his philosophizing and to the intellectual power he represents—cannot be countered by degrees of ruthlessness, since his own is total. It is total in principle, even though not outwardly, perhaps. In fact, it is the opponent who decides about the need for such ruthlessness.

Turning to the particular cases: what must be said about Feder is that he himself voluntarily started his impotent fight against Kant, and that eventually he kept it up because the insight into the brittleness of his foundations weighed too hard upon him. In a sense, it was his own obtuseness that ruined his career, seven years after Kant had attacked him.

As for Eberhard, he on his part fought with an obstinacy never matched by Kant's. For eight years he kept pursuing his thesis, and three thousand printed pages, more than twice the volume of Kant's three *Critiques,* were the result. Unlike Kant, he never quit; he kept up the struggle in other forms, as did Feder. Compared with Eberhard, Kant seems more ruthless only because of the greater extent to which he saw through his opponent.

In Fichte's case there are no definite signs that Kant was slyly waiting for the right moment to strike, as Schelling thought he had been. Rather, he struck at the necessary moment—and then indeed without mercy. He thus met Fichte, the opponent, in perfectly adequate fashion, although one might wish that he had met the thinker of genius in some other way.

But does this square the balance? Are these arguments not largely attempts to exonerate Kant? Is it not a fact that his battles against some opponents were no longer merely defensive, that they were fights to the finish? Is the hanky-panky not demonstrable?

If we were called upon to decide whether in his polemical use of reason Kant himself lapsed into "practices," into the bickering he disdained, we would say this: there is no fact which allows of no other interpretation; but there are some that do not exclude this interpretation, and there may be only one—"falsification"— for which it is plausible. And that in fifteen years of fighting for the existence of a philosophy, against opponents for whom tricks were the stock in trade of polemics. A case of similar discipline in a struggle of the same intensity would be hard to find. Kant's practice will not cause us to deny the legitimacy of his mode of combat.

Debate

In the course of analyzing Kant's polemics we come upon a mode of combat that is the opposite of exclusionary. There, the partner's struggle is found to be ultimately motivated not by ill will but by a love of truth. His person, therefore, will not be accused but honored; his claims will be countered, not with irony, but with enlightening seriousness; his case will not be demolished, but it will be clarified. Preceding this mode of polemics is readiness for frank discussion; but the discussion will not be fanatical and does not exclude the possibility of silence. Its mark is not ruthlessness but nobility. The man engaged in it wants to acknowledge; hence he appreciates existing achievements as they deserve. He wants to see; hence he inquires into premises and their possible consequences. He wants to understand; hence he clarifies the central questions. He wants to philosophize; hence he advises studying philosophy. He feels, beyond every division on issues, a unity in the way of thinking, in the state of mind, and on that basis he finds unanimity in the reflective medium, by way of a controversy between friends. This mode of controversy is what we call debate. We look for its typical characteristics mainly in Kant's replies to Garve and Herder, but occasionally also in the ones to Jacobi, to Forster, and to Constant.

Causes and Courses of These Polemics

Garve. After the publication of *Prolegomena,* in which the first reviewer of *Critique of Pure Reason* was so sharply challenged to emerge from his incognito, Kant heard from a man he had for years been ranking with Baumgarten and Mendelssohn, as one of "our greatest analysts."[255] Christian Garve wrote to inform Kant that he could "in no way" recognize the printed review as his, but that he did have "some part" in it. The review he had written was too long, and Feder, on his own responsibility, had turned it into a shorter one. A few lines of that—one-third, perhaps— were his, Garve's; but they made up only one tenth of his own review. Unbeknown to him, the review on which he had concentrated all of his strength and attention had become "not merely futile, but harmful."[256]

What spoke for Garve was not the story as such—already detailed here—but the manner of its presentation. Instead of the arrogant tone of the published review, Kant found in this letter the simple language of one who will admit his failings without vanity. "I confess to you that I know of no book in the world that would have cost me so much effort to read; had I not considered myself bound by my given word, I would have deferred its perusal for a better time, when I would have been mentally and physically stronger." Garve did not employ canny practices to dodge a direct encounter; he gave himself into his opponent's hand by sending him the unabbreviated review. "If you are as dissatisfied with this review of mine as with the one from Göttingen, it will prove that I have not enough penetration to judge so difficult and profound a book, and that it is not written for me." Instead of a tendency to discount and dismiss, the letter indicated a sincere endeavor to understand and freely to acknowledge the achievement of another; instead of anticipatory overall judgments, it expressed cautious doubts "whether I have properly considered the whole"; instead of a fundamental hostility spawned by ill will, it showed a receptive capacity for friendship. To meet a scholar who really cared more about his reputation as "an honest man"[257] than for the odor of a profound metaphysicist—this experience so mollified Kant that his answering letter, beyond its material content, also paid virtual homage to the addressee. And that mutual esteem stood up for the fifteen years that followed, until Garve's death, although subjected to many a test by the mediocrity of Garve's cognitive powers.

The first such test proved to be Garve's review—which did not reach Kant until he had dispatched his own noble and generous letter.[258] Unable at first to give it more than a "cursory scanning,"[259] he sent it to Schultz with a request for an appraisal. This arrived some days later and was perfectly accurate. Schultz replied that the original review was "very much better," but not up to the work it dealt with; "taken for all in all," it left Critique "still under a detrimental shadow."[260] Kant thereupon read Garve's review himself. From Hamann[261] we know that he was not happy with it, although he probably did not make the detailed comparison with Feder's that would have shown him what Arnoldt's[262] analysis and comparison of the two has made clear to us: that, except for the final judgment, Garve was responsible for all the errors and misunderstandings in the first review. He had read the new work more carefully, but his understanding of the crucial points had been no better than Feder's. His good will did not enable him to overcome his cognitive limitations; nor did his later studies of the Kantian works.

In 1792 Beck wrote that Garve, though defending *Critique,* had confessed to Eberhard "that critical idealism and Berkeleyan idealism were entirely one and the same"[263]—to which Kant rather brusquely replied that this opinion deserved "not the slightest notice."[264] Kant himself had then just had a sample of Garve's slight understanding: he had read Garve's *Essays on Several Subjects from the Realm of Morals, from Literature, and from Social Life,*[265] in which Garve had written a long footnote on the goal of humanity.[266] He saw that goal in happiness in the sense of the eudaemonistic ethic, and he wrote that Kant, while claiming to see it in perfect morality alone, was retracting such a view by regarding virtue from the standpoint of making rational beings worthy of happiness. Garve was suspicious of this distinction between being happy and being worthy of happiness. He could grasp the separation of the concepts "very well with my mind"; but the separation of the aims was one that he could "not find in my heart." In fact, he was altogether doubtful that these aims might be distinguishable in action. Such refinements already got lost "in reflection upon particular objects," Garve opined; in action they got lost "entirely."[267]

Garve developed his ethical principles as follows. Happiness is "a series . . . of good conditions."[268] To be recognized and named as such, it must be preceded by sensation. The sensation of happiness therefore precedes the alleged final goal—being worthy of happiness—and it is also the true impelling force behind the law. For every law is based upon a motive, and motives rest upon the distinguishing of conditions which are better from conditions which are worse. "The perception of this difference is elementary for the concept of happiness."[269] It is the motive for complying with the moral law. The conclusion Garve drew from all this was that happiness is the goal of all sentient beings and the mainspring beneath their laws.

Kant, in the first part of the essay on theory and practice, tried to resolve these misconceptions. Yet none of this could ever make him doubt that Garve was "a philosopher in the genuine sense of the word" (37: VI, 206), and Garve knew it. In 1798, after his attempts at interpretation had miscarried, he showed his gratitude nobly, sending Kant his last book,[270] which he had dedicated to Kant. Garve knew he was near death. For several years he had been suffering from cancer in the right half of his face. The book had been written during the most cruel illness; it marked Garve's psychological conquest of his illness. The document of this victory was dedicated to Kant as a token of thanks for their past correspondence, and with the wish "to resume this connection with you at the goal of my life, or during my approach to that goal."[271] Kant thanked him with the "greatest admiration" for this "loving and soul-strengthening" gift.[272] He honored Garve with an important letter that raised an unusual monument to the truthfulness of their relationship: in the last paragraph, Kant—convinced, as if it were self-evident, that even at the point of death nothing could matter more to Garve than to be delivered from an error—lodged one more protest against a misinterpretation on Garve's part.

Thus Kant's first controversy about critical philosophy occasioned not only an opponent's destruction but the birth of a friendship. Friendship and enmity had a common point of departure. This first controversy is the perfect case in which to observe the grounds, the methods, and the courses of two quite heterogeneous modes of combat.

Herder. Three points strike us in the controversy with Herder.

1. Only here—in his review of Herder's *Ideas*—does Kant seem to be the aggressor, while all his other polemics against contemporaries are replies to challenges. But we must add at once that in a deeper sense Kant was the aggressor always and everywhere, and that all attacks upon him were attempts to counter the new, all-contesting, and "all-crushing" philosophy.

2. The two opponents employed different modes of combat. Kant's criticism was not destructive. It climaxed in friendly admonitions to a former student. There is some irony in it, but not very much in comparison with the exclusionary polemics. Herder, on the other hand, was fighting to exclude critical philosophy, not

to serve it as a monitor but to set himself up as a judge over it and eventually as its executioner. The mainsprings of his struggle were affections: anger, at first, and hatred later.

3. A gradual change occurred in the relationship between the two men. On Herder's side it was extraordinary, ranging all the way from the enthusiastic reverence of his young years to abysmal hatred in old age. As for Kant, we have already found him flexible in his relation to Garve, but there this trait led from the possibility of an exclusionary polemic to a controversy between friends. In the battle with Herder, as in the fight against Feder, the change went in the other direction, although, from a certain moment on, Kant gave no further literary expression to it. The relationship grew visibly worse on both sides, if not in the same measure. It ended with Herder, in his later years, trying to "annihilate" critical philosophy in a large-scale offensive, and with the aged Kant—already skeptical of this "great artist of mirages"[273]—quoted by Hasse, the Orientalist of Königsberg, as rendering the "almost passionate judgment that [Herder] wished to be a dictator and liked to proselytize."[274]

To Kant, the encounter with Herder was not much more than a disappointing episode. In his years as a *Magister* he had the good luck to find among the divinity students at the university an extremely talented youth who received his ideas with virtually tempestuous zeal and enthusiastic worship. He tried, as he did with all students, to teach him to philosophize—in other words, for all the influence he was exerting, to lead young Herder to reflect independently and to weigh carefully Kant's own thought as well as everyone else's. In part, he was successful. When the young man left Königsberg after two years, he had become independent, self-confident, indeed self-certain. Kant let him go in the hope that, once "the warm motion of youthful sentiment slows down to that tranquillity which is, so to speak, the philosopher's contemplative life,"[275] he might turn into a philosophical poet, perhaps even into a thinker. He watched Herder's further course and heard of his early renown "with a certain vanity"[276] and—as shown by the only letter he wrote to Herder—with a certain concern.

In 1784, twenty years after Herder's departure from Königsberg, Kant suddenly found a point of thematical contact with Herder's creative work. He was occupied with questions of the philosophy of history when Herder published the first volume of his *Ideas to the Philosophy of the History of Mankind*.[277] By then, Kant was no longer the elegant author of *Observations on the Feeling of the Beautiful and Sublime,* nor the intuitive genius of *Universal Natural History and Theory of the Heavens.* He had become the strict academic critic, while Herder, from a philosophical point of view, had remained the student of 1764 or, as Haym put it, the "philosophical amateur."[278] Kant rediscovered the gifts that had marked his pupil, now applied to a wealth of material, and he rediscovered the perils that had threatened him, deepened by decades of habit. In his review he could praise the things he had always been able to praise, and he warned of the ones he had always been obliged to warn of. But Herder could no longer tolerate an instructor. His occasional answers in the second volume of *Ideas*[279] smacked of cold rejection. To Kant, what followed did presumably not come as any great surprise. Herder's thought, seemingly organized in beautiful, conclusive harmonies, revealed itself after some hesitation as bitterly hostile to a philosophizing enlightened by critique. Herder became the enemy who was of no further interest; in the end, he no longer needed to be taken seriously even as a seducer. Kant left his attacks to others to handle, and to time.

To Herder, all this made a completely different picture. For him, the relationship had three unmistakable, emotionally characterized peaks: worshipful enthusiasm in youth, involuntary rivalry during maturity, hate-filled enmity in old age.

Next to Hamann, Kant was the great experience of Herder's Königsberg period. In Kant he found a teacher whose sole objective was teaching his students to think. He kept them far from all discipleship, allowed them to share his own thoughts, which seemed only just to be originating, and simultaneously invited contradiction. His broad mind seemed to encompass the universe; his profound reason, to cover the absolute in man; his good cheer amid cogitative rigor, to unite humanity. To understand him was to find freedom to think for yourself, the open-mindedness to understand others, and consistent courage to be yourself. Young Herder awkwardly expressed this experience in poems. He felt as though a god had given him Kant, thereby delivering him from the chains of ignorance,[280] and as though Kant had freed him to be himself: "Kant! I heard and dared with half a tongue a novel song . . ."[281] He glorified Kant's name so that it might light up "eternity's night, past eclipsing."[282] Thirty more years would pass before Herder found the proper literary form for this enthusiasm, in *Letters for the Furtherance of Humanity.* We are indebted to it for the most beautiful literary portrait of Kant as a young man.[283]

With his peculiar intensity, Herder read Kant's *Cosmogony,* the *Observations,* and the other early works accessible to him. Kant favored him with a few private conversations. It was by the two cited works, above all, along with Kant's lectures, that Herder's thinking was influenced and may have been determined for the rest of his life. This, at least, was the opinion of Haym, still the man best acquainted with Herder.[284]

Twenty years later, Herder was recognized as one of the best-known and most fertile writers in the German language area. Ties of friendship linked him with Germany's outstanding men. His fame had long surpassed that of his teacher, whose early writings were all but forgotten already and whose new work was yet unknown. In Herder's years of writing on the most diverse topics, one idea had more and more clearly emerged: the idea of the evolution of all things. Language, religion, humanity—anything that had to do with man at all—could not, he felt, be understood in a different manner from that in which nature is understood. Natural history came to serve him as a model for the history of mankind. Giant dimensions encompassed a rich thought material in which man was to be evaluated not just from a cosmic point of view but anthropologically, historically, and theologically. The combination of these ideas had to become the *summa* of mankind, so to speak, and this was what Herder strained all his energies upon, from 1782 on. He was consciously bringing about the happy union of his greatest literary effort with his total intellectual life, and it is not inconceivable that now and then he was looking forward also to his one-time teacher's approval. In a sense, after all, Kant's *Universal Natural History and Theory of the Heavens* constituted the basis of his undertaking; important fields of material came from Kant's early lectures; and Kant's former lecturing method—consistently to pursue an objective in thoughtful, entertaining language, without committing himself to any system—had helped to form the thinking style of *Ideas.*

The expectation came true in a rather painful manner. In November 1784, under a pretext, Kant's *Idea for a Universal History, Cosmopolitan in Intent* appeared in *Berliner Monatsschrift*. The very title was bound to strike Herder like a blow. To his "ideas"—which meant notions, opinions, possibilities—Kant opposed an "idea," a guiding thought so well founded in itself that it could carry history from its source to its goal; and that on a few pages, not in four volumes. Heavier yet was the blow dealt by the guiding thought itself, for this history was no triumphal march of innate humanity; it was the unfoldment of passions whose ruinous force could be halted only by founding a state and, in that state, by establishing freedom. Then, before Herder had even read this essay, an anonymous review of volume 1 of his *Ideas* appeared in 1785 in the newly-founded *Allgemeine Literatur-Zeitung*.[285] It impressed him as zealous praise of nonessentials coupled with malicious distortion of the book's basic ideas and schoolmasterly censure of its fundaments. It was not hard to recognize Kant in the reviewer, and Herder, in letters to friends, made no secret of his outrage at such "icy, wretched, doglike flunkyism."[286] Against his will, he had been forced to oppose his former teacher, obliged to attack some passages of Kant's *Idea for a Universal History* in his own volume 2. Kant reviewed this sequel also, dwelled ironically on Herder's attacks, and followed up by publishing *Presumable Beginnings of Human History* (49), an essay in which Herder was not mentioned, although no reader of *Ideas* could take it for anything but a retort to Herder's book 10.

Since the new basic questions of Kant's thinking were not clear to Herder—he still had not read *Critique of Pure Reason* —it seemed to him that Kant, his once so beloved teacher, was occupying himself with invidious attacks on one who had surely not been the worst of his pupils. And when this error had been cleared up by Hamann[287] and Herder had been assuaged and was prepared to make peace, he still could not ignore the fact that Kant's new works were in direct conflict with at least some of his own ideas. By 1792, when Kant's treatise on radical evil appeared, all that Herder could see in it was a radical distortion of his idea of humanity. Having studied Kant's works in the meantime, he came to conceive their opposition in particular philosophemes as expressing a totally hostile way of thinking, a hostility not to be countered by other than total attack.

At the beginning of the third phase, Herder presented this attack as a defense of Kant's spirit against the "unspirit" of the Kantians. It was to be an apologia for the pure cause of Kant. Herder especially despised the theologians among the Kantians, because what they postulated in the name of reason was a cold religion of duty, alienated from humanity and advanced without an inkling of either reason or religion. But the attacks on them which Herder launched in *Christian Writings*[288] came to be more and more clearly directed against Kant's own philosophy of religion. They finally culminated in Herder's attempt to create a high school course that would protect future theologians from the noxious influence of critical philosophy. "To enable young theologians to do without this philosophy and to keep it out of their reach is something I consider both worthwhile and feasible."[289] The man who once upon a time, as a divinity student, owed all his major inspirations to Kant's teaching was now, as General Superintendent of Education, trying to bar students from receiving the same teaching. When this plot against academic freedom misfired, Herder plunged into what was perhaps the most luckless venture of his life: the attempt systematically to destroy the whole Kantian system and thus to give a new direction not just to the study of theology but to the spirit of the times. He wrote a *Metacritique of Critique of Pure Reason*,[290] appended to it a burlesque of *The Debate of Departments*, and concluded his enterprise with *Kalligone*,[291] a metacritique of *Critique of Judgment*. Here we shall deal only with *Metacritique*, and only with Herder's mode of combat in it.

Herder gave his *Metacritique* a veneer of objectivity. He was, he said, "talking of a book, not of an author—certainly not of an author's gifts and intentions, but of a book's content and effect."[292] To this book he wanted to do justice: "To lay bare the core of his writings has been the principal endeavor of this metacritique."[293] What entitled the author of *Metacritique* to undertake it was his long familiarity with Kantian thinking: "For more than thirty years he has been familiar with the principles that gave birth to *Critique of Pure Reason*. He has known them in the bud and in flower; hence *solus et totus pendet ab ore Magistri*."[294]

In the preface, this avowal of objectivity follows upon a parable. A youth falls asleep while journeying "into the valley of

academic wisdom." Hugo, the "spying thought," appears to him
in a dream and teaches him the principles of thinking as an
eternal quest: "Learn to know before you decide. . . . Understand
what you hear. . . . Learn for yourself, for none other." When
Hugo has vanished, Hägsa, "the well-known sorceress," appears
with seductive presents for the youth: a blowgun from which he
can blow the forms of visuality, the categories, and the postulates;
a box named Critical Idealism in which reason, a nothern light
fighting itself, and all things at large are seen in pleasant confinement; a disciplinary scourge with which canonless reason may
be chastised; and the architectural drawings for all possible cognitions. He who knows how to use them is relieved of toil, a
"self-thinker" allowed to become a despot. Mindlessness, Vogue,
and Cabal, three young witches, will come to his aid and lead him
into his "alphabet house."[295]

What interests us is not so much the interpretation of the
parable with respect to Kantian philosophy as the significance
of its function with respect to Herder's fighting method. In fact,
the avowal of objective examination is preceded by a disparagement of the examinee. That which will be tested is disqualified
beforehand as the insinuation of a witch. What we can expect
of Metacritique is a trial of Critique of Pure Reason at which
reason, in the Kantian sense, appears to sit in judgment, while
behind its facade of objectivity a General Superintendent plays
the Inquisitor's role, hunting that same reason down as a witch
and delivering it to public condemnation. The separation of
person and work, so strictly adhered to that Kant's name is not
mentioned anywhere in Metacritique, serves as a means to hit
his person indirectly, to discredit the man to whom Herder could
not stand up face to face. Nowhere can we speak of an endeavor
to "lay bare the core" of Critique. Herder picks out passages,
calls his opponent to account for them as long as he pleases,
interrupts him, bids him keep quiet, mocks him, derides him—
and all this in the petty, hypochrondriac spirit of schoolmasterly
censoriousness, seeking to trap the opponent and always ready to
generalize on his weak points. Where something laudable cannot
be suppressed, it can be relativized and combined with a note of
disapproval: others have said the same thing before, and said it
better. The many witnesses whom Herder calls to testify—invariably against Kant, never for him—are all taken seriously as

philosophers, at least; the defendant alone differs from the great philosophers not in degree but in kind, since his philosophy is unphilosophy pure and simple, error raised to a system.

Herder always had the gift to make methodical use of polemics and to vary it to fit the opponent. His criticisms of Spinoza and Lessing differed from his criticisms of Klotz, Schlözer, Spalding, and Nicolai, because in polemicizing he remained aware of each man's rank. In his polemic against Kant this sense was totally lacking. He treated Kant the way he treated Klotz, with utter contempt for an inferior spirit. Since he knew better, this can only mean that he was trying to bring Kant down to a level on which he would be easier to destroy. Herder's is a polemic rendered mendacious by hatred.

What came out of this sort of polemicizing did not even fit Herder's own spirit: it was a parody, built upon passages told out of the context of what he meant to destroy. Paradoxically, it owed to the opponent not only its existence but whatever light it shed. The hatred that blinded Herder robbed him of the possible fruits of his metacritique. There is no doubt that it might have grown into a genuine critique of Kant, a critique aware of the opponent's intellectual rank and achievement, though countering him with thoughts based on another power. Instead, it became a volume of which Goethe said, "If I had known that Herder was writing the book, I would have begged him on bended knee to suppress it."[296]

The others. Three other debates belong to this group: the controversies with Jacobi, Forster, and Constant.

Friedrich Heinrich Jacobi occupies a special place among the addressees of Kantian replies, since he challenged Kant not by objecting but by expressing agreement. He was not, of course, agreeing purely for the sake of the matter; Jacobi's agreement was a polemical weapon, for use in his battle with Mendelssohn. He spoke of Kant as like-minded, and it escaped him, perhaps, that he was thereby turning Kant's thought into an instrument of his own plans without agreeing with Kant on basic principles. This did not escape Kant, however. He soon felt obliged, in a reply that supported neither Mendelssohn nor Jacobi, to detach himself from the thought principles of both men, and thus to clarify publicly the difference between the fundaments of their philosophy and of his own.[297]

Georg Forster, long active as a natural scientist, wrote the first critique of Kant's approach to science without having made that approach clear to himself. He opposed Kant, not with principles, but with reflections based upon a wealth of natural observations. He did not care for new theories; his sole concern was the advancement of natural research. Whatever Forster suspected of hampering this research came under his attack. On the surface, the attack was a loose sequence of references to specific Kantian theorems; but what it amounted to was a critique of Kant's principles of deductive natural science—of his predilection for quick theorizing, his gift for cursory syntheses, his frequently premature willingness to follow guiding ideas before sifting all of the material. It is precisely because of the rudimentary accuracy of this critique that one would wish Forster had thought it through more systematically. His failure to do so made it too easy for Kant to rebut his every criticism of a principle.[298]

Benjamin Constant, in 1797, published a political treatise[299] in which Kant's application of moral principles were attacked in passing. Constant maintained that the categorical imperative, in following a line of total generalization and ignoring the historic circumstances of a situation, leads ethicallly acting individuals in the world into aporias and paradoxes—that this could be avoided only if Kant's moral principles, which were correct in themselves, were correctly specified with respect to the constellation given in each particular case.

That Kant could not accept Constant's objections is obvious. They would have led to the insight that the Categorical Imperative is inapplicable, and ultimately to a separation of theory and practice, of morality and politics, of ethics and law. To avoid such serious breaks, Kant wrote a strange retort venturing to carry the consequences to the point of absurdity—perhaps under the delusion that they might be avoidable altogether.[300]

Basic Posture in Debate

Kant's basic posture in debate is characterized by a willingness to talk, by respect for the opponent, and by chivalrous manners.

That Kant was really willing to talk can be seen time and again. Even while assuming that sheer malice had motivated the author of the first review of *Critique of Pure Reason*, he did state the premises of any possible discussion, and Garve no sooner approached him with that respectful and honest letter than Kant opened the colloquy. He seemed almost grateful to deal with the awkward objections, and the questioning tone impressed him as a sign of "kindness." He virtually begged Garve for enemies: "And now, sir, if it should please you to do more in this matter, I ask that you use your influence and reputation to find enemies for me—not of my person (for I am at peace with all the world), but enemies of my book." His only condition for taking them on was that they would "proceed in good order,"[301] i.e., would reflect for the sake of cognition, systematically, and without ill will.

Garve never produced these enemies; but he himself continued to philosophize in such hostility to Kant for fifteen more years. And Kant, at every occasion, would enter into discussions with him, until that last letter shortly before Garve's death. As a matter of fact, he kept the controversy going beyond Garve's death, in *Opus postumum*.[302]

That nobody pushed Kant into the debates with Forster and Constant is certain. Having recognized Forster's honest mentality, Kant responded to his "concern" (53: VIII, 160). And although not affected literally by Constant's allusion, he took it up and answered in full. Not for an instant did he try to evade the possible consequences of his premises, which had caused the argument; instead, he personally carried them to the point of absurdity, weakening his own stand in those discussions.

With Herder, finally, he began the literary argument himself, without being challenged and although he was already skeptical about Herder's philosophizing (cf. 75: XV, 399; 912); and he continued it until he felt not only a hostile power in the other's philosophizing, but a hostile person in the other thinker.

Such willingness to talk is not just an expression of general amicability. It is the result of an insight: that communication is the chief calling of man as a rational creature—for reason is not created "so as to isolate itself, but to enter into communion" (75: XV, 392; 897). Reason's way of doing this is to turn into language. Kant is willing to talk, therefore, as long as talk can contribute to communication and thus to the spread of reason. Such a contribution can be made even in a clash with dogmatism, for dogmatism can be overthrown if only reason is not corrupted by ill will and not blocked by a lack of freedom.

On these premises, Kant's entrance into a debate is already an implicit show of respect for his opponent. This respect is shown explicitly as well—limited at times to the gifts of the other's mind, but in most instances extended to his entire person.

Forster is called a man "of eminent talent, youthful strength, and flourishing fame" (53: VIII, 160). He is told directly that he has not understood Kant, but the misconceptions are never pointed out in a derogatory tone of voice. The opponent is treated as a peer.

Constant is described as "well-minded" (63: VIII, 427). Kant recognizes that Contant's concepts will not stand up under analysis, but he does not suspect intrigue behind this failing. He knows that "the good man" (63: VIII, 428) is troubled, like every ethicist who cares more about the application of a principle than about the principle itself. Constant is given to understand that claiming the right to lie in exceptional cases makes one a potential liar, but this warning does not lead to a charge of mendacity, as it does in the second reply to Schlosser, for example. It simply expresses an insight.

In the letter to Jacobi, Kant's respect is stated in emphatic terms. He ranks Jacobi with the men "of talent, science, and probity," whom he will always meet "with respect," and he hopes that in his essay Jacobi will "not find the slightest trace of deviation from that principle."[303] In the retort, too, Jacobi is numbered with the "friends of the human race" (51: VIII, 146) and the men of "broadened mentality" (51: VIII, 144) whose vocation it is to spread reason around the globe.

The purest tone of respect for a person is heard in relation to Garve. He is the man "of a punctilious and conscientious honesty and a humanly sympathetic way of thinking." In Garve, Kant finds "righteousness and purity of mind" as well as "gentleness and compassion."[304] He is the "worthy scholar" (59: VIII, 385 note), the "sage," and the "philosopher in the genuine sense of the word" (37: VI, 206) rolled into one. Kant's every public reference to Garve is an encomium to the man's noble figure, though he could never praise him as a thinker.

It seems odd that no such displays of respect can be found in the relations between Kant and Herder, the only one of the philosophers mentioned whom Kant knew personally. He did tell Herder in his letter that he was taking this occasion "to demonstrate the respect and the friendship which my usual negligence

in writing may have caused you to doubt,"[305] but this respect
was paid mainly to the brain and the talents which are appreciated anew, and extensively, even in the reviews of *Ideas*. There is
no trace of personal appreciation to be found in the reviews, in
any case. The reason, we think, appears in the letter to Jacobi:
Herder's talent for assimilation and combination struck Kant as
"syncretistery"[306] and made him doubt Herder's sincerity. It
shows how close to exclusionary polemicizing he came in this
relationship.

His expressions of respect should not be taken for a conventional game played with an eye on mutuality. Kant may have been
the one great thinker who consistently placed personal purity
above science. Of course, he was never fool enough to deny a
man's extant scientific achievement on grounds of his moral
questionability; to a scholar, great scholars will always be objects of admiration (34: v, 78) even if he knows the flaws in their
character. But to Kant, a local intellectual honesty was outweighed by the encompassing personal honesty. For only the
latter keeps reason—which is more than science—open for its
every stirring, and thus for its dominion over all things.

That debate in itself is a sign of respect for the opponent
shows in the nobility with which Kant conducts it as a struggle
between equals. Its governing principle is not to measure others
by any standard we would not want to have applied to ourselves.
"I do not know," Kant commented on the attacks made upon
Jacobi, "how otherwise good and sensible men can often get it
into their heads to see merit in what they would find highly unfair
if it were done to them."[307] This commandment of chivalry
prohibits attacking our opponent's nonessential weaknesses and
looking for psychological motives behind those weaknesses. It
requires a presumption of the opponent's purity of mind as long
as no other certainty is forced upon us by his combat methods. It
will not let us use irony against him. It always keeps the door
open for unanimity, indeed for a possible friendship, and it can
—as demonstrated by the controversy with Garve—keep such a
friendship intact through all alterations.

To be chivalrous is not to be good-natured. It does not mean
to look the other way when the opponent goes wrong. The very
premises of his essential failings are uncovered; his misconceptions are called by name; the dangers they pose to philosophy

are not made to seem innocuous. But the goal to be achieved is never victory but insight, understanding, and the preservation of the freedom to philosophize.

This basic posture determines the characteristics of debate, which we now have to analyze.

Characteristics of Debate

Debate as appreciation. Aside from the fact that the very act of answering was in Kant's eyes a form of appreciation, he liked explicitly to stress "the true merit"[308] of an opponent's achievement. In Constant's attack he saw this merit in the reflections on intermediary principles, which were conceived "correctly" (63: VIII, 427), even if not correctly applied.

In Jacobi's essay *On the Doctrine of Spinoza* he found it in the clear presentation of "the difficulties . . . that surround the teleological road to theology."[309]

In Garve's case he saw it in the early years in the clarity of analysis; in later years, more and more, in the philosophical form.

Finally, Herder's merit was appreciated in many ways. His "wide-ranging vision"; his "sagacity" in discovering analogies; his "bold imagination"; the stimulating liveliness of his mind (45: VIII, 45); his ability to give beautiful expression to noble thoughts; above all, his freedom of thought—"that inner freedom . . . from the shackles of accustomed concepts and of ways of thinking reinforced by general opinion; a freedom so very uncommon that even those who merely profess philosophy have only seldom been able to work their way up to it" (45: VIII, 57f.) —all these qualities, and their extraordinary measure that elevated the author above the mass (45: VIII, 45), Kant saw and appreciated in Herder's work.

Debate as a clarification of misunderstandings. Before deciding whether and to what extent the opponent is essentially an adversary, it is necessary to clear the way to the essence of all stumbling blocks: of false expositions of concepts, of misunderstood principles, of incorrect interpretations. Kant tried to elucidate those, but first he would reflect upon the question how he was to conceive them as critique at all. In the retort to Garve's doctrine of happiness he said, "I call the denials of my propositions *exceptions* taken by this worthy man to points about which (I hope) he wants to reach an understanding with me. I do not call them attacks, derogatory assertions designed to provoke a defense, for which there is neither a place here nor an inclination on my part" (56: VIII, 278 note). The exceptions as such, however, if they are meant to apply to Kant, are "nothing but misunderstandings" (56: VIII, 281). Psychologically, one may attribute them to the general human tendency to judge new ideas in the habitual paths of the old. Materially, Kant conceives them elsewhere as the result of two causes: on the surface, so to speak, it is the mere failure to understand another's language, the "linguistic discord" (53: VIII, 168), that leads to these exceptions; in a deeper sense it is the "misconception of a principle" (53: VIII, 161) —which will in turn open a vista on the principles of the opponent's own philosophizing.

Kant's way to counter misunderstandings due to linguistic discord is to define his concepts. Such analyses were needed in almost all the retorts. In the reply to Forster he draws the lines between the concepts of race and variant and of natural description and natural history. In the reply to Constant he divides the indefinitely used concept of truth into its heterogeneous elements, *veritas* and *veracitas,* and the general phrase "do harm" into *nocere* (to cause harm by accident) and *laedere* (to cause it with malice). When he is writing about the debate on pantheism, his very title—"What does it mean to take one's bearings in thought?"—reflects the effort to clarify a term that invites misunderstanding.

To show how Kant proceeds in these analyses, we take up his clarification of the concepts of "happiness" and "mankind" in the second review of *Ideas.* We choose this Kantian reply to two exceptions of Herder's, taken in book 9 of *Ideas,* because they show directly that the elucidation of concepts itself corresponds to a philosophical concern.

The principle, Herder had written, which makes of man an animal that needs a master and owes its happiness to him, or to its connection with him, is easily grasped but evil;[310] Providence aims at the happiness of individuals, not at that of "large societies."[311] Kant differentiates between these two concepts of happiness. Herder, he says, speaks of a merely subjective felicity whose contents may change within epochs—within a lifetime, in fact—depending upon the dreams connected with it by the individual. Against this, Kant puts an intersubjective concept of happiness, one whose sole substance can be "a state constitution ordered in line with concepts of human right" (45: VIII, 64). What is worthwhile in the pursuit of those other shadow pictures is the felicity of conditions of existence; in the construction of this free order it is existence itself. Herder's objection would not apply to Kant if Herder did not place the individual happiness of beautiful conditions above the happiness of a mankind organized along lines of freedom and justice. That Herder was doing just that, of course, was very clear to Kant.

In the second passage replied to, Herder had objected to Kant's setting different goals for the individual and the species: to say that the human race has to be educated, not the individual human being, is to attribute to the general concept what one denies to the individual concepts.[312] Kant answers that this objection is misinterpreting the term "mankind." Herder posits the equation "man : mankind = horse : equine species." As the equine species contains only the sum of the characteristics common to horses, he thinks that mankind contains the sum of the characteristics common to men. But Kant, in his writings on the philosophy of history, has an entirely different conception of mankind. His concept designates not what is common to all men but "the entirety of a series of generations extending into the infinite (undefinable)" (45: VIII, 65). The series may be compared to an infinite line, and a mathematician might use the thought model of a hyperbola to explain that the possibility which Kant conceived—of this line's infinite approximation to the definition—was indeed conceivable. Philosophically, the result can be expressed as follows: The definition of mankind is infinite progress to a perfection given only in the idea, and not attainable except in the idea.

If all these analytical dissections are performed "with some finickiness," as Kant himself puts it, this is not in order to get out of quandary by means of hairsplittings and sophistries. What matters to Kant is that such differentiations may suddenly cast a new light upon the sciences, and upon thinking at large. They open doors to criteria of distinction, and thus to "many genuine fonts of cognition" (53: VIII, 162).

More profoundly than in the clarification of concepts, the phil-

osophical concern shows in the illumination of principles. To
demonstrate this, we choose the replies to Garve and Forster.

To illuminate the moral principles attacked by Garve, Kant
had to develop his explications *ab ovo,* as it were.

He began by saying that if he viewed morality as a science
that teaches how one might come to be worthy of happiness, he
was not for an instant calling for man to renounce "his natural
goal, happiness" (56: VIII, 278). All he asked was that men
should abstract from that happiness in their definition of duty.
And if in this context he liked to link duty with the thought of
sacrifice, this was only because the connection made morality
more clearly visible as a pure motivation. The world's ultimate
end, to him, was neither morality alone nor happiness alone; it
was their union. Yet this could only be effectuated globally by
God, so to speak; what the individual could achieve was not the
factual coincidence of morality and happiness in the world, only
the possibility of that coincidence in himself—and this was what
he, Kant, called "being worthy of happiness." He agreed with
Garve's objection that no man could ever say for sure that he
had been acting purely on grounds of duty. No one can look
into the human heart, not even into his own heart; and as for the
phenomenological understanding of human acts, the motives
behind any such act can be explored ad infinitum, and its totality
is not purely transparent. But this, said Kant, was not the issue
here; the issue was the moral purity the law requires. If Garve
maintained that he could not find this requirement inscribed in
his heart, Kant wished to defend him from such self-accusations.
The requirement could indeed be found in Garve's heart; it was
only concealed from Garve's customary method of psychological
speculation. And at this point, having clarified the principles,
Kant comes up against the hostile power—against that other center of philosophizing about which he told Garve that he could
not but "loudly and zealously contradict" (56: VIII, 286).

Forster's fear that a preconceived principle might do violence
to science is laid to rest by elucidating the principle of teleology.
The rule is that research without a guiding principle is a "merely
empirical groping in the dark. . . . Only the methodical acquisition of experience can be called observation" (53: VIII, 161). It is
true, of course, that ideas keep being carried into observation
itself, but this is a methodological lapse that cannot invalidate

the basic rule. Everything depends on knowing how to use principles. Principles are not imposed on nature by the intellect; they are merely inserted in nature for the purpose of observing it. They are hypotheses, not theses; means of orientation, not definitions of being; premises of our ability to see, not the things we see. They have a touch of the fictitious, but without the moment of randomness, and they have a touch of the necessary, but without the moment of objectivity. They are subjective means for the guidance of human understanding; means inserted in nature for the purpose of observing nature; means to make the phenomenality of nature, which is unintelligible in itself, appear so that man can understand it—in other words, means to make it appear as the product of an intellect.

The point Kant would like to make clear is fundamental: if a man knows how methodical thought may proceed in not knowing and how it may not proceed, his voice will not jeopardize the freedom of reason even where a mere observer is reduced to silence. Such a man's voice will restore thinking, rather, from the power of silence to the freedom of speech—thus dispelling Forster's real fears as well.

As the word itself says, misunderstandings are expressions of a failure to understand. But this failure may be due to utterly different causes. If it is caused by insufficient information, or by a failure of judgment, elucidation will remove the misunderstanding; but if its cause is an autochthonous, alien philosophizing, a philosophizing in which alien contents are involuntarily adopted or rejected in an original fashion, the clarification will exacerbate the sense of contrariety and point out the hostile cogitative power with which battle must be joined.

Debate as exposure of the hostile power. Herder's premises were uncovered by Kant in a "supplement" attached to the first review of *Ideas.*

In part 1, Herder had tried to outline man's position in the realm of nature, and the constancy and evolution of his soul in that realm. The purpose, ultimately, was to raise pure humanity to the rank of a schema of all evolutionary history, to show that in the infinite realm of Creation there is an animating, all-organizing force that leads earthly creatures to that humanity in ever higher stages, through all forms of creatureliness. The entire organization was conceived in analogy to observable natural formations of matter, and as carrying the individual's development beyond his death, in the direction of the final goal.

The secret impulses behind this undertaking were exposed by Kant in three places.

1. There is a sudden break in Herder's principle of analogy, for Herder conceives the individual's death as a mere "step of nature to still more refined operations" (45: VIII, 52) on one and the same individual. Elsewhere, Herder carries the analogy over different stages of organization, each embodied in a particular species. Analogously, he would have to take man for such a species; to conceive the road as capable of completion at all, he might, for example, presume higher stages of mankind in the inhabitants of other planets. Instead, it is for man alone that he extends the analogy to the individual and naïvely carries it beyond his death—and that is supposed to be natural observation, free from all metaphysics.

Kant rejects this claim. For, he says, in nature we find simply nothing to justify such a transcending of death. The palingenesis from the caterpillar to the butterfly occurs to the state of the larva, not to death. Nature teaches one thing only: Death is the extinction of the individual. To speak of an analogy despite this fact, Herder would have to show us certain animals which nature, after their death, resurrects from a state of putrefaction, in more perfect forms. This, however, is downright impossible. "There is thus not the slightest resemblance between the gradual elevation of the same human being to a more perfect organization in another life and the scale as which we may conceive wholly different species and individuals in a realm of nature" (45: VIII, 53). Herder's analogy is not posited in the spirit of a natural scientist. The fundament of his *Ideas* is a humanitarian faith permeated with Christian conceptions of a Beyond. It is metaphysics, all avowals to the contrary notwithstanding, and Kant's only further interest in it is whether it is critical metaphysics.

2. To clarify that question, he takes up another hypothesis: Herder's invisible realm of active and independent forces. Not without some acidity, he asks what is to be thought of this at all, with Herder trying only "to explain the incomprehensible by means of the still less comprehensible" (45: VIII, 53). Laws of nature can be observed, at least, even if in the end one does

not understand their causes. Herder's procedure is systematized despair at the difficulties of real cognition of nature; it is a substitute drawn from the "fertile field of poetic power. . . . This too is always metaphysics, even a most dogmatic metaphysics, however much our author may disavow it because it is not in fashion" (45: VIII, 54).

3. And, indeed, the typical characteristic of dogmatism, the confusion of the regulative with the constitutive, can be found in Herder's scale of organizations. The unity of organic force and evolutionary series, the affinity of evolutionary stages—and specification as well, by the way—these are guiding ideas of research. But Herder presents the great unity "from a single generating maternal womb" as a research result, a product of science. In the garb of natural description he engages in dogmatic speculative philosophy, causing "great havoc" (45: VIII, 54) in science itself. Always to know more than he can know, this is his dangerous achievement.

The hostile power in Herder is thus recognizable as a historical-theological dogmatism misunderstood and presented as scientific. If Kant stays relatively gentle in fighting it, this is because he considers it primarily a product not of mulishness but of the bursting abundance of genius that cannot adjust to cautious philosophizing. His advice to Herder is to use such caution, not to rush into a different philosophy.

In his paper on the controversy about pantheism, Kant looked for ways to orient a transcending reason, and he found one in interpreting the phrase "to take one's bearings in thought" initially as a need of reason. This interpretation took him at the same time to the two guidelines used by Jacobi and Mendelssohn: to the "sound" reason anchored in speculation, which Mendelssohn also called "common sense" or "plain human sense," without giving a closer definition of that faculty; and to an intuition guided by transcendence itself. In these he found the powers really inimical to his philosophizing.

Mendelssohn's sound reason as the final means of orientation is a weakened form of rational insight. By accepting it, one inescapably denies that the transcendent realm is a realm of not knowing. He has come to overestimate theoretical reason, has succumbed to the old romantic mania for reason.

Jacobi's rational intuition is another form of romanticism, not a cold and rationalistic one, however, but a romanticism that is a transcendent visitation, so to speak, and tends to eccentricity. Both are estranged from critical reason. And yet Kant can find a useful element in both. The rationalistic romanticist knows that nothing but reason may be the means of orientation, and thus the final authority, in the transcendent domain; the eccentric romanticist knows that nothing but faith can be the guideline in that domain. Kant, excluding the two romantic elements, takes the middle way and combines the two useful ones. His guideline is rational faith—a faith because it can rest only on subjective maxims for which one will never be able to cite objective reasons; and rational, because these maxims are only the consequence of that subjective ground which Kant calls "the need of reason." Grounded in this rational faith, aware of its lack of insight, reason dares to think freely. It posits the postulates because it chooses itself without overrating itself. It is on this basis alone that, in transcending, reason will lapse neither into anarchy nor into coercion.

The hostile powers in Mendelssohn and Jacobi are different forms of dogmatism, but equally dangerous to the freedom of thought.

Kant opposed Garve also for freedom's sake. For Garve, in the footnote in his *Essays,* was not content to criticize, but opposed another principle of action to Kant's ethics.

To Garve, as we have seen, happiness was the cover concept for a series of good conditions. Judgment decides what is good, comparing various conditions on the basis of material sensations. Garve's concept of goodness is thus an empirical concept. As such it can designate only what is more or less good, what is comparatively good. But the pure concept of morality would have to name that which is good pure and simple. Garve exalts his comparative goodness to absolute goodness and makes it the motive for obeying the law and at the same time the sole reliable point we can hold on to when directing our actions. This is the same as to say that nature and inclination can make laws for freedom, and thus to annul freedom. Garve's ethic destroys the fundament of all ethics. It is the basic perversion of eudaemonistic ethics, in a form that seems humane. Kant, therefore, coldly rebuffs what Garve has to say about the principle of ethics, calling it "a dogmatic assertion" (56: VIII, 281) that contents itself "with the accustomed principles of psychological explanation" (56: VIII, 285) and at the same time ventures, with those principles, to take on the Absolute. This empirical, psychologizing way of thinking, which seems so liberal and yet cannot help ending in reflections on the Absolute—reflections in which it unfailingly turns dogmatic—this is the hostile power behind Garve's philosophizing.

Herder's dogmatism, unreflected upon and waxed in an air of genius; Jacobi's intuitive romanticism and Mendelssohn's rationalistic one; Garve's psychologizing empiricism and Constant's unreliable political thinking[313]—these hostile powers meet with Kant's opposition. But he opposes them neither in cold scorn nor with a will to destroy. In amicable argumentation he bares the fundaments, reflects upon their possible consequences, and then, presupposing the opponent's righteousness, admonishes him to change his way of thinking.

Debate as a call for change. Veiled or unveiled admonitions to change in speculation can be found in most of the Kantian retorts.

The one to Garve is a warning that an ethic based on merely empirical-psychological foundations is lost in view of the necessity to act. Aware of Garve's cognitive weaknesses wherever he had to leave his beaten paths, Kant presented the warning in the visual form of a case model. He worked out an experiment, so to speak, for testing the capacity to act in line with his own and Garve's ethics.

A man of kind and charitable disposition, impoverished through no fault of his own, holds a deposit whose owner has died. The heirs, haughty and extremely wasteful people, do not know of it and will probably never know. If he keeps the deposit, the good man and his family will be saved from privation; if he returns it, the money will be as senselessly sunk in an already vast fortune as if it were dropped into the sea. What to do? Kant has the two ethicists reflect. The Kantian is finished in no time: he returns the deposit on the single ground that it would not be right to keep it. The Garvean one has heavy going. Returning the deposit goes against his own happiness; if he does, he may perish miserably—he'd better keep it. But the fact might come out after all, and then his reputation for honesty would be ruined —he'd better return it. But this money in the hands of violent people would be a threat to mankind, so he'd better not return it. But he would have no chance to use it, for everyone would ask where it has suddenly come from; from the point of view of happiness it would be a senseless investment. So, better give it back after all . . .

There is no necessary end to this interplay of reflections. We hear the warning clearly: the eudaemonist will get lost on his course of considering endless circumstances. If all he knows is that things can always turn out differently from the way he happens to think at the moment, he will scarcely be able to make up his mind to act. The more conscientious he is, the longer the time for which in the jungle of reasons he will do—nothing. It is precisely the empirical ethic that fails the test of experience.

The warning to Herder is couched in the friendly tone of the former teacher, and the chances are that Kant had given it to his student before, in occasional conversations. In any case, we already find it in the letter of 1768,[314] then in the first review, in a more exact phrasing, and finally, in shrouded language, in the second: "Devoutly to be wished, however, is that in continuing his work, when he will find solid ground ahead, our brilliant author will place some restraints upon his lively genius; and that philosophy—the practice of which consists more in pruning than in bearing luxuriant shoots—may guide him to the consummation of his enterprise by distinct concepts rather than by hints, by laws observed rather than surmised, by broadly drafting but cautiously exercised reason rather than by winged imagination, be its wings derived from metaphysics or from emotions" (45: VIII, 55).

Thought, not poesy; concepts, not hints and metaphors; explanations, not synonyms; truths, not allegories; laws, not surmises; cautious reason, not extravagant emotion and imagination; observation, not metaphysics—this is the warning. What it asks of Herder is no less than that he quit his previous, genius-style philosophizing and submit to the discipline of an academic procedure aimed at insights rather than brilliant notions. In a certain sense the warning summoned him back to the classroom, to begin all over.

More urgent in tone was the admonition Kant addressed to his learned contemporaries who were embroiled in the battle over pantheism. Whether siding with Jacobi or with Mendelssohn, these men professed a dogmatic type of thinking, a thinking which unhesitantly passed the bounds of insight; what they were in danger of gambling away, in Kant's view, was the very freedom of thought. For him, the note he struck this time was quite unusual. It was the tone of a political manifesto: "Men of intellectual capacity and broadened mentality! I revere your talents and love your human feelings. But did you give careful thought to what you are doing, and where your attacks upon reason will lead? Beyond doubt, you want the freedom of thought kept from harm; for without that freedom even your own free flights of genius would quickly come to an end" (51: VIII, 144).

The consequence of either form of dogmatism would be loss of the freedom to think, followed by the rule of unreason. Kant therefore ends his treatise with a second, still more insistent warning to place the one judge, reason, above all faith, all arguments, all opinions: "Friends of the human race, and of that which is most sacred to that race! Accept what seems most credible to you after careful and sincere examination, be it facts, be it rational grounds—only, do not deny to reason what makes it the highest good on earth: the privilege of being the ultimate touchstone of truth" (51: VIII, 146).

If we compare our analyses of Kant's debates with those of his exclusionary polemics, the first fact we note is quite surprising. The opponents, each time, are dogmatics, but they are treated in totally different fashion—in one case as morally reprehensible ignoramuses who must be silenced; in the other, as venerable contestants who can be talked with. It comes as a surprise because the theoretical fundament of philosophizing would justify an exclusionary polemic in both cases. Evidently dogmatism as such is not enough to decide the form of a polemic. The reason why it is not enough can be stated: dogmatism is the "natural" philosophy from which a thinker ought to depart as he changes his way of thinking, and from which a man of insight will depart. This is why the dogmatic who really wants insight can be met as a like-minded person. It is not until he subordinates that quest to something else and that other thing renders him inaccessible to arguments—in other words, not until he becomes cognitively dishonest—that he will be unworthy of philosophical opposition.

Dispute

Finally, we have to mention three of Kant's writings in which yet another form of polemics predominates: *On the Volcanoes in the Moon* (46), an essay printed in 1785; *On the Moon's Influence upon the Weather* (57), which appeared in 1794; and *Settlement of a Mathematical Dispute Based upon a Misunderstanding* (61), a reply to a newspaper article published in 1796. The first protested against an overgeneralizing interpretation of the crater phenomena in the moon by contemporary astronomers; the second tried to clarify a fact which Lichtenberg had expressed in a paradox: "The moon ought not to influence the weather, but it does influence it" (57: VIII, 317); the third removed a seeming dispute between Kant and the younger Reimarus about the rational relations of the sides of a right-angled triangle.

The titles and topics alone justify the assumption that the form of controversy in these writings is the dispute. For our purpose, only the third will be analyzed in detail.

In his essay against Schlosser, *On a Newly Introduced Gentility of Tone in Philosophy*, Kant had referred among other things to a form of romanticism already prevalent in antiquity, principally in Pythagoras and Plato: the predilection for philosophizing about mathematical problems. One might, for example, ask with a certain wonderment: "What causes the rational relation of the three sides of a right-angled triangle to be none other than of the numbers 3, 4, 5?" (60: VIII, 393). A man who began to philosophize about this might think he was encountering a mystery, whereas genuine philosophers come to see only that they have to leave this field to the mathematicians, who find problems and solutions but are not looking for mysteries. The philosopher ought to keep the old warning in mind: *"Quaerit delirus, quod non respondet Homerus"* (60: VIII, 393)—Here a romanticist seeks what is beyond answering.

Three months later, the *Berliner Monatsschrift* carried a retort by Johann Albrecht Heinrich Reimarus, professor of natural history in Hamburg, under the title "On the Rational Relations of the Three Sides of a Right-angled Triangle."[315] Reimarus denied Kant's statement that there is but one rational relation of the three sides of such a triangle and demonstrated that, on the contrary, there are indefinitely many such relations. Only two months after that, Kant inserted a brief letter of response[316] in the same journal, under the aforementioned title *Settlement of a Mathematical Dispute Based upon a Misunderstanding*.

He began by saying that it seemed as if Reimarus and he were involved in a mathematical controversy, but this appearance was due to unclear language. It could be shown that—as he put it in a draft of his letter—"both can be right" (109: XXIII, 203).

What Reimarus wanted to say was that in "the infinite multitude of all possible numbers" (61: VIII, 409) the rational relation recurs indefinitely many times. But what he, Kant, had meant to say was that in "the series of numbers which in the natural order follow immediately upon each other" (109: XXIII, 202) the rational relation is found only in the numbers 3, 4, 5. There were strict proofs of both statements, and neither Reimarus nor Kant had invented one or the other.

The one remaining question was thus, "Who bore the guilt of this misunderstanding?" (61: VIII, 410). Had his essay dealt with a mathematical problem, the culprit would presumably be Kant, since he would have endowed a proposition with a generality to which it was not entitled. He had, however, offered only an instance of the mischief wrought in mathematics by the Pythagorean mysticists, and he could therefore expect that his exposition would be taken in the sense "in which a mysticist could see himself finding something strange and esthetically remarkable in the qualities of numbers" (61: VIII, 410). The proposition which Reimarus had exerted himself to prove had not been doubted by anyone as yet. Kant hoped that he would not be given the blame.

It was a rather curious way to solve the guilt question, and another solution—more correct, it seems to us—can be found in the drafts of the letter: Both men are guilty, Kant says, since neither one added the necessary qualifying clause to his proposition. Nevertheless, the guilt "weighed mostly on the latter" (109: XXIII, 204)—meaning Kant himself—for he alone would have been obliged to state the restriction.

In the matter as such we can find no reason why Kant's public statement turned this admission into an attribution of guilt.

What are the particular characteristics of this materially insignificant dispute?

a. The dispute is finite. In his letter, Kant says of the facticity of scientific debate that "in general, the like of it is almost unheard of" (61: VIII, 409), and in the drafts he calls it a "scandal" (109: XXIII, 202). The fact of debate in a scandal wherever the controversy might be settled cogently by arguments—that is to say, in the sciences—but in mathematics this scandal is unheard of because the objects of mathematical concepts are a priori given in visuality, and their contents, therefore, cannot remain ambiguous. Hence Kant's formula: "In pure mathematics there can probably be no debate proper on grounds of misunderstanding . . ." (109: XXIII, 201). In other sciences, controversy cannot always be avoided, but it can be cogently resolved. Since a dispute is the process of this resolution, its first essential characteristic is to be finite. The brevity and succinctness of Kant's *Settlement* is the expression of this finite character.

b. The medium of resolution is the factual argument. We can observe this in enlargement, as it were, in the structure of Kant's letter. In the exposition he compares the problematics of the two conflicting statements, establishes their contradictoriness, and calls for it to be resolved. In the resolution, he opposes the two statements to each other once again, but now with the limiting conditions attached. With exclusiveness removed from their interrelation, contradictoriness falls by the wayside; the cause of the misunderstanding has been cleared up. The procedure is the following: argument—counterargument—establishment of the contradiction; purified argument—purified counterargument —resolution and judgment.

The same, in principle, is the structure of *On the Moon's Influence upon the Weather*. Lichtenberg's paradoxical sentence is divided into its two contradictory wings, which relate to each other like thesis and antithesis. Kant posits the thesis, states the reasons for it, and defends it. He then confronts it with the antithesis and states the reasons for that. The resolution follows; it is the "settlement of this contradiction" (57: VIII, 322).

In each case there are three steps: argument—counterargument —judgment. It seems to be the old scholastic procedure that bore its most effective fruit in the *Summa Theologiae* of Aquinas: reasons pro—reasons contra—*respondeo*. Kant's answer, however, is always a "settlement," a compromise, never the mere acceptance and subsequent vindication of one of the two propositions. Peculiar to the compromise is a moment of mediation, of exalting both individual positions into a third in which they are absorbed without losing their own substance. From a technique of the Scholastics Kant leads the way to the three dialectical steps of Hegel.

c. The atmosphere of a dispute is impersonal. Persons are named and involved only insofar as they represent an issue; at stake is the issue alone.

From this point of view we can say of the ending of *Settlement* that it is not so much a discussion of the guilt question—although Kant says it is—as an inquiry into the factual cause of the misunderstanding. For the issue, the point is not who bears the guilt but what has caused it.

The reason why we regard the dispute as noteworthy at all does not lie in these minor writings, which have now become materially irrelevant; it lies in Kant's claim that the new metaphysics is science pure and simple. Because of this claim, elements of dispute will be found in all the altercations about transcendental philosophy. In fact, in debate as well as in the polemical use of reason, passages showing all the characteristics of a dispute recur again and again.

One may, perhaps, go so far as to say that in all of Kant's attempts to solve specific problems the mode of controversy he was really striving and calling for was the dispute. Even when striking hard in exclusionary combat, he would leave a way open for getting together again in reflection upon the issue. Up to this point we have been submitting debate and the polemical use of reason to typological analysis and examining the respective writings solely for those typical characteristics; but the pure types must now be broken up again from the standpoint of the dispute. The tract against Eberhard, for instance, is not exhausted by the characteristics we have analyzed, and the large remainder contains problem treatments that are impersonal and fruitful in themselves and have made *On a Discovery* a treatise of importance to the understanding of *Critique of Pure Reason*. Our analysis has disregarded this impersonal side because we consider it a characteristic not of exclusionary polemics but of dispute. Characteristics of dispute will be found in all of Kant's major polemical writings.

In conclusion, we have to return to the larger context of this book and to end our analyses with a question: What is the significance, if any, of all that we have set forth, for a future interpretation of politics? Let us suggest three points.

1. Kant proceeded against his contemporaries with political prudence. He always believed, of course, that the superiority of critical philosophy would make it prevail in the long run; but not for one moment did he delude himself that time alone would hand this victory to his generation, regardless of the efforts of philosophizing individuals. They had to gain the victory by fighting for it, with chivalry, factuality, or ruthlessness, depending upon the opponent. The size of the opposition made this impossible without political prudence. Kant employed prudence up to the limit of guile; that he ever took the step to untruthfulness cannot be clearly proved. He never lost sight of a sober appraisal of reality, but neither did he ever forget the demands of practical reason.

2. This procedure accords with Kant's political conduct. What little evidence we have of this—above all, that controversial evidence he himself gave in *The Debate of Departments*—shows the same characteristics of prudence. There, too, he goes up to the limit of guile, and where freedom is threatened he permits himself the actual use of guile; but he publicly admits it later and leaves his conduct to be judged.

3. Kant's polemical conduct corresponds to the guidelines he established for *Realpolitik*. These can be summed up in the verse "Be ye therefore wise as serpents, and harmless as doves," and the correspondence is traceable all the way down to the details.

Kant demanded that any war be waged so that its practices would not exclude the possibility of future peace. In polemics he fought all practices based upon malice, which exclude factual discussion.

With his principle of publicity, Kant moved political action from the cabinet rooms into the public forum. In polemics he would drag his opponent into the open and seek refuge there for himself.

It seemed to Kant that the neighborhood of a state with a nonrepublican form of government might make war unavoidable. In dealing with his contemporaries he found himself forced to fight again and again, despite his frequently manifested aversion to polemics.

It does seem that in looking at Kant the polemicist we get to know Kant the politician.

7. THE IMPORTANCE OF POLEMICS TO KANT'S WORK

We have now discussed Kant's fragmentary drafts of theories of polemics and his factual polemics against contemporaries in the 1780s and 1790s. What remains to be done, as far as possible, is to determine the place of polemics in his creative activity, and to outline what polemicizing meant to that activity. We shall inquire, first, into the role of polemics in his lectures, shall cast a glance on his polemical relations to the great philosophers, shall view the polemics against his contemporaries in a larger context, shall point out his polemics against himself, and shall attempt, then, to use all of this to assess the significance that polemics had for his work.

The Role of Polemics in Kant's Lectures

Kant began his lecturing activities in the winter term of 1755–56 and presumably ended them in the summer term of 1796. In these eighty-two semesters he was lecturing up to thirty-four hours a week, and never less than eight hours. As an assistant professor he averaged twenty hours a week; as a professor, fourteen hours until 1789, nine hours thereafter. He lectured on logic, metaphysics, ethics, anthropology, physical geography, pedagogics, natural law, philosophical encyclopedia, natural theology, theoretical physics, mechanical sciences, mathematics, mineralogy, and in his younger years perhaps on fortification and pyrotechnics also. Some of these lectures were repeated more than thirty times, the one on physical geography almost fifty times. The total number of lectures given (including *repetitoria*) may approach twenty-five thousand. Something he said as a young man was probably true of his entire lecturing career: "I for my part am daily facing the anvil of my lectern, wielding the heavy hammer of lectures indistinguishable from each other, keeping identical time."[1]

In one class, often repeated, he also lectured on polemics. Georg Friedrich Meier's *Excerpt from the Doctrine of Reason*,[2] a book Kant used as a compendium for his lectures on logic, contains a brief methodology of "learned controversy."

To get a picture of this lecture, we take a look at the model itself, then at the marginal notes Kant made in it, and finally at the lecture notes taken by his students, some of which are now available in print.

"A learned controversy," say Meier, "consists of the rebuttal and defense of an opinion."[3] Against the thesis set forth by the defender, the attacker advances an "antithesis." The debate cannot begin until the issue has been clearly drawn; otherwise it will be a mere "battle of words" *(Logomachia)*. This does not mean a *"controversia philologica,"* in which a word becomes the issue; it means a debate in which the difference does not lie in the issue any more, only in words.[4]

Meier outlines the methods of attack and defense. Flaws will be sought in the proof offered by one's opponent, to refute at least the way of thinking he followed in building his case, if not the case itself. It will be demonstrated either that the disputed thesis is false or that the antithesis is true. It will be shown— either purely systematically or by pointing out exceptions ("instances")—that the thesis does not deserve the universality claimed for it. The claim that has been made will be turned back upon its defender when he is shown that the consequences of his thesis speak against him ("retorsion"). Finally, it will be demonstrated to the opponent that the consequences of his error are harmful, ridiculous, and dangerous. The purpose of this exposure, this discovery of "his unintelligence and wickedness of heart,"[5] is cognition alone; if it serves ends of defamation, it will deteriorate into "consequence making," which is "abhorrent to all honest men."[6] To all these means of attack there are antidotes composed, in principle, of the same elements.

Meier himself does not want these methods to decay into mere techniques. He makes them subject to two restrictions: (1) they must be used for the sake of insight, and (2) they are limited by the duty a man owes to his opponent. Hence the theoretical as well as a practical foundation of all polemics. From this foundation spring Meier's last words of advice: not to make a profession of refuting others; not to argue about trivia; better not to respond to senseless attacks (refusal); but to fight back "with consummate thoroughness"[7] wherever it is worthwhile.

In *Reflections,* the section on logic contains some marginal notes which either deal with the point of polemics in principle, specify particular arrangements, or cite examples of disputed cases. The point of polemics is said to lie in accord (79: XVI, 847; 3458). Polemics has two sources: the will to truth, and the will to victory (79: XVI, 857; 3473). Polemics is a method of instruction (79: XVI, 839; 3442). The distinction between κατ' ἄνθρωπον and κατ' ἀλήθειαν that plays so large a role in critical philosophy makes its first appearance (79: XVI, 850; 3464). Most of the reflections that give examples have (like the rest) an anti-nomical structure: "The author teaches a lesson pro and contra" (79: XVI, 848; 3460). "When learning is said to better the will, wicked scholars provide counterevidence" (79: XVI, 852; 3469).

The lecture notes of Blomberg, Philippi, Pölitz, and Dohna-Wundlacken show that Kant incorporated his reflections in his lectures, that indeed they held a major place in each one. Kant used to stick to the structure of the model. The lecture's main weight seems always to have been placed upon the explication of technical terms; yet general remarks kept interrupting. "Our task is to convince, not to persuade" (119: XXIV, 601). "It would be best to abolish all altercations and, if two were in disagreement, jointly to endeavor to eliminate all misunderstandings and to find the truth" (119: XXIV, 602). "In fact, all arguments ought to be *argumenta* κατ' ἀλήθειαν, which I base upon something I really hold to be true" (119: XXIV, 602).

There is not much more to be gathered from the lecture notes. In *Manual of Logic,*[8] which Jaesche published in 1800, the remarks of learned controversy are not included—probably because Kant was of the opinion that as a matter of principle they did not belong to logic (cf. 119: XXIV, 601). But that he did take a great deal from Meier is evident from what we know of the factual polemics. Various combat methods (retorsion, restriction, prohibition, distinction, baring the consequences, attacking the proof, exposing unintelligence and wickedness) can be found there, as well as the twofold fundament of all polemics.

Meier claimed that learned controversies "have their uses."[9]

He did not further explain this contention, but Kant built part
of his instruction on it. He not only lectured on polemics; he
held polemical seminars. In the schedule of lectures for the summer term of 1758 we read: "In a class on Wednesdays and Satur-
days the theses discussed in the days previous will be considered
polemically, which in my view is one of the most perfect means to
arrive at thoroughgoing insights" (13: II, 25). Kant gave this sort
of polemical class—called *disputatorium*—several times until
well into the 1780s. What happened in them must remain conjec-
ture; but there, too, Meier may have shown the way in some
paragraphs which his *Excerpt* devotes to the dispute.[10]

A formal dispute, he wrote, is an oral controversy between
two present parties. The "opponent" attacks the thesis of the
"respondent" with an "antithesis," which he is required to prove.
The respondent has an assistant called "praeses," who may conduct the argumentation for him. In the controversy, both parties
observe the rules and proceed by the methods of scholarly debate.

In his lectures Kant evidently spoke only briefly of this. The
opponent, according to the notes of Dohna-Wundlacken, uses
arguments to reach a conclusion which "directly contradicts the
respondent's thesis" (121: XXIV, 783). Kant then made a characteristic change in the role of the praeses: "As the respondent's
assistant, the praeses seeks to compromise the issue" (121: XXIV,
783). Yet as a compromiser he must assume the thinking posture
of one standing above both parties; as far as his function in the
discussion is concerned, he must—as the notes of Pölitz say of
the teacher in general—"consider himself in the middle" (119:
XXIV, 601–2). According to the notes of Philippi and Blomberg,
"disputing might be very useful if it were not a *certamen personarum,* and if truth were pursued by way of agreement rather
than of debate."[11] As long as it remains this *certamen personarum,*
however, disputation will make sense as an *"exercitium Scholas-
ticum,"* at least (118: XXIV, 490).

This scant material makes two things apparent: (1) Disputation
as such has an antinomical structure. We may assume, therefore,
that the polemical discussions in the *disputatorium* were anti-
nomically structured also. (2) The debate is supposed to have
an end. The settlement is accomplished by the praeses, presumably acting as the representative, as it were, of impartial reason.

Beyond that, it is not clearly evident whether in those seminars

Kant was, so to speak, playing both parties and the praeses, or whether the two antithetical roles—or even all three, perhaps —were assigned to students. A line of Borowski's, about Kant's "disputing exercises with his students,"[12] permits us to infer that the students took an active part.

What was the point of these exercises? Kant himself stated it: polemics is the most perfect means to arrive at thoroughgoing insights. It is a method of seeking truth, not a mere technique of production. That too would be conceivable, after all; Herder, for one, made methodical use of polemics in this function, producing antithetical theses against the background of his vast knowledge. Another example in which we can study the procedure is Nietzsche's revaluation of all values; but next to Kant's employment of polemics as a method, Nietzsche's seems like a mirror image of the progress of a dogmatism living by negation. Part of the Kantian method was to have thesis and antithesis present at all times, to give reasons for both, and to judge them rationally. This presupposes a thought posture of refusing to sign up with either side. Herder and Nietzsche, on the other hand, invariably appear as adversaries. They are opponents, while Kant is the praeses whose achievement of a compromise places him above opponent and respondent.

These two summary compilations of references to scholarly debate and to the *disputatorium* cannot give us an exhaustive picture of the role of polemicizing in Kant's lectures, not even a picture of its essential function. That function shows only in the intent of all the lectures, and in the manner of their presentation.

According to Kant, any teacher at a university is expected "to cultivate in his listener first the intelligent man, then the rational man, and finally the scholar" (23: II, 305). The listener will be intelligent and rational once he knows how to make his own use of his intellect and of his reason. Enlightenment must free him from tutelage in their use. This precisely is what the instructor ought to teach him, insofar as it can be taught at all. In the course of instruction he must not serve as the student's support, only as his guide in the use of intellect and reason. To make a scholar out of the student, however, the instructor must make him capable of independent movement in the field of learned matters. There, everything depends upon how we define the object of scholarship in the field of philosophy, and how we define a

philosophical scholar. To Kant, the object is thinking itself, philosophizing—not the various thoughts, nor any distinct philosophy—and the scholar is solely a philosopher, not a philosophy
professor in today's sense. The point, therefore, cannot be to
teach students a distinct philosophy and definite ideas so that
they will be turned into *cognoscenti*; the point can be only to
teach them how to think and to philosophize so that, as far as
possible, they will become philosophers. We have an inescapable
criterion for telling whether a man is a philosopher: he must be
able to philosophize. Hence, to become a philosopher, he must
learn to philosophize. "But philosophizing can only be learned
by practice and the use of one's own reason" (67: IX, 25), and
philosophy cannot be learned at all: "How should philosophy be
learnable? Every philosophical thinker builds his own work, so
to speak, on another's ruins; yet none of these works has ever
been wrought so as to endure in all its parts. If for no other
reason, philosophy cannot be learned because it is not yet given.
And even supposing a philosophy were really extant: no man
who had learned it would be able to call himself a philosopher,
for his knowledge would always remain subjective and historical"
(67: IX, 25).

When it has thus become clear that we ought to learn philosophizing rather than philosophy, thinking rather than thoughts,
we have still to ask how we might learn to philosophize. There
an additional difficulty appears. No classic form of philosophizing
can be found anywhere—none that would enable us to take its
established method for our model pure and simple. We must
dare to train ourselves in the use of reason, and if we do this
against a background of thoughts from past history, those
thoughts are merely pieces of material on which our reason trains
itself. He who "would learn to philosophize may . . . view all
systems of philosophy only as the *history of the use of reason*
and as objects for exercising his philosophical gifts" (67: IX, 26).
To put it in a nutshell: learning to philosophize presupposes a
total lack of respect for past thinking. There is no classic author;
there is no classic philosophy; there is no classic method of philosophizing. All things must be tested afresh, and our reason must
dare judge them all. The text we take up is not a primal image
but a stimulating "occasion to make our own judgment about it,
and indeed against it" (23: II, 307).

Meticulous rethinking of the thoughts contained in a text is the premise of this free association. In learning to think, Kant chiefly pays attention to the method of both the thinker and the man he is thinking about, not to the contents to which the method brings them. We analyze the method of the man we think about, because someone else's procedure will let us learn to philosophize. The method of this analysis—that is, our own, the thinker's method—is "one of testing rather than deciding" (3: I, 213). "The peculiar method of instruction in worldly wisdom is zetetic, as some called it in Antiquity (from ζητεῖν), i.e. exploring" (23: II, 307). This method of, not teaching, but always only learning and liberating from mistaken thoughts and from mistakes in thinking —this is what Kant in his lectures called the "polemical" method.[13] It is by means of this method that one will learn to philosophize. No matter how he may have polemicized in spots, the intent of Kant's lectures made his method of presenting them polemical for so long as he could not dogmatically teach a philosophy conclusive in itself. Since that point was never reached, we can say of Kant's lectures that they were polemical in principle.[14]

That they could not be anything else is confirmed by reflecting upon the form of their presentation. In all his lectures with the exception of physical geography, Kant went by a compendium. The reason probably was twofold: first, the use of compendia conformed to the General Regulations issued by the Ministry of Education; second—and this seems more important to us—Kant saw in the closed system of a compendium a polemical means to counter his own teaching method. The point of the polemical method was to raise radical doubts about all traditional methods and contents; the danger it involved was that doubt might come to be a dogma. In order to raise doubt but at the same time to counteract it, Kant confronted the doubt with well-built academic concept systems: "Polemically, then, metaphysical concepts serve against dogmatic doubt, to keep its objections within bounds" (81: XVIII, 97; 5119).

For use in his classes he preferred compendia by Wolff, Baumgarten, Baumeister, Meier, Achenwall, Eberhard, Feder, and others. He never lectured on the basis of his own books: the ones he used were always more in conflict than in accord with his own thinking. From several sources, however, we know that Kant's procedure was not really to read from these compendia, but to use their structures and materials as a basis for reflecting extemporaneously upon their methods and contents. In the early years his way of doing this may have been to put the author on a new track "by a slight twist" (23: II, 308); later it was more and more to complement, criticize, and rebut the author, or simply to talk about things that were not in the compendium at all. In time, his own thought would infiltrate the models and blend into a philosophizing that was en route from academicism to Criticism. Kant himself described this process: as a young man, he said, he had already been "not merely commenting but sifting and weighing" his models, "trying to reduce them to principles which seemed better to me" (70: XIII, 538). His own ideas had been "flowing into my listeners' copybooks in fragments, little by little; what was kept in view on my part was a system I carried in my head" (70: XII, 361).

Today the manner of this penetration cannot yet be demonstrated in detail. It will take access to notes from many more semesters to make this process of decades perceptible in vague outline, by comparison with the many marginal notes that have been preserved. The theories of a radical critical upheaval in Kant's philosophizing will presumably yield, then, to a fragmentary insight into the organic evolution of his thought. In part, his *Reflections* allow us to assess this evolution even now. We need only mention the *"creatio mundi,"* a concept central to the doctrine of antinomies and thus to the genesis of critical philosophy; thanks to their dating by Adickes, the diverse explications of that concept in the lectures enable us to observe how, starting out from academicism, Kant's thinking gradually came to be critical thinking.[15] The point of departure in the process was always a model from which Kant detached himself in constant struggle. The number of specifically polemical phrasings that got into the lectures does not matter; the mere fact of divergence, of his own thoughts moving away from the model, means that the lectures could be nothing but polemical in nature. Insofar as his own thinking grew in these polemics, they played a system-building role as well.

In this triple function—exposure of errors in particular thoughts and in the method of thinking, medium of the search for truth, medium of the formation of a system—the polemical teaching method may have put its stamp upon Kant's lectures in the following ways.

Polemicizing was the cathartic that turned the lectures into investigations, above all, of flaws in the method. The thinking posture was that no one knows what is philosophically right, that everything can be wrong. What is wrong becomes determinable when we can show it to be due to some tangible mistake in the method. By way of this demonstration we train ourselves in the methods of philosophizing. We learn to philosophize.

As a medium of the search for truth, polemicizing turned the lectures into hours of "research" in new methods, and in the contents arising from those methods. There the basic frame of mind was that it must be possible to find out what is philosophically right—not, however, by preferring specific contents, but by experimenting, as it were, with the antithetical procedure that regenerates the contents as products of a purified method.

As a medium of system formation, polemicizing turned Kant's lectures into hours in which the gains of the past were synthesized in the direction of an entirety that was never shown but was envisioned as an idea. The lectures came to be the genesis of the new system. The basic posture was that the real philosophical evidence of the truth of thoughts lies in their fitness for a system. Philosophizing is the path of thinking in the direction of that entirety.

It was thus in three respects that polemics became a constitutive element of Kant's lectures. Failing to see this, we shall be hard put to understand how much cogitative intensity underlies the notes, which often sound rather cozy, and it will be difficult to comprehend how the students could be so fascinated by their teacher's presentation. Their notes are the static remnants of a process in which philosophizing was always present, and always en route to a philosophy; but the classes were the process itself. Although no student, and not even the teacher, can have surveyed the whole process, those who were thinking with him did feel involved; in thinking, they had an experience of the way philosophy comes into being, and so they came to philosophize with Kant. The pattern of the process was the pattern of infinite becoming—the never-ending struggle for a perfection that does not lie in time.

Kant's Polemical Dealings with
Great Philosophers

In dealing with the great philosophers, the young Kant was
guided by the idea that no thinker yet had left the enduring philosophy behind; the old Kant, by the conviction that he himself
had laid the foundation, at least, and the principles of that
philosophy. Both of these premises brought a polemical element
into the relationship—the first, because its consequence was the
necessity to rethink everything that had been thought before;
the second, because it amounted to the intentional conception
of past thought as erroneous in view of what had to be thought
from here on out, or to a distinct claim which meant the unintentional rejection of all previous philosophy.

Knowing that philosophy as a science had not yet been discovered freed Kant from dependence on any of the great thinkers
of the past. All of them were subject to examination and to a
reappraisal of their utility. They were the background source of
stimuli for a thinking that was independent, not obliged to anyone; they were the material available for the expansion and illustration of that thinking. No antiquarian or philological research
about those men could be of significance, nothing but a new,
ever-productive reflection upon their philosophemes to the end
of doing one's own thinking. The point was not to put the great
substance of past thinkers on display again; the present time was
called upon to do some radically new thinking. Wherever the
fame of great men impaired a man's freedom to think for himself,
that fame had to be fought for the sake of insight. Unreasonably
venerated greatness comes to be a detriment to mankind, and
any veneration that paralyzes free thought and the public use of
reason is unreasonable.[16] Since the truly great philosophers desired this freedom above all, the only way to deal with them that
fits their spirit is the polemical way.

The basic polemical trait that had thus been injected into the
relationship was brought to twofold development by Kant's claim
to have personally laid the lasting foundation. In consequence of
this claim, the great philosophers were conceived either as great
men gone astray or as great trailblazers for Kant. In the first case
their thought remained instructive only as error; in the second,

it was significant as a sign of things to come. With this double meaning all reverence could recoil into condemnation, and all condemnation, into reverence. The ambivalence in relation to the great thinkers is demonstrable throughout. Plato had linked his concept of the ideas with the notion of an intellectual visuality, a notion Kant found romantic; but Plato did deserve credit for having helped Kant (presumably via Cicero[17]) to the concept of the ideal (30: A 568f./B 596–97). Aristotle had drawn up his categories without a principle, in merely "rhapsodistic" fashion (30: A 81/B 106); even so, he had shown their necessity and had simultaneously provided an instructive example of how *not* to find categories. The consistent eudaemonism of Epicurus was the radical perversion of the principles of practical philosophy, but at the same time it was Epicurus' way of helping to bring forth the pure concept of morality. Descartes, while never overcoming his skeptical idealism, had thereby pointed the way to critical idealism, as a step yet to be taken. Leibniz, followed by his entire school, had falsified the concept of sensibility; but the philosophemes arising from his falsification had contributed to the revision of the concept. And the great reversal in the way of thinking had been brought about by the errors as much as by the discoveries of Locke, Berkeley, and, above all, Hume.

In all these relations, veneration and polemics were close neighbors, and they remained neighbors wherever Kant could look upon the earlier thinking as a portent of the new. It was only where he lost that view, where he felt he was no longer seeing anything but error—as in Spinoza, for example, or in the Scholastics—that he grew excessively unjust and at times, it may seem, even ignorant in his rejection.

Side by side with this intentional partial polemics against the great philosophers goes the unintentional total polemics arising from Kant's philosophical claim. "It sounds arrogant, selfish, and to the ears of those who have not yet renounced their old system it may sound belittling, to claim that before the rise of critical philosophy there had been no philosophy at all. Whether or not this seeming presumptuousness is censurable depends upon the question *whether there might be more than one philosophy.* Various ways of philosophizing and going back to first principles of reason, so as to found a more or less successful system upon these principles—there have not only been such attempts, but there could not help being many of them, each deserving well by our present one. Yet as in an objective view there can be but One human reason, there cannot be many philosophies either; i.e., not more than One true system of philosophy resting on principles is possible, no matter how diverse and often contradictory the ways men may have philosophized about one and the same proposition" (37: VI, 206–7).

On grounds of these objectifying premises—almost literally encountered again in the young Hegel[18]—the new philosophy must, to be consistent, bid all the old ones farewell. "If one announces a system of philosophy as his own product, this is as much as to say that before this philosophy there had not been any other. For if one were to concede that there had been a different (and true) one, there would have been two kinds of true philosophy on the same topic, which is self-contradictory. When critical philosophy is therefore announced as one previous to which there has been no philosophy anywhere at all, this is nothing other than what has been done, will be done, and indeed must be done by all those who design a philosophy according to plans of their own" (37: VI, 207).

A man who makes this claim, in such plain language, is condemning the entire history of philosophy as if it had become obsolete at one stroke. From the tacit polemicizing of these lines it is but a step to the total, explicit rejection of past thinking. All philosophies are then "essentially indistinguishable save for the critical one" (89: XX, 335). They are the "excrescences . . . of the mere confluence of accumulated concepts" (30: A 835/B 863). Whether or not the claim is followed by such judgments does not matter; its definite form makes it polemical to the point of total rejection.

What interests us here is not the question whether one would wish Kant to have had a different relation to the great tradition; our sole concern is to show that this relation was polemical at all times. The whole history of metaphysics—which Kant considered the intrinsic history of philosophy—was a battleground. Kant's retrospective entrance into it was not made to describe fights that had been; what he meant to do, armed with new weapons, was to join the battle royal. In combat, however, the great thinkers came to stimulate his construction of the ever-unfinished system. Polemics thus became the midwife at the birth of his works, of which we can say what Lessing once said of his *Nathan der Weise:* they are children of the onset of old age, delivered by polemics.[19]

There are a few names from history, nonetheless, which put a stop to almost all of Kant's polemicizing. Jesus is the model human being who most purely fulfilled the demands of practical reason. Newton is the great scientist who dared—though even he not every time—to think of the universe as evolved solely in line with laws of physics. But where is *the* great philosopher? Is it Socrates? He must be admired for his genuine love of wisdom, for his ability to ask questions, and for his turn to practical philosophy, accomplished by knowing that he did not know (cf. 67: IX, 29). And yet he seems to lack the extensive material knowledge without which he was bound to remain a barbarian.

Is it Hume? His incorruptible mind is exemplary; and yet he stopped at the halfway mark of reason.

Is it Leibniz? He was the encyclopedic scholar, with all the material equipment for turning into a great thinker; and yet his intellect did not enable him to find the way out of dogmatism.

The great philosopher is not to be found. It was the hope that he might yet become a reality which led Kant to polemicize against all others.

The Polemics against Contemporaries

We have already analyzed Kant's polemics against his contemporaries of the 1780s and '90s. They were not his only feuds with contemporaries, however. Kant went in for polemics in his very first publication, *Thoughts on the True Appraisal of Living Forces* (1). With this paper Kant involved himself in a fight which the followers of Descartes and those of Leibniz had for sixty years been waging over the determination of the forces of bodies in motion. For our purpose, the only important point is the way Kant treated the contemporary physicists on that occasion. He did not take any of them for a model but submitted them all to a stiff reexamination of their proofs. The premises were compared with the conclusions, to see whether, perhaps, one had a restriction imposed on it, or a universality supposed in it, that was not found in the other. The result: not one of the contemporary physicists passed the test in every respect. At twenty-two, Kant ventured to polemicize by name against Bilfinger, Johann and Daniel Bernoulli, Hamberger, Madame de Chastelet, Jurin, de Mairan, van Musschenbroek, Wolff, and others. A constant detachment from earlier theories and proofs was the gradual process in which his own took shape.

Nor is that *Appraisal* the only work in which Kant pronounced judgment on his scientific contemporaries. He did it again in some smaller publications and, above all, in *Universal Natural History*. His early scientific writings also had polemics serving as midwife.

So had his early metaphysical and logical writings. These rarely name names; but if the scholastical academic activity is kept in mind as a repulsive background, the polemical element will be impossible to overlook. The first metaphysical treatise, *Nova dilucidatio,* strikes at those who overestimate the theorem of contradiction as the fundamental principle of metaphysics. *A New Didactic Concept of Motion and Rest* shows by its very claim of novelty that it is a polemic against the old concepts. *A Reflection on Optimism* deliberately intervenes in a debate that has been going on for years. The essay on false hairsplitting in syllogistical figures takes dead aim at the school activities in logic. By *The Only Possible Proof to Demonstrate God's Existence* all other arguments are *eo ipso* excluded. *An Attempt to Introduce the Concept of Negative Quantities into Mundane Wisdom* struck Worländer already as "a thrust against contemporary school metaphysics."[20] The introduction to *Inquiry into the Clarity of the Principles of Natural Theology and of Ethics* calls the "present task occasioned" by the vacillating views of "academic sects" (21: II, 275).

Only twice did this basic polemical trait of the early metaphysical writings find a clear outward manifestation: in *Essay on Optimism* (14), and in *Dreams of a Spiritualist*.

In one of his earliest letters Kant reports that the announcement of his lecture on optimism had set off a polemic. In October 1759, Daniel Weymann obtained the *venia legendi* for philosophy in Königsberg. His habilitation paper, *De mundo non optimo*, joined in a debate that had been started by the 1753 prize question of the Berlin Academy, "On demande l'examen du système de Pope, contenu dans la proposition: Tout est bien." One day before

Weymann's habilitation, Kant filed his own paper with the dean's office. Unlike Weymann, he professed the optimism of Pope and Leibniz. According to him, the opponent he had in mind was not Weymann but Crusius,[21] but he was not ignorant of Weymann's treatise. He knew about it, in any event, for Weymann had asked him to take the opponent's role at Weymann's own defense of his thesis. Since Weymann was citing Crusius, Kant could not hit Crusius without hitting Weymann; and that he was quite unaware of the circumstances, a day before Weymann's habilitation, is hard to imagine. In this situation it is understandable, at least, that Weymann felt perfidiously attacked and struck back swiftly with a paper entitled *Reply to the Attempt to Raise Some Questions about Optimism*. Kant did not respond; it was the first time he refused battle. His stated reasons are characteristic: he had already declined to be Weymann's opponent, because of his "well-known immodesty"; now he was answering the indecent challenge "to exchange fisticuffs with a cyclops . . . in the most decent manner, that is, by silence." Of his rival, the new "meteorum,"[22] no more was heard in any of Kant's later letters or writings.

A matter of quite different weight is the anti-Swedenborg treatise. People had been asking Kant at times what he thought of Swedenborg,[23] whose telepathic and prophetic faculties were being discussed all over Europe. He wrote Swedenborg a letter,[24] said to have been favorably received; but the promised reply did not arrive. Kant thereupon bought Swedenborg's works and read them.

What he found there was the mania of uncritical thought turned to imagery. The world's final secrets were unlocked. The spirit realms became transparent. The "fantasts' paradise" (24: II, 317) opened its gates. The result of this "fanatical vision" of the Beyond amounted to "eight quartos full of nonsense" (24: II, 360).

In dealing polemically with this nonsense, however, much that Kant may have been thinking before that time assumed a more lucid form. He became certain that "the divers phenomena of life in nature and nature's laws are all we are granted to know; that the principium of this life, however—i.e., the spiritual nature, which is not known but surmised—can never be a positive conception" (24: II, 351). The separation of *mundus sensibilis* and *mundus intelligibilis* was carried out, albeit only as a hypothesis at first, which still required reflection. One thing was clear: the two worlds would need completely different sorts of thinking. Cognitive judgment had to be confined to the realm of possible experience; the job of metaphysics was to clarify in each case whether the point at issue was "defined by what we can know" (24: II, 367). "In this sense, metaphysics is a science of the *bounds of human reason*" (24: II, 368). The consciousness of method in the design of metaphysical hypotheses was revealed, and at the same time Swedenborg's nonsense served as an occasion for getting rid of some nonsense of one's own.[25] One quit asking theoretical questions where it was apparent that they must remain unanswered. The anti-Swedenborg polemic brought Kant several decisive steps closer to critical thinking.

Contemporaries of one sort always seemed to find Kant receptive, no matter what their offerings: namely, the innovators. When a mind revealed originality, Kant was an extremely liberal and generous critic. One of the first to recall this was Kraus, a student and later a colleague of his: "The most original authors, however paradoxical they might be, were his favorites. Even Moscati, who described man's erect posture as the source of many diseases and therefore not natural, was defended in a Kant review. Thinking, and always thinking something new if possible, soaring above the usual concepts—this was what his agile mind required. Hence his love of all the most paradoxical writings."[26]

Yet this does not mean that innovators would escape the Kantian polemics. He let their charms enchant him for a while; but then he started questioning the validity of their reasons and polemicizing against them as against others. We can observe this in his relation to Rousseau, the greatest innovator among his contemporaries.

Kant's first thorough contact with Rousseau left him fascinated with the Frenchman's acumen, with the "noble élan of his genius" and his "sensitive soul" (86: XX, 43), but chiefly with the all but inexhaustible productivity of his mind. Great perspectives opened up to him: as Newton's gaze had pierced the secrets of the universe, Rousseau's was penetrating man's "deeply hidden nature" (86: XX, 58). There was in man something like an analogue to the great cosmic order; only it had to be realized first, by means of freedom. But human freedom was a matter of education (86: XX, 167). It was foolish, therefore, to take one's eyes off man to study what seemed like the only order, that of the cosmos; you had to see to it, rather, that men were educated in freedom, and for freedom. "Rousseau has set me straight" (86: xx, 44). The discovery of the great potential order was proof: "According to Newton and Rousseau, God is justified . . ." (86: xx, 59). The impulse given by these thoughts is difficult to overestimate in the history of Kantian thinking.

Yet thinking soon broke the spell. It began with Kant's deliberate estrangement from that which enthralled him. "I have to keep reading Rousseau until his beautiful expressions will no longer distract me at all, and then, for the first time, I shall be able to examine him rationally" (86: xx, 30). The examination was swiftly followed by misgivings at "strange and absurd opinions" (86: xx, 43), at the affectation of "playing the eccentric" (86: xx, 44), at the hypochrondriac side of the man's character. After all, when things were viewed with cold reason they were lesser than they had seemed to the imagination. The radical critique of Rousseau set in, and what took place in it was a cleansing of all the ideas that had sprung from the impulse received. Only thereafter did Rousseau affect Kant's works—not in unbroken enthusiasm any more, but in many forms diffracted and purified by the polemical cleanser and not infrequently turning against Rousseau on the surface, in points which transcend the merely doctrinal.

It is as true of the physicists and metaphysicists among the youthful Kant's contemporaries as of Rousseau and Swedenborg and those with whom he took issue in the 1780s and '90s that they benefited Kant primarily as objects of polemics. He did not treat contemporaries any differently from the great philosophers, nor great philosophers any differently from his contemporaries. All of them were food for thought and occasions to do your own thinking. By inviting contradiction they showed a way which they themselves had not seen, and which ran counter to their ways. It will be hard to name a contemporary thinker with whom Kant might be said to have thought in pure accord. And who should have escaped his polemics, since he himself did not?

Kant's Polemics against Himself

Kant was a philosopher whose thought was subject to incessant change. We may conceive his writings as points marking that change. If we compare them side by side, as static products, they reveal breaks, of which the largest separates the precritical thinker from the critical one. For a long time people saw nothing but this break and accordingly split Kant into two, as it were: a precritical Kant, who was no longer to be taken seriously, and the real, critical Kant. The year 1781 was considered the great divide, and Kant himself appeared to justify this in his remark on the nascent *Critique of Pure Reason:* "By this treatise of mine, the worth of my previous metaphysical writings has been wholly obliterated" (81: XVIII, 42; 4964). Later, he spoke out several times against a new edition of the precritical works.

Yet even Kant himself was sometimes not quite clear about the real upheaval's location in time. In a letter to Tieftrunk[27] he placed it previous to the year 1770: his fourth dissertation, he said, ought to be numbered with the critical writings. Elsewhere he indicated that at least the ideas of the earlier works might still be salvageable, and now and then he kept thinking about a "revision"[28] that might be republished.

The more questions Kant researchers asked about the true turning point, the more difficult they proved to answer. The total change certainly came with *Critique of Pure Reason.* But the letter to Markus Herz[29] that outlines *Critique* was written as early as 1772, and by the methodologically clarified separation of the sensible and intelligible worlds a critical idealism was conceived as early as 1770. And was this the first time? In *Dreams of a Spiritualist* the separation was already executed, if only as an experiment.

This upheaval also led farther back into the past: to *Remarks on Observations on the Feeling of the Beautiful and Sublime,* the most important document we have on Kant's early evolution. It was there that the turn to man as a moral being occurred; and thus the turn to anthropology, a premise of *Critique,* would have to be placed in the year 1763, at the latest. *Observations* was its first fruit.

The number of upheavals had now risen to five. But this was not all, for the critical Kant was found to be not monolithic either. In *Critique of Judgment* it was a new way of thinking, the faculty of reflective judgment, that seemed suddenly to be critically developed. The perspectives of that work opened up the view of an encompassing whole in which the sensible and intelligible world were equally enclosed. And those perspectives pointed to *Opus postumum,* in the first volume of which the attempt to start out from unity—rather than to lead up to it—is made time and again, and fails time and again. Accordingly, seven points of fracture had been encountered: 1763, 1766, 1770, 1772, 1781, 1790, and 1796. In each of the representative works (early physical and metaphysical writings, *Observations, Dreams,* fourth dissertation, letter of 21 February 1772, *Critique of Pure Reason, Critique of Judgment, Opus postumum)* crucial points seemed to have been penned by a different Kant. And when more questions were raised—such as: Where and when did the evolution of the critical method begin? Where and when do we note the first signs of the antinomy problem? Where is the new understanding of metaphysics as a delimiting science suggested for the first time?—it appeared over and over that within those changes there were others going on, quite apart from the fact that in delving into *Reflections,* into the lectures, and into the letters one got a sense of discovering yet another Kant. Specification, it turned out, was never definitive and exhaustive.

With this possibility of endless specification it is plausible to conceive the various upheavals simply as moments of a continuous process. In single works the process is scarcely perceptible. In the many volumes of *Reflections,* the collected material which Kant, in some four decades, jotted down on scraps of paper or in the margins of compendia, it can be traced already. A complete publication of the lecture notes taken by students would manifest the process more clearly yet.

But what must have been going on inside the thinker in whom the process occurred? Time and again his attitude toward himself and his thought was questioning and hostile. He seemed to feel constantly under an obligation to refute himself, to overthrow the systems he had begun, to revise his own insights. In the young man the process was like a vortex; he spoke of years in which he had been turning "my philosophical reflections to every conceivable side"[30] and overturning "the whole edifice repeatedly, profoundly indifferent to my own and other people's opinions."[31] It was a permanent revolution, so to speak, but within its several upheavals there emerged the outlines of a process which gradually, in newly gained methods and insights, appeared to be coming to rest.

Appeared to . . . Kant's system was complete in the idea, perhaps, but his thinking went on. Even the aged Kant happened
suddenly to be facing certain cogitative problems of his own as
if he could no longer understand them.[32]

From the moment he proclaimed himself a static thinker,
Kant's inner polemicizing against himself was bound to look like
a ceaseless self-refutation. It could not but seem as though the
thinking process, once begun, were continuing regardless of
the thinker's will. That the process continued in fact is demonstrated by the work Kant left behind. He could not rest in his
polemicizing against himself, though with advancing age it became more and more inward. His relation to his own thoughts
also can be called polemical in principle, no matter how much or
how little he may have outwardly polemicized against himself.[33]

The Weight of Polemics in Kant's Work

To sum up: we may say that all of Kant's creative activity can
be understood as polemicizing—against the great thinkers of the
past, against his contemporaries, and against himself. The formula "delivered by polemics" applies to his work as a whole.

How are we to reconcile this with the accounts of his
contemporaries?

We do not deny Borowski's contention, for instance, that Kant
had an "unpolemical heart"; we merely add that the unpolemical
heart was joined to a polemical spirit. It is only when Kant's
rather quietistic emotions are projected into his thinking that we
have to protest—as against Alain's pronouncement that "la part
de la polémique est, en lui, très petite."[34] What this interprets is
not Kant but the ignorance of his interpreter.

In Kant's work, polemics is the medium of progressing. Viewed
like that, it is the creative motor, not an incidental appendage.
The parallel to the sustaining ideas of his early philosophy of
nature and of his late politics becomes evident, and we may say,
in this sense, that Kant's idea of a gradual realization of progress
in the medium of struggle is also the key to the history of his
own thinking. If only for the sake of purely historical research on
Kant, therefore, it will be necessary to pay more attention to
that idea, as well as to the entire complex of the problems of

antagonism and unity in general. A hypothesis of Kantian drafts of that idea proves to be at the same time the carrier of Kant's cogitative existence. In a deeper sense we find this confirming the physicists' principle *hypotheses non fingo*.

All science rests on guiding principles. If Kant's philosophy is understood not as merely evolved but as a perpetual becoming, research about it will be based upon his own schema of becoming —the schema of an infinite process heading for a goal posited in the idea, of a process driven toward that goal by the medium of antagonism. Since the process is infinite, each point in it may become the center. This may be a thought not without importance to the interpretation of Kant. As a thinker, Kant is this infinite process, not one of its static points. The researcher must be allowed to choose every one of the static points as the center, the early Kant of physics as well as the Kant of the *Critiques* or the Kant of *Opus postumum*. In doing so, of course, he should be aware that this "fixed" Kant will have to be restored to the free flow of the process. Neither the thoughts of the early Kant nor those of the critical or the late Kant show us Kant as such—for Kant as such was not a certain field of thoughts but the act of thinking; not a distinct philosophy but the act of philosophizing. Mindful of the warning he often uttered, we would have to say that what must be known, to understand Kant, is not his philosophy but his philosophizing, and it is not just his thoughts but his thinking. Grasping this will then become a process interminable in itself, a process in the course of which we must give up any claim to have understood it already.

PART THREE

FROM CONFLICT TO PEACE IN CRITICAL METAPHYSICS
Kant as a Metaphysical Peacemaker

> Outward peace is mere semblance. It is the germ of the temptations that must be eradicated, the germ that lies in the nature of human reason; yet how can we eradicate it if we do not give it the freedom and indeed the nourishment to sprout weeds and uncover itself, so that we may extirpate it with its roots? (30: A 777f./B 805–6)

In part 2 we considered Kant's philosophizing historically, as a process of everlasting struggle. We took time to present its various forms, without examining what the struggle rests upon and what it aims at. Now we look for its foundation in the roots of reason's conflict with itself, and for its direction toward a reason unified by critique. We discuss the relevance of conflict—and thus of major polemics—to the history of reason, and analyze this with an eye to the peace which critique is to bring about in metaphysics. We shall see conflict itself as a way to peace, and Kant, as a metaphysical peacemaker. The impelling problem in his politics—how to achieve unity on adequate principles which simultaneously assure the greatest possible freedom—will emerge as the leitmotif of his philosophizing. Kant's seemingly peripheral political thought rests upon the core of his metaphysics and thus turns out to be eminently central.

8. CONTROVERSY AND ITS SETTLEMENT IN THE REALM OF THEORETICAL PHILOSOPHY

Controversy

In his presentation of theoretical philosophy Kant makes rather sparing use of images, and he does not always use them with the same skill. This is understandable in him as a transcendental philosopher, for his philosophy is not concerned especially with particular experiences and the scope of their imagery. Rather, it aims at what precedes all experience: at the forms of experiencing in the cognitive faculty, and at the scope of that faculty in reason as such. From the viewpoint of such a philosophy all direct imagery involves the danger that philosophical cognition—to Kant, essentially an aprioristic "autognosis" (94: XXI, 106) of reason—may be dulled into a surface cognition of things. The image, instead of engendering reflection, would doom cognition to a fate of "deflection" from itself. By shunning direct imagery, transcendental philosophy is to be saved from that fate.

Still, as a means of cognition the image is useful and necessary even to Kantian philosophy. It is useful for purposes of elucidation wherever thoughts are hard to represent didactically; it is necessary where the thoughts are ideas, which transcend knowability as such and are not thinkable except in symbolic analogies. In both cases the image does not govern the thought but serves it, rather, as an implement of clarity and interpretability.

Among the metaphors we meet in these functions, in the field of theoretical philosophy, are some from navigation,[1] representing the relation of the knowable to the unknowable (of a continent to the vast ocean) and the course of thought that remains possible on the borderline (along the shore). We come upon metaphors from astronomy (30: B xvif.),[2] which help (by way of the zenith of the sun) to understand the possibility of taking our bearings in what we cannot survey; we encounter metaphors from architecture (30: A 707/B 735 and others), which confront the proud pretensions of metaphysics (the tower it seeks to build) with the modest results (the solid foundation); we meet metaphors of road clearance,[3] not infrequently carried by a chiliasm of reason and opening paths that lead to assuredly scientific metaphysics.

More frequent and important than these, however, are the metaphors from politics: the images of combat and war, the thought
model of peacemaking, and, above all, the image of legal process
that encompasses all of *Critique of Pure Reason*.

It is not impossible that at the time Kant wrote that first
Critique he was not fully aware of its pervasive political imagery.
It may not have struck him until he had written the tract *Perpetual
Peace*. Soon after, in any event, he wrote his second reply to
Schlosser's attacks, *Announcement of the Impending Conclusion
of a Tract on Eternal Peace in Philosophy* (62), which in the
metaphysical field is deliberately and humorously tied to the
language and the imagery of a political tract.

In fact, Kant had written a tract on eternal peace in philosophy
as much as fifteen years earlier—not as a mere proclamation
of peace, however, but as a voluminous file of material on
peacemaking.

If this were just a matter of a certain likeness between images
used in politics and in general metaphysics, it would suffice to
point out the metaphor or, perhaps, certain analogies. But the
likeness goes deeper. Beyond the metaphor it comprises basic
problems, thought forms, thought structures, and finally whole
processes of evolution, with metaphysics and politics tied so
closely together that, for example, the origin of the republican
state (which did not exist yet) can be visualized from the genesis
of metaphysics (for previous to *Critique,* to Kant's mind, that did
not yet exist either), or the ideal course of metaphysics from the
course of the projected history of mankind. And it is by no means
clear whether thoughts on the genesis of metaphysics supplied the
model for the origin of the ideal state and the republican world
order, or whether basic political thoughts shaped the draft of the
new metaphysics. The only thing that is historically certain is
that the *metaphysica generalis* was elaborated ahead of political
thinking—but in such a way that political thinking, as a world
of images and as material, was already present in that elaboration.
If we are reminded of Kant's early adoption of political ideas
from Rousseau, Montesquieu, and Hume, and of his later en-
twinement of these ideas as images in the evolution of metaphysics, we are not going to view the reminder as sufficient when
we know that the basic political ideas were pre-formed, so to
speak, in Kant's philosophy of nature long before these authors

became known to him. Philosophically, by the way, seeing that the various branches of Kantian metaphysics spring from one metaphysical root is more relevant than determining what sequence they have grown in. The formal likeness of the history of thinking and the history of outward freedom is an impressive indication of that one root.

The Fact of Controversy in Dogmatic Metaphysics

To Kant's critical eye, the story of dogmatic metaphysics seemed like an endless struggle for an unattainable goal. New theses were advanced "despotically" (30: A ix) by individual thinkers or entire schools, systems, and epochs, each claiming at this very moment to chart the course of metaphysics once for all. What ensued from their collisions with the old was hardly ever a discussion, but a supposed manifestation of the earlier thinking as void. The latest always manifests itself as the best, and its producer—a metaphysical intelligence to whose wisdom nothing can be added, and from whose delusions nothing can be taken away (cf. 18: II, 170)—is entitled by cleverer arguments, or by the claims of sheer power, to strut for a while as a little conqueror. Later, his doctrines also suffer "the fate of opinions" (21: II, 283). They make room for new doctrines, without leaving any "unanimity" (30: B xiv) "on this stage of debate" (30: A 853/B 881). What remains is a thicket of contradictory statements, each promising what it cannot give: accuracy and general validity. The promise of metaphysics comes to look like constant self-deception on the part of reason, and the effort of metaphysics, like the restless labor of Sisyphus (cf. 81: XVIII, 94; 5115) and an object of quarrels to boot. It comes to be suspect and despicable (cf. 30: A 844/B 872) to others, and ultimately to itself.

A close look at the battle of the metaphysicists, finally, will make it seem that the only true philosopher is he who laughs at philosophy. A fight for territorial gain in the "field of the noumena" (30: B 409) is waged with "rationalizing assertions" (30: A 422/B 450). The last attacker will win; his victim will succumb. All that one needs to risk a clash at any time is sufficient skill in rebuttal and sufficient nerve in assertion. Looking more closely at his conquests, however, a man will find that he has won imaginary areas which have always been his, and whose possession no one could really have denied him. His struggle, then, will strike him as mere "shadowboxing" (30: B xv), and his victory as a pitiful "nonentity" (30: A 423/B 451). Both are disappointments which eventually turn even a dogmatic into a skeptic.

Despite all this, the possibilities of sneering at the struggle are limited for several reasons.

1. As mere *entia imaginaria,* the objects of combat are indeed nonentities for our knowledge; but as ideas which we cannot reject they are simultaneously the ultimate directions for our thinking. In that sense the debates about questions of the world's finiteness or infinity, about the limits of divisibility and thus the immortality of the soul, about God's existence, and about freedom have always touched upon pillars of metaphysics. Whoever engaged in metaphysics had some right to attribute central significance to those debates.

2. Sneering at the metaphysical debates seems to presuppose that we can relate to metaphysics without conflict. Yet how?

When the skeptic spurns everything, when the absence of success to date leads him to turn mistrust into a universal maxim (cf. 54: VIII, 226–27 note), the folly to which he succumbs may be respectable in dogmatic ages (81: XVIII, 294; 5645); and yet, all unawares, he is making his own metaphysic out of the statement that there is no metaphysics. In his disdain of the metaphysical battle he will be latently embroiled with whatever appears as metaphysics.

When one tries to make certain of peace by accepting a particular metaphysic, he is simultaneously raising a random one to the rank of the only one, and as a result he will have to fight many others.

And when one combines several in a synthesis, "mediating" himself into a chance of agreement, he will emerge with a metaphysic that bears in it the germs of many contradictions. He will have to fight his own metaphysic.

There can be no dogmatic metaphysics without being fought over—which is why, although distrust has been kindled by conflict, we do not only distrust conflict as such. Conflict is the surface indication of trouble in the depths. To a thinking like Kant's, a thinking based upon the theorem of contradiction as an indubitable premise, the fact of conflict must serve as a constant warning not to latch on to a system yet, but to propel thought far enough ahead to move without conflicting with itself. Even if we had to deny all merit to the struggles of dogmatic metaphysics, those struggles would have the merit of furnishing the occasion for metaphysics proper.

3. Whoever holds metaphysics in contempt will find his justification in the contemptible doings of the metaphysicists. He starts by viewing their struggles as absurd and ends up taking the utterances of metaphysical combativeness for products of unreason. But what if the ultimate cause of this fighting were not the failure of individuals but the weakness of all human reason? What if this weakness were recognizable—even if not removable —because the fighting alone drew attention to it? The fact of conflict, then, would not be an expression of unreason; it would be a product of reason which for the moment is not understood, and which leads reason to know itself. Conflict as such would cast suspicion upon the right place: not merely on the premises of particular metaphysics, but on the sources of all metaphysics in the cognitive faculty of the subject, and on its methods of unfoldment. Fighting would not just be the constant objection to all old metaphysics, nor the offense that impels men toward some new one; it would come to awaken them, rather, to a wholly new mode of philosophizing, a mode in which they would know that before asking about the last things they must ask about the first things. They must ask about the basic relations of human reason, about its mode of being in the world, about its metes and bounds, its a priori forms that mold cognition, and the possibilities of its making statements beyond its bounds. In a word, the factuality of antagonism in metaphysics is the objection to dogmatism that we cannot fail to hear, and at the same time it is what awakens us to criticism.[4] Reason commands that there be no conflict, and yet reason is the beneficiary of the conflict that was. For in pursuing its commandment, reason inquires into the conditions of the possibility of conflict and thus comes to be transparent to itself.

The Source of Controversy

If we proceed in the sense of Kant's transcendental method, taking the factuality of conflict in dogmatic metaphysics for our point of departure in searching for the subjective conditions of its possibility, we come upon an "illusion" (30: A 297/B 353). It is the temptress that induces reason to contend against itself. This illusion is not a product of malice on the part of certain sophists, nor is it the delusive result of flawed thinking; it is "a transcendental semblance" (30: A 297/B 353) which "ineluctably attaches" (30: A 298/B 354) to the use of reason—and, in consequence, to the use of all cognitive faculties as such—just as certain optical delusions (cf. 30: A 297/B 353–54) are inevitably bound up with the use of our senses. Rational enlightnment enables us to see through the illusion and thus to keep from being further deceived, but the semblance as such cannot be made to disappear. Kant therefore calls it "natural" and "unavoidable" (30: A 298/B 354).

What does the illusion consist in? What is its delusiveness? Where lies its fraudulence? And how does it tempt reason to conflict with itself? There are various ways to approach it through its effects: by mistaking space and time—the subjective forms of visuality—for objective things, for example. The subjective form of the phenomenality of the world is reversed, then, into an objective reity in which the totality of conditions, the absolute, will be quite rightly but unsuccessfully sought (81: XVIII, 400–401; 5961). Another consequence of the illusion is the false evaluation of logic—this canon for judging whether subjective statements are formally correct—as an organon, a guarantee of the material correctness of objective knowledge. A third effect lies in misusing empty concepts for cognitive ends, in confusing their mere unfoldment with synthetic cognition, and in misapplying the intellect beyond the bounds of possible experience.

What happens in all these cases is a misconception of our ingrained subjectivity, and a subsequent distortion of that subjectivity into objectivity. In case the distortion should already result from the illusion, it would have to be rediscoverable in the authority that guides us in putting the intellect to use, decides about the possibility of logic, and explores the roots of cognition. This authority is reason. It is in reason that we look for the seat of the unavoidable delusion.

Whatever use we make of the intellect aims at the realm of possible experience. It unifies the diversity we see, unifies it under concepts, without being unified itself. This is why, above itself, it needs a faculty of unity. This faculty, reason, is to bring about unity. Reason does thus not relate to objects directly; it relates to the intellect, rather, serving to systematize and discipline its employment, and within the bounds of possible experience to keep it open, endlessly, on all sides.

As the intellect unifies the objective diversity by means of intellectual a priori concepts, the categories, so does reason unify the diversity of intellectual cognition by means of rational concepts, the ideas. Unlike the categories, ideas have no corresponding visuality. As concepts, all of them are empty. Therefore, while serving cognitive purposes, they have no direct cognitive value.

There is no concluding the realm of possible experience, and no way for the intellect to come to anything absolute as it explores conditions. But reason extends the perspective of the intellect to infinity, so to speak—by a "necessary rational conclusion" (30: A 339/B 397) whereby the categories are expanded "up to the absolute" (30: A 409/B 436) in analogy to experience, but without empirical premises. Reason thus drafts the idea of the absolute in three ways: in relation to the subject; in relation to the diversity of phenomenal objects; and in relation to the unifying premise of all objects of thinking at large. The absolute unity of the transcendental subject is conceived in pure apperception; the absolute unity of the premises of all phenomena is conceived in the concept of the world; and the absolute causal unity of all objects of thinking at large is conceived in the necessary being.

These ideas cover "what all experience is part of, although it is never an object of experience itself" (30: A 311/B 367). We have "no concept" (30: A 338/B 396) of their object. In our senses we can find no congruent visuality, and yet ideas are rational conclusions drawn from the known upon the unknown; they are "not arbitrary fictions, but are given by the very nature of reason" (30: A 327/B 384). Their function in regard to the intellect is to serve the collective unity of intellectual concepts as a regulative that will simultaneously permit those concepts to achieve "the greatest possible expansion" (30: A 643/B 671). The intellect will, of necessity, lag behind ideas, but it will continuously approach them in "asymptotic" fashion (30: A 663/B 691).

Thus the use which speculative reason makes of ideas is merely regulative. And now the natural illusion becomes apparent: the subjective maxims of reason have a thoroughly objective appearance. Their subjective character can be recognized only in critical self-reflection. Proceeding without reflection, our reason cannot but mistake the subjective maxims for objective principles. It will succumb to the appearance of objectivity; it will aim the ideas directly at objects and pervert their "vitally necessary regulative use" (30: A 644/B 672) into a transcendent and constitutive one; it will open the vast field of dialectics[5] in which the "sophistications . . . of pure reason" (30: A 339/B 397) become sophisms of antireason. From the idea of pure apperception, the "vehicle of all concepts in general" (30: A 341/B 399), and from the analytical unfoldment of that idea, reason will draw fallacious conclusions in paralogisms upon the subject's nature as a possible object.

From the idea of absolute totality in serial synthesis, an unreflected reason will infer that the world is finite or infinite, that matter is finitely or infinitely divisible, that natural causality is omnipotent or that it may be interrupted by spontaneity, that chance is endless or that there is a necessary being. Each time, it will turn out that both alternatives, the thesis that would settle the absolute in the world and the antithesis which denies it altogether, have the same weight of evidence in their favor. The conclusions drawn from a given relative thing upon something absolute that is now given instead of given up—these conclusions put reason into a "condition" (30: A 340/B 398) of arguing against itself. It is in this "antinomy of pure reason" that the endlessly embattled character of dialectics finds its favored arena, even if not its only one.

From the idea of the absolute as an absolute unity of all premises of thinkability as such, the deluded reason will infer a supreme being, and an analysis of the "concept" will let it draw conclusions on the qualities of that being. The "ideal of the most real being" is thus, "even though it is just a conception, first *realized,* i.e., objectified; then *hypostasized;* and finally, by reason's natural advance to complete unity, *personified*" (30: A 583/B 611 note).

The doors to three dialectical fields—rational psychology, rational cosmology, and rational theology—have been opened by the constitutive use of ideas. Their entire area, an area that contains the central metaphysical questions, is one of conflict in principle. It will continue to be that until critique sees through the source of error, through the "confusion of the subjective with the objective" (81: XVIII, 75; 5058)—until the subjectivity of maxims and ideas have been recognized and their seeming objectivity has been, not expunged, but uncovered and rendered harmless. This insight is linked with the turnabout from a supposed knowing in the transcendent field to not-knowing—a change that strikes the uncritical thinker as regressive, the critical one as progress to *docta ignorantia*. In a sense, it is the homecoming (cf. 81: XVIII, 79–80; 5073) of reason to itself. What reason finds in that turnabout is unity instead of conflict, sense instead of supposed knowledge; and instead of straying presumptuously in a "bird's eye" use of the intellect it finds a serviceable regulative guidance of the intellect in its "domestic" use (30: A 643/B 671).

We were looking for the premise of the possibility of conflict within reason, and we came upon an illusion. The illusion can be characterized: it is the direct result of a transcendental semblance of pure reason, which cannot but lend a seeming objectivity to the subjective maxims and ideas of that reason. This unavoidable delusion becomes a fraud where reason fails to see through it. Subjective maxims are confused, then, with objective principles, and a consequence of this confusion is that the regulative use of reason will be perverted into a constitutive one. The resulting judgments are sophistical and transcendent, one and all; their reversal is fully justified. And indeed, they never cease battling.

The illusion provides only the condition on which antagonism is *possible*. Conflict is not bound to result from its possibility, for the illusion may be perceived as such. To explain conflict, therefore, a premise of its *reality* needs to be found in addition. Negatively, this condition is the lack of rational critique, and positively it is the wrong use of reason.

The fact that the transcendental illusion is anchored in the nature of reason itself does not mean that reason is by nature contradictory. It does harbor the ultimate premise of the possibility of controversy; but rational men are still free to choose. Where their reason chooses itself, so to speak, it will be unified in critical self-knowledge. It will not turn antinomical until it misconceives itself and turns dogmatic.[6]

Controversy's Place in Reason

Antagonism, we have found, originates in transcendental semblance, where the premise of the possibility of dialectics lies, and it originates in the wrong use of reason, where the premise of the reality of dialectics lies. This, it seems, is all there is to be said about its location. It lies within reason only insofar as reason, on whatever grounds, fails to see through its natural dialectics. The place of conflict, therefore, is the old metaphysics, the one that must be dismissed. In other words, it is dogmatism.

But is the severity of this conclusion justified? It not enlightened reason too inevitably antinomical in structure? Is conflict not inescapable in the field of a critical *metaphysica specialis,* at least, where there is no knowledge to help us make out a thing?

We pursue these questions—and with them, the question of locating the real battleground of enlightened reason—in the fields of *metaphysica generalis* and *specialis.* The bases of our pursuit at this point are *Critique of Pure Reason* and *Prolegomena.*

Metaphysics, Kant says, has been real at all times "as a natural disposition" (30: B 21), but never yet as a science. In the dogmatic unfoldment of this gift of nature, reason "liked to build" (31: IV, 256). Ceaselessly it put up edifices whose scientific nature was tacitly assumed, without ever asking *whether* there could be metaphysics at all. Kant's basic question, ahead of all investigations, is the questions of this Whether: "My intention is to convince all those who find the occupation with metaphysics worthwhile that it is inescapably necessary to suspend their labors for the time being, to regard whatever has so far been done as undone, and above all to begin by raising the question whether such a thing as metaphysics is at all possible throughout" (31: IV, 255).

What Kant casts doubt upon is not a specific philosophical knowledge but the fundament of philosophy at large. But has he really ever raised the question with candor? In *Prolegomena*[7] see his "whether" tilt almost instantly into a "how"—at first, of course, so as to answer the first question along with the second. But when we ask "how," are we not presuming "that"? Besides, Kant inquires whether there can be metaphysics at all, but not whether a possible metaphysics would be scientific. Instead, he always presumes that if metaphysics should turn out to be possible at all, it would be a metaphysical science. We note here an unquestioned point in Kant's radical critical questioning, and in any case, we find no evidence to show that at the time of *Critique of Pure Reason* he seriously doubted the scientific character of metaphysics—although at earlier times he had done so,[8] and although in fact, as we have shown, he did allow exceptions to the claim. In questioning the possibility of metaphysics as a whole, of course, he also questioned the definitions of its nature. We cannot question without opening the door to doubt. Yet Kant opened the door only so as promptly to shut it again—to shut it, he opined, more thoroughly than it had ever been shut; to shut it so that for the first time it was going to stay shut forever.

However this may be, enlightened reason makes us want a metaphysics "able to appear as science" (31: IV, 253). It leads "necessarily to science" (30: B 22), where it will not be in danger of "being refuted" (30: B xliii). Whatever it is that philosophers may be pursuing, they must pursue it "by way of science—the one way which, once cleared, is never overgrown and permits of no aberrations" (30: A 850/B 878). He who will not help to clear that way and take it, then, is turning "work into play, certainty into opinion, and philosophy into philodoxy" (30: B xxxvii).

We must keep in mind how strictly and at the same time how differently from our present usage[9] Kant explains the concept of science. The only source with which we can check here is *Metaphysical Foundations of Natural Science*, which originated in close proximity to *Critique of Pure Reason* and to *Prolegomena*.

Science, according to Kant, means "any doctrine if it is to be *a system*, that is to say, an entirety of knowledge arranged according to principles" (33: IV, 467). The principles may be principles of either the empirical or the rational conjunction of cognitions. Real science conjoins them according to rational principles. It demands apodictical certainty. Hence the inductive inference of the natural sciences cannot satisfy it. Kant says of chemistry, for instance, that while it amounts to a systematic whole and is therefore called a science, this designation does not really fit because chemistry rests only on empirical laws that imply "no sense of their *necessity*" (33: IV, 468). In the strictest sense it does not deserve the name of science. Kant would prefer to call it a doctrine of nature, like all of the empirical natural sciences.

Strict science is to him a closed system of cognitions that have been obtained methodically, are apodictically certain and aprioristically intertwined according to rational principles, and have been deductively unfolded from their entirety. Metaphysics as a strict science would have to display all of these characteristics.

That in transcendental philosophy, his *metaphysica generalis*,

Kant laid claim to this strictly scientific character is beyond doubt. As a science, he says, transcendental philosophy must be "critically pursued and methodically introduced" (34: v, 163) and conclusive as a whole. "For metaphysics is in its essence, and in its final intent, a complete whole . . ." (88: xx, 259). Its maker, pure reason, is the faculty of cognition from principles a priori, and thus predestined, as it were, to be strictly scientific. Its object, reason, is a closed entirety and thus fully representable in a finite system. "And as far as *certainty* is concerned, I have pronounced my own sentence: that in this sort of reflection it is quite impermissible to *opine*, and that whatever part of it bears as much as a likeness to a hypothesis is contraband goods. . . . For the will to be taken for downright necessary is proclaimed by every cognition that means to stand a priori—and how much more by a definition of all pure cognitions a priori, by a definition that is to serve as the yardstick, and thus as the model, of all apodictic (philosophical) certainty" (30: A xv).

Presumably, Kant was not only trying to make metaphysics conform to the concept of strict science; he probably copied that concept from the idea of metaphysics. For at one point in *Critique of Pure Reason* he says that of all sciences that have an object, none but metaphysics has the rare good luck to grasp the whole field of the cognitions pertaining to it, and to be able to hand down its finished work to posterity (30: B xxiii–xxiv).

Thus even Kant drew a line between philosophy and that which we today call science. Curiously, though, the line consisted in philosophy's having to be more scientific than science.

We return to our question. Is there a place for controversy in the critical *metaphysica generalis?*

Metaphysical debate rests on a rational illusion that has not been seen through. No metaphysic built on an illusionary *ratio* can be scientific. Yet any metaphysic that is not scientific is debatable. Of course, in its very debatability it displays the mannerisms of a science; but all the grounds of objective judgment it purports to offer are disguised, unrecognized subjective principles. Seeing through the illusion takes the kind of reason whose realm has been fully surveyed by pure reason, in line with a priori principles. Methodically cognizant of the mode of validity of its conclusions, the *metaphysica generalis* of such reason may claim to have a scientific character. In the realm of a critical *metaphysica generalis*—that is to say, in transcendental philosophy—conflict, as hitherto it used to break out between the several metaphysics and even in the mere unfoldment of dogmatic reason, has been overcome. Measured by the strictly scientific nature of this metaphysic, a debate that cannot be settled would here, as in mathematics, be "all but unheard of" (61: VIII, 409). The establishment of scientific metaphysics by critique is essentially an act of metaphysical peacemaking.

This may be acceptable as long as the object of reason is reason itself (81: XVIII, 9; 4851). But how about *metaphysica specialis*, the metaphysic "proper" (81: XVIII, 709–10; 6414–15)? In that, reason turns transcendingly to objects that differ from it and do not really have an object character, since they are never given: to God, to freedom, and to immortality. Kant calls them "the ground of the importance of all metaphysics" (81: XVII, 475; 4241). In their domain, is controversy not compulsory?

To Kant, *metaphysica specialis* is an area for the application of transcendental philosophy (81: XVIII, 710; 6415). What has been worked out in the latter is projected upon the former—which is therefore equally subject to the commandment of being scientific, and equally referred to in the confident line that "in metaphysics there is no uncertainty" (81: XVIII, 71; 5042).

And yet we speak here of an altogether different kind of science. It follows cogently from transcendental logic that concepts without visualities are empty, and that visualities without concepts are blind. There is nothing visual corresponding to mere rational concepts such as the objects of *metaphysica specialis*. It can be apodictically stated that they are insufficient for knowledge. Philosophy as *Metaphysica specialis* is thus a "philosophy of ignorance" (81: XVIII, 36; 4940). The ignorance is not merely partial or comparative; it is total. We can derive a synthetic knowledge of it, on grounds a priori, from the sources of knowledge. "Hence that knowledge of one's ignorance, which is made possible solely by the critique of reason itself, is *science*" (30: A 758/B 786)—and controversy is thus banished from the realm of *metaphysica specialis* as well.

Let us be somewhat more cautious. The issue here was not the meaning given to transcendent theses by the subject; it was only the view which speculative reason has of a domain in which it recognizes itself as not knowing. For the time being, all that is scientific and thus removed from irreconcilable strife is this knowledge of not knowing. As for the meanings given to transcendent propositions by each distinct thinking individual—what role controversy might play in that process we have tried to show in our treatment of polemics in part 2.

Critique of Pure Reason gives a simple answer to our search for the place of conflict in reason. Starting from the way it understands its own metaphysic, the work replies that debate, the characteristic of dogmatic "grandiloquence" (30: A 757/B 785), must be eliminated by critique. Reason will thus purge itself of both the fact and the suspicion of inner contradictoriness—"for what else should reason, the one thing called to do away with all errors, rely upon if it were blighted in itself, unable to hope for peace and tranquil possession?" (30: A 743/B 771). In critique we hear a postulate of reason that calls for peace in philosophy. Here, too, reason casts its veto against war. Critique is assigned the task of making peace.

The Road to Peace

In the previous section on controversy in metaphysics, political parallels might have been pointed out now and then. When dogmatic metaphysics was interpreted as a battlefield, for instance, one might have recalled the interpretation of the political state of nature as a theater of war. Or the objection to metaphysical strife that is lodged by speculative reason might have been compared to practical reason's veto of political warfare. Finally, it could be shown that war has no more a place in the idea of a perfect world than controversy has a place in the idea of scientific metaphysics. We shall now pay more attention to such parallels, beginning with the question of the function of metaphysical conflict.

The Function of Controversy

"Whatever nature itself prescribes is good for some purpose" (30: A 743/B 771). This teleological axiom forms the basis for Kant's inquiry into the point of conflict. And at the same time it suggests the answer: even though antagonism has no place in enlightened reason, it does have a function in enlightening it. How can this function be circumscribed?

Man's natural cognitive tendency inclines him not to criticism but to dogmatism. There he need not strain his reason at the start, fathoming principles of cognition; he may accept them unquestioningly, rather, and see to their application. Dogmatism agrees nicely with a natural bent to indolence, while at the same time imparting a sense of broadened knowledge not just in the empirical realm but all the way to the bounds of thinkability. Dogmatism seems to justify indolence, whereas the labors devoted to critical investigation are ill rewarded: they assure us of knowledge where we were not doubting in the first place, and where we do want to know—in the realm of the absolute—the only knowledge we get is that of not knowing. By this knowledge, criticism burdens the thinker with the weight of freedom, and thus with the hazard of faith. Dogmatism, on the other hand, in addition to all its other advantages, bestows the benefit of succeeding to a supposedly scientific character. It is man's very confinement in his little frailties, in indolence, cowardice, and the need for tranquillity, that makes him linger in dogmatism.

In its dogmatic period, therefore, reason is in peril of yielding to every superficially conclusive system it encounters. Dogmatism serves it as "a pillow to go to sleep on" (62: VIII, 415). But nature has taken two steps to make sure, as it were, that reason will not inevitably succumb.

First, it has imbued natural reason itself with that illusion which gives rise to thought results that are logical and yet contradictory—and that in the very realms aimed at by all metaphysics. All those transcendent propositions have equally compelling arguments for them and against them. Their view plunges reason into the antagonism which makes it conscious of its discord, much against the will of dogmatic thinkers. It is reason's own natural bent that runs counter to the natural need for tranquillity. At the same time, nature takes care that the discord will clearly come to light. Instead of giving man only a will to agree, it has endowed him with self-consciousness (62: VIII, 413). This is what spurs the independent use of his cogitative powers; it is what impels him to play with mere concepts, to "bring his philosophy into polemical friction with others," and—as this does not easily occur without affects—to "*quarrel* on behalf of his philosophy and finally, massing against one another (school against school, as army against army), to wage open war" (62: VIII, 414). By such warfare, nature saves man from the misfortune of "rotting alive"

(62: VIII, 414). The diversity of philosophies and the discord between them is not just a consequence of dogmatism; it is also the antidote to dogmatism. It is what preserves the spirit.

In the natural state of reason it is the conflict of systems and their gaping contradiction that has kept the human intellect "free of utter decay" (81: XVIII, 33; 4936). Every negation of past thought, even if it should stray into a fixed position, will engender doubt; and what the endless series of metaphysical negations evokes—athwart any dogmatism, which each one sought only in another fashion—is the basic skeptical feeling that there must be something wrong with the known modes of philosophizing. This is why we owe a debt of gratitude to all negative thinkers even if their thinking was exclusively negative, even if they produced nothing but a new occasion to negate. What all of them really wanted for philosophy may have been to let it come to rest, at last, in a new system; but their destructive unrest was the means by which, quite unintentionally, they preserved philosophy. Without the act of constant negation it would have grown vacuous "in a stupid tranquillity" (81: XVIII, 34; 4936).

Nor does this exhaust the function of debate. There can be conflict only between parties concerned with each other, parties which ultimately live by some kind of unity: "We cannot conceive a diversity without (absolute) unity, if the entire diversity is to be conceived by reason."[10] Implicit in every conflict is the idea of the One, and thus the very postulate of unity to which as a conflict, it keeps giving offense. And if, moreover, the conflict erupts in reason, in the place where one would locate unity pure and simple, it is a sure sign that what looks like reason is not reason yet. Conflict thus leads to a skeptical posture—by which we do not mean perennial neutrality but a mistrust of past unfoldments of reason, since all of them ended in conflict. Debate aims human reason at the cause whose visible result it is; and so it starts the self-canceling process that is completed in scientific metaphysics. Debate indicates the need for critical philosophy. The more fiercely it rages, the sooner will "a mature critique arise, upon whose appearance all these controversies must fall of their own weight" (30: A 747/B 775).

Debate itself cannot, of course, furnish that system; so we can really not speak of a process of self-cancelation. But the factuality of debate is a constant warning to look for the system in which it will be eliminated. Eventually, in fact, the emergence of critique becomes compulsory when the intensity of debate turns it into a threat of anarchy and a menace to the continued existence of metaphysics and of reason. For when that happens, when the misuse of reason threatens its very existence, rational men will save reason by changing their way of thinking. In that sense, debate is the father of critique.

There is a rather malicious epigram of Kästner's titled "On Eternal Peace" and unmistakably alluding to Kant's political tract and to the continuing polemics over transcendental philosophy:

> There'll be an end to wars, provided
> The sage's word is not forgot;
> Men will keep peace, live undivided;
> Philosophers alone will not.[11]

But in response Kant could rightly point to the import of that war between philosophers. It kept thinking men from yielding unquestioningly to coercive systems and from making fools of themselves; it preserved the freedom of philosophizing; it aroused skepticism of every doctrinal concept built solely on the ruins of another (86: XX, 150f.); and finally, it guided reason to itself and awakened it to the idea of critique (31: IV, 338).[12] As a phenomenon, the philosophers' war remains an aberration before the postulate of unity; but it is still "the most beneficial aberration . . . into which human reason has ever been able to fall" (34: V, 107). Understood in this fashion, Kästner's epigram does not "bear ill tidings" to philosophers but a "message of congratulations" (62: VIII, 417).

Accordingly, although unable to assign to debate a place in reason, Kant takes a wholly affirmative view of it in reason's history. Reason needs it "very much indeed" (30: A 747/B 775), and one might wish only that it had always been carried on without restrictions.

When we consider the function of debate in the history of reason we find it corresponding in every detail to the function of war in the history of mankind.

In the political state of nature it is the war waged by all against all that forces men to galvanize their energies for the most extensive settlement and cultivation of the earth; and so does the antagonism of reason in the anarchic state of metaphysics compel thinkers to keep their thinking awake and to extend it to all possible objects.

The political antagonism that takes effect everywhere lays the foundations of culture and builds upon them; the antagonism of reason urges it to keep designing new systems until at last, having pondered everything, it will find the fundament that holds.

In the evolution of the political order, laws are used to confine that antagonism within firmly delimited areas; in the formation of schools in metaphysics—"a makeshift . . . to collect the restless multitude about some great man as the point of union" (54: VIII, 247)—anarchy is removed locally by adopting common premises and ways of thinking.

Antagonism grows more violent in the interrelation of states; debate grows more intense in the interrelation of schools. In its most violent form, war jeopardizes the existence of mankind; in the most confused discord, controversy threatens the existence of reason. By both war and controversy, men are forced to change. One calls for a political order that is not belligerent; the other, for a metaphysics that is not controversial. In both, henceforward, differences are not to be temporarily suppressed by victories, but to be permanently voided by judgments. The course of politics and the history of reason both end in a rational establishment of eternal peace.

As war is Kant's secret motor of political evolution toward a lawful order that will simultaneously afford the greatest freedom, so is the conflict of reason his impulse to a system that will find supreme freedom in supreme legality. In both cases, the evolution is also conceivable as impelled by nature itself, by its cunning employment of human destructiveness to produce order by the chain of negations, as nature does wherever it is at work. "In such manner, nature's own course finally leads its beautiful, if mostly mysterious, order to perfection by way of destructions" (81: XVIII, 34; 4936).

These are plays upon thoughts, however, and Kant himself views their immediate constitutive statement value in empirical situations as nil. But their regulative significance carries weight when they direct human action where the counsel of reason ought to direct it anyway—to a course that will abolish war in politics, and controversy in metaphysics.

Premises of the Road

To Kant, we said, the goal of metaphysics is to void its inner conflict with itself, and that in turn must be accomplished in a way which it is the philosopher's task to prepare. This raises the question of principle of what matters more to Kant: preparing the way and being en route, or setting the goal and arriving.

First, it is a matter of course that without a goal the way becomes a blind alley, and without a way the goal becomes a mirage. The way is to aim at a goal; the goal is to define the way. Philosophizing is neither a brief errand (always undertaken only so as to arrive) nor a ceaseless pleasure trip (never undertaken so as to arrive). Instead, it lives by the irremovable tension between the way and the goal. Accordingly, one may perhaps reply that our question has been wrongly put, that neither the way nor the goal can claim priority. Both exist only together, are meaningful only as they relate to each other.

But this does not mean a flat rejection of the question. Even if we see that the interrelation is necessary, we can ask what sort of interrelation it must be. Is the goal to be desired unconditionally, so that every way to reach it should be taken? Or is there one qualifying way, one that will remain meaningful even if—though constantly aimed at the goal—it will not take us there; The goal is given by reason, as a postulate, in the idea. But the road to the goal is a task of reason. It must be taken. What happens on it is decisive. This is why in a subjective respect the road matters more than the goal.

We do not find this problem discussed by Kant abstractly, in principle; but it does appear in his writings under various guises and is always solved in the same fashion. He says, for instance, that truth in itself has no value, that the value lies in the manner of arriving at the truth (cf. 86: xx, 175). Or: the real good lies not in the possession of perfection but in progress toward it (81: xviii, 455; 6103). Or: philosophy itself is not the goal of mankind, nor is the knowledge of that goal all there is to it; rather, philosophy is the way by which men would like to reach the goal.[13] In these three cases of relating the way to the goal, priority is granted to the way.

The same thing happens when Kant comments on a political product of his time. In the 1760s Tahiti was discovered (see 76:

XV, 785; 1500 note), and it was described in travel books as an island paradise whose inhabitants, favored by rich gifts of nature, spent a life of pleasure in eternal peace. It seemed like a country that had completed its evolution and happily reached its goal. Kant read about it, but unlike his contemporaries he was not enchanted. The question to ask in view of that happiness, he felt, was not what the natives' beautiful existence was worth, but what their existence as such was worth. It was not *how* they lived, but what they lived *by,* and to what end. And the only answer to this was that the island might as well be inhabited "by happy sheep and cattle as by human beings happy in mere pleasure" (45: VIII, 65). Men in such happiness "seem only to fill out the emptiness of creation" (76: XV, 891; 1521). A people that has completed its evolution and does nothing but enjoy is superfluous: "The world would not lose anything if Otaheite perished."[14] For in that paradise man misses his "original destiny" (44: VIII, 39) of being en route.

Here, as plainly as one might wish, Kant prefers the way directed at a goal to the goal that has been reached and lacks a way now. The road to peace, whether in metaphysics or in politics, matters more to him than peace itself. Indeed, such peace makes no sense at all unless it opens and directs a way—in other words, unless it has not been achieved yet. This is paradoxical: "So there appears here a puzzling, unexpected course of human events, just as elsewhere, when we contemplate that course at large, almost everything in it is paradoxical" (44: VIII, 41). Peace is not an end in itself, and Kant's striving for unity is not unqualified. Desirable, therefore, is not any odd path to it, but a distinct, preeminent one: the path of enlightenment.

Before we characterize this road more closely, let us speak of its two most important premises: the right to be free in the public use of reason, and the subjective right to truthfulness.

What puts reason itself on the path of enlightenment and on the path of its self-elucidation is antagonism. It shows in the antinomical structure of each individual dogmatic reason, but even more clearly in the discussion of rational men. In their community, antagonism must come to light if only they are permitted to make use of reason. The indispensable premise of the road to peace in metaphysics, therefore, is the freedom to use reason with a scientific intent. Kant calls this the public use of reason (44: VIII, 37).

From this freedom, the still undetermined "germ of temptations" receives nourishment to "sprout weeds and uncover itself" (30: A 777f./B 805–6). Even where reason seems to be using its freedom to incite men against other men's reason, it will still serve unity. Reason does not undermine itself. It is kept within bounds by reason alone, not by dogmas that one sets around it like "sentries" (30: A 747/B 775), nor by the resistance of a citizenry which one "summons as if to put out a fire, so to speak" (30: A 746/B 775). The very denial of the freedom of this reason may testify to its freedom. The peace of reason is imperiled only where restrictions are placed on this freedom, where the decision what reason shall be is made, no matter why, before reason is used—and then that peace is in danger even if it should be feigned by a coerced external unity.

And where the freedom of reason is actually suppressed, reason itself will be lost along with peace. To suppress it would mean "to violate and trample the most sacred rights of mankind" (44: VIII, 39), the fundamental rights which enable men to enlighten themselves, and it would mean to stifle the germ which nature "most fondly tends, namely, the inclination and vocation to think freely" (44: VIII, 41). The result would be a sick reason whose use would infect everything, eventually even civic life. A healthy reason calls imperiously for freedom. For how long? As health "is a ceaseless falling ill and recovering" (62: VIII, 414), it requires a constant remedy which gradually brings the condition into the sort of balance that is "hovering on a pinpoint" (62: VIII, 414). This remedy is critique—still understood here as the encompassing right to test and examine all things. "And in view of the benefit, nothing is so important, nothing so sacred, that it might escape from this testing and searching scrutiny, which is no respecter of persons" (30: B 766).

Kant deals with all objections that might possibly be raised against this freedom. That the process takes him across the line to the political realm is not a lapse at all; rather, it means that this freedom of reason is also a premise of politics, provided the politics is rational. Whatever is done about reason will have public consequences. This is why, as far as consequences are concerned, merely to elucidate or to obscure human reason is a political act.

We shall deal briefly with the main objections.

a. It is said that radical freedom to criticize presupposes mature judgment. Where this not given, freedom may abuse itself, and it will be reason itself, then, that has to pay for this freedom. It is therefore in the interest of reason partly to restrict the freedom of the young, including academic students, until their judgment has ripened.[15]

Kant replies: In the long run, whatever grounds may be advanced for tutelage are senseless. "For it is quite an absurdity to expect enlightenment from reason, and yet, ahead of time, to prescribe to reason what side the enlightenment will have to take" (30: A 747/B 775). Rather, enlightenment is man's departure from all sorts of tutelage, a departure that cannot be prepared for by new guardians, only by the courage to put one's own reason to use. Hence the slogan of enlightenment: *"Sapere aude! Dare to use your own mental faculties!"* (44: VIII, 35). In the final analysis, the case is similar to the withholding of freedom from young nations or from serfs. There simply are no grounds on which freedom ought to be withheld, or why the use of reason should be censured. Just as man learns to use freedom only by handling it, he can acquire the maturity to use his reason "in no other way than by attempts of his own" (36: VI, 188 note). The right way is not to withhold the right to criticize, but to give instruction in critique and to extend full freedom.

b. Another objection is that radically free critique will stop at nothing. Carried to the point of impinging even on religious matters, its chilling character is bound to hurt people's feelings and to evoke the reaction of fanaticism, which then in turn will pose a threat to freedom. Here again it is said to be in freedom's interest to limit freedom.

And again there is no misunderstanding Kant's reply. A radical critique of religion, of the ideas of immortality and the existence of God, poses no danger to reason itself, not even if the critique takes a position of dogmatic atheism. Critical readers—and they are the vessels of reason—will not fail to notice that here an author is overreaching himself. Without succumbing to his dogmatisms, therefore, they will look at the interesting features of his presentation and will judge him by the quality of his mind rather than by an accidental sympathy with specific opinions. Here too the counsel of reason says, "Let these people just carry on; if what they show is talent, if it is profound new research—in a word, if only it is reason—reason will win every time" (30:

A 746/B 774). Even where a harsh critique should stir up fanaticism, it will awaken the counterforces as well, since they are what it lives by. In all religious matters it is thus to be hoped that the uncalled potential guardians, church and state, will "let these things take their course and will favor science and reason; for no other way can lead to the lawful freedom of thought (instead of anarchy) and to the supremacy of reason (instead of the despotism of orthodoxy)" (81: XVIII, 505; 6215).

c. Finally, the weightiest argument that can be made against the freedom of the public use of reason is that it may undermine the foundations of the state. It thus runs counter to the will of all, we hear, and the will of all must therefore be in a position to restrict it.

Kant's answer: It is one thing to call for resistance to the common weal and thus to negate its existence; it is something else entirely to discuss its fundaments with a scientific intent and with the will that, in principle, it should exist. The first is destructive rebellion and cannot be tolerated by a state. But the second is the spread of reason within the state and must not be restricted; for all civic conditions are consequences of reason, whose only judge is itself. From reason alone can we hope for gradual progress. This is why public criticism is sacred also in political matters, indeed quite especially in those matters. It is the sole inalienable right which every sovereign must accord to his subjects, in the interest of all, if there shall be reason in the world.

The common rule applying to all three objections is that the possible abuse of rights cannot determine whether they are to be granted. That way of thinking would be bound to bar all freedom, since freedom always includes the possibility of its abuse. No ground suffices, therefore, to justify imposing any kind of scientifically intended restriction on the freedom of critique, "the most innocuous of all that may be called freedom" (44: VIII, 36). No tutelage, whether domestic or academic, whether ecclesiastical or political, does anything to spread reason (cf. 76: XV, 898f.; 1524).[16] The thinker's task is to dispense with all of them, to take the risks of incorruptibility, to "void the mirage wrought by misinterpretation" (30: A xiii) everywhere, and thus, through critical reason, to convey upon the age the dignity of an age of enlightenment: "Our age is the intrinsic age of critique, which all must bow to. Religion, by its sanctity, and legislation, by its majesty, commonly seek to escape from critique. But then they arouse justified suspicion of themselves and cannot demand the unfeigned respect which reason grants only to those able to withstand its free and public testing" (30: A xi note).

One reservation can be made, of course—not really against the right of public criticism, but against the point of it: freedom to criticize is senseless as long as truthfulness cannot be found somewhere. Without truthfulness, critique is endless talk that enlightens neither reason nor anything else. Hence the right and duty to be subjectively truthful that goes with the right to criticize. Veracity in dealing with ideas is a premise of peace in philosophy. It is "the first requirement" (81: XVIII, 603; 6309), but it is possible only by means of freedom.[17] As the "supreme *principium formale* of morality" (83: XIX, 145; 6737) it is an inalienably valid demand even if it should cause us to be "denied all favors of fortune" (81: XVIII, 548; 6280). What is truth is always difficult and frequently impossible to make out, being subject to possible error; "but to be truthful is possible in any case, if only one has the serious will" (81: VIII, 603; 6309). A man can err, but he ought not to deceive (62: VIII, 421). To deceive is to lie, and the lie is "the truly rotten spot in human nature" (62: VIII, 422) and the destruction of human dignity as such (37: VI, 429). There is "not one conceivable case"[18] in which even a "white lie" deserves exculpation. Not even God, let alone an emergency, can "liberate" (83: XIX, 142; 6727) from the *obligatio essentialis* to tell the truth always and everywhere. "If the commandment *Thou shalt not lie* (be it with the most pious intentions) were received into the core of philosophical principles as a doctrine of wisdom, it would not only establish eternal peace in philosophy but might assure it for all time to come" (62: VIII, 422).

We were inquiring into the premises of peace in metaphysics. It is not a secret peace among thinkers that is presupposed here, not an intellectual solidarity that goes ahead of critique; it is to be free to fight, and to be entitled to truthfulness in combat. Those are the premises on which critique gradually turns from its premature object-relatedness to a reflective conduct that will bring it into a new relation to objects. This turnabout shifts the fight away from individual combatants and toward the fight itself. Rational peace becomes possible, but only in veracity and freedom.

In Kantian politics we find parallels to all of this, and often identical thoughts. We already mentioned that the "inalienable rights" (56: VIII, 303) which a state's subjects have against its head require "freedom of the pen" (56: VIII, 304). This freedom to criticize, "the sôle palladium of a people's rights" (56: VIII, 304), is itself rooted in "mankind's natural calling" (56: VIII, 305) to communicate whatever concerns man at large. What shows here is a natural will to truth which every statesman, according to Kant, ought to utilize by allowing philosophers, the men predestined for critique—to speak, not in order that he do as they say, but in order that he hear what they know. For it is in these men, who are not corrupted by power and not the captives of interests, that critique may most likely be truthful. A prudent statesman will not recklessly forgo their help; he will assure himself of it by a secret alliance in which he includes all those truthfully joining in thought.

The postulate of truthfulness is set forth in the first Preliminary Article of the tract *Perpetual Peace*. What Kant demands there is that no peace that has been concluded with secret reservations about future wars be deemed a peace. The *reservatio mentalis* has no place in politics. Its manner of shrouding things, burdening the publicly uttered words with the weight of secret reservations, is Jesuitical casuistry, unworthy of a politician. Political peace starts with calling things by their right name. The principle of the lie is the principle of war. But the only assurance that a ruler wills the right—the right which in turn rests on truthfulness —lies in the will to publicity in both the domestic and the foreign field. "All acts which affect the rights of others and the maxim of which does not agree with publicity are wrong" (59: VIII, 381). It is the radical No to secret diplomacy, to cunning as the last resort of the *raison d'état*—in short, to the politics of untruthfulness. Without this No, trust between states is impossible. It is essential, however; for a free league of states, which cannot be subjected to compulsion, depends upon such trust. In politics there cannot be peace either, except in freedom and veracity.

The Short Ways and the Long Way

It is precisely where the postulate of unity is heard in all its urgency that unity is in danger of being pursued in the wrong ways. Kant calls them the short ways.

We might, for instance, try by coordination and censorship to enforce an outward unity of reason in the form of general homage to one dogmatic system—to a universal system, as it were.

Or we might make peace in metaphysics by resolving to agree at any price. Kant views the ensuing mediation attempts as products of deficient sincerity. He scornfully calls them "syncretistery."[19] Their sponsors, the syncretists, are "false peace-makers" (38: VII, 51), to be considered more dangerous than militant dogmatics.

Or—seeking at least to imitate criticism, the "middle way of thought"[20]—we use a fixed recipe, such as the principle of the middle, to draft in-between things of which one "can make what he will" (60: VIII, 396 note).

Or we indulge in "moderatism," the pacifism of philosophy, so that all men will have "a roof," at least, "an occasional shelter,"[21] where there is no common edifice.

All these shortcuts to unity require us to sacrifice either freedom or veracity, if not both. We seem to be offered only one way —skepticism—that will let us stay nonviolent as well as truthful. But skepticism is neither a way to peace nor peace itself. Where it should become the goal, its artificial, impermissible ignorance undermines the foundations of all cognition;[22] its sheer distrust of reason brings it to do violence to reason. And where it is to serve as the way, it is a way without a goal, senseless because, having long despaired of the possibility of progress, the skeptic takes an invidious satisfaction in distrust. All that skepticism can provide is a resting place where reason, having gone astray, may perhaps find the way back to itself again. Skepticism, moderatism, and syncretism—all are forms of coming to rest on the surface. They smoothe out the outward signs of conflict without extirpating "the germ of temptations" (30: A 777/B 805). Their tranquillity is a "seeming" one (30: A 777/B 805).

In contrast to these short ways to unity stands a single long one. It takes its departure not from skepticism but from the skeptical method. What Kant means by that is the cogitative posture of viewing the argument over objects with sovereign calm —not with the intention of arrogantly rejecting both parties or modestly backing either one, but with the will "to discover the point of misunderstanding" (30: A 424/B 453). Through the patent antitheticality of statements which uncertainly sweep reason back and forth, this thinking posture seeks the only certainty, its nomothetical side.

On this course the concept of "critique" gets a new, capital meaning. Hitherto, when there was talk of freedom or of the universality of critique, it was still widely taken to mean "belittling, adding up mistakes, exposure and due rejection of shortcomings."[23] Critique was an object-related negative conduct of reason. To understand the change in meaning, we must consider it from two different angles: historically from its significance in eighteenth-century aesthetics, and systematically from reason's relation to itself.

In the aesthetics of the eighteenth century, "critique" means the normative laying down of rules that govern the judgment and the creation of works of art. This legislative faculty springs directly from the faculty to decide, detach, delimit, separate—in a word, from κρίνειν. The negative conduct of reason performs an aboutface in the process and turns out, in legislation, to be positive.

The type of this legislation is more closely determined as reason refers back to itself. For a start, it does this by turning away from all objects to the general subjective faculty of cognition, which Kant calls the rational faculty in the broadest sense. This is why, instead of measuring the metes and bounds of past systems or of any external objects, critique will measure "those of the rational faculty as such, in respect of all the cognitions for which it may strive *independently of all experience*" (30: A xii). Critique is the determination, by reason, of reason's own extent and limits, and the giving of laws for its use. Decisive are the principles a priori that are inherent in reason itself, not empirical facts of any kind. Accordingly, critique as a reflective conduct means the delimiting measurement of the entire realm of reason by its self-knowledge, in line with principles a priori.[24]

But does Kant, when he speaks of critique in a capital sense, really mean only this reflective conduct of reason? Probably not. It is only the basic step of critical reason. Kant calls for a second step, since he wants critique also applied to quite definite objects: education, civic order, and religion.

In defining itself, reason assigns to its several faculties (to the faculty of concepts, to the faculty of ideas) their particular realms, and designs the methods of its unfoldment upon those realms. Its object-relatedness can be called critical in a capital sense when it has been preceded by the self-enlightenment of reason about the premises on which it can refer to objects. Object-related critique is the unfoldment, according to principles and methods a priori, of a reason enlightened by self-knowledge. As critique (in a positive sense) our talk of objects is a projection of rational laws and the resulting establishment of norms by pure reason. The projection may refer to education, to the state, or to anything else.

Thus, on the long way to peace, reason, after a skeptical look at controversy, turns away from all objects and toward the source of utterances and of utterability at large: to reason. This about-face in the way of thinking is an "inscending" of reason to its surveyable realms, with the skeptical method of external contemplation passing into transcendental inward measurement and legislation. It is the basic step of transcendental philosophy, the critique followed by the second step of reflecting upon all things. Not until, in turning from the objects of debate to its subjective conditions, reason has surveyed itself and staked out its own limits will the point of misunderstanding become comprehensible as one "of reason with itself" (30: A xii). In this point reason will find the condition of the possibility of controversy, and thus the access to unity.

As part of the way, this basic step can be conceived as terminable and interminable at the same time. It is terminable insofar as Kant conceives reason as a finite whole and accordingly subject to elucidation in time; it is interminable insofar as even the enlightened reason can be obscured again and must therefore be elucidated not once but over and over. The enlightenment that is conceived as finite is describable in a finite process; the enlightenment that has to be accomplished time and again is infinite as a subjective endeavor. It is the infinite propaedeutic. A propaedeutic for what? For the second step, the projection of reason into the field of the thinkable. This part of the way too can be conceived as conclusive and inconclusive at the same time: conclusive insofar as the objects in each case are conceived as fixed, so to speak, against an absolute background; and inconclusive insofar as the objects in each case are given only in the realm of relativity, in which there is no end to critical reflection. The process of elucidating them continues.

Kant prepared this way in his first *Critique,* which he himself called a "tract on method" (30: B xxii) and which we may understand as a road sign to eternal peace in metaphysics. The road is "the true middle way" (31: IV, 360) and, as such, the only lawful way. Preparing and originally indicating it is what Kant called "the most onerous business of all" (30: A xi); traveling it is an "infernal journey of self-cognition"[25] for reason. In retrospect, both indication and travel seemed to him so strenuous that "at no price"[26] would he want to repeat them, and yet so important to peace in metaphysics that even less would he wish to have missed them.

We cannot describe this way as a whole; we shall point out only one, the basic one, of its stations. In the self-examining analysis of its faculties, reason comes upon the faculties of concepts and of ideas. For concepts, it finds given visualities, pure or empirical; for ideas, it finds none. Since it takes a conjunction of concept and visuality to make cognition possible, however, ideas remain empty for our knowledge. Our thinking cannot reject them, for it is in them that we think the absolute which corresponds to the contingent things we find given everywhere. In ideas we think the transcendent without knowing it. It is this recognition by reason, its recognition of its ignorance in the face of ideas, that makes peace in philosophy possible. The resolution of the antinomies presupposes on the one hand that we think about transcendence; but on the other hand it presupposes the resignation of knowing that within these thoughts we do not know. This means that in the space of immanence alone peace cannot be gained at all, and that the road to it, as a whole, therefore cannot be finite. The link with transcendence is twofold, however. In boundary concepts it is merely conceived; but in order to conceive it, we must have had previous contact with it in our way of thinking. When Kant says that the road to peace presupposes freedom of critique and truthfulness, this means that in the call for truthfulness the absolute is existentially touched already. One who thinks along its lines will not reject it as a boundary concept, and for veracity's sake he will not pretend to know anything about it. As self-measurement, critique is not just an intellectual achievement; it is an existential achievement without which there could be no rational peace. It thus applies to metaphysics already that without transcendence there can be no peace.

We briefly indicate the similarities in politics. Here, too, we are offered many shortcuts to peace: the road without freedom, in universal monarchy; the road without truthfulness, in secret diplomacy; and the middle way that has been calculated, as it were, in a balance of power. The last-named, by the way, was already mentioned in Kant's early philosophy of nature. One question he considered in *Universal Natural History and Theory of the Heavens* was whether the laws of equilibrium would keep separate world systems in the right relation to each other, and he rejected this notion on the ground "that the slightest shift would have to cause the downfall of the universe" (4: I, 311). Very similarly he says almost forty years later that a league of states based on a balance cannot endure—that it resembles the house that was built in perfect accord with the laws of equilibrium and promptly collapsed when the first sparrow lit on its roof (56: VIII, 312).

What all these shortcuts take us to is only the short peace, the postponement of hostilities. Against them there is but one long, lawful way, with freedom and equality implied in the fact that it is lawful. It is the strenuous way of states gradually evolving into organisms ruled in the republican manner and then joining, freely and truthfully, in a worldwide federation—with the result that the domestic political peace that has already been achieved by each of them will expand into world peace. This road too is difficult and onerous, and there is no completing it in time; but at each of its stations it can rest upon the supersensory, the ground of its completion. This road too requires a relation to transcendence.

Neither in metaphysics nor in politics is there more than one road—Kant calls it "the only true" road (32: IV, 441)—leading to the only peace that may be called eternal.

Truth, Error, and the Middle Way

That the way to peace is a middle way goes back, among other things, to the concept of truth, to the thought movements that spring from it, and to the concept of error.

The concept of truth in the sense of correctness is explained by Kant as *adaequatio rei et intellectus,* as "agreement of cognition of its object."[27] The weight of this purely "nominal" or "verbal explanation"[28] rests on *adaequatio.* The truth we are talking about lies neither in the intellect nor in the object but in their concordance as manifested in the judgment. "Judgments alone are true or false" (79: XVI, 244; 2124).

Left open here is what we are to understand by "the object." Two possibilities are conceivable. Formally, Kant's "object" may mean the laws of thinking; materially, it may mean the definite things thought about.

In the first case, truth lies in the agreement of cognitions with the laws of thinking. Truth is purely logically understood, then, as "concordance of cognition with itself" (67: IX, 51). "Totally abstracting from all objects" (67: IX, 51), it is the "negative condition" (30: A 59/B 84) of material truth—a condition that precedes material truth and, being materially empty itself, serves it at the same time.

In the second case, truth means the agreement of a cognition with an object. But here the thinker will run into difficulties. For the object is "outside" of him, while the cognition lies "in" him (67: IX, 50). To be compared with the cognition, the object itself must be turned into a cognition. All that is comparable, therefore, is "whether my cognition of the object agrees with my cognition of the object" (67: IX, 50). Cognitively, the thinker moves in diallela, in circles. Kant, in his transcendental philosophy, tries to break out of the circles as the conditions of the possibility of cognition allow him simultaneously to find the conditions of the possibility of its objects. All objects are thus "within us at the same time" (81: XVIII, 281; 5642), since their form is the product of the conditions of their phenomenality, which lie within us. But the diallelon shows up anew, in exacerbated fashion: lest cognition be a game played with empty forms, the materiality of its object must be qualified also—how, is not demonstrable—by something objective outside us. Kant calls this outside thing "transcendent," and he says of it that it is "wholly unknown to us and useless as a criterion of truth" (81: XVIII, 281; 5642). Thoughts in which we tried to approach it would entangle us in the circles of mere logical forms. What applies to this diallelon as to the other is that breaking through it is "downright impossible for any human being" (67: IX, 50). It is by no means sure that in cognition we do not circle farther and farther away from the object outside ourselves. Hence the most urgent question: "Whether and to what extent there is any certain, general, and usefully applicable criterion of truth?" (67: IX, 50).

The general formal criterion of logical correctness is the accord of cognition "with the general and formal laws of the intellect and of reason" (30: A 59/B 84). Since these laws are given, they permit us to test the accord.

But where lies the general material criterion? It is not thinkable.

The specific object we want to get to know differs from another object by its qualities, which are always specific. They are precisely what a material criterion would have to cover. But as a general criterion it would have to disregard them at the same time, and to test all objects for their common features. The concept of a general material criterion is self-contradictory.

This does not mean, however, that we have no truth criterion at all for our knowledge of definite objects. The transcendental criterion of the truth of any cognition about objects within us is the empirical context throughout, according to principles and laws of phenomenality. The reason is that the conditions of the possibility of both are identical.

Yet how is the reexamination of truth to be performed by means of this inner criterion? Kant gives no details, pointing to the *"criterium veritatis externum"* (39: VII, 128), to the outward criterion of truth. This, he says, is not the only, but "still the greatest and most useful means to correct our *own* thoughts" (39: VII, 219). This implement, "a subjectively ·necessary touchstone of the correctness of our judgments in general" (39: VII, 219), is discussion. In discussion we come to compare cognitions. The differences between them are hints, indications of semblance; the agreements are indications of truth. They are indications— not proof. That is to say: as a test of truth, discussion alone will not suffice either, although for testing all cognitions, even in mathematics (39: VII, 129), it is indispensable.

At many points in his work, therefore, Kant suggests a dialectic of ways of thinking that will prepare the middle way and will prove the best possible test of truth at the same time. It has three maxims, which at one time he calls "general rules and conditions for the avoidance of error" (67: IX, 57), at another time "maxims of common sense" (35: V, 294), at a third, "unalterable commandments" leading "to wisdom" (39: VII, 228), at a fourth, "maxims of reason" (75: XV, 186; 454). They are: (1) Think for yourself! (2) Think in every other man's place! (3) Think consistently!

Think for yourself! This means: Dare to have a mind of your own, and to look to yourself for the supreme principle of truth (51: VIII, 146). Such courage starts "man's most important inner revolution" (39: VII, 229)—namely, his exit from "self-caused tutelage."[29] It is a maxim of "unprejudiced" (35: V, 294), "en-

lightened" (67: IX, 57), and "never passive" (35: V, 294) thinking,
the premise of which is the autonomy of reason.

Think in every other man's place! That is to say: Do not isolate yourself in your thoughts. They may be wrong. "For it is
not my view that . . . once convinced of something, I ought to
leave it undoubted. In pure philosophy that isn't done."[30] Instead,
new thought should always be given to what has already been
reflected upon; it should be ceaselessly turned over in my mind,
from changing standpoints. I must provide my opponent with
"an advocate in me" (75: XV, 484; 1089), must detect the "optical
delusion" by means of the "parallaxes" (24: II, 349) that result,
and must thus continually rid myself of opinionativeness. It is
the will to test my judgment "against other men's intellect"
(39: VII, 128) that takes me into the public world shared by all
rational men, into the world where my judgment can be "measured, as it were, against the entirety of human reason" (35: V,
293) and my accidental limitations can be disregarded. Thus, in
infinite reflection, my thinking heads for the standpoint common
to all, the standpoint of reason itself, in order to make the insight
of all my own. This maxim of an "expanded" (35: V, 294) and
liberal way of thinking includes the necessary courage for publicity, indeed the will to publicity. Even my solitary thoughts
should constitute a discussion that liberates me from subjective
delusions.

Think consistently! This maxim of a "succinct" (67: IX, 57)
way of thinking "is most difficult to achieve" (35: V, 295) and
at the same time most necessary, for to be consistent is "a philosopher's cardinal obligation" (34: V, 24). Reflections that have
digressed in expansion are unified by this maxim under the guidance of *one* thinking—which is now no longer the potentially
obstinate one of the first maxim, but the potential thinking of
all, freed from logical obstinacy by the spirit of publicity.

None of these maxims suffices in isolation. Thinking for myself
alone may mire me in the obtuseness of a self-isolating intellect.
Thinking in the place of other men only, I may—if I do not know
what matters—lose myself in the endless play of reflection. Consistent thinking alone may end in arid, unsubstantial "consequence making." Only a continuous, vivid dialectic of the ways
and faculties of thinking, one that includes free use of the intellect,
candidly communicated and received reflection, and the courage

of reason to go to the heart of the matter—only such a dialectic can, detached from all individual subjectivities, lead to the middle way, which through rational consistency is at the same time a middle way of principles. In thinking up the unifying metaphysic of all, this dialectic provides a criterion of truth.

Like the concept of truth, the concept of error also prepares the way of metaphysics as a middle way.

The place of error is in judgment. But judging is the activity of the intellect; it is thinking. Kant's formal explication of the concept of error is therefore "the form of thinking contrary to the intellect" (67: IX, 53). This already shows the problem: how should it be possible for the intellect to think contrary to itself? It is as difficult to understand this as to understand the physical problem "how any force should deviate from its own essential laws" (67: IX, 53). Since spontaneity is neither a quality of that physical force nor one of the intellect as a natural faculty, the deviations of both can only be understood as being due to a deflecting outside impulse. But then all material cognition is obtained by joint action of the only two cognitive roots: the senses and the intellect. Error and cognition are equally caused to originate by the interplay of sensibility and intellect. Sensibility is the source of cognition as long as it remains inferior to the intellect, "as the object to which the intellect applies its function" (30: A 294/B 351 note); it becomes a cause of error "when it invades the intellect's action itself and determines its judgment" (30: A 294/B 351 note). "The original cause of all error will thus have to be solely and exclusively sought in the unnoticed influence of sensibility upon the intellect, or, more precisely put, upon judgment" (67: IX, 53).

What follows from this definition of the concept is that error can never be total, since in total error the intellect would have to cease being an intellect. It would have to be not merely deflected by the senses but destroyed by them—and then no judgment could be made at all. Positively, this means that every judgment must have something to it. "An error is always partly true" (79: XVI, 286; 2250). Purely from the viewpoint of love of truth there is thus no sufficient reason against considering the judgments of other people. All of them are not just potentially true; there really is partial truth in them, if only truthfulness may be presumed on the part of him who judges.

Even from the viewpoint of all possible erroneous judgments, the way to an internally unified metaphysics is a middle way in the sense of partly sublimating every one of them. No insight and no judgment will be negated altogether; rather, that way is the synthesis of what is true about them, the synthesis which unifies all positivity and precisely thus becomes the way for all.

Once again the political parallels are demonstrable. What has been shown in regard to metaphysical thinking applies equally to political thinking, for the stated rules are maxims of thinking as such. But where lies the parallel to political action, which is a function of the political will?

Kant conceives the infinite political way as a function of the general will. In the course of theoretical metaphysics, judgments are not unified as general insights unless they are the pure insights of inwardly unified reason also; and neither is political volition unified unless, as the general will, it corresponds to the inwardly unified rational will. A twilight zone surrounds the empirical determination by comparisons of any general insight, because that sort of determination is indispensable and yet inadequate at the same time—and so, to Kant's mind, twilight shrouds the empirical determination of the general will in a democratic institution in the present sense, because this determination must be understood as both approximating what is really intended and essentially apart from what is really intended. Formally, however, the rule is that the infinite middle way leads in one case to the insight of all, and in the other case to the will of all and thus to peace.

Peace in Metaphysics

Peace

Clarity about the way will clarify the goal. Just as there are metaphysical and political shortcuts to peace from which, for all our will to unity, we draw back, so are there false forms of metaphysical and political peace, forms arising from sources that are unfit for unity. One of these is the metaphysical peace that grows out of the believer's need and will eventually be justified in religious fashion, as a peace above all reason. Such peace is preceded by sacrifice with which reason cannot concur. The claims of reason are unified by being abandoned, all at one stroke. The end of controversy would be the end of reason.[31]

Nor can men of reason give the name of peace to any arrangement based overtly or covertly upon a happiness principle, whether on that of contentment or quite generally on that of pleasure. Principles of happiness are unfit for unity because everyone will see their object in something different. Ultimately they are principles of war, sufficient to uphold only a peace in which conflict is shunned out of laziness, a peace which on that very ground will remain a preserve of conflict. Peace based on a need for tranquillity is a similar case; it appears morally justified by the modesty of demands, but this accidental continence is not taken seriously by reason, which would content itself only with a continence due to a knowledge of its limitations. Peace based on the will to absolute permanence also runs counter to reason. Imagining that reason, at some point in time, might put a stop to thought, that the thinking subject's thoughts might, so to speak, stand still forever—this is an insult to the imagination (58: VIII, 334). Absolute rest would be the extinction of thought. "The permanent state of things is death" (94: XXI, 118).[32]

Thus, in behalf of reason, Kant rejects all forms of peace that do not spring from reason itself and cannot aim at a worldwide expansion of reason.

He confronts them with the one peace which reason prepares for itself—gradually, but never definitively—in its self-knowledge. This peace is possible solely when reason has the will to be itself, when it is continually enlightened from its own sources and perpetually expanded in freedom. In this peace we give up no knowledge other than a pseudoknowledge, and we accept no faith other than the rational faith. We do not want to rest otherwise than by sublimation in the continuous activity of reason, and we want no happiness other than that of the unity of reason with itself.

Similarly, Kant rejects any political peace derived from false sources. A peace that aligns all men with one empirical will, whether arising from violence or from the need to believe in an ideology, is a servile peace. A peace born of the need for happiness as a worldwide condition of well-being and being well off—such a peace spoils the nations' way of thinking (cf. 35: V, 263) and ends up in boredom. A peace due to the need for beautiful tranquillity in a new golden age is but an "empty longing" (49: VIII, 122) of the poets, for whom Kant has nothing but ridicule. These forms of peace have laws aimed at felicity instead of liberty and justice. But tranquillity will not offset injustice, and contentment cannot take the place of freedom.[33] All these poetical forms of peace take their bearings from the happiness of cattle and sheep; they are less worthy of mankind than a war that is waged for freedom and in which right is held sacred.

Confronting these forms is the one peace that will spread justice around the world in the greatest possible freedom, because reason wants justice to reign. It is the peace that can be reconciled with human dignity—in fact, it is the peace required if man as *homo politicus* is to win his proper dignity by the union of politics and ethics.

This peace is an idea. In world history we see nothing that corresponds to it, and nothing visible will ever fully correspond to it. In the field of sociological thought it is an empty concept that acquires substance only insofar as political mankind, guided by a will to extend the right, brings political conditions asymptotically closer to it.

Yet if it is true that in both politics and metaphysics there are forms of peace that cannot mean peace at all, forms which not infrequently mean worse than war, namely, not just the end of individuals but the end of justice, of liberty, and of reason—if that is true, a peace that is understood as a mere interruption of conflict and postponement of hostilities is not the absolute goal to be sought at any price. In the intelligible order, this peace —like man's physical existence—is outranked in the merely existing realm by reason, by right, and by freedom.

For both metaphysics and politics, peace must therefore be neither the happiness of "stupid sheep" (76: XV, 891; 1521) nor a rest "upon supposed laurels" (62: VIII, 417); nor must it be a congealment in pure permanence. Essentially it is indeed "eternal" (59: VIII, 343f.), but not so as to be immune in time to change, the characteristic of temporality. The idea cannot be transplanted into the existing realm; only existing realm can, in an infinite process, be brought closer to the idea. Every state of peace along this road is relative. Its worth is derived from the source it came from, from the conditions it rests upon, and from the goal it aims at—not simply from its state of peaceableness. As an "armed condition" (62: VIII, 416) it remains embattled, and it is from battle, in a "militant posture" (62: VIII, 417), that it constantly regains the right, freedom, and reason. Peace itself remains a way to peace. In that sense it always remains conflict, but no longer a lawless one in quest of victory and destruction; it is a lawful conflict seeking judgment and lasting community.

Hope for this peace is justified. As a possibility and as a challenge it is ever present in ideas of reason. For reason wants unity. A believer in reason looks forward chiliastically to eternal peace in both metaphysics and politics. He knows, of course, that reason itself must produce the object of its hope, in an infinite process. Rational chiliasm[34] is not romantical. Although in exuberance, and not without irony, he may speak at times of an "imminent eternal peace" (62: VIII, 413, 419) and of the one and only metaphysic that will soon be completed, the believer in reason will always keep the door open for a return to clear, basic relationships, and to the awareness that in metaphysics as in politics the realization of possible peace remains always an infinite task.

Reason in Peace

In principle, the wars between dogmatism and skepticism and between the several dogmatic schools have been overcome by the self-knowledge of reason. Too, the focus of all metaphysical debates has been exposed by critique, providing a means to see through their triviality and to achieve unity. And yet reason is incapable of voiding the *possibility* of debate. For that possibility is inherent in the nature of reason itself, and its transcendent use can make conflict a reality at any time. The exploratory activities will quickly take it to the bounds of the explorable, without satisfying it within those bounds; and since it may not always resist the temptation to exceed them, reason needs an authority above it, one that will continually purify its use. Kant gives various names to this authority; he calls it now "experimental reason," now "judicial reason," now "critical reason." In metaphysical peace, reason fails to turn into a naïve unit. Critique cannot transport it into a mystical *unio sui*. Rather, it is precisely by critique that reason remains self-related, and thus always dichotomous.

Kant likes to show this self-relatedness in diverse ways in a picture of legal proceedings. We cite a passage in which the parallel development of metaphysics and politics is illuminated very clearly:

Critique of pure reason may be viewed as the true tribunal for all rational controversies; for in those controversies which are directly concerned with objects, pure reason is not involved. It is set up, rather, in order to define and to judge the rights of reason at large, according to the principles of its first institution.

Without that institution reason is in a state of nature, as it were, and cannot enforce or secure its assertions and claims otherwise than by *war*. Critique, on the other hand . . . gives us the tranquillity of a state of law, in which we do not settle our controversies by any other means than *legal process*. What terminates quarrels in the first state is a *victory*, boasted of by both sides and mostly followed by an uncertain peace established by the intervening authorities; but in the second case it is a *verdict* which covers the controversies' very source and must therefore establish an eternal peace. Also, the endless quarrels of purely dogmatic reason oblige us finally to seek tranquillity in some critique of this reason itself, and in giving laws based upon it—as Hobbes says that the state of nature is a state of injustice and violence, and that one must necessarily leave it and submit to legal compulsion, which alone will so restrict our freedom that it can coexist with everybody else's freedom and precisely thereby with the common weal [30: B 779f.].

In *Critique of Pure Reason*, variants of this metaphor appear so often that it may well be said to encompass the whole work.[35] Putting its several elements together, we find the roles assigned about as follows. Pure reason is the tribunal; critical reason sits in judgment; accused are the searching intellect if it has passed the bounds of immanence, and reason as a designer of ideas, if it has invaded immanence with constitutive statements. Judicial reason adjudicates their cases according to laws it has imposed on itself in taking its own measure. The laws are on file in *Critique of Pure Reason*. What goes on, as in every legal proceeding, is not an awarding of victories but a pronouncement of verdicts. They have absolute legal force, since judicial reason, relieved of all bias, can recognize the root of the transgressions.

The metaphor is well chosen because it clearly shows the perpetual task which reason faces in peace. Although the mere filing of *Critique* means that a definitive verdict has been reached against metaphysical controversy, there is always a chance of reason straying anew and causing more and more outbreaks. This possibility requires, in addition to the filing of *Critique,* that reason constantly reflect upon itself, and also that it constantly purify itself. Objectively, critique is on file once for all, but its effect will last only so long as reason will reiterate it in subjective efforts. The proceedings are carried through again and again, based on files that are always the same. Reason is the permanent judge, and at the same time the permanent defendant. The trial of reason is its own self-imposed, infinite task of self-enlightenment and self-purification. The peace of reason is thus not a state of trustful rest but one of vigilance and self-examination.

Again the parallel to political eternal peace is unmistakable. That peace is won by worldwide expansion of right, in freedom. In its realm of justice, violations of right are not impossible; indeed, their possibility is guaranteed by freedom. This is why freedom must watch over itself, lest it decay into license, and the idea of justice must watch the statutory law, lest it turn into institutionalized injustice. This applies equally within the fixed boundaries of a state and in the worldwide interrelation of states. Eternal peace is necessarily bound up with living liberty and a vigilant sense of justice. Both must be enforceable in institutions, so that the conflicts which are always possible will not end in lawless combat but will be settled legally, in the form of a trial. This presupposes a code of international law, a world parliament, and a world court. Yet even those cannot provide a definitive assurance of peace; they can maintain it only for so long as it is fought for and won in the institutions, by freedom and the sense of justice. Where either one lies down in trust or in search of repose, peace has been lost in principle. It remains possible only when there is more critique in it than there is trust, and more of a legal struggle than of repose.

The Basic Relations of Diversity and Unity

In this section on theoretical philosophy we have sketched the road of reason from war to peace. Included in this road is a philosophical history of philosophy—one whose basis is not *cognitio ex datis,* but *cognitio ex ratione.* The author of this history is reason itself, and its object is the evolution of reason, i.e., philosophizing (cf. 89: XX, 340). The road from war to peace in metaphysics is thus a philosophical autobiography of reason, so to speak, from "archaeology" (89: XX, 341) down to the passage into metaphysics proper.

Reason can write this history because it narrates only the evolution of rational trends. The evolution in turn is already laid out in the trend. To be able to write its history, reason must see through itself. But critique is the process of its self-knowledge and at the same time the foundation of the new metaphysics. In critique, the predisposition of reason becomes transparent to reason. Knowing itself, it can write its history. It writes it retrospectively and yet aprioristically, as a road that leads philosophizing to critique.

In this history of reason, which needs critique to become possible, the facts of history are not ignored even though originally it is not a historical narrative. It need not be justified by those facts, but it raises the accidental element of history to the rank of a historic sign and justifies it by lending historic relevance to it. The exact *cognitio ex datis* makes it possible to show how history coincides with the rational schema of the history of reason—as if the philosophers had "had this schema itself before their eyes and followed it in this knowledge" (89: XX, 342). The empirical element is thus unified in the rational schema; but this deprives it of its peculiarity. It becomes a function in the direction of critique and is henceforth evaluated as critique only, whether positively, as a sign of history, or negatively as an object lesson to demonstrate aberrations.

We visualize this road as a narrative, in order later to comprehend its formal structure and finally, by means of that structure, to get a grasp on the basic relationships of diversity and unity in theoretical philosophy.

Reason takes its first steps "in full confidence" (88: XX, 262), without reflecting on the condition of its possibilities. It trusts in itself—not because it knows itself, but because it knows that it has already had many successes. Finding evidence in mathematics that it is capable of cognition a priori, it confidently hopes to have the same success in metaphysics, without becoming aware of the fundamental differences between mathematics and metaphysics. In this hope it concentrates upon avoiding contradiction, passes all bounds as it does so, and plunges into dialectics. Under the delusion of being unity itself now, it finds all of its most crucial transcendent theses contradicted by equally true antitheses. It constantly debates itself, but this fight only strengthens its will to unity. It tries new systems, upon which it founders again. Pervaded by a sense of failure, it emigrates into skepticism and there seeks satisfaction in denying its own faculties. In this state it sways back and forth—now relapsing into its past carelessness and with that into controversy, now making a principle of incapacity—until it resolves to go the whole way once more from the beginning, but now turned inward, not just to external objects. On this journey it measures its own circumference, content, and limits and uses those to draw up laws for the employment of its faculties. It recognizes itself as knowing in the realm of that which can be experienced, as not knowing in the immeasureably larger realm of transcendence. It speculatively conceives that second realm, to complete the interminable immanence in ideas. There, knowing that it does not know, it remains united in itself. By way of critique, for as long as it remains critical, it will find peace.

This way from dogmatism via skepticism to criticism can be summed up formally, as follows.

Theoretical philosophy begins in controversy. But it wants peace. It finds peace, not by settling external contradictions, but by removing its inner contradictoriness in self-knowledge. It recognizes its own relativity, within which it finds unity. Its unity it not the absolute unity of the One pure and simple—this would be transcendent; reason can point to it, but without either knowing it or being it. But as long as it is unity at all, reason remains linked with the absolute unity by a twofold relation to transcendence. Existentially, the link is truthfulness, the condition that must be met for reason to be able to come to its own unity at all; and speculatively it is the boundary concept, the condition that must be met for reason to be able to be a unit. Since it must, over and over, come to the unity it is—and since this unity remains related to the idea of the One and is continuously approaching it—the road to reason is infinite and interminable.

The basic relations that ensue for the problematics of diversity and unity are as follows.

In immanence, diversity is a datum; but the absolute unity of the idea is transcendent and a challenge only. It cannot be transposed into immanence, but immanence can approach it. A unity that can be realized in immanence is merely relative—or, if we want to put it paradoxically, it is absolute only within the bounds of relativity. It is therefore contingent. It is desirable on the conditions of freedom and veracity. Hence the rule: discord is better than unity without freedom and veracity; but unity in freedom is better than discord.

These are basic relations that will keep crossing our path in Kant's metaphysics, and in his politics as well.

9. FROM CONFLICT TO PEACE IN PRACTICAL PHILOSOPHY

What has just been demonstrated in the thematics of theoretical philosophy—that philosophy begins in conflict but wants peace —might be shown to evolve in the history of reason throughout the fields of critical philosophy. For the foundation and exposition of all those fields is always a bit of theoretical philosophy, even if thematically entering other areas. Hence Kant's own reference to a "parallelism" (34: V, 3) of practical and speculative reason. In its practical use, pure reason also "tried all possible wrong ways" at first, uncritically, until the right way, the "only true" (32: IV, 441) way was found. This way must be based as much upon principles that do not contradict themselves as upon principles that do not contradict each other. If the inner contradictions of natural practical reason are not concealed, therefore, they compel "a complete critique of its own faculties" (34: V, 109). This critique provides the fundament for a "doctrine of wisdom . . . as a science"[1] that claims to solve whatever practical philosophical questions are soluble at all (34: V, 67). Once again, the antagonism of uncritical reason proves to be a beneficial aberration and an impulse to unity.

We shall forgo a demonstration of this entire parallel evolution. Without completely expounding practical philosophy, we take up some of its basic problems that will let us show how, and under what conditions, conflict can and cannot be turned into unity. Our purpose is to uncover a structure that recurs time and again.

Freedom and Its Use

When Kant speaks of freedom in the field of pure practical philosophy, he means the idea of a faculty that must be given if rational beings are to be conceived as determining their own will (cf. 32: IV, 446–47). In the idea, freedom in a practical sense is thus a causal faculty for the determination of the will. As an intelligible principle we cannot derive it from anything else; as a *realitas noumenon* it is united in itself. Its own direct ground is the One.

Our freedom and the reality of what we ought to do are mutually entwined, but not in the form of a circle. The fact of the moral law enables us to recognize that there must be freedom, since the possibility of the moral law requires freedom. Freedom is the *ratio essendi* of the law, and the law is the *ratio cognoscendi* of freedom. Yet this definition tells us only *that* there is freedom; *what* it is remains indefinite, an "undemonstrable concept" (35: V, 343). Definitions of this concept are misdefinitions and must be rejected. Freedom is not the stopgap of a causality we have not seen through; it is no special form of natural causality; nor is it the mere possibility of the will shaping the temporal future. All these definitions would locate freedom in time and rob it of its transcendental unity along with its intelligible character. But in the realm of phenomenality freedom is past saving. It lies in the intelligible act alone. It has about it "nothing at all that might qualitatively correspond in experience" (35: V, 343). Keeping freedom pure of everything empirical remains a condition of its existence.

Man uses his freedom in determining his will. The use of freedom, as distinct from freedom itself, is not a matter of natural unity; a freedom of which only one use could be made would not be freedom. Its nature includes the variety of possibilities and uses. Accordingly, Kant does not endow freedom with any exclusive moral qualification. It is "the greatest good and the greatest evil,"[2] depending on the use one makes of it. In fact, the varied use that is actually made of freedom makes it the premise of the possibility of contradictory actions. As such it must "be the greatest evil in our eyes" (83: XIX, 282; 7202), for it seems to bring forth "nothing but confusion" (83: XIX, 280; 7202), and certainly "no unity of my will" (83: XIX, 284; 7204). Events of nature are tied to a principle of unity by the category of causality, beyond all determination of the will; now they are to be confronted with action due to a freely determined will, an action subject to a self-imposed law, a principle of unity. Ethics is the science of searching for this principle and its premises and making its practical necessity heard (83: XIX, 284; 7205). The guiding idea of ethical inquiries is the regulative of all *realitas noumenon,*" lest it contradict itself."[3] Only if freedom and its use aim at a law that creates the capacity for unity throughout will they become "the greatest and properly absolute good in every respect" (83: XIX, 282; 7202).

The use of freedom in its purely natural character is thus embroiled with itself. Freedom is the guarantee of both this struggle and the possibility that it will lead to unity, which is the true task of freedom. The use of freedom also needs a way to peace, a way on which free unity will come more and more to be the ground of all action. Uncovering this way are Kant's *Groundwork for a Metaphysic of Morals* (32) and *Critique of Practical Reason.* Its decisive factors are the grounds on which the will is determined: whether it happens "out of the *principio* of unity" or merely out of "principles of empirical ends" (83: XIX, 284; 7204).

The Struggle of Subjective Principles

The use of freedom indicates something which is the fundament of that use. For its unity, everything depends upon the determining factor in the ultimate ground of the will. This ground is either one absolute thing—the law—or a diversity of contingent things: objects of the faculty of desire, moods, emotions, inclinations, all of them pointing to an infinite regression. Where they act as the ground of the will, the will must act diversely as a cause in the service of something else, which is always variable. The will does something because, beyond it, something is desired somewhere else. It is subordinated without exerting a subordinating, lawmaking effect of its own. In this heteronomy its direction remains as variable and divergent as the determining grounds themselves.

All these empirical determining grounds of the will are principles of happiness. But this title does not define anything specific. What each individual looks upon as his happiness depends on ever-particular feelings of pleasure and displeasure. These feelings refer to matter, not to forms of legality. They get their bearings from experience. They may achieve a measure of relative unity, but they never arrive at the legality that implies an awareness of its necessity. In the determination of the will, therefore, the principles of happiness are embattled and mutually exclusive. Inclination combats inclination; objects of the faculty of desire fight against other objects; a sense of pleasure battles other pleasures. Perverted, these principles sometimes determine the maxims, the subjective principles of volition, and if they were to be generalized into principles of objective laws there would "arise the extreme opposite of agreement, the worst antagonism, and the total destruction of the maxim itself and its intent" (34: v, 28). Without the veto of reason, which "defies outshouting" (34: v, 35), the not merely logical but practical conflict of those principles would be so confusing, it would have to ruin morality altogether.

There is no way to reconcile eudaemonistic principles in the determining position. They may, of course, be so interrelated by clever calculation that they will exert pleasurable, perhaps even salutary effects on the individual subject without promptly destroying themselves. But in their broadest generalization as lawmaking factors for rational beings as such they would invariably have to commence a process of mutual self-cancelation. The rule of eudaemonistic principles leads to a chaotic multiplicity whose point of reference to unity remains undiscoverable. There is no end to their conflict until a more general principle is found. The conflict may be pictured as a war upon which no peace can be expected to follow. Positing eudaemonistic principles as the supreme determining ground of the will controverts not just a Kantian view but the whole formal structure of Kant's metaphysics. When his philosophizing turns to ethics, therefore, it begins with the fight which the absolute determining ground wages against the rule of contingent principles.

The Absolute Principle's Fight against the
Rule of Contingent Principles

The most general ethic we can conceive is recognizable by its *universal* unification of the autonomous will. It does not link individuals as individuals, nor as human beings, but as rational beings. Since the Kantian ethic claims such universality,[4] it must rest on a principle that is absolute in the strict sense. Its fundament is an absolute law, a law based upon the *ratio universalis*, not just on the *ratio humana*. Kant generally calls it "the moral law." It is the absolute condition of every good will.

What this law is cannot be seen in examples or explained by examples. Examples are visualities for what is relative in the realm of possible experience. But the moral law is not directed at experience, at material actions in time; it aims at the formal principle of action. It is purely formal. In the eyes of this law the actor is responsible for the intelligible principle of his act, not for the act as a phenomenon and for its consequences in reality. The moral law demands a pure state of mind before the law; it is not satisfied by purity of the intention with which a particular act is committed. It is the autonomous, aprioristic, formal, universal, categorical law of reason, the law that obliges each limited and fragile individual will to work *on account* of the law, not just *in accordance* with it. But it constrains the will only by means of that which, as good will, it is itself always willing. The moral law confronts the will with an unrestricted ought, which good will would unrestrictedly acknowledge as its own volition. In view of this law, the will may therefore regard itself as legislating in the measure in which it is a good will (32: IV, 431). It is good when its maxim, "turned into a universal law, . . . can never conflict with itself," or when the will itself "can never conflict with itself" (32: IV, 437). Only as such can it really be a will. The law that constrains it is also a law of its freedom.

The law of the *ratio universalis* is a law of the intelligible world. As such it finds no adequate expression in language and no adequate representation in visuality.[5] It is as undefinable as freedom itself. It claims as absolute a unity and universality as is never given in the phenomenal realm. Since its commands are absolute, Kant calls it the "categorical imperative." By its pure formality, the utterable formula of the law—"Always act as if the principle of your action were to become a law of nature"— points to that intended absolute unity. The formula is an attempt to use the model of a natural law, adopted here as the type of the intended legality pure and simple, to bring the diversity of principles of action into the unity without which they cannot be moral. The point is to turn our thought from externals to the principle. But that the formula is not yet the flatly unifying factor, that it is not yet the moral law itself, is apparent from the impossibility of finding the one wording that could not be exchanged for another. In *Groundwork* alone there are more than ten different ones,[6] though always aimed at one goal: to establish the principle of action on a legality whose rigor and universality would be comparable to the legality of natural laws.

If we see the moral law itself in the wording of the categorical imperative, we inevitably take that wording for a kind of magic, by means of which we can manipulate total generalization so as to advance to the intelligible principle. For morality's sake we want to reach the intelligible by means of skill—and thus we lose all morality. Even the formula of the categorical imperative keeps presupposing the one *ratio universalis;* without that, it is an invitation to abuse. It serves our faculty of judgment as means to unite historic action in its suprahistoric source; but it is not the source itself.

As the sole principle of the determination of the will, the law of the *ratio universalis* would unite all action in one source. Yet man, as a twofold creature, exists from two sources—reason and sensibility. The absolute principle of the determination of the will must prevail over the onrush of contingent principles. Man is inevitably subject to the practical law, but not exclusively so. Rather, he feels in himself "a powerful counterweight to all commandments of duty . . . in his needs and leanings, whose entire satisfaction he sums up under the name of happiness" (32: IV, 405). The principles of happiness affect the will pathologically and steer the maxims, the subjective principles of volition, "against the . . . known practical laws" (34: V, 19). Kant allegorically personifies the fight of practical against pathological motives as "the good spirit's struggle against an evil one" (89: XX, 346).[7] They are fighting neither to achieve certain outward goals of the moment nor to exterminate each other; they are fighting for primacy in the supreme determining ground of all maxims.

Two principles which conflict, but of which neither one can be eliminated, are unifiable either by coordination or by subordination. In our case, this means that unity of the determination of the will arises either when concurring practical and pathological principles jointly affect the will, or when one subjugates the other and imposes the terms on which the other may continue in effect at all.

In the ideal of the beautiful soul, Schiller designed the first of these possible unities in his essay *On Charm and Dignity*, a work Kant praised. In the first part of *Religion within the Limits of Reason Alone*—a work Goethe scorned[8]—Kant himself called for the second mode of unity. Let us briefly consider the two.

Schiller speaks of a beautiful soul "when the moral sense has finally become so sure of all human sensations that it may permit affects to guide the will without ever running the risk of conflicting with affective decisions."[9] A beautiful soul does not merely produce particular moral acts; its entire being, its character, is moral. It so forms a man's actions that they will infallibly and effortlessly appear beautiful and virtuous. Its sole merit lies in being as it is. In it, reason and sensibility, duty and inclination, bring about the One without a struggle. Rather than subjugate either of the two principles, a beautiful soul reconciles them with each other; it does not put a stop to their conflict "dictatorially" (37: VI, 378) but overcomes it easily, cheerfully, and freely. In perfect harmony it blends the duality of the twofold being into one.

And, after all, why not? Did Kant himself not give his consent to the draft? In a short reply in *Religion* he declared himself "in accord with the masterfully composed essay . . . on the most important principles" (36: VI, 23 note). More than twenty years earlier (about 1770), he himself had thought of a similar possibility of unity. The practice of morality, he had written then, consisted "in so forming our tendencies and our taste that we will be able to make acts aimed at our pleasure correspond to moral principles. The man of virtue, then, is he who knows how to conform his leanings with moral principles" (83: XIX, 113; 6619). Even in those days, of course, Kant thought only of adjusting one's leanings to moral principles, certainly not of adjusting the principles to the leanings—but as a general rule their union seemed possible to him. And so we ask once more: Why not?

Replying to Schiller's point, Kant interpreters sometimes recall Schiller's own distich entitled "Scruples of Conscience" (from the series *The Philosophers*):

> Gladly I serve my friends,
> but regret to say that I like it.
> Often I'm irked by the lack
> of any virtue therein.[10]

We are told that a misunderstanding of Schiller's comes here into plain view: that the crux is not whether he liked or disliked serving his friends; that all Kant forbade was serving them only *because* one liked to. Schiller's irony, we hear, does thus not touch Kant at all. A poet, and a far from inattentive reader of Kant, is lectured here on the value of words—a rather quaint undertaking. Besides, a misconception on Schiller's part is here quite out of the question. Schiller's essay makes it perfectly clear that he knows how to draw the necessary lines. With Kant, he holds that, "in the field of pure reason and moral legislation," subjective principles are rightly "spurned altogether"; it is only "in the realm of appearance and in the real exercise of moral duties" that the objective moment must always be reached by way of the subjective one. "Therefore, no matter how much things done *because* one likes to and things done *because* one ought to may conflict in an objective sense, it is not the same in a subjective sense; and man not only *may* but *should* bring his pleasure and his duty into conjunction. He should enjoy obeying his reason."[11]

Schiller rejects Kant's model of subordination only for the appearance of morality, not for the intelligible grounds of morality as such. In other words, he is not refuting Kantian principles but complementing Kant from a standpoint that opens a vista of the subjective conditions of morality in man. From that point, the contradictions turn out to be merely seeming contradictions.

At first glance, this reduction of duality to unity by demonstrating that the contradiction is only apparent reminds us of the formal resolution of the antinomies. One might think that formally Schiller's solution is more Kantian than Kant's. This would be a delusion, however. A closer look proves it to be un-Kantian on several grounds.

a. When he dispenses with constraint, Schiller may lay himself open to the objection that all this sounds "as if we might ever get to the point of doing without a respect for law that is combined with fear, or at least with apprehension, of transgressions—to the point where we, like the deity that is above all dependence, might ever come to possess a *sanctity* of will on our own, by a sort of natural and immovable concordance of our will with the pure moral law (which, since we could never be tempted to betray it, might well cease in the end to be a commandment for us)" (34: v, 81–82).

Schiller obviously failed to see something fundamental. The moral law is not an anthropological law; it is precisely not a law of the ever-fragile *ratio humana,* but an absolute law of the *ratio universalis.* Yet man, who ought to live up to it, is always seen anthropologically by Kant, as a creature that keeps foundering and is thus always in need of constraint. Man comes up against a law that is absolute, a law not made to his measure. The cost of Schiller's conception of unity is either an anthropological relativization of the law or an elevation of man from the anthropological realm into that of the absolute.

b. On the formal side of unity, Schiller does something completely un-Kantian. He "reduces" the objective duality (acting because one ought to, or because one likes to) to a subjective unity. The unity is obtained by declaring the objective contradiction to be subjectively a mere apparent contradiction. Kant always proceeds the other way: to him, the subjective contradiction proves to be objectively a mere apparent contradiction. From the subjective split he returns to an objective unity, cutting through the surface divisions in order to point to the unity in the depths. What Schiller does in vaulting the divisions in the depths, so as to have unity on the surface, is the opposite of what Kant wants; Schiller achieves an outward peace instead of the inner one between conflicting principles. Kant views this peace as delusive. Since the dualism here is between something absolute and the contingent, Kant cannot envision the unity save in a realm that encompasses all dualisms. When Schiller establishes unity in appearance, he is relativizing the absolute.

c. Schiller's construction is a blow at the universality of the law. Kant would be the last to deny that a coincidence of inclination and duty may occur by chance in the individual human being; we can conceive of men inclining toward the law. But this unity would still be codetermined by something material, by an object of the inclinations. The law would be emotionally craved; it would have turned into matter. Yet the material objects of volition have proved to be precisely that which is not unifiable. The beautiful accord of duty and inclination is an accidentally valid unity. Since it brings "sensibility . . . into play" (36: VI, 23 note), it is not entitled to the universality Kant is seeking. The beautiful soul may be conceivable as a beautiful accident, but its principle of union does not suffice for a general principle of unity.

For these reasons, what we can justly see in Schiller's coordination of duty and leaning is not the completion of Kant's endeavors, only their beautiful distortion.

Kant takes the consequences. He rejects the coordination of the principles and achieves their possible unity by subordination. In doing so, he does not negate the contingent principles as such; their claims are legitimate as long as they do not try to qualify as an objective principle in the supreme determining ground of all maxims. "Moral order" (36: VI, 30) wants the objective principle to have primacy in the last determining ground. In that order, subordination prevails once for all, but it must always be restored in a continuing struggle. A fixed order in the supreme determining ground would have to make freedom superfluous. Man would be inevitably subject to the moral law, and precisely that would place him beyond all morality. While the primacy remains potentially in dispute, however, every decision must be an intelligible free act. Hence morality—always realized in decisions only—presupposes the possibility of conflict. It always tends to a fixed order, of course, but it involves the knowledge that this order "is always only just *becoming*" (36: VI, 75). The self-realization of morality is the road to this order.

The absolute principle's struggle against the rule of the contingent principles can come to an end in the idea, but not in reality. As in the antinomies, conflict here assumes a function in the history of reason. It is the stimulant that calls for a decision and will not let freedom come to rest; it is the offense on which morality trains itself and gradually gains strength. It keeps man open for different possibilities and thus confronts him with the necessity of having to decide, forcing him, moreover, to keep repeating his decision newly and originally. As the conflict of antinomies drives man to the free use of his reason and thus to the independence of having to answer for his knowledge, so does the conflict of the two principles drive man to the autonomy of his will and to the freedom of choice in which—now responsible in practice—he aligns his actions with the objective principle. The principle of the *ratio universalis* does indeed always demand this alignment without restriction; but the fragile *ratio humana* can meet that absolute demand only in infinite approximation. The way to peace in morality is a single and interminable way *on* which—not *in line* with which—the crucial things take place.

For morality too the conditions of unity are the relations to transcendence, freedom, and reason. The relation to transcendence is always realized in moral action by the mere fact that its principle is absolute. Freedom is made possible by the fact that good will, recognizing its own willing in the law's constraint, always knows it is autonomous. And reason is omnipresent because in its absolutely pure form as *ratio universalis* it establishes the moral law.

Embattled Modes of Faith

Morality is "sufficient unto itself" (36: VI, 3). Its only premises are reason and freedom, linked by the not deducible but empirically reinforced awareness that there can be reason in practice. Its demands of the moment carry their own authorization, for a man can do what he ought to do, if the ought is a commandment of reason.

Reason does not permit us to doubt this conclusion, for in order to doubt it we would have to give up reason itself. At the same time, however, our intellect shows us the gaps in the seemingly seamless conclusion. For example: Can I really do what I ought to do? If the qualifying relations of duty and inclination have been reversed in a man, if there is "radical evil"[12] in him, his will is no longer free. He may hear what he ought to do, and he may do what he will; but he can no longer will what he ought to. The supreme ground of all maxims is ruined.

Or: The counsel of reason in me cannot help serving its opposite now and then. It demands justice of me, but it leaves behind a discrepancy of good conduct and wellbeing. It thus comes to be usable for injustice and may seem like a mockery of the ideas of justice.

Or: The moral law in me demands inexorably that I do what I

ought to do, always and under any circumstances. It calls on me to act as if I were a saint. In other words, it overtaxes me in principle. And finally—a paradox surpassing everything else— morality commands purity of mind, the purity of the intelligible principle. Yet the inside of man is shown to him only as it comes into appearance; the intelligible principle of his acts remains hidden from him. Reason demands of him something to which he has no rational access, something for which he cannot knowingly account to himself. It calls on him for morality and leaves him unsure whether he is really moral. Its challenge seems to bypass the specific human sort of rationality, for which there is knowledge in the phenomenal realm only.

Reason discovers these gaps in reflecting on its practical activity. They are not accidental gaps; they are pits which rationality cannot get over. They show to reason its need for complementation, and they simultaneously challenge it to prove capable of complementation. Reason cannot solve this task by an increment of knowledge—for there is definitely nothing to be known here— but solely by a superstructure of faith that will let moral action appear to make sense as a whole, and thus to make sense even across those gaps. Their complements are not guidelines for cognition (in other words, not ideas of speculative reason) but ciphers that lend meaning to action, i.e., postulates of practical reason. As such postulates Kant cites God, immortality, and freedom. God is the idea of the moral person which sees the intelligible and judges by it. Immortality is the idea of the premise on which the accord of good conduct and wellbeing might become a reality. And freedom is the premise of the possibility to reverse the wrong contingent relationships, for, thanks to it, a free man can do what he ought to.

As transcendent concepts, all these postulated complements are empty. It takes their use, the direction of immanence, to lend significance to them. But what they can signify to immanence, to action in time—this in turn is decided, not by their contents as such (for those are transcendent, and thus empty), but by the modes in which they are believed and from which, in relation to something else, they derive their contents.

Faith, like the will, can spring from two sources that differ in principle. It can spring from the absolute moral law, i.e., from reason itself; or it can spring from word about something, which is relative but is declared to be absolute. The resulting modes of belief are opposed to each other. In one, its postulates are known to be mere products of reason, products whereby reason complements itself. In the other, the postulates are taken for facts disclosed to the fragile *ratio humana* by divine revelation. Belief in reason and belief in facts are mutually exclusive and cannot coexist except in conflict.

Faith in facts, if it is to claim universality, presupposes divine revelation. It is belief in that revelation. If it is to link all men, the revelation must not be a merely individual manifestation of truth; it must be a singular manifestation, one that claims to be valid for everyone and whose reality may rest on writings. Those alone serve to assure the faith of a large measure of immutability. They turn belief in revelation into belief in information. It is thus a historical faith, but one whose believed facts elude historical and rational reexamination. It does not involve a sense of necessity, but it postulates it and sanctions it by making itself the premise of salvation. Promoting that premise to the one and only premise, it demands absolute validity. It regards itself as universally communicable by means of statutory formulations; but its communicability extends no farther than the word of it. It remains an accidental communicability. The legality of such a faith is supposed to be proved by statutory laws and observances; but these, viewed from the lawful principle of practical reason, are mere "surrogates" (36: VI, 173), "pious toys and faineancy" (36: VI, 173).

The faith in facts commands belief although "permitting . . . no imperative" (38: VII, 42). As *fides imperata,* it summons the *fides servilis* and ends up as a "humiliating means of coercion" (36: VI, 123 note). Its instruments of sanction—fear, hope, threats, violence, excommunication—all rest on the delusion of being able to compel a moral cause by physical means. It is the "delusion of possessing an art to bring about supernatural effects by wholly natural means" (36: VI, 177). It claims an origin of its own while turning itself into a piece of theoretical holding-to-be-true. It publicizes itself as a faith of love and damns the unloved (they always are the unbelievers) with "the dread voice of orthodoxy" (36: VI, 130). It regards itself as the chosen faith and ends in "idolatry" (36: VI, 169 note), in "religious mania" (36: VI, 168), in "sham divine service" (36: VI, 170), in a servile "bondsmen's and hired hands' faith" (36: VI, 115). Finally, in justification by faith, it seeks to create a new man in another world and begins by forcing temporal man to give up his reason, either in the *sacrificium intellectus* or in outright lies. While pretending to give everything to God, it withholds the one thing God would have to cherish: the moral state of mind (36: VI, 172). In a word, wherever you touch this faith it bears the stigma of evil—contradictoriness. In principle it is always at war with itself, as clearly shown wherever it encounters other contents of faith.

As regards the "different kinds of belief in divine revelation" (38: VII, 36), these are merely "different forms of the sensory kind of conceiving the divine will" (38: VII, 36). As long as no more than a necessarily "symbolic presentation" (36: VI, 176) is drawn up in this kind of conception, its sensoriness is not yet a bar to unity, for it is really an unintended sensoriness. But where the presentation does more than suggest that which is to be presented, where it seeks to call it by name—and all types of the faith in revelation end in this perversion—the faith becomes a faith in experience or in miracles. This cannot be universal, and so there are always other faiths in revelation beside it, to be fought for good or ill. The phenomenon is paradoxical: all types of faith in revelation arise from the same wrong principle, but between them lies "a vast distance in *manner*" (36: VI, 176). It is over that distance that they quarrel. Absolutizing the relative, they view themselves as different in principle. Although in principle they are as one, their principle does not qualify for unity. In agreement on the essence, they are bound to quarrel about nonessentials because they have raised their perversions to essential rank—a fight to the death about trivia, based on a delusion.

This type of struggle is easily recognizable. We have met it before—in the fights of natural metaphysics, in the political battles of mankind or of nations in a state of nature, later in the struggle of subjective principles in the determining ground of the will—and we are going to meet it once more in the interest-based struggle between judgments of taste. It is the lawless struggle in which one aims at the opponent's annihilation, seeks victory at any cost, and fights himself in the process. Yet this seemingly senseless battle of religious parties has an unintended beneficial effect: not unlike war in a politically decayed world, it preserves the freedom that it would not mind suppressing. Its task in the history of faith is to keep freedom alive, though in limited measure, until a united faith can agree with freedom and enter into it.

This unity must be able to base itself upon a "legal title" (cf. 36: VI, 6off.). It can do so only when a rational faith carries with it a sense of necessity and general communicability. Such a faith "proves itself" (36: VI, 129). No experience qualifies its communicability; it communicates itself wherever there is reason. Its characteristic in the realm of reason is the line that about it there "can be no conflicting opinions" (36: VI, 131). It rests on the flatly unifying practical principle of the *ratio universalis*—in other words, on the moral law. It is not the premise but the consequence of morality. For practical action awakens a "rational need" (36: VI, 104) for a power that unites the whole of moral endeavors in an effect harmonizing with the final goal, and for a time span in which the highest good can become a reality.

The rational faith thus lends meaning to the individual moral effort by involving it in a possible entirety that is never given, though it is always a challenge. This makes that faith the awakener of moral impulses. At the same time, establishing confidence in the future moral force as such, it turns into a power that is the carrier of moral action, if not its original producer. Hence the "mere faith in reason" (36: VI, 102) is a moral faith—free, since it springs from morality whose *ratio essendi* is freedom; unique and universal, since it rests on the unique and universal principle of the *ratio universalis;* and the only saving faith because, if shown by practical action to be a living faith, it is the only one that makes a man worth saving. It is an appeal to the human self, not a holding-to-be-true of definitions of transcendent being; its supreme principle is not an external divine service but the inner betterment of man; its outcome is not passive submission to another will, but the "salvation of the souls" (36: VI, 8) that can be gained by free acts. It is an animating faith, not a didactic one.

The faith in reason is not its own opponent, but this does not mean that it is in the world without a struggle. As long as belief in revelation is considered meritorious, the rational faith finds in it its adversary. It is not free to fight or not to fight that foe. To be passive toward the exclusionary is to abandon oneself. The existence of the faith in revelation compels the rational faith to do battle. The history of faith is therefore "nothing but an account of the constant struggle between the moral religious faith and that of divine service" (36: VI, 124).

Outwardly this struggle may look alike in both modes of faith, but its essence in the two is entirely different. What the faith in revelation combats in rational faith is reason itself; what rational faith combats in the faith in revelation is irrationality. The first seeks to destroy the free faith; the second, to free the exclusive faith. The first excludes tolerance; the second, the principle of intolerance. The faith in revelation takes its stand on the principle of isolation; the faith in reason, on the principle of universality. This universality shows in the fact that rational faith alone can absorb its counterpart without abandoning itself. It does not absolutely exclude faith in revelation. If that faith comes to a new understanding of itself, if it sees itself as a "mere sensory vehicle" (38: VII, 37) that is "changeable in itself" (38: VII, 42) and capable of "a gradual purification to the point of congruence" (38: VII, 42) with rational faith—in that case the faith in revelation, now a servant of rational faith, can gradually enter into rational faith itself. Even this transition is conceived by Kant as a struggle, but no longer as a struggle to exterminate each other; it is a struggle for purification, by rationality, of that which can be changed in the sensory realm. In this struggle, ecclesiastic faith dismisses its own "supreme interpreter" (36: VI, 109) in religious faith. Due to this struggle, it gradually comprehends that dogmas in themselves are worthless—that everything depends on awakening the moral impulses and allowing them to take effect in free acts.

The antagonism of the modes of faith shows us two models of struggle. One is the fight waged without reason, the life-and-death combat between various forms of the faith in revelation; the other is the fight waged by reason to get all things gradually involved in rationality. The first form is a lawless, arbitrary struggle waged in the hope for a violent peace in time; the second is a lawful, rational struggle aimed at a peace which, on account of freedom, can in time be won only in infinite approximation. Since the lawless struggle goes of necessity with the faith in revelation, and since the fight over the modes of faith themselves rests upon man's twofold origin (as a creature of the senses he makes something sensory of the divine; as a rational being he negates this transformation)—for these reasons, the struggle begins and ends not *in* faith, but *with* faith. Faith is thus condemned to be a struggle for all time. It is impossible for believers not to fight. But in time they have a chance to turn their struggle from a lawless one into a lawful one that comes more and more to be reason.

Corresponding to the two forms of struggle are two forms of unity. One springs from the one principle and is thus united in its very source; the other's origin bears the germ of temptations. One is a triumph of reason; the other, a triumph of violence. One comes about by the expansion of freedom; the other, by its suppression.

And once again we find Kant rejecting a unity without freedom. He pursues only the unity that presupposes reason and freedom and provides the sole ground on which rational men can unite.

The Union of Rational Men

The challenge of the moral law is addressed to each individual, but to each as one of a group, the group of rational beings. The task it poses for everyone, "man's ultimate destiny," is to found and expand "the kingdom of God on earth" (75: XV, 608–9; 1396). To approach this idea, man needs an ever-growing and eventually global "society according to laws of virtue" (36: VI, 94)—a society whose point and principle of union is morality. At one time Kant calls this society the "ethical state" (36: VI, 94), at other times the "realm of virtue" (36: VI, 95), the "realm of morals" (34: V, 82), or the "moral world" (30: A 808/B 836).

All these are names for "a *corpus mysticum* of rational beings" in the world, "provided their free arbitrary will forms a consistent, systematic union under moral laws, both with itself and with everybody else's freedom" (30: A 808/B 836). Since the laws of this intellectual world are laws of freedom, not coercive laws, and since as inner laws they do not permit any sanction, they must be regarded as "commandments of a common lawmaker" (36: VI, 98), in which "God's will is originally graven into our hearts" (36: VI, 104). And since man is denied any chance to observe their observance, the common maker of those laws must be a "teller of hearts" who can see through "everyone's innermost state of mind" (36: VI, 99). The bond of the intellectual world is not the law; it is morality, and the idea of God that springs from morality (cf. 75: XV, 518; 1171). The ethical state is thus based on the moral law and necessarily on the moral faith that grows out of that law. It is a kingdom of faith, an association that unites all believers in reason under the immediate moral world government of God. If it were freely accepted by all mankind, it would bring about that state of the world which might, without distorting it, be called a terminal state.

The way to the ethical state is to expand pure morality. But that idea of a *corpus mysticum* of the rational is the idea of the invisible church. This is not something ever achieved in the world; it is the idea that keeps all achievements headed toward the real goal. In the world we can see only the several churches. Their relation to the invisible one—which alone can be the world church—makes out their value. Their importance to the world's evolution lies not in the way they are at any time; it lies in their relation to the idea and in their capacity for changing with respect to the idea.

Churches are the visible schemata of "an invisible kingdom of God on earth" (36: VI, 131). They are not this kingdom itself; they are its possible mundane representations, required at all times to realize the kingdom. Essential to them is therefore an awareness that the way they are is accidental (they are mere vehicles and provisoria), but also an awareness that their existence is necessary (they are indispensable to the expansion of God's kingdom). They are the sources from which an incessant conquest of their accidental side is to bring forth the necessary side.

Where the churches have come to understand themselves in this way, they are many communities bound for the one religion. Despite their various shells, they know they are united in the one principle. But where the sense of the indispensability of their existence turns into a feeling that the manner of their existence is indispensable, there the churches are bound to take their facade for the essence. This makes them pagan[13] societies that cite revelation to justify their orthodoxy. As such they are exclusionary in the sense of mutual destruction. Since "conflict can never be avoided" (36: VI, 115) between them, they are the true obstacles to unity and the "shackles" (36: VI, 121) of religion.

Religious communities based on revelation are essentially "despotic" (36: VI, 180) even if, as may happen, they affect a conciliatory demeanor. Their exclusiveness shows in their quest of the wrong unity, of unity by force. Unification efforts by churches that hold revelation to be essential are plots against human freedom. According to Kantian principles, the worldwide joyous participation in those efforts must be viewed subjectively as an expression of general thoughtlessness, and objectively as a sign of evil in the world. The wrong ecclesiastic unity is not better than the wrong political unity, but it is more perfidious. For it would violate the state of people's minds, not only their outward actions.

But here again, in principle, distortion always exacts its own vengeance from the visible churches. Since the revealed content of faith is to them the essence, this content inevitably keeps blocking their unity. The visible churches' external, necessary antagonism preserves mankind from the worst of fates, which would be a world religion based on revelation. Though lawless, their conflict is a beneficial aberration. It affords a remnant of religious liberty, and it finally compels the churches to understand themselves. They constantly preach unity and live in discord; but in the end, to escape the general contempt of thinking people, they must remember their own principle, reverse their reversal of it, and then, on grounds of reason and morality, establish the faith that includes all rational men. With that faith they will found the pure religion. "In the long run, a religion that does not shrink from declaring war upon reason will not be able to stand up against reason" (36: VI, 10).

Pure religion is "not the sum of certain teachings as divine revelations . . . but that of all our duties in general, as divine commandments" (38: VII, 36). It is a "religion of good conduct" (36: VI, 175), whose only purpose can be "to form morally better men" (38: VII, 66). It recognizes its only divine service in the service of practical reason. Like morality, it is "purely a matter of reason" (38: VII, 67) and "hidden within" (36: VI, 108); indeed, it is really morality to which we grant admission by the idea of God. Its characteristics, therefore, are universality (numerical unity; hence no division), purity (absence of unbelief; hence no belief in revelation), freedom (absence of coercive laws; hence no powerful clergy), and immutability (absence of accidental factors; hence no belief in history). This religion alone is a world religion in the true sense of the word, because no other is absolutely united in itself and simultaneously qualified for universality.

Visible churches are militant churches because their principle is contradictory in itself. Their violent victories over others are fonts of new conflicts which also fail to end in definitive triumphs. The invisible church alone will ultimately be the "triumphant" (36: VI, 115) church. But the existence of the militant churches obliges it to fight, and the fight must be exclusionary until the visible churches bow to the terms of the invisible one. It is too much to hope that they will do so voluntarily, but the threat of disdain and the repeated experience of their own impotence against reason will compel them. Their decision to enter into a new conditional relationship with reason lends a new dimension to the struggle. In the history of reason it can now be seen as a fight in which the *ecclesia triumphans* seeks gradually to lift the *ecclesiae militantes* to their proper level. As such, the struggle is no longer exclusionary but inclusive. It is a fight for an ever larger community.

The visible churches' approach to the invisible one is not going to result in a state of empirical perfection. It remains a "continuous progress" (36: VI, 136). That is enough. For, in a sense, the whole already lies hidden in the principle of approximation as a "developing and subsequently regenerating germ" (36: VI, 122). In that sense the principle of peace may be viewed as being peace already. But this peace is not absolute rest; it is lawfully ordered motion.

Thus the road to the *ecclesia triumphans,* to the union of rational believers across all lines of states and outward religious creeds, begins in controversy. The controversy is lawless as long as the visible churches found themselves on the wrong principle, on a belief in revelation. Where this foundation turns into one of reason, the exclusionary struggle widens into an inclusive one. As such it persists and impels the churches more and more to approach the guiding idea.

Once again, the premises of unity are the principles that qualify for unity—reason and freedom—and the product of those principles, morality.

Basic Relations of Conflict and Unity

In this section on practical philosophy we have been discussing freedom and its use, the principles of morality, the battles between modes of faith and between churches, and in every case we have observed something similar. It appeared that freedom may, in license, miss the absolute source; that morality may, in eudaemonism, lose its absolute principle; that faith may turn an accidental principle into the essential one, and the church may base itself upon a merely accidental faith. Each time, the one objective principle of morality has been displaced by contingent, subjective principles that will be perverted and looked upon as absolute. They will seek absolute unity without being qualified for universality. The consequence is war, with license destroying license, with finite principles of ethics banishing each other, with modes of faith replacing one another, with churches doing what they can to make each other perish. It is the hopeless struggle without a true counterpart, the unconditional pursuit of victory that never leads to a definitive victory—a senseless back and forth over trivia. But it does have a function. Each of the perversions claims unity and universality; not being entitled to them, each resorts to coercion; and what conflict does, again and again, is to break this coercion whenever it seems to grow total. The power of the arbitrary will proves to be limited; the principles of morality turn out to be relative; the modes of faith, to be accidental; the churches, to be sects. Conflict thus maintains the possibility of freedom and a minimum, at least, of its reality—just enough to let a man remember to what end freedom is a principle, what the principle of morality is, what faith is based upon, and what upholds the church.

In this recognition of principles, man is discovering also the roots of past evils. Those he can now eradicate. From the one absolute principle which reason qualifies for unity and universality, man designs the ideas of freedom, of morality, of faith, and of the community of faith. At these ideas he directs his volition, his action, his faith, and his temporal churches. Now the idea stands firmly established; but the human being that is to approach it is fragile and keeps missing the idea. Conflict is not removed from the world by the idea of the absolute as a ground and carrier, but it has received a different structure. It is now a struggle waged on grounds of the absolute and for the end of including all rational things in this core. It is a lawful struggle which in principle does not exclude; it includes, rather, within universal horizons. It is a fight for the continuing approach to the idea, a fight that is necessarily endless because the idea is transcendent. It is peace, since the principle of peace is at work throughout it; but this peace is also a way throughout, since the unity pursued is only an idea.

Again we comprehend a few basic relationships. Just as there are forms of unity—unity in freedom and unity by violence—so are there two forms of struggle: the lawless one for a unity without freedom, and the lawful one for unity in freedom. The first must have an end in time; the second must not. The first comes to an end only by passing into the second. Once it has fulfilled its finite function, it discards that function and assumes an infinite one grounded in the law.

10. FROM CONFLICT TO PEACE IN JUDGMENT

Critique of Judgment as a whole is a work of synthesis, both in a historical and in a systematic respect. Historically, the book resolves specific problems of aesthetics and teleology that had been discussed for a century in Italy, France, England, Germany, and Switzerland, and the resolution almost invariably seems like a systematic synthesis of the many previous opinions. Systematically, the third *Critique* is the bridge between the two earlier ones. Unlike those, it is not critique for the sake of a doctrine; there is no doctrine of judgment. Its sole aims are the illumination a priori of the principles of the connecting cognitive faculty, judgment, and the discovery in those principles of the possibility of a unified system.

Both the historical synthesis and the systematic connection might provide all sorts of opportunities to trace that fundamental line of Kant's philosophizing, from diversity to the One. Even in this part, however, we shall concentrate upon his way of recognizing antagonism in specific philosophemes within the systematic presentation, upon the functions he ascribes to it, and upon the manner in which, and the conditions under which, he seeks to unify what has been split.

We do not give a complete interpretation of the third *Critique,* nor any exhaustive analyses of particular problems. Instead, with an exclusively formal interest, we make observations that seem to us important in view of things not discussed here in so many words. We are going to talk only of pleasantness and beauty, in other words, only of *Critique of Aesthetic Judgment*—which does not mean to say that for an interpretation of Kantian politics this alone matters. *Critique of Teleological Judgment* is of great significance to such an interpretation—materially (by the draft of a philosophy of history) as well as methodologically (by the clarification of the use of teleological principles) and formally (by the distinction of machine and organism). No exegesis of Kant's political thinking would be able to avoid recurring frequently to *Critique of Teleological Judgment.* It is less important only to the passage from antagonism to unity, which concerns us here.

The Controversy about Pleasantness

As *Critique of Pure Reason* establishes the unity of cognition and *Critique of Practical Reason* the unity of the will, *Critique of Aesthetic Judgment* inquires into the unanimity of feeling and sensation. The first *Critique* advances to the conditions of the possibility of human knowledge; the second, to the absolute principle of volition as such. In both, the ground of unity is discovered, which is why in their fields it is possible to bring judgments into accord. But where is the basis for a unanimity of feeling, and how should judgments about it ever come to agree? The chances are poor; feeling and sensation are subjective realms in which no individual can substitute for any other. The judgment measuring these realms is not a pure cognitive judgment; Kant's name for. it, somewhat confusingly, is "aesthetic judgment." The faculty that subsumes in it does not define; it merely reflects. The question is whether these three factors make it impossible to arrive at unanimous judgments of taste.

The faculty of judgment is the third, the middle one, of the cognitive faculties, the one which by subsumption mediates between the intellect and the imagination. As determinative judgment it assigns given particulars to predetermined universals, according to rules given to it a priori by the intellect. On the basis of the unified data it achieves a unified assignation.

As reflective judgment, on the other hand, it is never given more than a link in the chain of mediations, nothing but the accidental particular. The universal is unknown to him who makes the judgment; to be able to subsume at all, he has to find it first. No calculable procedure can say how to find this universal in a particular case. The process of reflective judgment is a critical mental movement which in the sphere of the particular aims at a whole that is not defined, but is guiding. Since it lacks a predetermined universal, and since the universal established in reflection is not a general concept, its kind of subsumption remains an indefinite motion. Reflective judgment seems to be an obstacle to unanimity in judgments of taste.

The field of reflective judgment is vast, but it is limited. Kant divides it into (a) the conception of a general legality for the contemplation of nature and (b) the vision of beauty. Accordingly, he calls the faculty of reflective judgment either teleological or aesthetic, and he structures its critique in two corresponding main parts, each based on its own principle.

The field of aesthetically reflective judgment covers a particular way to judge. Kant calls it aesthetic judgment. What this "aesthetic" characterizes is not a relation to the pure forms of sensibility, as in *Critique of Pure Reason;* here it means a relation to the subject and to its feelings of pleasure and displeasure. All that one may look for in aesthetic judgment is a subjective definition. Something is attributed to the subject: "By voicing an aesthetic judgment about an object we indicate at once that while a given conception is related to an object, the judgment is understood to define, not the object, but the subject and its feeling" (87: XX, 223).

Yet the verbal sequence "aesthetic judgment" seems to be contradictory in itself. A judgment that is aesthetic, i.e., sensory, is not conceivable. Our senses do provide material for judgments, of course, but they themselves never judge; judgments are always made by the intellect alone (87: XX, 222). This is why Kant may admit in an apologia (39: VII, par. 8–11, 143ff.) that we are neither confused nor deceived by our senses: "One may rightly say that the senses do not err—not, however, because they always judge correctly, but because they do not judge at all" (30: A 293/B 350). The word "aesthetic," therefore, cannot refer to the act of judging. What justifies the term is not the judgment as such but its reference and its determining ground, both of which point to a matter of the senses.

The reference to the subject can be characterized more exactly. It covers the feelings of pleasure and displeasure in which the subject, as a conception affects it, "feels itself" (35: v, 204). An object, the form, is accorded something only insofar as for subjective ends the form is "a sensory conception of the state of the subject" (87: xx, 223)—of a state which in turn is "sensible" (87: xx, 223). The determining ground of an aesthetic judgment lies in a sensation directly linked with the feeling of pleasure or displeasure.

As a judgment based upon a feeling, aesthetic judgment is not a general but an individual judgment. As a judgment referring to the subject it has no objective concepts. Its predicate does not convey cognition, just a reflective statement that characterizes an object only insofar as it puts the cognitive faculties sensibly into free play. It therefore does not seem qualified for unity at all.

The crux of the question of its general validity, however, is what this sensation, on its part, is based upon. If its ground lies in the direct empirical visuality of an object, or in its conception, the aesthetic judgment is a mere judgment of the senses; but if the ground lies in the harmonious play of two cognitive faculties of judgment (intellect and imagination) that have yet to be reflected on, the aesthetic judgment is a judgment of reflection (87: xx, 224). In the first case, the sensation is a product of interested participation in the existence of the thing conceived; in the second case it is a product of aesthetic distance, to which the very possibility of reflecting is due. The judgment of the senses contains a material purposiveness; the judgment of reflection, a formal one. The predicate of the judgment of the senses expresses a direct reference to the conception of feelings of pleasure or displeasure; the predicate of the judgment of reflection expresses a reference to the interplay of cognitive faculties. The first judgment has no principle at all; it is left to the discretion of the individual subject. The second rests upon a principle that permits general communicability. Hence the mere judgment of the senses cannot claim general validity, but the judgment of aesthetic reflection can. Its claim, of course, requires an authorization, and this will be furnished by demonstrating the ground of the possibility of accord—which does not imply a possibility of enforcing an accord.

To our question we can now reply that even if the power of reflective judgment, the aesthetic judgment, and the relation to the subject are obstacles on the way to conceptual unity, the prospect of a possible general validity still remains open. The crux is the location of the judgment's determining ground, and if that lies in pleasure, of course, all hope for unanimity must be abandoned.

Kant delimits pleasantness from beauty and goodness, explicating as follows. Pleasant is that which pleases the senses immediately, in sensation; beautiful is that which pleases by means of reflection, by its form; good is that which pleases cogently by means of reason, by its mere concept. Pleasant things delight us individually, without concepts; beautiful things please generally, without concepts; good things meet with universal respect due to concepts. Pleasant is thus what delights the senses of one individual at a time, by direct sensation.

Whatever delights the senses by direct sensation produces by its existence a lustful feeling that is the expression, not of a detached approval, but of relish. Relish is an unreflected reception of stimulations and emotions whereby the pleasant thing acts upon the subject. The subject's relation to things pleasant is therefore that of inclination or that of desire. With respect to those things the subject proves needful, restricted, and thus limited in its freedom. The subject is interested in the existence of pleasant things.

This has consequences for our judgment about these things. Since they always please the senses of individuals by materiality, our judgment about them is not based on the free interplay of cognitive faculties, but on a "private feeling" (35: V, 212). As a private feeling, this is left to the individual subject's discretion. Where it appears at all, universality in judgments about pleasant things is always only comparative and accidental, never general or universal.

A comparison of judgments would have to show, therefore, that conflict between them is limitless and lawless. We can never hope for unanimity, because the grounds of their antagonism do not lie in the cognitive faculty itself. This antagonism is not dialectical, and thus not removable by critique. Here all efforts in behalf of unity are futile. A debate about pleasantness as such is not to be taken seriously. The difference in views may be established empirically, but a debate about it would be "folly" (35: V, 212).

Governing the field of pleasantness is an antagonism qualified by its random nature, which is bad subjectivity. In that sense we can compare it to the antagonism of precritical metaphysics, of eudaemonistic ethics, of the faith in revelation, and of the embattled churches. The only differences are that this random antagonism cannot be eliminated as a controversy, that it has no function, that no postulate is addressed to it, and that it cannot find a new basis in reason. Controversy about whether things are pleasant or unpleasant is everlasting and meaningless.

We have established that Kant sees conditions of unity in freedom, in the relation to transcendence, and in an existential element (truthfulness or morality at large). The question is to what extent this still applies here. That aesthetic judgments also require freedom is only negatively apparent in the case of pleasantness. Our dealings with things pleasant lack the moment of reflection. Reflection is possible only in aesthetic detachment, which delivers from the object's claim and leaves room for contemplative vision. That vision alone would permit a general aesthetic judgment. The inability to achieve unity turns out to be a consequence of the lack of freedom—although, as we have yet to see, of a freedom peculiar in kind.

But what about the second condition of unity, the existential moment? In aesthetic judgment this has not been mentioned so far, and there seem to be two reasons why it cannot appear as a condition of the unity of that judgment. First, the existential moment belongs in the realm of practical reason, from which all objects of aesthetic judgment are separated by a wide gulf; what decides about them is a different use of reason. Furthermore, the incompatibility of judgments of the senses may seem to be due to the very truthfulness of the individual about what strikes him, and perhaps him alone, as pleasurable. Here a clarification will not be possible until Kant legitimizes the claim of general validity made in behalf of the aesthetically reflective judgment.

Finally, as regards the transcendent relation, we can only say that in the realm of pleasantness it does not appear, and that its absence is clearly one more negative reason for the lack of general validity.

Unanimity of Judgments about Beauty

Judging what is beautiful seems to be rather like judging what is pleasant. Experience shows no unanimity in either case; what looks beautiful to one man will look ugly to another. There is no conceptuality that might compel agreement. Everybody has to trust in his own findings. One must dare to make a judgment.

And yet there is a difference. Judgments about beauty manifest an expectation to agree; one seems "to have a general voice for oneself and lays claim to everyone's concurrence" (35: v, 216). This voice does not justify postulating an agreement; for such a postulate it would have to be able to rest upon a logically universal judgment citing objectively sufficient reasons. The voice does not demand; it "only *expects* that everyone else will agree" (35: v, 216). If concurrence is withheld, the man who makes the judgment claims the right to lay the other's different judgment to a lack of taste. What makes him do so—or, more generally put, by what authority is general validity claimed for judgments of taste?

If it is correct to say that a negative reason for the divergence in aesthetic judgments of the senses was the absence of freedom, it must be possible to show that a mode of freedom is a condition of the possibility of judgments of aesthetic reflection with which men are asked to agree. Since all aesthetic judgments are subjective, it is in part the liberation of the subject that will enable it to pass from judgments of the senses to those of reflection. Wherein does this liberation show?

Reflective taste judges "by a *wholly disinterested* liking or disliking" (35: v, 211). In this line lies a liberation of the subject that amounts to a virtual liberation from finiteness. Every finite being is needful, dependent in its existence upon existence of other beings and things. To exist is to be interested. In the realm of existence, the finite subject's relation to things is naturally determined by the will to appropriate. Where there is no such will, and thus no interest, there seems to be no need either. The subject contemplates in pure contentment, then, leaving the object free at the same time and receiving it as a pure phenomenon, in contemplative vision. Private desires and conditions fall by the wayside. Within its subjectivity, the subject achieves an objective posture that might suffice to let it hope for general consent.

The subject is now free also in its feelings of pleasure. Beauty pleases. In being pleased, the subject is not directed toward the satisfaction of a moment of relish, which always presupposes captivity in the realm of the senses; rather, it is given room for detachment from the object and thus for reflection upon its own state. Only in being pleased can there be pure contentment enlightened by reflection.

To estimate the freedom of this pleasure, we must compare it with the pleasure we take in goodness. "Good is that which pleases by its mere concept, by means of reason" (35: v, 207). What pleases in the sense of goodness must first of all be recognized by reason as either good in itself or good to some end. In both cases, reason is interested in the existence of the good. This interest is a binding obligation, to be fulfilled in freedom. Included in liking the good is thus an appeal to go beyond mere contemplation, to advance to bringing it about.

The essence of liking beauty is a "freedom from"; the essence of liking goodness, an appeal to "freedom for." The first delivers us from the will to possess as well as from that to produce; the second imprisons us in the reality of moral existence. Only our liking for beauty is free in every respect.

A further deliverance shows in the separation of beauty and goodness: our deliverance from objective expediency. What is good is decided by purposive concepts given by our reason; what is beautiful is decided by a disinterested liking. To begin with, beauty has no purpose beyond itself. Whatever end we might posit for it would have to evoke an interest again. It would be incompatible with disinterested liking. Hence our failure to ask for either the theoretical or the practical significance of beauty. We really meet it unquestioningly. In the encounter it turns out to have a purpose for the subject individual, the purpose of putting his cognitive faculties into free play. This purely subjective pur-posiveness without a purpose is nothing but the form of pur-posiveness any more.[1] It always goes with disinterested liking.

The deliverance from interest and purpose also frees the subject from any tie to the materiality of the presented object. The judg-ment of aesthetic reflection aims not at the "what" of the object, but at the "how" of its presentation. What we mean by this is not just the manner of presenting; we mean the condition that proves to create the possibility of the presented object. This qualification of the object's possibility is what Kant calls its form. That form, not the materiality of the object, is subjectively expedient for the play of cognitive powers.

Freed from striving for utility, the beauty-judging subject stands outside the realm of existence, so to speak, outside the realm filled with embattled interests. Freed from the tutelage of concepts, it moves in a sphere not ruled by consciousness at large, in a sphere in which decisions are not cogently made by the intellect. Freed from objective expediency, it judges outside the moral world, the world in which obligations would weigh upon it. Free from the ties of enjoyment, morality, and cognition, the subject finds the way open to judge by sheer liking, to make judgments which it expects to be generally valid.

One moment in the subject's liberation that is surely crucial for the possible general validity of aesthetically reflective judg-ments is deliverance from all individual subjective desire. But this is only a negative ground of unity, its *conditio sine qua non*. For the positive ground we must look elsewhere; it must be sought in the transcendental and transcendent foundation of taste.

Findings of beauty spring from a kind of pleasure. But in the structure of such findings something comes before the pleasure; it is preceded by an element of reflection on the interplay of cogni-tive faculties. The pleasure rests on an awareness of the free mutual furtherance of intellect and imagination. It is the effect of this interplay, grown sensible in the subject. Related by reflection to the cognitive faculties, the pleasure is kindled, not by their lawful concordance in a cognition, but by the playful and yet not lawless way in which those faculties—without any actual cogni-tion—open the door to possible cognition. In the process, intellect and imagination stimulate each other so that, as though by accident, they will fit into the legality of interaction. In this play, freedom and the law are one.

Although the pleasure of beauty cannot be conceptually produced, it does rest upon a relationship common to all men. It is therefore generally communicable. The judgment of taste that communicates it may expect to be generally valid. We may accordingly say that judgments of taste have one voice in favor of their unanimity, because the liking in which those judgments are registered refers to a transcendental ground in the cognitive faculties.

The transcendental place of that accord is reached by reflection. But how to register the reflection itself? The expected general validity of the judgment of taste presupposes a registering principle that measures concordance and the relationships favoring it —a principle by which the general feeling that rests on a mood must be made communicable without the mediation of a concept. Kant calls this principle a "common sense" because human faculties are experienced in it as common and made communicable, and because it is common to all men. The principle is taste.

With this transcendental foundation of its general validity we have not yet attained the ultimate ground of the judgment of aesthetic reflection. Kant goes back to that ground in the transcendent foundation of taste: "This is the *intelligible* aim of taste. . . . Nor is it in any other respect that [beauty] pleases with a claim to everyone else's agreement" (35: v, 353). The intelligible is the fundament that brings our cognitive faculties into accord. Beauty always rests upon this fundament, for beauty also comes to be in the accord of two or all cognitive powers. In play, beauty points beyond itself and at transcendence. This gives it the scope that trains men for liberality. Since Kant considers transcendence accessible in morality alone, he couches the connection between beauty and transcendence in the words "Beauty is the symbol of the morally good" (35: v, 353). Insofar as this line confers on beauty a distinct and limited function, it narrows the scope of beauty; Kant has better luck showing the ground of beauty when he says that beauty points up "something within and without the subject that is not nature, is not freedom either, and yet is linked with freedom's ground, the supersensory" (35: v, 353). In this ground he finds "the theoretical faculty united with the practical in common and unknown fashion" (35: v, 353). Beauty is the symbol of moral goodness because in play it penetrates to that ground from which man, in the ought, hears the appeal to his morality.

We started out from the question, What is the condition on which general validity may be claimed for a judgment of aesthetic reflection?

Here too the basic conditions of unanimity are freedom and the anchoring in transcendence, with freedom understood as the subject's liberation from all ties to distinct and determining reality, and transcendence understood as the intelligible ground that encompasses nature and freedom. That a transcendental ground of unanimity (which in the intellectual and rational realms was given) must be demonstrated in the subjective realm is a matter of course. Unanimity about judgments of taste is thus assured in a way we know. The very thing which materially, due to the character of beauty as a symbol for moral goodness, may seem like a sudden invasion of aesthetics by morality—this very thing is thoroughly in line with Kant's systematic thinking if considered from the structure of the conditions of unity. There is no unity without transcendence. Even where this unity, as unanimity, is conceptually not discoverable, though to be expected in practice—even there, the expectation cannot be legitimate without a relation to transcendence.

The demonstration of possible unanimity in judgments of taste does not mean that in discussing what is beautiful there can be an unequivocal end to conflict. It means no more than that discussing what is beautiful makes sense. Judgments are arguable; but in each argument there lies the hope, if not the guarantee, of gradually arriving at an agreement. It is possible to understand one another. The struggle waged in discussions of beauty is communicative, and it shows the characteristics of a lawful struggle.

Is there a *way* to unanimity in judging beauty?

Judgments of taste are subjective and determined by a feeling, not by concepts. The ground of their unanimity must lie in the subject, not in a regular object. The way to unanimity of taste is thus a way of the contemplating subject. It is, first, a way of deliverance from individual subjective desire. Next, it is a way of practicing the use of one's faculty of judging beauty—in other words, of training one's taste. Empirically this is done by contemplating exemplary models. That is not enough, however. The models change in time. The models themselves seem to indicate that there may not be any unanimity of taste. Taste is a heteronomous faculty as long as its principles come from experience alone. In the final analysis, Kant considers only one way to train one's taste as sure: since beauty is the symbol of moral goodness, and since taste is the faculty of judging the pictorial representation of the idea of moral reason, "the true propaedeutic for a foundation of taste [is] the development of ethical ideas and the cultivation of the moral sense" (35: V, 356). Training in morality is training in taste. Again, the stations of the road to unanimity are freedom and ethical practice, and it is an infinite road.

Conflict and Unity of Spirit and Taste in Genius

Another possibility of conflict lies in the production of beautiful things. For it is there that the really productive force, the spirit, ought to be originally active and yet to submit to a canon, to taste; and it is there that the spirit can conflict with taste, and taste with the spirit. But true beauty comes to be only where the two—no one knows how—become as one in its production.

Kant terms production in the sense of nature an "acting or working in general," and in the sense of art, a "doing." What has come about by working is called an "effect"; what has come to be by doing, a "work" (35: V, 303). Doing is thus a production directed at, and unified in, a work. To make that direction possible, the doing must be preceded by a planning anticipation of the work, and this in turn is made possible by cognition and conception. Accordingly, doing presupposes a knowledge or vision as the basis of a skill. What the knowledge anticipates, however, has yet to be accomplished by the skill, by a special faculty. It is equally true of artistic and of merely technical production that envisioning a work is one thing and realizing one's vision is another. It is one thing to know what a shoe must be like, and it is quite another thing to make it. The vision is formed into a work by the artist's creative activity; the known plan is transformed into a product in the artisan's manufacture. Both creation and manufacture are modes of production. But there are differences. Artistic creation is a free production, a sort of play that carries its justification in itself, while manufacture is purposive production, justified by an outside goal. Creation is singular, while manufacture can be repeated at will. Creation is playfully guided by the vision of the work; the course of manufacture is determined by foreknowledge of the product. Manufacture can be learned. Creation cannot; it is self-engendered.

There is a peculiar relationship between creation and rules. All production that is based on freedom occurs according to rules— "for every art presupposes rules, upon whose foundation a product that is to be called one of art must be conceived, first of all, as possible" (35: V, 307). In manufacture, the rule of production is thought out by the producer. Guiding its conception is the purpose: the product. The rule must prove efficient for the purpose. In a sense, it is deducible.

But what if the product is purposeless, like a work of art? The rule of production is not deducible, then, and not conceivable. The producer has no method of production that might be known or learned. And yet the rule is the condition that must be met if his creative activity is to be unified in a work. If the rule is not freely conceivable, it must be furnished by nature. But how and where? In the artist's creative activity. In the mental disposition of the subject, nature lays down "rules for art" (35: V, 307). The artist's work as a creative process is not transparent, but it is infinitely purposive in the direction of a work that is without a purpose. In externalizing the subjectively disposed rules, the artist creates things of beauty. These rules are autonomously laid down insofar as no other work, not even an exemplary one, provides them, and the artist alone applies them originally to his work; they are heteronomously laid down insofar as the producer does not conceive them freely but receives them freely from nature, the source of all productivity. If that originality speaks out of the producer, Kant calls him a genius. Hence his line: "Art is possible only as a product of genius" (35: V, 307).

But what is genius? It appears from the previous expositions that "genius is the innate mental disposition (ingenium) whereby nature lays down rules for art" (35: V, 307). His unique relation to the rule lets us see some of the essence of a genius, an essence that defies clear definition.

A genius is original. Since he does not create by knowable and deducible rules but produces precisely that "for which no definite rule can be given" (35: V, 307), his natural gift is not just a talent for some skill but a power of original productivity. What he creates is unique and unrepeatable. He "takes the product from the sources" (75: XV, 361; 812). What he creates is not a work of imitation; it is the exemplary model on which another genius may perhaps catch fire and find the way to his own productivity. Genius is not a result of influences and therefore not historically comprehensible; it is a gift of nature. Ideas occur to a genius without his knowing how they "find their way hither" (35: V, 308). His work comes to be without his being able to "describe, or to indicate scientifically" (35: V, 308) how, by what means, and to what end it grows. His creation occurs, in enthusiasm, without being subject to disposition or planning (75: XV, 361; 812).

This means negatively that whatever the intellect and the will permit us to learn, whatever "lies on the natural course of research and cogitation according to rules" (35: V, 308), has not been brought into the world by genius and requires none. In the constellation of consciousness at large, of technical skill, of inventiveness and constant application, it may presuppose a great brain, perhaps; but the difference between this and the little brain that need only exert itself more to go the ways of learning is simply one of degree. In the sciences there are no geniuses. To Kant, comparatively speaking, the difference between Newton and any physics student is a quantitative difference, one which in principle can be overcome, whereas the difference between Rembrandt and a painter who may have talent but lacks genius is fundamental, qualitative, and not to be bridged by diligence and a strong will. In the sciences we can say of a man, "If only he is intelligent and will work hard . . ." In the arts we must say, "Without a touch of genius there is no hope."

Scientists communicate by nature. They are predestined for collaboration. Their results are passed on, handed down from one to the other; they jointly build a scientific universe. If they are true scientists, they will rejoice in the sort of progress that promptly leads beyond them.

Geniuses are lonely. They themselves do not make progress in their fields, nor do they have any progress to expect of others. They are inexhaustible and naturally limited at the same time. Collaboration would be bound to hinder their autochthonous work rather than to help it.[2] Contemporaries across time, they are perhaps akin to each other only in being "nature's favorites"

(35: V, 309)—linked, at best, in the sense that one of them will kindle the light for each other. Mostly they are as apart as alien worlds.

Genius, the originally creative element in art, is productive thanks to a peculiar gift, to the spirit. Spirit is not merely a special talent;[3] it is an "original animation which . . . comes out of ourselves and is not derivative" (75:XV, 415; 934). It is "the animating principle in the mind" (35: V, 313), which puts the mind's activities into free play (75: XV, 364; 817) and keeps all the talents in motion; and at the same time it is the peculiar force that imparts life to the works of the mind (75: XV, 326; 740). Without spirit, the artist cannot be a genius, and his work can be no work of art. The spirit is the intrinsically ingenious element in genius and in the work. Hence Kant: "Instead of genius, we can also use the word spirit alone" (75: XV, 414; 933).

The spirit works by way of productive imagination. For this "is most powerful in creating another nature, so to speak, from the material furnished to it by real nature" (35: V, 314). From this material it creates its own infinitely modifiable and playfully reconstruable world, a world whose unfeignedly natural laws are analogous to the laws of the given world, and yet "lie higher up in reason" (35: V, 314). Free from the coercion of empirical associations, imagination creates out of the old world material a new world that is not a copy but "surpasses nature" (35: V, 314).

How does the spirit work? This is the riddle that cannot be cracked, only circumscribed. The spirit produces beauty so that it will ceaselessly animate. But beauty occurs in the playful accord of two powers, of imagination and the intellect. Both are kept in constant motion by the spirit. To the intellect it must give food for thought, and to productive imagination it must give material for forming—and that in order to make imagination's gift for original modification inexhaustible, and to keep the intellect's will to exhaust that gift endlessly busy. There is no conceiving what will be wrought visually by the spirit. Intellectual thinking founders on the experience that it cannot come to an end, and on the knowledge of trying something that is beyond it. The experience is not one of disappointment at one's incapacity, but one of delight in inexhaustible play. It is an experience that shows a way of thinking beyond the intellect.

Wherein does the spirit work? In producing visions that are

not exhaustible in concepts. Kant calls them aesthetic ideas. Who produces them in the end is not quite clear. Now we read that "the ground that spawns ideas is the spirit" (75: xv, 414; 933); now, that the spirit is "the faculty of representing aesthetic ideas" (35: v, 313–14); and now, that "the aesthetic idea is a . . . conception of the imagination" (35: v, 314; 316). What is clear is their relation to the rational idea. As the rational idea is a concept which nothing visual can represent, the aesthetic idea is a visualization to which no concept can be adequate. The first is a concept of the unknowable; the second, a vision of the ineffable. Both transcend the intellect—one in the medium of reason that foils all sensibility; the other in the medium of sensibility, in such a way as to foil the intellect.

The spirit, we may conclude, is the source of the creative being that expresses the ineffable—expresses it in a way that is original, always animating, and not to be stated in rules. This gift of nature involves major risks.

The "peculiar spirit" (75: xv, 326; 740), originality, may lose its way in perversions: in arrogant, incommunicable conduct and speech due to a sense of singularity,[4] in undisciplined boorishness due to a sense of originality,[5] or in the eccentric doings of "apers of genius"[6] and adepts who can experience their inadequacy but not accept it. Freedom, without which genius is not conceivable, brings instability and license in its train. "A genius depends on moods" (75: xv, 361; 812). His productivity declines, then, to mere imaginative romanticizing (cf. 75: xv, 393; 899), to an imaginative and therefore seductive kind of madness,[7] and finally to the production of nonsense out of misguided wealth (cf. 35: v, 319) or to a departure from all legality as such. These mistakes are "privileges, as it were, of genius" (35: v, 318). Kant's dealings with them are not always consistent in detail, but by and large his unmistable tendency remains to confront freedom with an obstacle wherever it becomes license, and thus an obstacle to freedom.

The first such obstacle is met in the material. Whatever the spirit forms and transforms must materialize—in language, in stone, in color. In these fabrics, freedom encounters an obstacle to prove itself on, as if it were all a game. The artist's performance in the creative process requires a technical skill which studying develops in a talent. This is why every art involves "something mechanical" (35: V, 310), something for which rules can be laid down and which is never the true source of art, although a condition for it. One must have learned much and studied formally "if genius is to have a fabric" (75: XV, 393; 899). Even for a genius, learning is "the modest and sure course" (75: XV, 340; 778) to art.

The work is another obstacle. It gathers the artistic efforts into a unit. Where a genius aims his productivity at a work, it will always counteract flights of romantic fancy.

More important is the third and intrinsic obstacle to license: taste. Genius is the natural gift to express aesthetic ideas so that the presentation will make a subjective mood communicable (35: V, 317). This mood is the interplay of imagination and the intellect. Taste is the capacity to register and judge their accord (76: XV, 828; 1510). All representation is accordingly addressed to taste and must stand the test of its judgment. As the "polish of judgment" (75: XV, 356; 806), taste is the intrinsic "discipline of genius" (35: V, 319). It will teach genius how far its audacity may go to serve the purposes of presentation. It clarifies the abundance of thoughts and makes ideas "durable" (35: V, 319) .

Primarily, however, taste is a faculty of judgment. How should the spirit, the force of original productivity, agree with it? The two may jeopardize each other. We can think of discrepancies and antagonisms between them. They clash patently in works that realize the possibilities of genius without taste, and of taste without genius.[8]

What conforms to taste "is not for that reason a work of the fine arts."[9] Rather, it is precisely its exemplary regularity that can make a work boring.[10] Too much taste may rob it of the spirit. What remains is a production which, lacking genius, will never be more than toil[11]—a work whose innocuous flawlessness will make it insufferable in the long run, and a creator whose original touches of genius evaporate in mere virtuosity. Hence Kant's warning of taste. Taste does slick down boorishness, but it also takes "some of the content" (75: XV, 356; 806) away from genius. It disciplines and civilizes, but at the same time it clips "the wings considerably" (35: V, 319). It does help in learning the necessary mechanics, but "mechanism stifles genius" (76: XV, 824; 1509) and the introduction of mechanism ruins it as a matter of principle (75: XV, 370; 829).

If taste without genius will thus produce only everyday flaw-lessness and imperil the essence of genius, this does not mean that a genius without taste is the true creator of beauty. Such a genius may produce brilliant art, perhaps, but never beautiful art. For beauty in art, taste remains not only an essential condition but "the indispensable condition *(conditio sine qua non)*" (35: v, 319). It is "the foremost" (35: v, 319) element we have to look for in art.

This leads to a paradoxical situation. Without taste there is no art; but, on the other hand, taste will be the ruin of art. No rational advice can show us a way out of the dilemma. Kant him-self seems to be wavering, now taking the "mechanism of talent"[12] for the fundament of art, now considering a critique that precedes the work "most harmful" (86: xx, 28) to genius. At one time he is ready to accept anything for the spirit's sake—for where "the spirit shines forth, all flows are made good" (75: xv, 375; 844); at another, he thinks that some sacrifices "on the side of genius" (35: v, 320) may have to be made for taste's sake, because as the highest cultivation of the senses taste must take priority.

The irremovability of this paradoxon does not rest upon a lack of lucid insight; it is a consequence of Kant's concept of genius. For that concept encompasses two downright irreconcilables, na-ture as well as freedom, and thus, so to speak, playfully unites all things. Kant therefore calls it the "unity of the world soul" (75: xv, 416; 398) and, as such, "a paradox" (75: xv, 549; 1242). To deprive the Kantian genius of this paradoxicality is to reduce it to mere talent.

The paradoxicality is not senseless; it means that no insight can tell us how a work of art comes to be. To the man who cannot originally produce it, no advice will suffice. Here, in an ultimate sense, is something that cannot be learned. It remains the mystery of genius, the mystery which no genius ever understands.

For our problem, that of leading conflict back to unity, a strange situation results. We cannot see how the antagonistic mental faculties are to be united in genius—and yet in a work, if it is a work of art, they are united. Ultimately, though, that unity is not achieved by man as a result of his freedom, of freely being himself; the unity is nature's gift to a free genius. In a sense, nature has "impregnated" (75: xv, 415; 936) the genius, has imbued him with the original rule and thus covertly reconciled his conflicting faculties on the level of talent. In the product, nature brings about precision without finicality (35: v, 307); in productivity, the right mean of boldness and reserve; in the creator, the unity of imagination and the intellect, of spirit and taste (35: v, 320). There are all sorts of displays of unity in a coincidence of opposites, without our knowing the way.

Can the points made here mean anything to us with respect to our basic question? We have inquired into the forms of antagonism, of struggle, of unity, and about the road that leads to unity. Is there not a discrepancy between this reaching of a goal without a way and the rest of Kant's philosophizing? We do not believe so. Rather, we think we have here a variant of the basic relations frequently met before.

Thus far the way to perfection always appeared as an infinite road which man never surveys as a whole and has never traveled as a whole. In art alone is this road finite, because the work of art as a whole lies in time. But Kant, when he withdraws this finite road from our consciousness, is giving its infinity back to it, so to speak. The intellect will not come to an end in its reflections upon that road. In letting nature travel it, as it were, Kant removes it from human perfectibility. What has traveled this road is not man; it is something transcendent in man, which Kant calls nature. For a talented man without genius it would be an infinite road.

Though this is all we can say about the road to unity, we can still name the conditions of its possibility.

Genius alone can take that road. But "the form of genius is freedom" (75: xv, 361; 812). Form, in Kant's sense, is what makes genius possible. The condition of its possibility is freedom. Its creation grows in freedom, for as we have seen, genius is not tied to any demonstrable regularity. This freedom is entwined with taste, however. Since taste is discipline, Kant calls it an "analogue of morality" (76: xv, 837; 1512). Since it is based upon morality, moreover, and practiced only in developing one's moral sense, the artist's creative activity also needs an existential moment, in the Kantian sense. The relation to transcendence, finally, is demonstrable: as genius is the faculty of aesthetic ideas—in other words, the faculty of visually elaborating the ineffable—the work of genius is essentially transcendent even though it lies in the realm of the senses. In artistic creation, this transcendent element is produced within the sensible media.

Where freedom is discarded as the basis of both the creator
and his creativity, there can be neither genius nor a work of art.
There may remain a virtuoso and a tour de force—in other words,
a technician and his product. Where the discipline of taste is
lacking, eruptive production and the manner of genius may
remain; but that is not enough for a work of genius. Where the
relation to the inexpressible is lacking, experts and their skills
may remain, or the "apers of genius" and their rubble. The only
work deserving of the name of a work of art is the incomprehensible union of opposites in which freedom, discipline, and the
ineffable meet in the play of the senses. The conditions of this
union are freedom, morally based taste, and the transcendent
relation. Once again the old basic relations are reencountered;
only we cannot tell how and by what ways they bring unity out of
the contradictions.[13]

Basic Relations of Conflict and Unity
in Aesthetics

In the field of beauty we were inquiring about the relations of
conflict and unity, about the function of conflict, the forms and
premises of unity, and the road that leads to unity.

The possible antagonism appeared as a conflict of aesthetic
judgments in looking at beauty, and as a conflict of mental forces
in producing it. Both cases, we suggested, were familiar forms of
conflict: in dealing with pleasantness it was lawless conflict along
individual subjective principles; in dealing with beauty there
were two forms of lawful conflict, waged on grounds of principles
that are indeed subjective but are founded on the absolute. The
struggle for the judgment of aesthetic reflection opened the prospect of a unanimity which no discussion can compel, but which
can be approached with an ever-broadening understanding. It is
a communicative struggle. In producing beauty, controversy could
be shown to exist, but there was no telling the way to unity. From
the viewpoint of the result, however—of the work in which that
struggle has actually led to unity—the way becomes recognizable;
it is directly productive and ends in perfection. It has the characteristics of lawful debate, except that here it is nature, not man,
which establishes its unknown law.

In aesthetics, too, antagonism has a function. We did say that the clash of judgments of the senses is not only lawless but meaningless; but we can now supplement our statement: that clash does have a function, since it makes clear that a judgment of aesthetic reflection must not rest on individual subjective principles alone. This is why something like a postulate for reflective judgments issues from that conflict, a postulate calling on the subject to free itself from the barriers of mere pleasure. We may say, perhaps, that even though lawless controversy is meaningless in judgments of the senses, it does have a function in aesthetic judgments at large: involuntarily, it indicates the principles from which even subjective judgments get a prospect of unanimity.

A clear function belongs to the lawful conflict of aesthetically reflective judgments. Controversy of this kind cleanses the subject of its ties to pleasure and accidental liking, expands its limits in struggle, and spreads that liberality in which one learns to understand the grounds of judgment that are not capable of proof.

In producing beauty, finally, antagonism is the indispensable means of the tension without which a finite work would come to be tedious. It adds flavor to flawlessness, imparts discipline to genius, and thus, in a work, comes to be the motor of a living perfection that encompasses the antitheses.

The various forms of unanimity and unity recall the well-known types we have often encountered.

In judgments of the senses, unanimity could only be coerced. It would be unity without freedom. Unanimity of reflective judgments is possible, however, just as forces of the mind can be really unified in works. Each time, of course, there are indispensable premises. If reflective judgments are to be unanimous, the subject must be set free and its taste cultivated and transcendentally and transcendently based; if the work produced is to be unified, there must be freedom in its production, discipline in its direction, and the faculty of representing the ineffable. Although unity and unanimity in aesthetics mean something other than unity in politics or ethics, their realization in principle still depends on the same premises as in the two other fields.

In the area of things pleasant we can find no road from antagonism to unity. In judging beauty, it is the subject's road to liberation from all interests, the training of taste, and the cultivation of moral feelings. The way to unanimous reflective judgments serves thus to point out a practical way which in mankind is never finished. It is a signpost which permits us to say that unanimous reflective judgments are indeed a postulate, but one that will never be purely realized—no more than the moral law will. Men will always argue about beauty. Only a perfect mankind could be of one mind about it; but even that unanimity would not be capable of proof (because there are no objective grounds of beauty), only of universal understanding.

The road to unity in works of genius is beyond cognition. Only one thing is certain: wherever nature takes that road, it will make use of the freedom and discipline of a genius, and it will be thanks to them that the transcendent mysteriously finds an expression in the sensory realm.

In aesthetics, too, there is *one* road leading to the goal, in the judgment of beauty as well as in its production. In one instance it is the long way, the infinite way. Only a genius, "nature's favorite," creates perfection in time, arriving at the goal by a finite way. But Kant forbids us to see through that way. Our intellect would no sooner reflect on it than it would confront us with infinity in time. If a man tried to take that finite way without the aid of nature, he would not come to an end. For the finite intellect, this road too is infinite.

11. CONFLICT AND UNITY IN REGARD TO POLITICAL THOUGHT

What remains to be done is to summarize the results we have obtained in part 3, to connect them with the results of our two previous parts, to point out the originality and relevance of Kant's political thinking, and to uncover the main traits of its future interpretation. To this end we are attacking the theme of conflict and unity once again from the outside and extending it to political thought. We first take a look at the outward indications of the burden of our theme in Kant's work; then, going a step deeper, we inquire into the material significance of contradiction and controversy in Kant's work as a whole. In a third step, we recapitulate the formal basic relations of antagonism and unity. In a fourth section, we project these upon political thought, use them for a kind of a priori draft of the main features of a Kantian politics, and rough in the outlines of its future interpretation. In conclusion, we ask whether Kant's philosophy is an endeavor on behalf of peace at all, whether his metaphysics can already claim political relevance, and whether his political thinking may be accorded a central position within his metaphysics.

Outward Indications of the Burden
of the Theme

Purely on the outside, the polarity of antagonism and unity keeps reappearing in Kant's work throughout his life. In his very first piece of writing, *Thoughts on the True Appraisal of Living Forces* (1747), the young student took up an "issue" (1: 1, 14) which in the early eighteenth century divided physicists all over Europe into two camps. Beyond an occasional "presumption of victory" (1: 1, 14), no decision had been reached in the first four decades. Now the twenty-two-year-old Kant proclaimed his intention, "before the tribunal of the sciences" (1: 1, 18) and subject to "the jurisdiction of mathematics" (1: 1, 97), to "uncover the roots of the notorious debate" (1: 1, 34) and by this "sole means" (1: 1, 34) to "settle one of the greatest divisions now prevailing among the geometrists of Europe" (1: 1, 16). Though in this "greatest contest of the intellect" (1: 1, 33) he could not hope to make peace all by himself, he could "lend a hand, taking some steps not incompatible" (1: 1, 15–16) with peace. "Be that as it may, I dare predict with confidence that this debate either will shortly be settled or will never cease" (1: 1, 16).

Thus, in the very first treatise we find the metaphors we know —the images of controversy and of war, of a court of law and a trial—and the entire effort of that first treatise is already aimed at removing the issue from the world by legal ways, by discovering the "roots of evil."

More than fifty years later, in 1789, at the end of his literary career, Kant published *The Debate of Departments;* and in that last work which he himself completed (along with *Anthropology,* published in the same year) he tried to bring the controversy between the superior and inferior academic departments to the "conclusion of a peace" (38: VII, 61) by means of a verdict.

Kant's work is accordingly framed in the polarity of conflict and unity, and in the pursuit of whatever unity can be established. Reappearing within this framework, time and again, is a leitmotif we find in several titles: *Perpetual Peace, Settlement of a Mathematical Dispute Based upon a Misunderstanding, Announcement of the Impending Conclusion of a Tract on Eternal Peace in Philosophy.*

The leitmotif also determines the structure of various writings. The two on peace have to be cited again, also *On the Moon's Influence upon the Weather, Settlement, The Debate of Departments,* and above all, *Religion within the Limits of Reason Alone.* In the last-named, a glance at the chapter headings suffices to show the thoroughgoing proximity to the political way of thinking. We read, for instance, "On the battle of the good principle with the evil principle for the governance of man" (36: VI, 57); "On the good principle's legal claim to govern man" (36: VI, 60); "On the evil principle's legal claim to govern man, and on the battle between the two principles" (36: VI, 78); "The victory of the good principle over the evil, and the establishment of a kingdom of God on earth" (36: VI, 93); "Philosophical conception of the good principle's victory as the establishment of a kingdom of God on earth" (36: VI, 95); "Man is to depart from the ethical state of nature in order to become a member of an ethical community" (36: VI, 96), and so forth. Time and again Kant's *Religion* recalls his political thought—which is another far from accidental reason why the work gave offense to the politicians.

Next, in a larger framework, Kant's metaphor has to be mentioned again. Not only *Critique of Pure Reason* but his work as a whole is replete with imagery from the political realm. The metaphors relating to the jurisdiction of reason are found in his very earliest writings, and his last work remains concerned with a verdict.

Finally, the occasion of the various writings is another of these external characteristics. From the earliest natural scientific treatises down to the late metaphysical ones, Kant's direct intervention in debate was far more frequent than most men are aware of. How much weight he himself attached to this intervening and battling shows in the relatively large number of rudimentary theories of polemics that can be found in his work. Here, too, the first draft appears in the early writings and the last in *The Debate of Departments,* while the two in between are located in the most important works.

Whether in the structure of his writings, in their metaphor, in polemical intervention in a debate, or in the design of a theory— the point is always to eliminate the issue if it is lawless, or to provide the means for its elimination. Every debate aims at a possible unity, though never at its unconditional pursuit.

Thus the motif of antagonism and unity keeps recurring even on the surface of Kant's work. This does not constitute its significance, however. To grasp some of that significance, we ask how relevant the principle of conflict is as a theme in Kant's philosophizing.

The Theorem of Contradiction and the Principle of Antagonism

When Kant discusses the theorem of contradiction, as he does in *Logic* (67: IX, 51–52), for example, he sees in it no more than a canon for the formal side of statements—a canon incapable of stating anything positive about material truth although applying to all statements as a negative condition, a *conditio sine qua non.* What is self-contradictory cannot be. The theorem is the touch-stone of analytical judgments and of possibility as such; it must not be more. When it is used to guarantee material truth and to evaluate synthetic judgments, it opens the large field of dialectical metaphysics in which reason no longer finds anything but a supposed certainty. The critique of reason starts, therefore, with a restriction of the theorem of contradiction to the realm of formal logic and analysis. This means that as a principle the theorem belongs to formal logic. The field of its validity is the formal side of any statement, not its material side. Within the formal side, however, Kant applies it strictly. Contradiction is never accepted as the intentional form of dialectical statements; it is exclusively a sign of error, always to be avoided or to be removed. To Kant, the theorem is an inviolate principle, and, indeed, its restriction is more apt to be breached than its validity. For in some cases its import appears to go far beyond logic.

The first such instance appears in the doctrine of antinomies. All the dialectical theses and antitheses are deduced in strict accordance with the theorem of contradiction. At no point in their chain of proof is a repugnancy to be discovered. But various statements, noncontradictory in themselves, have contents which do contradict each other. Reason itself, not the logic of particular propositions, comes to be suspected of not agreeing with itself and has to dispel that suspicion by resolving the antinomies. The principle of antagonism is the guiding idea of this resolution, and that in the form, not only of smoothing contradictions on the surface of statements (for there are none), but of eliminating the germs of future contradictions in the conditions under which such statements can be made. To do this, reason must plunge deeply into *metaphysica generalis*. It takes that plunge in a new understanding of space and time as mere forms of visuality, in an understanding which makes it possible for everything phenomenal in the world to be one, for categories to be confined to an immanent use, and ideas, to a regulative use. In consequence of this limitation, reason will find the way back from its seeming contradictoriness to an identity with itself. A noncontradictory dialectics comes to serve as real proof of the correctness of transcendental aesthetics and logic. Thus the principle—if not the theorem—of contradiction leads beyond the purely logical form of statements, into metaphysical depths.

To Kant, the theorem of contradiction remains undisputed as the highest possible principle of *metaphysica specialis*. Here, in the conception of ideas that can never claim to be materially true, possibility is the sole criterion of testing. As *definitio impossibilis* (6: 1, 391), the theorem of contradiction guarantees or denies this possibility. On grounds of thought, the theorem can no longer warrant the existence of transcendence, but this inability impairs its import only for a dogmatic *metaphysica specialis*, not for the critical one.

In another field the principle of antagonism comes even to have ontological relevance. In practical philosophy men look for unity in the use of freedom—legally, by devising external laws to bring everyone's freedom into accord with everybody else's and to make legal verdicts void all forms of civil strife; morally, by citing inner laws to align the principle of subjective volition with a general will and thus prevent the struggle between opposites of license; ethico-theologically, by uniting all moral laws in their epitome, the idea of God, and leading the visible *ecclesiae militantes* into an invisible one that does not conflict with itself. What applies to all practical laws, however, is that the will must be "capable of willing" (32: IV, 424) the supreme generalization of their principle into a natural law. This is said to be "the canon of their moral appraisal as such" (32: IV, 424). Here again, the principle of antagonism is only the *conditio sine qua non;* it cannot tell what the law should be, only what it cannot be. But the principle does carry out this function regarding the unity of goodwill in the intelligible world. Only if this will does not contradict itself is it directed at the ought, the point of contact with being. As the unified use of reason as such is the premise of rationality,[1] the unity of freedom—and thus the unity of good will —is the premise of morality (cf. 83: XIX, 28off.; 7202).

Unity and antagonism themselves are thus invested with an all but moral significance that shows quite clearly in Kant's way of qualifying them both. A lack of unity—in other words, contradiction and controversy—is the font of all evils: "All evils come from the lack of unity in the world as a whole. This is the source of antagonisms. When there is perfect unity, not only regarding substance but regarding forces as well, everything must agree with the natural essence and must therefore be good" (81: XVIII, 213; 5541). Conflicting forces dwindle in effect, or else they become totally ineffective. Ineffectiveness, however, is the mark of evil: "For evil has the peculiarity that among all things that exist together it is not unanimous, and that it conducts itself so as to bring forth no result save by the rule of the good" (84: XIX, 491; 7687). Dogmatic metaphysics; license that conflicts with itself; politics as a history of wars; faith as a war of extermination against other faiths—these and everything that controverts itself share the fate of evil, which is never substantial to the end: "All false art, all idle wisdom lasts its time; for in the end it will destroy itself, and its highest culture is simultaneously the moment of its fall" (31: IV, 366). Unanimity alone, the "community of directions,"[2] can work by the rule of the good. This rule is legality as such, in which all things find their way back to unity.

All of Kant's philosophizing is a removal of contradictions, controversies, and debates. It is their logical removal, a voiding of contradiction in the formal structure of any statement. It is their gnoseological removal, an elimination of contradictory germs in the premises of possible cognition. It is their metaphysical removal in resolving the antinomies; their "ontological" removal in directing volition toward a general will capable of willing itself; their aesthetic removal in parting with divergent private feelings. And it is a political removal of antagonisms, a conquest of the state of nature and of war.

·All this appears to mean that Kant inperceptibly expands the theorem of contradiction beyond the limits set upon it. But this is not so. The theorem remains a principle of Kantian logic. Alongside it, however, we find in Kant something like a principle of controversy cast not only in one form but in many, and accordingly calling for unity in manifold ways. It is not a logical principle but a generally metaphysical one, and thus more encompassing than the theorem of contradiction. Indeed, the theorem of contradiction may perhaps be said to be no more than that principle's particular phenomenon in the field of logic. Kant, it seems, never became clearly conscious of the principle and therefore never put it into words. But it is at work everywhere, and important enough to put all of his metaphysics onto that course from conflicting diversity to unity.

Where the removal of antagonisms is more than just a logical operation, it appears as a way to unity that is a "middle way" in line with principles. Kant has followed this way many times. Historically we can demonstrate it in his thinking as a way from rational dogmatism to skepticism, and on to criticism. His philosophizing mirrors it in diverse forms, of which a typical one shows in the very first treatise. The occasion for Kant's *Thoughts on the True Appraisal of Living Forces* was furnished by the debate that had been raging for decades about two formulas for the determination of living forces. To measure them, Descartes had posited the formula "energy = mass × velocity"; Leibniz, the formula "energy = mass × velocity." The two calculations were mutually exclusive, and so it seemed that one of them would have to be accepted and used to combat the other, as many physicists had then been doing for years. Not so Kant. He assigned each formula to its own realm of validity: the Cartesian one to the realm of mathematical bodies (in which there can be no living forces, of course), and that of Leibniz to the realm of natural bodies. In separate domains both are true; as soon as they step out of those domains, both become false. The type of resolving the antinomy of freedom is thus given as early as in Kant's first-work.

Aside from this form of the "middle way" there are numerous other types: links, syntheses, mediations. We are not going further into those.[3] The crucial fact is that they are not preshaped media of an approximate compromise such as the principle of the middle; rather, they are middle ways to be newly derived from principles in every case. For all of them, the road to unity does not go via skill, primarily, but via the spread of reason.

Basic Relations of Conflict and Unity
in Kantian Metaphysics

To get to a deeper level than merely demonstrating the material effectiveness of this principle, we have to uncover the basic relations that serve to make it effective. Having observed these basic relations of conflict and unity in Kant's metaphysics, we can do no more now than sum up the results obtained before.

Natural metaphysics, eudaemonistic ethics, the faith in facts, revealed religion, material aesthetics—all of these are fields dominated by lawless struggle, by a struggle aimed at the subjugation and destruction of the adversary, at the definitive victory of forcible unification. There is no place for this struggle in reason itself, but it has a function in the history of reason; it urges rational men to reflect upon all possibilities, and it forbids their natural reason to go in for a perverted unity. Politicians dream of universal monarchy, priests of a world religion, aesthetes of a codified, universally valid beauty, and philosophers of the *philosophia perennis* in the form of a system. But the means by which they seek to realize their dreams, the lawless, violent conflicts, turn against their own goal: metaphysics perishes in controversy; empires crumble; faith succumbs to doubt, and once beauty is known, it yields to the ugliness that follows. Natural reason needs tranquillity, but the lawless struggle will not let it come to rest; in each of its expressions—in knowledge, in speculation, in practical legislation, in faith, in the view of beauty—the struggle drives our natural reason to know itself, which is to purify itself at the same time. Natural reason discovers the root of lawless controversy and can tear it out. The root is always a perversion of subjectivity into objectivity—of knowledge within human bounds into an absolute certainty of being; of ideas into real things; of the purely subjective eudaemonistic principles into an absolute principle of ethics; of accidental facts into an absolute basis of faith; and of private feelings into determining grounds of aesthetic judgments that are universally valid. All these are reversed by the self-knowledge of reason. It shows the relativity of knowledge and the subjectivity of speculation; it lays down the absolute principle of the determination of the will and the absolute fundament of faith, and it guides aesthetics to a subjectivity that offers a solid hold. This laying of a new foundation makes lawless conflict unnecessary. Its function proves to be finite. It turns into a legal conflict, into the controversy about a more and more comprehensive unity in greater and greater freedom—a debate that cannot cease and has therefore an infinite function.

The unity pursued by critical reason is characterized by its terms. It is a free unity that does not limit other people's freedom beyond its own measure. The boundary concept relates it to the intelligible substrate. It is a unity of the idea and thus cannot be transplanted into time; but if man makes an honest effort, he can bring reality continually closer to it. It is the free unity that cannot be achieved without an existential moment, and presupposed in it is a relation to transcendence.

The interrelation of antagonism and unity is the same thing in many guises. Corresponding to the two forms of struggle are two forms of unity, and two forms of the way. Unity without freedom and without transcendence is pursued in lawless struggles, by shortcuts; free unity is pursued by the infinite way of a lawful struggle that is understood as a challenge. Lawless struggle, the short way, and violent unity are in conflict with themselves. They are the labors of Sisyphus, the to and fro of misdirected efforts. Lawful struggle, the infinite way, and free unity on their part form another unity, one that even as a goal remains a struggle and a way—with the principle of unity contained in both the struggle and the way, which in a sense already are the unity. Critical reason denies itself all inner contradictions. But it affirms even the lawless struggle insofar as that struggle fractures and makes impossible the violent unity that is more violent than lawless struggle itself. The following order of rank applies to critical reason: lawless conflict, which preserves a minimum of freedom, is better than a perverted total unity; but free unity is better than lawless conflict. Hence the call of critical reason for conquering lawless conflict everywhere in lawful fashion. Free unity is a postulate in all fields of metaphysics.

Extension of These Relations to Political Thought

Knowing the basic relationships, we might draw up a rough a priori outline of Kantian politics. Like everything else, it begins with lawless conflict, with the state of nature, with a war of all against all. This war has its unintended function: it drives men apart, forces them to settle and cultivate the entire planet, and constrains them to reunite with one another. The lawless struggle itself compels the combatants to adopt laws. The laws eliminate the function of the struggle; but struggle as such does not become superfluous, for the law can be broken. Even where it holds sway, it has to fight for its rule. This lawful struggle for the rule of law will go on until the idea of a state with the greatest possible freedom for all has been realized. This is Kant's idea of a republican state. Its realization occurs by an infinite way; it is understood as a political effort that is at the same time a moral task and accordingly impossible without an existential moment and a relation to something transcendent.

In the establishment of the state, the lawless struggle is banished from firmly delimited areas but not from the interrelation of those areas. The state of nature prevails between states, and between groups of states. Lawless struggle is the final means of foreign policy. It is the means by which rulers keep trying to set up the wrong, forcible unity of a universal monarchy. But the tool of their choice—war based on the principle of license—keeps making them fail halfway. History turns into a senseless battlefield. Yet there again the lawless struggle serves a function: viewed in an infinite perspective, it compels politicians to choose between turning back and destroying the human race. Their only way to opt for mankind is worldwide political unity without violence. The global union of states is a free federation comprising the individual states as moral persons. It is the task for which mankind must struggle lawfully, along an infinite way.

If we are correct in our view of the basic relations, it is possible to outline the following basic features of a future interpretation of Kant's political thought.

Unity is not worth seeking without freedom. Both the foundation of states and their foreign policy rest upon freedom. Where Kant may be forgetting this at times, his material expositions might be purified on grounds of the formal basic thought assured by his metaphysics as a whole.

Unity is not desirable without an existential moment. Politics is therefore tied to practical reason. It is not morality, of course, and is not based on inner laws like morality; but its legality is based on the idea of law, and thus upon morality.

There is no unity without a relation to transcendence. The unity which Kant really pursues is therefore always one whose pure form exists only in the idea. In politics, the course of unification is oriented toward reason, not toward power.

Only the infinite way leads to unity. Hence there is no stopping, no resting on laurels, and no safety except in advancing toward the idea. What makes a state meritorious is not the way it is, but the possibility that it may change and come to be like the idea of the republican state.

Unity comes about by lawful struggle. It presupposes a will to the right and a will to freedom, not a need for peace and quiet. For freedom, the fundament of unity, guarantees at the same time that license may erupt again at any moment. Basic to the unity pursued is therefore the postulate of vigilance in behalf of freedom.

Unity is not opposed to struggle as such, only to lawless struggle. Hence war and peace, being finite, are not the ultimate fixed points of Kant's political thinking. They get their substance from the relation to their idea, and from the fundament they live by. Kant's will to peace is not a will to peace at any price. He is not a pacifist. He can conceive of a wrong peace, and to that he would even prefer the wrong war. War itself, if it is waged for freedom or the right, can be the beginning of a lawful struggle. Still, the mission of the law is always to transcend war. The postulate for all politics remains: There shall be no war!

According to this fundamental outline, Kantian politics must be the progress of mankind from war to peace—a progress which mankind not only ought to make but can make if it cares more for freedom than for violence, more for right than for might, more for morality than for cleverness, more for critique and lawful struggle than for peace and quiet, and more for relating to transcendence than for being satisfied with pure immanence.

Philosophy as a Way to Peace

With the pursuit of the One found like an ever new variation of a leitmotif in all the themes that carry Kant's metaphysics, some general conclusions may be ventured, perhaps, without running afoul of Kantian thought.

Philosophy begins in conflict, but it has the will to peace. In this will it may misconceive itself and seek the wrong peace, peace by violence. Once it has become transparent to itself, however, it has come to know the premises of peace. It approaches peace by an infinite way, a way on which the principle of peace is at work everywhere. Along the way, peace is thus always present, and whatever peace can be found in time remains always a way to peace.

Kant is the philosopher of that way. He is not a pacifist of metaphysics—after all, he rejects certain forms of peace—but in a profound sense he, more than any other thinker, may be the philosopher of peace. All his philosophizing is understood by him as being en route to the peace of reason. It is for this very reason that in him peace is already present.

Does this make Kant's entire philosophy a political philosophy? Yes and no. No—because thematically its most vital parts have other objects. Yes—because many conceptual and cogitative forms that come to be relevant to his political thought are laid out in his earliest writings; yes—because the basic structures of his political thinking can be found within all objects of critical metaphysics; yes—because this makes all Kantian metaphysics a propaedeutic for political thinking (though not *merely* such a propaedeutic), with the result that we can interpret his politics on the one hand as a variant of his metaphysics, and on the other hand as its capstone.

On the theory of its being a mere variant of the metaphysics we might say that what is shown once more in Kantian politics, in a different fashion, is how antagonism can be led to unity. It is Kant's old theme, the theme which in his best period he carried through in incomparably more sagacious style. The variant is important on account of the new content; but in its philosophical execution it lags behind other variants.

On the capstone theory, however, we might say that in a sense Kant's politics is the most lucid sample of his philosophizing. For in his politics, that secret basic structure of his metaphysics—the conquest of antagonism—has become the theme itself. In the transition from war to eternal peace it has been projected into universality and made the object of philosophizing. Understood in this way, Kant's politics is the concrete model of his metaphysics. It is of central significance.

Whether we look upon it as a variant or as the completion of the metaphysics, we can be sure of one thing: it is original politics, a politics based on the earliest forms of Kantian thinking and homogeneously related to the great metaphysics and the very history of Kantian thought. The politics itself has metaphysical rank. To deny this—be it only by ignoring all or part of that rank —is a philosophical failure and an admission that one of Kant's central thought forms has not been perceived. It is a failure that has helped to conceal the relevance of his thinking, and thus to rob that thinking of the political effect it might have had in the world. In this respect the minimizers of Kantian politics may even have incurred a political guilt.

NOTES

(See Note on Sources, page ix, and Register of
Kant's Works, page 357, for clarification of the
form of citation used in the notes.)

Introduction

1 In the seventh decade: 43 (1784), 44 (1784), 45 (1785), 49 (1786),
   51 (1786), 35 (1790), 56 (1793). In the eighth decade: 58 (1794), 59
   (1795), 31, part 1 (1797), 38 (1798), 39 (1798).
2 Depending on whether or not we include the writings on historical
   and legal philosophy.
3 30: A 316 ff./B 372 ff. 35: par. 65, 82 ff.; v, 372 ff., 425 ff.
4 The immediate occasions were mostly provided by controversies
   with contemporaries, or by the requests that kept arriving from
   the publishers of periodicals. Only one treatise can with some
   measure of certainty be traced to a real political occasion: the
   tract *Perpetual Peace*. It was Kant's reflection on the universal joy
   over the Peace of Basel. The treaty was signed 5 April 1795, and
   Kant sent his manuscript to Nicolovius on 13 August. Cf. L. 672,
   13. viii. 1795, to Nicolovius.
5 See also VIII, 470. Three months before Kant's publication, a
   treatise by Mendelssohn entitled "On the Question, What Do We
   Mean by Enlightenment?" had appeared in the September issue of
   Berlinische Monatsschrift. Kant heard about it on the day he
   penned his own essay and decided to publish anyway, giving his
   reasons as cited.
6 L. 621, 10. iv. 1794, to Biester.
7 L. 683, 15.x. 1795, to Kiesewetter.
8 The Kant editions contain a grammatical error.
9 L.883, undated, from A. Richter. All that we know about Richter
   is that he died as a professor in Vienna in 1827, at sixty-seven
   years of age.
10 Kant's reply has been preserved in a draft. Cf. L. 884, to Richter,
   from the year 1801.

11 L. 565, 2. iv. 1793, from Fichte.

12 L. 578, 12. v. 1793, to Fichte.

13 For instance, in Friedrich Paulsen's *Immanuel Kant, sein Leben und seine Lehre* (5th ed., Stuttgart, undated, p. 364): "The systematic elaboration in the metaphysical foundations of Theory of Law (1797) belongs to the period of senility. . . . The same is true of the second essay, incorporated in The Debate of Departments (1798)."

14 Locke held high state offices under Shaftesbury (the philosopher's grandfather); Hume was Under-Secretary of State from 1767 to 1769, handling the entire correspondence of the Foreign Office; Montesquieu was presiding officer of the *parlement (président à mortier)* from 1716 to 1725.

15 L. 564, 22.iii. 1793, to Spener.

16 L.s 693, 697, 699, and 733, the replies to which are either missing or lost.

17 The literature mentions Machiavelli, Hobbes, Locke, Hume, Grotius, Pufendorf, Thomasius, Leibniz, Wolff, Baumgarten, Vattel, Achenwall, Fichte, Humboldt, Gentz, Montesquieu, Rousseau, Voltaire, Condorcet, d'Argenson, Turgot, Mirabeau, de Sieyès, and others.

18 Kurt Borries, *Kant als Politiker. Zur Staats- und Gesellschaftslehre des Kritizismus* (Leipzig, 1928).

19 We cite some relative figures:
J. E. Erdmann, *Die Entwicklung der deutschen Spekulation seit Kant*, vol. 1 (Stuttgart, 1931), 8 out of 232 pp. Paulsen, *Immanuel Kant* (see note 13 above), 20 out of 420 pp. Bruno Bauch, *Immanuel Kant* (Berlin-Leipzig, 1971), 13 out of 470 pp. Ernst Cassirer, *Kants Leben und Lehre* (Berlin, 1918), 15 out of 460 pp.

20 Karl Jaspers, *The Great Philosophers*, vol. 1 (New York, 1962), Kant, pp. 230–381; the chapter "Politics and History," pp. 328–62. Cf. also the essay "Kant's 'Perpetual Peace' " in Jaspers's *Philosophy and the World: Selected Essays* (Chicago, 1963), pp. 88–124.

21 Cf. Pierre Hassner, "Situation de la philosophie politique chez Kant," in *La philosophie politique de Kant* (Paris, 1962), pp. 77–103.

Chapter 1

1 "Metaphysicae cum geometria iunctae usus in philosophia naturali, cuicus specimen I. continet *Monadologiam physicam* . . ." (10: 1,

473 ff.): Kant's second dissertation, upon which he based the public disputation of 10 April 1756. The treatise was written in the year before.

2 10: I, 477: "Substantia simplex, monas dicta, est, quae non constat pluralitate partium, quarum una absque aliis separatim existere potest."

3 Ibid.: "Corpora constant monadibus."

4 10: I, 482: "Monas spatiolum praesentiae suae definit non pluralitate partium suarum substantialium, sed sphaera activitatis, qua externas utrinque sibi praesentes arcet ab ulteriori ad se invicem appropinquatione."

5 Ibid.: "Vis, qua elementum corporis simplex spatium suum occupat, est eadem, quam vocant alias *impenetrabilitatem;* neque si ab illa vi discesseris, huic locus esse potest."

6 10: I, 483: "Corpora per vim solam impenetrabilitatis non gauderent definito volumine, nisi adforet alia pariter insita attractionis, cum illa coniunctim limitem definiens extensionis."

7 A brief orientation about preceding and contemporaneous attempts at a dynamic theory of matter is furnished by Erich Adickes in *Kant als Naturforscher* (Berlin, 1924), vol. 1, Leibniz, p. 163f. note; Hamberger, p. 164 note; Euler, p. 164 note; Boscowich, p. 171f. note. Boscowich's theory, which was worked out in full only after Kant's *Monadologia physica,* bears a special resemblance to Kant's.

8 It is not by accident that this concept is missing. In matter, attraction and repulsion can always exist only simultaneously. Each force is the other's *causa essendi.* Likewise, Kant conceives the drives to individualization and socialization as always working only at the same time. The relation of love and respect is different: "Beyond a doubt, respect is primary, because without it there is no true love either, although without love one can have great respect for another" (58: VIII, 337). The two can take effect separately; it just is not desirable that they should. Love is "an indispensable complement to the imperfection of human nature" (58: VIII, 338).

What Kant means here, of course, is not pathological love, which is always the result of affection. It is the moral love, which "as the maxim of benevolence" (37: VI, 449) turns other people's purposes into ours, the love whose duties are charity, gratitude, and compassion. In Kant's work the import of this love is not infrequently eclipsed by dignity and respect. One will therefore do well to keep the dynamic concept of matter on hand as a thought model for the interrelation of love and respect—an interrelation that is not given to practical reason, but is set before it as a task.

9 According to Emil Arnoldt (*Gesammelte Schriften,* vol. 5 [Berlin, 1909], pp. 338–40), Kant lectured on physics at least once a year as an assistant professor (fifteen times), and as a full professor in the terms of 1776, 1779, 1781, 1783, 1785, and 1787–88. In addition, he gave two lectures on mechanical sciences (1759–60 and 1760).

10 *Vorlesungen Immanuel Kants* (Berlin: Deutsche Akademie der Wissenschaften, 1961), section 1, vol. 1, pp. 93 ff.

11 Erich Adickes, *Kant als Naturforscher,* vol. 1 (Berlin, 1924), pp. 11f.

12 Kant's lecture on physics, p. 99 (see note 10 above).

13 *De mundi sensibilis atque intelligibilis forma et principiis,* 1770 (26: II, 385 ff.). The idea of the infinite divisibility of matter occurs for the first time in 1769. But there it is only the consequence of a hypothesis and has thus a hypothetical character even as an idea. Cf. 81: XVII, 377; 3986: "It may also be assumed that there are no substances in space at all, but a greater or lesser effectiveness of a single supreme cause at various locations in space. It would follow from this that matter is infinitely divisible."

As a firm statement, the idea does not appear until about 1775. If we nonetheless put its origin in the year 1770, this is because the fourth dissertation prepares the ground for the future transcendental aesthetics (in 26: II, 398 ff.; par. 14 f.) and because, while the division into a phenomenal and a noumenal world is not made there for the first time, it is carried through for the first time with methodical clarity, not just as a hypothesis (as in *Dreams of a Spiritualist,* for instance). The new interpretation of space and time and the clear concept of appearance lead necessarily to the infinite divisibility of matter.

14 Cf. the reflection (penned about 1775) in 72: XIV, 187; 42.

15 The circle that is strikingly evident here—using the existence of each force as proof of the necessity of the other—is also found in Kant, though in more sublime a form.

16 [A long note extensively reexamining Erich Adickes's inquiry into the question whether Kant's writings on natural science justify his characterization as a "natural scientist" was omitted here, chiefly because many of the terms and criteria used by Adickes in 1924 have been rendered obsolete by a half-century of scientific up-

heavals. With the author's consent several other notes were omitted for similar reasons, or because the references in them are to lesser works unavailable in this country. —E. B. A.]

17 It was not till fifteen years later, in connection with the new definition of space and time, that Kant had misgivings in principle about this thought of a creator. We may assume, he says in a reflection written about 1770 (81: XVII, 428 f.; 4134), that the existence of the world is due to God's decree; but we cannot conceive of its having been brought forth by God as a creator. We can conceive the beginning only *in* the world; the beginning *of* the world remains unthinkable, for it would have to suggest a previous period of time in which the world did not exist. At the same time, the beginning of the world would have to be the result of a beginning in the creator, but in the necessary being nothing can begin. We may say, therefore, that the world is everlasting, but not that it is eternal. "Everlasting" means only that it has been at all times, that there was no time before it. There is a qualitative difference between this all-permanence, which is still always subject to time, and eternity which lies outside of time. (Cf. also 81: XVII, 429; 4135.)

18 Cf. the concept of creation in the critical period (34: V, 102): "If existence *in time* is a mere sensory mode of conception on the part of thinking creatures in the world, and if accordingly it does not concern them as things in themselves, the creation of these creatures is a creation of things in themselves—because the concept of a creation does not belong to the sensory mode of conception in existence, nor to causality, but can refer to noumena only. Hence, if I say that creatures in the sensible world 'have been created,' I am viewing them as noumena." This accords with a line from *Opus postumum*: "No mundane matter can either originate or perish" (94: XXI, 29).

19 Kant consistently rejects all attempts to explain nature by direct divine intervention. If primal matter and the antagonistic forces are given, everything must be systematically explicable by mechanical laws. Newton had failed to pursue this systematics to the end; he thought it was God who solidifies planets and stars and invests them with centrifugal force. Even after all celestial bodies have entered into their courses and roatations there remain two ways in which Newton's God has to help. Both the moving forces and the movements gradually diminish in the universe, and when their loss

leads to a standstill, God must step in and give all things the proper twist again. He also must intervene when a gradual increase in the slight irregularities observed in the courses of the stars might threaten a collapse of cosmic order (cf. Adickes, vol. 2, pp 210 f.). To avoid chaos and standstill, God has to assist the laws he made. There must be something wrong with his laws—a conclusion which leads Kant to say that this kind of natural science is both diminishing God's wisdom and voiding nature: "The natural scientists who have gone in for such mundane wisdom will have to make solemn amends for it before the tribunal of religion. Then there will indeed not be a nature any more; the changes in the world will be wrought solely by a deus ex machina" (4: 1, 333).

20 The reference is to all of part 2, section 7, of *Universal Natural History and Theory of the Heavens* (4: 1, 306–22). If for no other reason, these pages are worth reading because they show a lover of the colossal, of gigantic thought dimensions. We almost feel as if here we were encountering Kant's time of genius. Since he later strove to shroud his every trait of genius, to sublimate it in discipline and modesty, we may never come to know him fully in his late works—and all of the critical writings are late works. The picture of the old Kant, reinforced by the portrayals of his friends Jachmann, Borowski, and Wasianski, may give an innocuous turn to our view of his mind and soul. This often happened in the history of Kant's image, with Heine and later Nietzsche as typical examples. To their Kant pictures we might reply, looking at the early works, that from adolescence on Kant had a tendency to be carried away by thoughts, speculations, and reveries. This was the soil that nurtured his philosophy, but at the same time it was a threat to solid philosophical craftsmanship. Recognizing the threat, Kant sought the "spirit of thoroughness" (30: B XXXVI). He outwardly discarded the touch of genius and couched even his poetic and imaginative thoughts in prosaically sober language. His is a prose that awakens the reader from the rapture of thoughts, to make him reflect upon their content. It is the language of criticism —cool, formalistic, dry, because the danger of speculative seduction is ever present.

21 This line of the old Kant shows a proximity to Heraclitus. We cannot tell from Kant's works how much of the Heraclitean fragments he knew; he mentions Heraclitus several times (19: II, 216; 24: II, 342; 75: XV, 622; 76: XV, 753, 832; 79: XVI, 59; 81: XVII, 555), but

all those passages are unimportant and suggest a very conventional and falsified picture. The proximity is not to be explained by direct knowledge.

22 Cf. 56: VIII, 299 f.; and 84: XIX, 591; 8045.

23 About the context of this line cf. L.s 842 and 865, as well as the reflections in 78: XV, 971–76; 1551–53; and 94: XXI, 13 f.

24 Our only concern here is the clear elaboration of the moment of relativity in motion. We want neither to present the theory of motion in full nor to show how 33 (1786) differs from the little piece of 1758 in regard to methodology or to the history of ideas. We therefore draw no sharp line between the elements of the early treatise and those of the late one. Rather, we use the advantages of both: the great visuality of 13 and the clear conceptuality of 33. We consider this procedure legitimized by the fact that both treatises maintain the relativity of motion.

25 Newton did regard all motion in empirical space as relative, but not that in absolute space. Cf. Adickes, vol. 1, 275 ff., and Kant, 72: XIV, 146; 40; 169 f.; 41.

26 In 33, Kant considers this "common explanation" (33: IV, 482) inadequate. It may suffice as long as we ignore the materiality of matter; once we include this in our consideration, we have to fix its location. In round bodies, for example, their location is determined by the center alone. A ball can move without changing its place, by rotating on its axis. Hence the definition applies only to a physical—i.e., mobile—point as the location.

27 This ultimate thing itself could not be material; if it were, it would be qualified, and thus not the ultimate. This is why Kant in 33 defines absolute motion as a motion "conceived without any relation of one matter to another" (3: IV, 556). One might think, perhaps, of the straight-lined motion of the total universe, the system of all matter; but here, too, space is presupposed. Hence Kant's phrasing (72: XIV, 193; 42): "There is no motion in absolute space. The universe is at rest." Correspondingly, he says (72: XIV, 132; 40) that "all motion as a whole is at rest." Both statements are uncritical, for rest also presupposes space. These statements about the whole inevitably takes us into the field of antinomies. The correct statement is paradoxical and would have to say: The universe as a whole is not in motion, and neither is it at rest.

28 That motion is mutual follows from the reciprocity of distances. 71: XIV, 39; 10: "All distance is mutually equal to one another, i.e.,

A is as far from B as B is from A." A and B are the two correlates of
a relation that includes the two identical relations B:A and A:B. A
shift in the correlate A changes the relation of B to A. The "stubbornness of language" (13: II, 18) wants a correlate to be at rest,
but even then it must be considered in motion. Kant gives a gro-
tesque example (13: II, 18 f.): A cannon ball is fired at a wall in
the vicinity of Paris, from east to west. To which of the two bodies
is the motion to be attributed, to the ball or to the wall? If only
their relation to each other is considered, the "phenomenon of
change" allows no perception except that of a mutual approach. If
I mentally place them into mathematical space—in other words, if
I abstract from everything outside the two—I must attribute to
both of them a motion inversely proportional to their masses. The
wall, therefore, is moving toward the ball.

29 13: II, 17. Cf. 33: IV, 559 f.; and 81: XVII, 453 f.; 4200.

30 This is not equally true of "perpetual peace," which is a rational
concept.

31 84: XIX, 601, 598, 475; 8070, 8062, 7640.

32 84: XIX, 599, 527; 8063, 7824.

33 49: VIII, 120: Between the city dwellers and the nations of herds-
men there was "continuous warfare . . . or at least an incessant
threat of war; and internally, at least, nations on either side could
therefore enjoy the invaluable treasure of freedom. For even now
the threat of war remains the only brake on despotism, since it
now takes wealth for a state to be a power, but without freedom
there will be no industry that might produce wealth." Cf. 49: VIII,
121: "We need but look at China, whose geographical situation
means that it may have to fear an occasional unexpected assault,
perhaps, but no powerful enemy, and in which every trace of freedom is therefore extinguished." In any case, war is less of an evil
than universal monarchy, "the grave of general autocracy" (36: VI,
34 note).

34 The community of concepts—if we may employ this term—is thus
not fixed by Kant in a conceptual pyramid that would permit concepts to be clearly circumscribed and definitely delimited on all
sides. The premise of such a pyramid would of course be ontology,
a thought edifice solidly construed as cognition of being. One of
the logical results of the surrender of ontology is that concepts lose
their definitively fixed limits.

35 Cf. the following passage from Karl Jaspers's *Nikolaus Cusanus*

(Munich, 1964), p. 34: "How are speculative writings to be read? We must enter into their thought movements, must experience the truth of those movements, must be involved in them. It takes a conceptual musicality to be able to hear what is done in that sort of thinking, and it takes training in this musicality to be able to penetrate and understand.

"Philological reading—the kind in which we compare, trace usages, show discrepancies, discuss historical dependencies—is a useful preparation for understanding. But it is disturbing at times, leading to rationalistic misconceptions, distracting."

Kant's writings, of course, cannot be called speculative in the same sense as can those of Nicholas of Cusa. But the elements of mobility and of an ultimate indeterminacy are to be found in him too, only more concealed and bound up in a stricter rationality. In a sense, therefore, the passage applies to his writings also.

36 Vaihinger's otherwise meritorious commentary to the *Critique of Pure Reason* is a striking example. Yet it is precisely Vaihinger who ought to be given credit in this point: he was one of the first to see clearly that the many divergencies in Kant's work and mode of expression need not have an absolutely negative significance. Cf. Hans Vaihinger, "Kants antithetische Geistesart, erläutert an seiner Als-Ob-Lehre (in *Den Manen Friedrich Nietzsches* [Munich: Weimarer Weihgeschenke, 1921], pp. 151–82).

Chapter 2

1 6: 1, 410: "Bina principia cognitionis metaphysicae, consectariorum feracissima, aperiens, e principio rationis determinantis fluentia."

2 Ibid.: "Nulla substantiis accidere potest mutatio, nisi quatenus cum aliis connexae sunt, quarum, dependentia reciproca mutuam status mutationem determinat."

3 6: 1, 412 f.: "Substantiae finitae per solam isparum existentiam nullis se relationibus respiciunt, nulloque plane commercio continentur, nisi quatenus a communi existentiae suae principio, divino nempe intellectu, mutuis respectibus conformatae sustinentur."

4 Cf. 72: XIV, 173; 41; and 72: XIV, 193; 42: "The fundamental conditions of community between matters, i.e., where there is no action without interaction, is attraction and repulsion at rest." Of

this antagonism, then, Kant says regarding man (75: XV, 590; 1353): "In the constitution of the world this is the mechanism which instinctively conjoins and segregates us."

5 Cf. 56: VIII, 307-13; 59: VIII, 354-57; and 37: VI, 343-51.

6 Kant's concept of substance is not unequivocal. We distinguish the one used here from only two others: first, from the concept of the early writings, which is identical with the concept of the monad—"Substantia simplex, monas dicta, est" (10: I, 477)— and, second, from the predominant meaning of the critical concept of substance as a pure relational category (see 30: A 80/B 106). In our case, substance stands in space in the sense of a real object, in the sense of 30: A 277/B333: "Matter is substantia phaenomenon."

7 Lecture on physics; 99 (see chap. 1, note 10, above).

8 Ibid.

9 56: VIII, 291-92: "But this consistent equality of men in a state, as its subjects, goes very well with the utmost inequality of the mass and in grades of possession—whether in physical or mental superiority over others, in external gifts of fortune, or simply in rights (of which there can be many) with respect to others—so that one man's welfare is greatly dependent on the other's will (the poor man's on that of the rich), that one must be obedient (as the child to his parents, or the wife to her husband) while the other commands, that the one serves (as a daily laborer) and the other pays wages, etc."

10 94: XXI, 54. Cf. 94: XXI, 9-10, 15, 17, 35, 48, 51; and 94: XXII, 49, 50, 120.

11 Cf., for instance, Karl Vorländer's *Kant und der Sozialismus unter besonderer Berücksichtigung der neuesten theoretischen Bewegung innerhalb des Marxismus* (Berlin, 1900), pp. 14-15: "Kant did not yet envision the full consequences of his categorical imperative, which modern socialism sees precisely in the fact that the prerequisite of political independence—*economic* independence, i.e., freedom from economic servitude—can be made possible *for all*, not just ideally, but actually. And a fair judgment will concede that under the economic and cultural circumstances of his time he could scarcely do so. After all, the lawmakers of the French Revolution did not go beyond our philosopher; for in making that distinction of active and passive state citizens they preceded him."

From the standpoint of our previous analogy, the answer is that Kant might well have done so. Vorländer's fairness is a license for inconsistency. Consistency may be philosophically breached in the name of a higher consistency; but breaching it in the name of conventions or in consequence of a concession, as Vorländer obviously means, calls for critique, not for fairness.

12 An example: if two bodies collide on a straight line, with the same speed, they are real opponents; if they draw apart at the same speed, they are merely potential opponents.

13 18: II, 194: "In all the world's natural changes, the sum of the positive, when counted by adding concurring (not opposed) positions and by subtracting really opposed ones from each other, is neither increased nor diminished." Kant says (18: II, 195) that in the physical world this proposition is a "long proven rule of mechanics. We express it as follows: Quantitas motus, summando vires corporum in easdem partes et subtrahendo eas quae vergunt in contrarias, per mutuam illorum actionem (conflictum, pressionem, attractionem) non mutatur." The second proposition (18: II, 197) reads: "All real grounds of the universe, if one adds up the concurring ones and subtracts from each other those that are opposed to one another, will yield a result equaling zero."

14 Kant's most important dogmatic treatise, 17, was written in 1761, one year before 18. The difference between logical and real repugnancy is already found in 17, in a passage about the supreme reality of the necessary Being (17: II, 85 ff.). Kant says of this Being that "in the most real of beings there can be no real repugnancy or positive antagonism of its own definitions, since the consequence thereof would be a deprivation or deficiency, which contradicts its supreme reality" (17: II, 86). In 17 the meanings of deficiency and deprivation are not yet clearly differentiated, however. The essay on negative quantities is apt to have been written largely for this differentiation's sake.

That the thought model of real repugnancy was constantly used in late critical metaphysics also is demonstrable by 39: VII, 230; by 36: VI, 22–23 note; and by 37: VI, 384.

15 Concerning the division into concepts of nature and freedom, and the division of philosophy at large into theoretical and practical philosophy, cf. 35: V, 171 ff.

Chapter 3

1 Schelling poses the question at various points of his work. On attempts to resolve it, and on the historical and systematic circle of

problems surrounding it, see Jaspers, *Schelling: Grösse und Verhängnis* (Munich, 1955), pp. 124–30.

2 Conceived as the transcendental ground in the transcendental dialectics of the *Critique of Pure Reason* is the idea of God; in the *Critique of Judgment*—used here for comparison—it is the intelligible substrate. There is no contradiction between the two answers, since God too is an intelligible being and thus that substrate itself. Even so, a comparative inquiry into the concepts of God and the intelligible substrate would be desirable and necessary for a clarification of Kant's transcendence.

Chapter 4

1 Emil Lask, *Die Logik der Philosophie und die Kategorienlehre* (Tübingen, 1911), pp. 245 ff.

2 Cf. Schiller's charge of rigorism (Schiller, *Sämtliche Werke,* Säkular-Ausgabe, vol. 11, pp. 218 ff.) and Kant's reply in 36: VI, 23–24 note.

3 30: A 666/B 694: "Reason has indeed but one sole interest, and the controversy between its maxims is only a difference and mutual restriction in the methods of satisfying that interest."

4 Schelling, *Sämtliche Werke,* 1856 ff., vol. 7 (1860), p. 354.

5 6: I, 414: "Insana etiam Manichaeorum opinion, qui duo principia pariter prima atque a se haud dependentia mundi imperio praeficiebant, nostro principio funditus evellitur."

6 In *The End of All Things* Kant discusses monism and dualism in a practical sense. He says (58: VIII, 328 ff.) that there are "from olden times two systems with respect to future eternity": that of the "unitarians" who would grant eternal bliss to all men, and that of the "dualists" who reserve salvation to a few elect.

In a practical sense the weight of reasons is said to favor dualism, for it opens "a prospect of eternity" that is linked with an idea of compensatory justice and conceives even death as governed by no other principles than those governing life. Dualism is thus directly connected with our self-judging conscience, whereas unitarism ignores guilt and merit and "seems to lull too much into indifferent security. . . . In a practical sense, therefore, the acceptable system will have to be the dualistic one."

But it does meet with many objections. Who can look into his heart, to judge by what principles he has been acting? Who can judge to which forces a so-called merit is due—to lucky chance or to circumstances in general, to lack of opportunity or really to a free moral decision? And finally, assuming the existence of an evil principle at work in all eternity: how could we reconcile it with a wise Providence that "even one single individual should exist only to be eternally damned"? Although agreeing with reason in a practical sense, dualism will never be conceivable without aporias.

7 In the second Preface to *Critique of Pure Reason* (30: B, xv ff.) Kant points out that the method of natural science is the model for the new method of metaphysics. As an example he cites the methodical turn carried out by Copernicus. Finding the courses of heavenly bodies incalculable on the basis of the hypothesis that they revolve around the observer, Copernicus tried the opposite assumption and discovered the laws. Likewise, it had so far been tacitly assumed in metaphysics that cognition must go by external objects, and it had not been possible to achieve synthetic cognition a priori. The hypothesis now being tried was that external objects, and thus experience as such, must go by the forms of the two roots of cognition, the subjective visual and conceptual faculties. The road to synthetic cognition a priori had thus been discovered, since knowledge in the realm of possible experience contained no more now than the knower himself put into it.

This about face in metaphysical method is sometimes called a "Copernican turn." The term invites a misconception. Copernicus lifted the subject out of the center of the world and made it revolve around the objects. But Kant, in a sense, put the subject into the center, into the focal point of everything objective insofar as it is an object of cognition. The Kantian turn is the opposite of the Copernican. They are alike only in reaching the goal by a radical turn away from the naïvely probable.

What the new metaphysical method has in common with the method of natural science is that the fitness of metaphysical concepts and principles must be experimentally confirmed. It happens by the twofold application of propositions in the realms of the sensible and the intelligible world. If the double view produces no contradictions, the experiment has proved the propositions fit; if it leads to insoluble antinomies, it has proved them unfit. The material of aesthetics and analytics must withstand the dialectical experiment, just as the doctrine of ideas must be found fit in the cognoscible realm as well.

8 81: XVIII, 408; 5970. Cf. 5971, 5973, 5975.

9 Kant calls this a "symbolic anthropomorphism." Unlike dogmatic anthropomorphism, this is permissible and necessary.

10 31: IV, 357: "Such cognition is one *according to analogy*—which does not mean an imperfect similarity of two things, as the word is commonly understood. What it does mean is a perfect similarity of two relations between quite dissimilar things."

11 On the problem of metabasis cf. 81: XVIII, 457–58, 546 ff.; 6110, 6280; also 94: XXI, 284–85.

12 83: XIX, 128; 6667: "Relations of law can be compared with those of bodies. Every body is at rest with respect to all others, except as it is being moved by others; and so does every man have duties of omission toward others, except as others concur with him in one will or alter his condition against his will. *Actio est aequalis reactione*. As much as a large body affects a small one, so much does the small one reaffect the large one. The common center of gravity, i.e., the common will, is the same before the act and after."

13 In 17: II, 132–33, Kant says that the principle of analogizing "covers what seems to me an important object of reflection for the philosopher: how such agreement of very different things on a certain common ground of uniformity can be so great and widespread and yet so exact at the same time. These analogies are also very necessary aids to our cognition; mathematics itself provides several. I refrain from citing examples, for it is to be feared that such likenesses, felt in so different a manner, may not have the same effect on every other intellect, and the thought I am throwing out here is unfinished anyway, and not yet sufficiently intelligible."

Chapter 5

1 13: II, 25. 79: XVI, 783; 3332. 79: XVI, 839; 3442.

2 79: XVI, 846; 3456: "The presentation is dogmatic or polemical. The means are critical, since the opponent is anticipated."

3 "Auf des Herrn K* Gedanken von der wahren Schätzung der lebendigen Kräfte." In Gotthold Ephraim Lessing's collected works, ed. Karl Lachmann, 3d ed., vol. 1 (1886), p. 41.

4 Here we must point out a passing homonymy. In the early writings the term "polemics" did not occur; we used it as a cover concept for all modes of argumentative controversy over certain claims. In *Critique of Pure Reason* the term is to be found—not in the en-

compassing sense we gave it, but in the derogatory one of dogmatic controversy. In this sense we must take it up for the time being, until, in the context of *Critique of Judgment,* we can replace it with the term "quarrel."

5 In G. W. F. Hegel, *Sämtliche Werke,* Jubiläumsausgabe, ed. Hermann Glockner, vol. 1: *Aufsätze aus dem kritischen Journal der Philosophie und andere Schriften aus der Jenenser Zeit,* 2d ed. (1941), pp. 171–89.

6 Ibid., p. 173.

7 Ibid., p. 174.

8 Ibid., p. 175.

9 Ibid.

10 Ibid.

11 Ibid., p. 189.

12 Karl Jaspers, "Can There Be Philosophical Polemics" in *Philosophy,* tr. E. B. Ashton (Chicago, 1969–71), vol. 1, pp. 24–30.

13 Ibid., p. 29.

14 Ibid.

15 August Stadler, *Kants Teleologie und ihre erkenntnistheoretische Bedeutung* (Berlin, 1874), pp. 35 ff. Our discussion is based upon that inquiry.

Chapter 6

1 Cf. *Immanuel Kant; ein Lebensbild nach Darstellungen der Zeitgenossen Jachmann, Borowski, Wasianski,* ed. Alfons Hoffmann (Halle, 1902).

2 Borowski (in *Immanuel Kant,* pp. 219–20): "Agreement with his own ways of thought and action was precisely not what Kant asked for. He paid little or no heed to philosophical opinions that might differ from his."

And Jachmann (p. 44): "To philosophers following another system—even to his opponents if they were really searching for truth and revealing no motives unworthy of a scholar—he always referred with unbiased appreciation of their merits. He tried to make clear to himself how his lesser opponents could quite naturally come to hold other views, and he lived fully confident of the final victory of truth."

3 Cf. Borowski, pp. 260–61.

4 Ibid., pp. 191–92: "Never, never did he resort to the wretched means of satire, or of gibes at other teaching colleagues."

5 Ibid., p. 197.

6 L. 275, 11. vi. 1786, from Biester.

7 Cf. L. 454, 15. x. 1790, to Herz.

8 Jachmann, in *Immanuel Kant*, p. 17.

9 Pörschke to Fichte, 14. iii. 1797, no. 286 in J. G. Fichte, *Briefwechsel: Kritische Gesamtausgabe*, ed. Hans Schulz (Leipzig, 1925).

10 Cf. Borowski, in *Immanuel Kant*, p. 260.

11 L. 134, early April 1778, to Herz.

12 Cf. L. 205, 7.viii. 1778, to Garve.

13 L. 313, 28.xii. 1787, to Reinhold.

14 L. 205, 7.viii. 1783, to Garve.

15 Ibid.

16 J. G. H. Feder, *Über Raum und Caussalität: Zur Prüfung der Kantischen Philosophie* (Leipzig, 1788), p. xii.

17 L. 210, 26.viii. 1783, to Schultz.

18 See note 14, above.

19 Johann Schultz, *Erläuterungen über des Herrn Professor Kant's Kritik der reinen Vernunft* (Königsberg, 1784).

20 C. L. Reinhold, "*Briefe über die Kantische Philosophie*," *Teutscher Merkur*, August 1786, pp. 99–141; January 1787, 3–39; February, 117–42; May, 167–85; July, 67–88; August, 142–65; September, 247ff.

21 Cf. Günther Röhrdanz, "Die Stellung Kants in und zu der Presse seiner Zeit," in *Zeitung und Leben*, vol. 29 (Munich, 1936), pp. 46ff.

22 *Deutsche Monatsschrift*, vol. 3 (1796), pp. 139–52.

23 J. G. Fichte, *Selected Works*, ed. Fritz Medicus, vol. 3 (Leipzig, n.d.), p. 69.

24 J. G. Herder, *Collected Works*, ed. Bernhard Suphan, vol. 18 (Berlin, 1883), p. 327.

25 See note 9, above.

26 Friedrich Nicolai, *Gedächtnisschrift auf Johann August Eberhard* (Berlin, 1810), p. 78.

27 This claim of Fichte's will be discussed later in detail. C. L. Reinhold, *Versuch einer neuen Theorie des menschlichen Vorstellungsvermögens* (Prague and Jena, 1789). J. S. Beck, *Einzig-möglicher Standpunkt, aus welchem die critische Philosophie beurteilt werden muss* (Riga, 1796).

28 Vol. 2 (August 1798), pp. 156–66.

29 54: VIII, 247. 70: XII, 371.

30 The figures are based on Erich Adickes, *German Kantian Bibliography* (Boston, New York, Chicago, 1893–96). This lists 2,832 items, 159 of which are Kant's own works and works dealing with their publication, while a number of others are from the literature published after 1804. Presumably our own estimates are all rather low.

31 Reinhold to Fichte, September 1799, no. 390, in Fichte's *Briefwechsel*.

32 Schelling to Fichte, 12. ix. 1799, no. 393 in Fichte, *Briefwechsel*: "Kant will probably not be immortal since they call him dead already. . . . Here, too, many have a Life of the dead K. prepared, complete with funeral poems. Since he is no longer lecturing and has withdrawn from all social activities except for his friend Motherby's house, he gradually comes to be unknown here, too; even his prestige is dwindling."

33 One can trace this in his correspondence. He let the exchange of letters with Hamann dry up in the last fifteen years before Hamann's death, due to the insight that "I, poor earthling, am not at all organized for the divine language of Intuitive Reason" (L. 86, 6. iv. 1774, to Hamann). Kant knew too well that beneath their occasional differences of opinion lay the radically different basic postures of two philosophers. Conversation could bring both of them to a comunicative awareness of the difference; in written altercations the gulf between them might easily have proved unbridgeable. Kant did not break off this correspondence in order to part with his friend, but in order to keep him.

His correspondence with Lavater came to a more rapid end, although Lavater had assured him that as a "philosopher à la Wolf" (L. 81, 8. ii. 1774) Kant had for "many years" been his "favorite writer," to whom he was "most sympathetic" (L. 90, 8. iv. 1774). True, Kant answered in one of the most important letters he ever wrote; but in one only. As in his relations to Herder and to Jacobi, he let this suffice for all time. It did not escape Kant that Lavater was a romantic (75: vx, 406f.; 921), a "phantast" (76: xv, 705; 1485), and indeed, in the final analysis, an extremely clever fraud (81: XVIII, 694; 6369), from whom it was better to separate.

Another correspondence was not taken up by Kant at all. In 1794 Samuel Collenbusch, a blind pietistic physician, had Kant's

Religion and *Critique of Practical Reason* read to him "a few times" (L. 649, 23.i. 1795). He then drafted several letters to Kant and sent him at least four (L.s 647, 649, 657, 698). To these invitations to a dialogue about the foundations of religion and morality, invitations couched in the tenor of the Glad Tidings and in part very beautiful, Kant did not respond even when Collenbusch begged him to answer "for the love of your own law's duty" (L. 698, 30.iii. 1796). To Kant's mind, the encounter with a faith in revelation that misconceives itself as faith in a higher reason would have been bound to end in a senseless quarrel better not entered into.

34 See note 29, above.
35 Ibid.
36 Ibid.
37 Ibid.
38 L. 201, 13.vii. 1783, from Garve.
39 Feder's review appeared in the Supplement to the *Göttinger Gelehrte Anzeigen* of 19.i. 1782, part 3, pp. 40–48. It is reprinted in the edition of Kant's *Prolegomena* by Karl Vorländer in Philosophische Bibliothek, vol. 40 (Hamburg, 1957), pp. 167–74. We quote from p. 167 of that reprint.
40 Ibid.
41 Ibid., p. 168.
42 Ibid., p. 169.
43 Ibid.
44 Ibid., p. 168.
45 Ibid., p. 172.
46 Ibid.
47 Ibid.
48 Ibid., pp. 172–73.
49 Ibid., p. 173.
50 Ibid.
51 Ibid.
52 Ibid.
53 Ibid.
54 Ibid.
55 Ibid., p. 174.
56 Cf. Feder's autobiography (*J. G. H. Feder's Leben, Natur und Grundsätze: Zur Belehrung und Ermunterung seiner lieben Nachkommen, auch Anderer die Nutzbares daraus aufzunehmen geneigt sind* (Leipzig, Hanover, Darmstadt, 1825), p. 80.

57 Cf. ibid., p. 88.

58 Ibid.

59 *Philosophisches Magazin,* ed. Johann August Eberhard (Halle, 1788–92); four volumes containing four issues each:

Year	Volume	Issues
1788	1	1, 2
1789	1	3, 4
	2	1, 2, 3
1790	2	4
	3	1, 2, 3
1791	3	4
	4	1, 2, 3
1792	4	4

60 Eberhard, *Neue Apologie des Sokrates, oder Untersuchung der Lehre von der Seligkeit der Heiden* (Berlin, Stettin, 1772). We quote from the two-volume "new and revised" edition (Frankfurt, Leipzig, 1787).

61 Ibid., vol. 1, p. viii.

62 Eberhard summed up the reaction to the book in Germany as follows: "One rebuttal, and a thousand vilifications!" (ibid., vol. 2, 4.). In the vilifications he evidently included Lessing's retort *Leibnitz von den ewigen Strafen* (*Sämtliche Schriften,* Lachmann ed., 3d ed., vol. 11, pp. 461–87).

63 Eberhard, *Allgemeine Theories des Denkens und Empfindens: Eine Abhandlung, welche den von der Königl. Akademie der Wissenschaften in Berlin auf das Jahr 1776 ausgesetzten Preis erhalten hat* (Berlin, 1776).

64 Cf. L.s 129, 28.ii. 1778 and 132, 28.iii. 1778, from von Zedlitz.

65 Eberhard, *Kurzer Abriss der Metaphysik mit Rücksicht auf den gegenwärtigen Zustand der Philosophie* (Halle, 1794), pp. iii–iv.

66 *Handbuch der Aesthetik für gebildete Leser aus allen Ständen in Briefen,* ed. J. A. Eberhard (Halle, 1803–5), 4 vols.

67 Eberhard, *Synonymisches Handwörterbuch der deutschen Sprache für alle, die sich in dieser Sprache richtig ausdrücken wollen* (Halle, 1802). The sixteenth edition of this, the most successful of Eberhard's books, appeared 1904 in Leipzig.

68 Eberhard, *Der Geist des Urchristenthums, ein Handbuch der Geschichte der philosophischen Kultur für gebildete Leser aus allen Ständen* (Halle, 1787–1808), 3 vols.

69 *Philosophisches Archiv*, ed. J. A. Eberhard (Berlin, 1792–95), 2 vols.

Year	Volume	Issues
1792	1	1, 2, 3
1793	1	4
	2	1
1794	2	2, 3
1795	2	4

70 Friedrich Nicolai, *Gedächtnisschrift auf Johann August Eberhard* (Berlin, Stettin, 1810), p. 54.

71 Ibid., p. 55.

72 *Philosophisches Magazin,* vol. 1, p. 1.

73 Ibid., 1, 3.

74 Ibid., 1, 4.

75 Ibid., 1, 5.

76 Ibid.

77 Ibid., 1, 157.

78 Ibid., 1, 334.

79 Ibid.

80 Ibid., 1, 335.

81 Ibid., 1, 6.

82 Ibid.

83 Ibid.

84 Ibid., 1, 306.

85 Ibid., 1, 9.

86 Ibid., 1, 23.

87 Ibid.

88 Ibid., 1, 29.

89 Ibid., 1, 289.

90 L. 353, 9.iv. 1789, from Reinhold.

91 Fichte, *Briefwechsel* (see note 9, above; in the following notes 92–108, 112–16, and 119 we cite only the numbers, dates, and addressees of these letters), no. 55, August–September 1790, to Weisshuhn.

92 Cf. no. 56, 5.ix. 1790, to Johanna Rahn.

93 No. 77, 2.ix. 1791, to Kant.

94 Cf. no. 61, 29.ix. 1790, to Achelis.

95 No. 68, 5.iii. 1791, to his brother Gotthelf.

96 No. 131, 20.ix. 1793, to Kant.

97 No. 140, November–December 1793, to Flatt.

98 No. 74, 7.vii. 1791, to Sonntag.
99 No. 75, 18.viii. 1791, to Kant.
100 No. 131, 20. ix. 1793, to Kant.
101 No. 56, 5. ix. 1790, to Johanna Rahn.
102 No. 57, 27. ix. 1790, to Weisshuhn.
103 No. 140 (see note 112).
104 No. 145, December 1793, to Stephani.
105 Ibid.
106 No. 135, October–November 1793, to Niethammer.
107 No. 140 (see note 97, above).
108 No. 135 (see note 106, above).
109 *Aenesidemus oder über die Fundamente der von dem Herrn Prof. Reinhold in Jena gelieferten Elementar-Philosophie.* The work appeared anonymously in the *Allgemeine Literatur-Zeitung,* Jena, 1794, nos. 47–49.
110 J. G. Fichte, *Über den Begriff der Wissenschaftslehre oder der sogenannten Philosophie* (Weimar, 1794), Preface to the first edition. In Fichte, *Werke,* ed. Fritz Medicus, vol. 1 (Leipzig, 1911), p. 157.
111 Review of *Aenesidemus,* in Fichte, *Werke,* vol. 1, p. 148.
112 No. 135 (see note 106, above).
113 No. 140 (see note 97, above).
114 No. 145 (see note 104, above).
115 No. 161, 2. iv. 1794, to Böttiger.
116 No. 157, l. iii. 1794, to Reinhold.
117 *Erste Einleitung in die Wissenschaftslehre,* in Fichte, *Werke,* vol. 3, p. 4.
118 Ibid., p. 14 note.
119 No. 291, 4.vii. 1797, to Reinhold.
120 *Erste Einleitung in die Wissenschaftslehre,* in *Werke,* vol. 3, p. 5.
121 *Vorlesungen über die Geschichte der Philosophie,* in Hegel, *Werke* (Jubiläumsausgabe), vol. 3, p. 610.
122 Cf. 70: XII, 364. Besides, we have to mention Garve's request (cf. L. 819, mid-September 1798, to Kant) as well as the challenge issued by Nicolai in his autobiographical essay (Friedrich Nicolai, *Über meine gelehrte Bildung, über meine Kenntniss der Kritischen Philosophie und meine Schriften dieselbe betreffend, und über die Herren Kant, J. B. Erhard, und Fichte* [Berlin, Stettin, 1799], p. 186). That Kant actually read the latter is of course not certain.
123 We quote from the reprint in the Akademie edition (XIII, 542–43).

124 Nicolai was a courageous fighter against all the abuses prevalent in his time; a witty, knowledgeable antagonist of orthodoxy and pietism, of the Werther fever in Germany, of the folk song fad, of romanticism, and of the obscurantism of the secret orders. In the nineties, when he atacked Criticism also, he was renowned both as a writer and as a publisher. His activities can best be compared to those of his revered French contemporaries, Diderot and Voltaire, although intellectually he was not their equal.

125 For a characterization of Schlosser's thinking, see Schiller's letter to Goethe of 9. ii. 1798.

126 His friendship with Goethe, his official career, his marriages to Cornelia and, after her death, to Goethe's friend Johanna Fahlmer—all this invested Schlosser's name with a certain glamor among his contemporaries. His writing contributed to it. Schlosser's German style was cultivated, indeed manneristic, with every page testifying to a comprehensive education. To both the aestheticizing and the Christian side of his way of thinking, Kant's writings and the whole of critical philosophy were the barbarian enemy of the age. Schlosser felt obliged to enter the lists against them.

127 Johann August Schlettwein was the most important German physiocrat of the period. After years in the service of Margrave Karl Friedrich of Baden, he was professor of political, cameral, and financial sciences at the University of Giessen. He loved to castigate his contemporaries in letters of paternally pious challenge.

128 L. 205 (see note 14, above).

129 L. 359, 12. v. 1789, to Reinhold.

130 L. 360, 19. v. 1789, to Reinhold.

131 L. 359 (see note 129, above).

132 L. 205 (see note 14, above).

133 Ibid.

134 Ibid.

135 Ibid.

136 Fichte, *Briefwechsel* (see note 9, above), no. 251, 30. viii. 1795, to Jacobi.

137 L. 784, 13. x. 1797, to Tieftrunk.

138 L. 795, 9. i. 1798, to Schultz.

139 L. 359 (see note 129, above).

140 L. 205 (see note 14, above).

141 L. 360 (see note 130, above).

142 L. 359 (see note 129, above).

143 L. 360 (see note 130, above).

144 L. 359 (see note 129, above).

145 L. 360 (see note 130, above).

146 Ibid.

147 Cf. L. 359 (see note 129, above).

148 Ibid.

149 L. 795 (see note 138, above).

150 70: XII, 370. Cf. 94: XXI, 307.

151 Kant's outwardly forcible interpretation is that even Leibniz had not understood the theorem of sufficient reason objectively, as a law of nature, but as a merely subjective principle referring to a critique of reason. Leibniz had understood, says Kant, that according to the theorem of contradiction nothing but tautologies are known. Cognitions that exceed those must have a particular reason. And since these cognitions are called synthetic, "Leibniz intended to say no more than that beyond the theorem of contradiction (as the principle of analytical judgments) another principle, the one of synthetic judgments, must be added." This was his "remarkable allusion" (54: VIII, 248) to future investigations which had been carried out since.

Leibniz's concept of monads had never claimed applicability to the real world of bodies. It had been an indication of their "unknowable substrate, the intelligible world" (ibid.), and had thus occasioned a new concept of sensibility, a concept which Leibniz had not put into words, but thanks to which his system "agrees with itself" (54: VIII, 249). The basis of his reflections on preestablished harmony could not possibly have been a will to bring body and soul into communication, for these things are by nature quite independent of each other. Rather, preestablished harmony was pointing to "the community between intellect and sensibility in the same subject" (ibid.), a community whose ground had then been shown by *Critique*.

152 *Philosophisches Magazin*, vol. 1, p. 258.

153 Ibid., 1, 259.

154 Ibid., 3, 214.

155 The theorem of sufficient reason did thus help Leibniz "not one whit in getting beyond the basic theorem of analytical judgments, the theorem of contradiction, and synthetically expanding himself a priori, by reason" (88: XX, 283). His system of predetermined harmony, having been "aimed at explaining the community be-

tween body and soul" (ibid.), is now "the most curious figment ever thought up by philosophy" (88: xx, 284). And his monadology leads to a "kind of enchanted world" (88: xx, 285). Cf. note 151, above.

156 Cf. *Philosophisches Magazin*, vol. 4, pp. 195–213.

157 Ibid., 4, 208.

158 A. G. Baumgarten, *Metaphysica,* § 520.

159 *Philosophisches Magazin*, vol. 1, p. 290: "Herr Kant accused the philosophy of Leibniz and Wolf of 'having falsified the concept of sensibility and appearance, and that by regarding the difference between sensibility and the intellectual realm as merely logical.' "

160 Ibid., 1, 298.

161 30: A 43: "That all our sensibility is thus nothing but the confused conception of things—containing solely that which belongs to things in themselves, but only under a conglomeration of characteristics and partial conceptions which we do not consciously discriminate—this is a falsification of the concepts by which the entire doctrine of sensibility and phenomenality is rendered useless and empty."

162 L. 360 (see note 130, above).

163 *Allgemeine Literatur-Zeitung* (Jena, 1789), vol. 2, p. 595.

164 Jena, 1789, no. 87, 730.

165 *Philosophisches Magazin*, vol. 2, pp. 244–50, 269–73; vol. 3, pp. 156 ff.

166 Ibid., 3, 156, 158.

167 Cf. L.s 405 and 412.

168 The same fact shows in the innocuous controversy with J. A. H. Reimarus, the professor of natural history in Hamburg, which will be discussed here later, in another context.

169 L. 345, 28. ii. 1789, from Jakob.

170 L. 353 (see note 90, above).

171 L. 359 (see note 129, above).

172 Ibid.

173 L. 360 (see note 130, above).

174 L. 359 (see note 129, above).

175 L. 366, 14. vi. 1789, from Reinhold.

176 *Philosophisches Magazin* 1, 307–32.

177 L. 366 (see note 190).

178 Jena, no. 174–76; 2, 577–97.

179 L. 366 (see note 175, above).

180 *Philosophisches Magazin,* vol. 1, pp. 435–68.

181 Ibid., 2, 1–28.

182 Ibid., 2, 391–402.

183 Ibid., 2, 403–19.

184 Ibid., 2, 420–30.

185 Ibid., 4, 255–70.

186 Ibid., 2, 429.

187 Ibid., 2, 406 ff.

188 Ibid., 4, 265.

189 Ibid., 4, 263.

190 Ibid., 2, 419.

191 L. 442, 16. viii. 1790, to Schultz.

192 L. 436, 29. vi. 1790, to Schultz.

193 Ibid.

194 L. 437, 2. viii. 1790, to Schultz.

195 Ibid.

196 L. 436 (see note 207).

197 L. 439, 5. viii. 1790, to Kästner.

198 Ibid.

199 Cf. L.s 572 and 573.

200 L. 441, 15. viii. 1790, to Schultz.

201 L. 488, 27. ix. 1791, to Beck.

202 J. S. Beck, *Erläuternder Auszug aus den critischen Schriften des Herrn Prof. Kant auf Anrathen desselben* (Riga, 1793–96), 3 vols.

203 Cf. L. 452, 14. x. 1790, from Jachmann.

204 L. 502, 24. i. 1792, from Jakob.

205 In Johann Christoph Schwab, Karl Leonhard Reinhold, and Johann Heinrich Abicht, *Preisschriften über die Frage: Welche Fortschritte hat die Metaphysik seit Leibnizens und Wolfs Zeiten in Deutschland gemacht?* (Berlin: Königl. Preuss. Akademie der Wissenschaften, 1796), p. 144.

206 Cf. Gerhard Lehmann's introduction to vol. 20 of the Akademie edition; xx, 479–88.

207 Cf. *Rechtfertigung des Directoriums der franz. Republik, wegen seines angeblich ungereimten Plans, den Krieg mit England zu ihrem Vortheil zu beendigen;* 70: XII, 381–82. Cf. also Wasianski (see note 1, above), pp. 298–99: "He admired [Napoleon's] artistry in trying so hard to conceal his true intent to land in Portugal."

208 Cf. L. 70, 21. ii. 1772, to Herz.

209 L. 149, 28. iii. 1779, from Feder.

210 Feder's autobiography (see note 56, above), p. 117.

211 Ibid.

212 Ibid.

213 Ibid., pp. 117–18.

214 Ibid., p. 118.

215 Ibid.

216 Ibid., p. 119.

217 Cf. L.s 233, 275, 279, and 297.

218 Feder's autobiography, p. 120.

219 Feder, *Über Raum und Caussalität* (see note 16, above).

220 Ibid., p. xi.

221 Feder's autobiography, p. 123.

222 *Philosophische Bibliothek,* ed. Feder and Meiners, vol. 3 (1790), pp. 1–13.

223 Feder's autobiography, p. 124.

224 Ibid.

225 Ibid., p. 129–30.

226 Ibid., p. 125 note (by Feder's son).

227 Ibid., p. 124.

228 L. 360 (see note 130, above).

229 Goethe, *Annalen oder Tag- und Jahreshefte,* 1803; quoted from the Gedenkausgabe of his works, letters, and conversations, ed. Ernst Beutler, vol. 11 (Zurich, 1950), p. 720.

230 *Schreiben eines Vaters an seinen studierenden Sohn über den Fichtischen und Forbergischen Atheismus* [1798].

231 30. viii. 1799, to Schlosser; quoted from Gedenkausgabe (see note 229, above), vol. 19, p. 387.

232 *Intelligenzblatt der A. L. Z.,* no. 109, 28.viii. 1799, columns 876–78.

233 Nicolai's autobiographical essay (see note 122, above), p. 81.

234 Ibid., p. 105.

235 Fichte, *Briefwechsel* (see note 9, above), no. 393, 12. ix. 1799, from Schelling.

236 Cf. ibid., no. 394.

237 Ibid., no. 393 (see note 235 above).

238 Ibid., no. 400, 20. ix. 1799, to Schelling.

239 Ibid., no. 401, 28. ix. 1799, to Reinhold.

240 *Philosophisches Magazin,* vol. 3, pp. 148–61.

241 Ibid., p. 151.

242 Ibid.

243 Ibid., pp. 152–53.

244 Ibid., p. 155.

245 Ibid., p. 153.

246 Ibid.

247 Ibid., p. 158 note.

248 Ibid., p. 158.

249 Ibid., p. 159.

250 Ibid., p. 149.

251 Ibid., p. 159.

252 Ibid., p. 153.

253 Ibid., p. 159.

254 L. 360 (see note 130, above).

255 L. 112, 24. xi. 1776, to Herz.

256 L. 201, 13. vii. 1783, from Garve.

257 Ibid.

258 Garve's review appeared in Nicolai's *Allgemeine Deutsche Biblio-thek* (1783), section 2, appendix.

259 L. 209, 22. viii. 1783, to Schultz.

260 L. 221, 21. viii. 1783, from Schultz.

261 Hamann to Herder, 8. xii. 1783: "[Kant] is said to be displeased with it and to complain of being treated like an imbecile. There'll be no reply forthcoming; but he will answer the Göttingen reviewer in case he dares to take on Prol[egomena] as well" (Hamann, *Briefwechsel*, ed. A. Henkel, vol. 5 [1965], p. 107).

262 *Vergleichung der Garveschen und der Federschen Rezension über die Kritik der reinen Vernunft*, in E. Arnoldt *Gesammelte Schriften*, ed., Otto Schöndörffer, vol. 4 (Berlin, 1908), pp. 1–118. Arnoldt sums up the interrelation of the two reviews in these figures:

Total of Feder's review	312 lines
Literally taken over from Garve	76 lines
Meanings taken over with slight changes in language	69 lines
Meanings taken over in shortened language	55 lines
Additions of Feder's, or very free reproductions of Garve's text	112 lines

263 L. 545, 10. xi. 1792, from Beck.

264 L. 549, 4. xii. 1792, to Beck.

265 Christian Garve, *Versuche über verschiedene Gegenstände aus der Moral, der Litteratur und dem gesellschaftlichen Leben*, part 1 (Breslau, 1792).

266 Ibid., pp. 111–16.

267 Ibid., p. 112.

268 Ibid., p. 114.

269 Ibid.

270 Garve, *Übersicht der vornehmsten Principien der Sittenlehre, von dem Zeitalter des Aristoteles an bis auf unsre Zeiten: Eine zu dem ersten Theile der übersetzten Ethik des Aristoteles gehörende und aus ihm besonders abgedruckte Abhandlung* (Breslau, 1798). Dedication, pp. 1–4.

271 Ibid., p. 3.

272 L. 820, 21. ix. 1798, to Garve.

273 L. 375, 30. viii. 1789, to Jacobi.

274 J. G. Hasse, *Letzte Aeusserungen Kant's von einem seiner Tischgenossen* (Königsberg, 1804).

275 L. 40, 9. v. 1767, to Herder.

276 Ibid.

277 Johann Gottfried Herder, *Ideen zur Philosophie der Geschichte der Menschheit,* part 1 (Riga, Leipzig, 1784).

278 R. Haym, *Herder nach seinem Leben und seinen Werken dargestellt,* vol. 1 (Berlin, 1880), p. 41.

279 Herder, *Ideen,* part 2 (Riga, Leipzig, 1785).

280 Cf. J. G. Herder, *Sämmtliche Werke,* ed. Bernhard Suphan, vol. 29 (Berlin, 1889), p. 240 note.

281 Ibid., p. 240.

282 Ibid., p. 241.

283 Herder, *Briefe zur Beförderung der Humanität,* 79th letter, in *Sämmtliche Werke,* vol. 17, p. 404:
"I have had the good fortune to know a philosopher who was my teacher. He in his most vigorous manhood had the gay liveliness of a youth which will, I believe, accompany him into his old age. His forehead, built for thinking, was the seat of indestructible serenity and joy; talk rich in ideas issued from his lips, joking, humor and wit were at his disposal, and his teaching lectures were the most amusing concourse. He examined with as much spirit Leibnitz, Wolff, Baumgarten, and Hume, as he followed the development of physics, the laws of nature as expounded by Kepler and Newton, and as he responded to the writings of Rousseau which were them appearing, his *Emile* and his *Héloïse,* and every new discovery he assessed, and he always returned to the genuine knowledge of nature and to the moral value of man. The history

of man, of peoples, and of nature, mathematics and experience were the founts from which he enlivened his lectures and his conversation; nothing worth knowing left him indifferent, no cabal, no sect, no personal gain, no vain ambition had the least attraction for him as contrasted with the expansion and elucidation of truth. He encouraged and forced one agreeably to think for oneself. Domineering was alien to his nature. This man whom I name with the greatest gratitude and respect is Immanuel Kant." [Tr. by Carl J. Friedrich in *The Philosophy of Kant* (New York: Modern Library, 1949), p. xxii—E. B. A.]

284 Haym, *Herder* (see note 278, above), p. 41: "In the main, albeit with a changing center of gravity, he was and remained a Kantian from the year 1765 on—so as eventually to fight the Kant of 1781 with the thoughts, the merely remixed and recolored thoughts, of the evolving Kant."

285 *Allgemeine Literatur-Zeitung*, 1785, no. 4, and supplement 1, 17a–20b, 21a–22b.

286 Herder to Jacobi, 2.ii.1785. Cf. Herder to Hamann, 14.ii.1785.

287 Cf. Hamann to Herder, 8.v.1785.

288 J. G. Herder, *Christliche Schriften*, 1st–5th collection (Riga, 1794–98).

289 *Über die Frage: Ob nicht bei den Studirenden, welche sich dem Predigtamt widmen, das Beziehen der hohen Schulen als eine Nothwendigkeit ganz abzuschneiden? dagegen eine Veranstaltung zu machen sei, den hiezu erforderlichen gnugsamen Unterricht selbigen durch eine beym Gymnasio hierzu zu machende Einrichtung geben zu lassen? ein Pflichtmässig erstattetes Gutachten. Sämmtliche Werke*, vol. 30, pp. 488–95, 492.

290 *Verstand und Erfahrung: Eine Metakritik zur Kritik der reinen Vernunft*, part 1 (Leipzig, 1799). *Vernunft und Sprache: Eine Metakritik zur Kritik der reinen Vernunft. Mit einer Zugabe, betreffend ein kritisches Tribunal aller Facultäten, Regierungen und Geschäfte*, part 2 (Leipzig, 1799).

291 Herder, *Kalligone* (Leipzig, 1800).

292 *Metakritik*. In *Sämmtliche Werke*, vol. 21, p. 8.

293 Ibid., p. 9.

294 Ibid.

295 Ibid., pp. 3–7.

296 Quoted from Haym (see note 278, above), vol. 2, p. 687.

297 Unwittingly and quite unwillingly, Kant had become involved in

the controversies that focused now on the religious views of Lessing, now on Spinoza's pantheism, now on rationalism—arguments summed up today under the name of "the debate on pantheism." (Cf. *Die Hauptschriften zum Pantheismusstreit zwischen Jacobi und Mendelssohn,* ed. Heinrich Scholz [Berlin, 1916], in *Neudrucke seltener philosophischer Werke,* publ. by the Kantgesellschaft, vol. 6.)

298 In 1789, in Vilna, Georg Forster read Kant's essays 48 and 49, published in *Berliner Monatsschrift* in November 1785 and January 1786. The essays satisfied his curiosity about nature on a side from which, he wrote, "my practical endeavors as a naturalist kept me far removed," and they evoked in him a train of thoughts "which vividly and agreeably occupied me for some time" (cf. *Etwas über die Menschenracen,* in Georg Forster, *Sämmtliche Schriften,* vol. 4 [Leipzig, 1843], part 1, p. 281). Since in Vilna, moreover, reading and writing had to "take the place of an association with thinkers" (ibid., p. 280), Forster did not let the year end before publishing an essay, *Noch etwas über die Menschenracen,* in *Der Teutsche Merkur,* 1786, 4th quarter, 57–86, 150–66. He began by considering the relationship of principle and observation and went on to touch upon a loose sequence of Kantian concepts.

299 Benjamin Constant, *Des réactions politiques,* Paris, An V (22. ix. 1796–21. ix. 1797).

300 The book's eighth chapter is entitled "Des principes" (pp. 116–27). According to Constant, a principle is the general result of a number of given particulars ("Un principe est le résultat général d'un certain nombre de faits particuliers," ibid., p. 64). If these are basic data (*données premières*), their result is a universal or fundamental principle (*principe universel*); if they are combinations of secondary data, their result is a connecting or mediating principle (*principe intermédiaire*). As the basic data affect all data in general, so do the fundamental principles affect the mediating ones. Indeed, the latter are really nothing but the means to apply those basic principles in a manner appropriate to the particular combinations.

An example from ethics shows this clearly, according to Constant. Telling the truth is one fundamental principle of ethics; but he who carries it into society in isolation from its connecting principles is said to make society impossible and to lapse into grave aporias. "We have proof of this in the very direct conclusions drawn from the principle by a German philosopher who goes so far as to call it a crime to lie to a murderer who asks us whether our friend, whom he is pursuing, has not taken refuge in our house." (Quoted from the German translation of Constant's book, *Von den politischen Gegenwirkungen*, publ. in the periodical *Frankreich im Jahre 1797: Aus den Briefen Deutscher Männer in Paris*, vol. 2, p. 123.)

By his "German philosopher," Constant did mean Kant rather than J. D. Michaelis, a theologian of Göttingen who had "expounded this curious view even earlier" (ibid., 123 note). In Kant's own works we cannot find the example, although we do find a similar one (37: VI, 431). Kant nonetheless accepted the challenge and, in his retort (63), turned Michaelis's example into an illustrative model whose absurd consequences he took upon himself.

301 L. 205 (see note 128, above).
302 94: XXI, 478. 94: XXII, 260.
303 L. 375 (see note 273, above).
304 L. 205 (see note 14, above).
305 L. 40, 9. v. 1767, to Herder.
306 L. 375 (see note 273, above).
307 Ibid.
308 Ibid.
309 Ibid.
310 Herder, *Ideen* (see note 277, above), part 2; *Sämmtliche Werke*, vol. 13, p. 383.
311 Ibid., p. 341.
312 Ibid., pp. 345–46.
313 Constant acknowledges the need for absolute principles to keep accidentality within bounds; but for their unavoidable connection with the accidental circumstances of history he seeks to relativize them after all, by principles of mediation. Kant affirms the idea of mediation but rejects its application to the "entirely" (63: VIII, 429) unconditional duty of truthfulness. His purely formal reflections are logically unassailable. In such mediation, he says, the absolute loses its absoluteness; where it must submit to any considerations it is already conditional. It cannot tolerate an "if." Concerning truthfulness, therefore, nothing mediative can be "inserted" (63: VIII, 428) beside the basic principle: whenever statements cannot be avoided, truthfulness in them is an absolute duty. To insert mediations anyway is to violate "the principle of law with respect to

all inescapable necessary statements" (63: VIII, 429) and thus to shake the credibility of the foundation of all legal contracts. When Constant, in considering possible consequences, doubts the absolute duty of truthfulness, he does so only, in Kant's view, because he fails to think the consequences through to the end. But since all particular cases take their departure from the end, it is always the principle as well. To harm it is to harm the source of all possible consequences even if the harm should not appear in all the consequences.

Kant thus aims at a different principle of reflection. It is not to reflect toward the historic circumstances of a particular case, but from that case toward the suprahistoric principle. Kant sees this in the categorical imperative, which has the pure intent of any act in mind and at the same time its extreme consequence for the principle. In this sense alone is Kant an ethicist of responsibility.

Kant does not name the hostile power that is at work in Constant, but it can be felt in the polemic. It is the politician's way of thinking—the thought of one who, starting from whatever is historically given and seeking to limit his own responsibility, will prudently tackle the problems of each particular situation and make a principle of adjusting his principles to the situation. If we assume that he is a man of good will, we find him claiming only the right to be arbitrary on the ground of respectable arguments. Kant names this very consequence of such thinking in the title of of his reply: "On a supposed right to lie from altruistic motives." Inevitably, the supponent will fall prey to chance even though this is just what Constant wants to keep from happening.

Should his political ethos really become a universal principle, however—without the tacit presumption of good will—the result would be Machiavellianism. We are not encountering Constant's reflections in an evil man, in his case, but their principle exposes them to political evil. Indeed, the question is in what measure they are not evil itself.

314 L. 40 (see note 305, above).
315 *Berlinische Monatsschrift,* vol. 28 (1796), pp. 145–49.
316 Ibid., pp. 368–70.

Chapter 7

1 L. 13, 28. x. 1759, to Lindner. For the figures cf. Arnoldt (see note 277), vol. 4, 319 ff.; 5, 173 ff.

2 *Georg Friedrich Meiers ordentlichen Lehrers der Weltweisheit und der berlinischen Akademie der Wissenschaften Mitgliedes Auszug aus der Vernunftlehre. Mit Königl. Poln. und Kurfürstl. Sächs. allergnädigsten Freiheiten* (Halle, 1752).

3 Ibid., §499.

4 Ibid., §500 ff.

5 Ibid., §512.

6 Ibid., §511.

7 Ibid., §513.

8 *Immanuel Kants Logik ein Handbuch zu Vorlesungen* (Königsberg, 1800).

9 Meier (see note 2, above), §513.

10 Ibid., §514–17.

11 118: XXIV, 490. 117: XXIV, 296.

12 Borowski (see chap. 6, note 1, above), p. 159.

13 Cf. 79: XVI, 839; 3442; 846; 3456, and 121: XXIV, 782.

14 The degree to which this can show in the outward structure of the comments is evident in a reflection from the time of 24, on the qualities of God. Invariably and promptly, a *contra* breaks in:
   "Existentia entis originarii: contra Atheistas . . .
   Existentia Intelligentiae summae: contra Deistas . . .
   Existentia personae summae: contra fatalistas . . .
   Immutabilis et impassibilis: contra anthropomorphistas . . .
   Substantialitas: contra spinozam . . .
   qvod sit ens extramundanum: contra stoicos . . .
   Unicitas: contra polytheistas.
   Summa perfectio: contra Manichaeos.
   Infinitudo: contra Anthropomorphistas.
   Omnipraesentia: contra stoicos.
   Omnipotentia. Intelligentia: contra deistas.
   Personalitas: contra deistas . . ." (81: XVII, 337 f.; 3907. Cf. 81: XVII, 338; 3908).

15 Cf. the reflections 3829, 3879, 3912, 4134, 4271, 4616 ff., 4742, 5544, 5548, 6450.

16 Cf. 79: XVI, 419; 2565: "The damage which great men have done by their greatness. It is not good to make an idol unto oneself and to conceive a man as great." There is a reference to this idol in a transcription of the lecture on logic (121: XXIV, 740): "Such an idol that has been exalted for admiration, as Aristotle, for instance, has done extraordinary damage to mankind and always kept it in bondage. For no one believed that this man might ever be sur-

passed; hence one was always merely imitating. The greatness of a man was then injurious to a posterity . . . which did not have the courage to surpass him."

17 Cf. Klaus Reich, "Die Tugend in der Idee: Zur Genese von Kants Ideenlehre," in *Argumentationen; Festschrift für J. König*, ed. H. Delius and G. Patzig (Göttingen, 1964), pp. 208–15.

18 Cf. Hegel, *Über das Wesen der philosophischen Kritik überhaupt, und ihr Verhältnis zum gegenwärtigen Zustand der Philosophie insbesondere. Werke*, Jubiläumsausgabe, vol. 1, pp. 177 ff.

19 Lessing to Jacobi, 18. v. 1779.

20 Karl Vorländer, *Immanuel Kant, der Mann und das Werk*, vol. 1 (Leipzig, 1924), p. 154.

21 Cf. L. 13 (see note 1, above).

22 Ibid.

23 Cf. L. 39, 8. iv. 1766, to Mendelssohn.

24 Cf. L. 29, 10. vii. 1763, to von Knoblauch.

25 Cf. L. 39 (see note 23, above).

26 Handwritten note by Kraus, to Wald's eulogy. Quoted from II, 515.

27 L. 784 (see chap. 6, note 137, above).

28 Cf. L. 303, 11. ix. 1787, to Jakob, and the public statement *An die Herren Buchhändler* (70: XII, 360) of 6 June 1793.

29 L. 70 (see chap. 6, note 208, above).

30 L. 34, 31. xii. 1765, to Lambert.

31 L. 40 (see chap. 6, note 305, above).

32 L. 634, l. vii. 1794, to Beck: "I notice, as I write this, that I do not even sufficiently understand myself . . ."

33 Cf. Gerhard Lehmann, "Kants Lebenskrise," in *Neue Deutsche Hefte*, no. 7 (October 1954), pp. 501–8.

34 Alain, *Lettres à Sergio Solmi sur la philosophie de Kant* (Paris, 1946), p. 8.

Chapter 8

1 Examples: 30: A 235–36/B 294–95, A 395–96, and others.

2 Cf. the first pages of *What Is Orientation in Thinking?* (51: VIII, 133 ff.).

3 30: B xii; B xxiii–xxiv; A 726/B 754, and others.

4 In 30: A 407/B 433 we read that the "entire natural antithetics" of reason preserves us "from the slumber of an imagined conviction."

According to A 757/B 785, controversy is a means to "awaken reason from its sweet dogmatic dreams in order to subject its condition to more careful scrutiny."

5 Kant calls dialectics either the "logic of appearance" (A 61/B 86) or the "critique of dialectical appearance" (A 62/B 86). In the first sense it is a sophistical art that employs inadequate means to lend to statements an appearance of objectivity; in the second, it is a critical resolution of transcendental appearance. Cf. 81: XVIII, 39; 4952. Kant's use of the term remains ambivalent.

6 This is why nothing but self-knowledge enables reason to resolve the antinomies. Inevitably connected with reason at large is only appearance, not deception.

7 Especially in §4, and then developed until §56.

8 As late as 81: XVII, 495; 4284 (dated variously between 1770 and 1775) we read, for instance: "Metaphysics is not science, nor is it scholarliness; it is merely the intellect that knows itself, and thus merely a vindication of common sense and of reason."

9 This concept of science has been clearly developed and distinguished from philosophy time and again by Karl Jaspers. We mention only his most detailed expositions: *Philosophy,* vol. 1 (Chicago, 1969), pp. 174–225. "Philosophie und Wissenschaft," in *Rechenschaft und Ausblick,* 2d ed. (Munich, 1958), pp. 240–59. *Die Idee der Universität für die gegenwärtige Situation entworfen,* by Karl Jaspers and Kurt Rossmann (Berlin, Göttingen, Heidelberg, 1961), pp. 41–61. In all these works (and in others) the concept of science is explicated in the same fashion. It is determined by three indispensable characteristics: (1) Science is methodically attainable and actually attained in being aware of one's method; (2) science advances in the field of the particular, in steps which to the intellect are cogently certain or whose degree of certainty is cogently known to it; (3) within that certainty each step is imitable and therefore universally valid.

The methodical system sought by Jaspers is the universe of the sciences. All single sciences are endlessly open toward the universe; indeed, inconclusiveness is the very mark of science. It makes endless progress by induction in the particular. The break with Kant lies at the point which for Kant is decisive: science is not a whole that can be deductively developed into a systematic structure.

10 81: XVII, 402–3; 4067. Cf. 81: XVII, 631; 4667.

11 *Abr. Gotthelf Kästner's zum Theil noch ungedruckte Sinngedichte*

und Einfälle. 2d collection (Frankfurt and Leipzig, 1800), p. 65, note 60.

12 The fact that for Kant, too, the clash of reason with itself became an awakening factor is attested in a letter to Garve (L. 820, 21. ix. 1798).

13 79: XVI, 70: 1667. Cf. 94: XXI, 155.

14 76: XV, 785; 1500 (Otaheite = Tahiti).

15 Kant considers the question in view of the early age at which students in those days entered the university—mostly between their fifteenth and their seventeenth year. Today, with the step taken up to four years later, he would presumably not raise the question at all.

16 Kant speaks of a threefold tutelage. We grow up in a state of domestic tutelage and are so raised, as children, "as if we should remain minors all our lives—should not think for ourselves but follow the judgments of others, should not choose ourselves but follow examples. . . ."

As adults we stay in a state of civil tutelage. "We are judged under laws we cannot all know, and according to books we would not understand. Our freedom and our property are subject to the arbitrary will of the very power that exists only in order to preserve freedom, and only to make it unanimous by means of the law. This has so impaired our independence that we could not govern ourselves even if that coercion were to cease" (899).

Finally, we stay in a lifelong state of "pious" tutelage. "Others, who understand the language of the sacred documents, tell us what we are to believe; we ourselves have no judgment. The place of our natural conscience is taken by an artificial one that goes by the verdict of the scholars" (899). Morality is replaced by observances.

The premise of any improvement in these conditions is freedom, "freedom of education, civil liberty, and freedom of religion" (899). This must be the goal of our efforts, in negative education, negative legislation, and negative religion.

In negative education the child is presumed to be good and allowed to grow according to his talents, without intervention and without compulsion. Negative legislation does no more than enable all to be free, under laws which are drawn immediately from reason. A negative religion drops all canons and accepts only the precepts of reason, required for the simple concept of a way of life pleasing to God.

17 81: XVIII, 605; 6309: "Freedom of thought alone can make sincere human beings. . . ."

18 Against this passage from *Education* (69: IX, 490) stands the following (75: XV, 540; 1225): "A white lie can be excused (on account of the frailty of human nature), but it cannot be justified."

19 L. 375, 30. viii. 1789, to Jacobi.

20 81: XVIII, 293; 5645: "Between dogmatism and skepticism, the median and solely lawful way of thinking is criticism."

21 62: VIII, 416. Cf. 62: VIII, 415.

22 Cf. 30: A 424/B 451 and 31: IV, 271.

23 Martin Heidegger, *Die Frage nach dem Ding* (Tübingen, 1962), p. 93. (English: *What Is a Thing?* Trans. W. B. Barton, Jr. and Vera Deutsch [Chicago: Regnery, 1968].)

24 Cf. Heidegger, "Was heisst 'Kritik' bei Kant?" in *Die Frage nach dem Ding*, pp. 92 ff.

25 The expression goes back to a line of Hamann's: "Nothing but the infernal journey of self-cognition can blaze our trail to deification." (Johann Georg Hamann, *Sämmtliche Werke*, ed. Josef Nadler [Vienna, 1949–], vol. 2, p. 164.)

Kant uses the expression in 37: VI, 441 and in 38: VII, 55—the first time in the context of moral self-knowledge, the second time, in that of the religious one. In neither case does it refer to the self-knowledge of reason; and yet, to Kant the problematics of self-knowledge has borne fruit, primarily in the problem of critique. Critique is the autognosis of reason.

26 L. 205, 7. viii. 1783, to Garve.

27 30: A 58/B 82 and 67: IX, 50.

28 Ibid.

29 44: VIII, 35 and 39: VII, 229.

30 81: XVIII, 69; 5036. Cf. 81: XVIII, 62–63; 5019.

31 In 58, Kant describes the mystical attempts to immerse oneself in absolute tranquillity. He comments: "All for the sole purpose that men might finally have an eternal tranquillity to enjoy after all, which would then make out their supposedly blissful end of all things—a concept, in truth, with which their intellect leaves them and all thinking comes to an end" (58: VIII, 335–36).

32 Cf. the section on absolute contentment in *Anthropology* (39: VII, 235).

33 Achenwall said in his *Iuris naturalis pars posterior*, §102 (xix, 373): "Ad securitatem pertinet TRANQUILLITAS, status a metu violentiae

vacuus." Kant's skeptical comment: "What goes on may be tranquil and yet very unjust" (83: XIX, 373; 7433).

34 One would have to count as philosophical chiliasm the many pasages in which Kant speaks of the imminent conclusion of eternal peace in metaphysics. As the very title shows, the "Annunciation" is the treatise of this chiliasm. Now and then Kant succumbs to the peril of confusing transcendental chiliasm with empirical chiliasm and then postulating perfectibility in time (cf. 81: XVII, 625–26; 4651).

Kant calls political chiliasm a chiliasm of reason if it asserts nothing but constant progress to better things by way of legality (38: VII, 81), and if it knows that the idea of this progress "can come to further" the progress itself and "is thus nothing less than romantical" (43: VIII, 27). It aims at "the condition of a perpetual peace based upon a league of nations as a world republic" (36: VI, 34). One can say of it that "the world is still young. . . . Man will yet achieve his destiny. . . ." (75: XV, 621; 1423). Cf. 76: XV, 784, 789; 1499, 1501.

A chiliasm that aims at the "complete moral improvement of the whole human race" (36: VI, 34) is what Kant calls a theological chiliasm.

35 A comprehensive and exhaustive compilation of the several elements of this image as well as all passages referring to it in *Critique of Pure Reason* can be found in Vaihinger's *Kommentar zu Kants Kritik der reinen Vernunft,* vol. 1 (Stuttgart, 1881), pp. 107–16.

Chapter 9

1 Cf. 34: V, 12, which says that the total critique of all rational faculties lays the ground "for a systematic, theoretical as well as practical philosophy as a science." At the end of 34 (V, 163) Kant calls science "the narrow gate leading to the doctrine of wisdom."

2 83: XIX, 288; 7217: "Freedom is the greatest good and the greatest evil. Hence the rules of freedom must be the most important."

3 83: XIX, 294; 7251: "The regulative principle of freedom: that it should only not conflict with itself."

4 Cf. 32: IV, 408, where Kant says that the moral law "is of such extensive significance that it must apply not merely to humans but

to all rational beings in general, not merely under accidental conditions and with exceptions, but as flatly necessary." Cf. ibid., 410, 411–12, and 425. Each time, Kant says sharply that the moral law is not an anthropological law. It is not a law of the *ratio humana,* which is merely relative and in need of supplementation.

5 The following interpretation of the categorical imperative may not be immediately and literally justifiable by Kant's own statements; but it can be justified by Kantian thought.

6 32: IV, 402, 403, 421, 429, 434, 436, 437, 438, 439.

7 This struggle is shown in *Religion* (36).

8 Goethe to J. G. and C. Herder, 7. vi. 1793: "On the other hand, even Kant, having spent a long lifetime cleansing his philosophical mantle of a good many grubby prejudices, has wickedly sullied it with the stain of radical evil in order to lure Christians, too, to kiss the hem" (quoted from Gedenkausgabe, ed. Ernst Beutler, vol. 19 [Zurich, 1949], p. 213).

9 Schiller, Säkularausgabe, vol. 11, pp. 221 ff.

10 Ibid., vol. 1, p. 268.

11 Ibid., vol. 11, p. 217.

12 Kant did not always see radical evil in the reversal of the qualifying relationships. In 75: XV, 542; 1233, he says that "radical evil is falseness. . . . " In 85: XIX, 640; 8096, he resumes the search for it: it cannot be either envy—for this is a means of perfection—or falseness, or ever the lie; for if this, as mendacity, were innate in man, all hope would have to be abandoned. Radical evil is "falseness in the judgment of our selves," the unwillingness to know ourselves. And in 1798, several years after the publication of 36, we read in 85: XIX, 646; 8103, that "the insincerity of men is the radical evil."

  For an interpretation of the concept of radical evil in 36, see Karl Jaspers, "Das radikal Böse bei Kant," in *Rechenschaft und Ausblick,* 2d ed. (Munich, 1958), pp. 107 ff.

13 On the concept of paganism cf. 38: VII, 50. Paganism consists in "presenting the external (nonessential) side of religion as essential." Ecclesiastic faith and the faith in revelation are "sheer paganism" when they view their statutes as the absolute fundament of faith. Where the visible church recognizes itself as a mere vehicle of the invisible one, it has no more than "a certain admixture of paganism." In Kant's sense, "pagan" can be defined as the faith which does not originate in reason.

Chapter 10

1   35: V, 236: "Beauty is the form of the purposiveness of an object if it is perceived in the object without conception of a purpose."

2   81: XVIII, 77; 5065: "I have a very high opinion of the genius of the old. We act in a body, which not only makes genius dispensible (as well as valor and skill at arms), but prevents it."

3   75: XV, 414; 933: "Spirit is not a special talent but an animating principium of all talents."

4   75: XV, 391–92; 896. 75: XV, 415; 936.

5   75: XV, 356; 806. 75: XV, 370; 829. 76: XV, 824; 1509.

6   76: XV, 825; 1509. 75: XV, 340–41; 778.

7   76: XV, 827; 1510: "The genius bordering on madness is vigor of imagination without judgment." Cf. 75: XV, 361; 812.

8   35: V, 313: One can, "in a work that is to be a work of the fine arts, often perceive genius without taste, and in another, taste without genius."

9   Ibid.

10   35: V, 242–43: "Everything stiffly regular (approaching mathematical regularity) has the quality of tastelessness: that its contemplation affords no longer entertainment, but will—unless expressly intended for cognition, or for a definite practical purpose—cause boredom."

11   75: XV, 361; 812: "A production without genius is toil."

12   75: XV, 409; 922: "Required for all this are, first, a mechanism of talent, and above that, finally, genius."

13   A further form of antagonism, and of the manner in which it is carried to unity, might be demonstrated with respect to the sublime. We dispense with a presentation, but it might be shown that there, too, the well-known basic structures recur in a new variation.

Chapter 11

1   34: V, 120: "The requisite of the possibility of any use of reason—namely, that its principles and assertions must not contradict one another . . . —is the condition for having reason at all."

2   75: XV, 618; 1420: "Whatever is to maintain itself must have a community of directions, and different purposes must be connected

in accordance with an idea which, even though not intended, does constitute the outcome in which all their conflicting tendencies can be united."

3 Cf. the general and the special introduction in Vaihinger's *Kommentar* (see chap. 8, note 35, above), vol. 1, pp. 1–70.

REGISTER OF KANT'S WORKS

1 Gedanken von der wahren Schätzung der lebendigen Kräfte und Beurteilung der Beweise, deren sich Herr von Leibniz und andere Mechaniker in dieser Streitsache bedient haben, nebst einigen vorhergehenden Betrachtungen, welche die Kraft der Körper überhaupt betreffen.

English: "Thoughts on the True Estimation of Living Forces" (excerpts), in *Kant's Inaugural Dissertation and Early Writings on Space*. Trans. John Handyside. Chicago: Open Court, 1929.

2 Untersuchung der Frage, ob die Erde in ihrer Umdrehung um die Achse, wodurch sie die Abwechselung des Tages und der Nacht hervorbringt, einige Veränderung seit den ersten Zeiten ihres Ursprungs erlitten habe und woraus man sich ihrer versichern könne, welche von der Königl. Akademie der Wissenschaften zu Berlin zum Preise für das jetztlaufende Jahr aufgegeben worden.

E: "Essay on the Retardation of the Rotation of the Earth," in 4 E (2).

3 Die Frage, ob die Erde veralte, physikalisch erwogen.

4 Allgemeine Naturgeschichte und Theorie des Himmels oder Versuch von der Verfassung und dem mechanischen Ursprunge des ganzen Weltgebäudes, nach Newtonischen Grundsätzen abgehandelt.

E: (1) *Universal Natural History and Theory of the Heavens*. Trans. W. Hastie; new intro. by Milton K. Munitz. Ann Arbor: University of Michigan Press, 1969.

(2) *Kant's Cosmogony, as in His Essay on the Retardation of the Rotation of the Earth and His Natural History and Theory of the Heavens*. Trans. Hastie; rev. and ed. with an intro. and appendix by Willy Ley. New York: Greenwood, 1968.

5 Meditationum quarundam de igne succincta delineatio.

6 Principiorum primorum cognitionis metaphysicae nova dilucidatio.

E: Appendix (pp. 213–52) to *Kant's Conception of God; a Critical Exposition of its Metaphysical Development together with a Translation of the Nova Dilucidatio*, by F. E. England; foreword by G. Dawes Hicks. London: Allen & Unwin, 1927.

7 Von den Ursachen der Erderschütterungen bei Gelegenheit des Unglücks, welches die westlichen Länder von Europa gegen das Ende des vorigen Jahres betroffen hat.

8 Geschichte und Naturbeschreibung der merkwürdigsten Vorfälle

des Erdbebens, welches an dem Ende des 1755sten Jahres einen großen Teil der Erde erschüttert hat.

9 Fortgesetzte Betrachtung der seit einiger Zeit wahrgenommenen Erderschütterungen.

10 Metaphysicae cum geometria iunctae usus in philosophia naturali, cuius specimen I.continet monadologiam physicam.

11 Neue Anmerkungen zur Erläuterung der Theorie der Winde.

12 Entwurf und Ankündigung eines Collegii der physischen Geographie nebst dem Anhange einer kurzen Betrachtung über die Frage: Ob die Westwinde in unsern Gegenden darum feucht seien, weil sie über ein großes Meer streichen.

13 Neuer Lehrbegriff der Bewegung und Ruhe und der damit verknüpften Folgerungen in den ersten Grunden der Naturwissenschaft.

14 Versuch einiger Betrachtungen über den Optimismus.

15 Gedanken bei dem frühzeitigen Ableben des Herrn Johann Friedrich von Funk.

16 Die falsche Spitzfindigkeit der vier syllogistischen Figuren erwiesen.
E: *Kant's Introduction to Logic and His Essay on the Mistaken Subtilty of the Four Figures.* Trans. Thomas Kingsmill Abbott, with a few notes by Coleridge. New York: Philosophical Library, 1963.

17 Der einzig mögliche Beweisgrund zu einer Demonstration des Daseins Gottes.
E: In *Kant, Selected Pre-critical Writings and Correspondence with Beck.* Trans. with an intro. by G. B. Kerferd and D. W. Walford, with a contribution by P. G. Lucas. New York: Barnes & Noble, 1968.

18 Versuch den Begriff der negativen Größen in die Weltweisheit einzuführen.

19 Beobachtungen über das Gefühl des Schönen und Erhabenen.
E: *Observations on the Feeling of the Beautiful and Sublime.* Trans. John T. Goldthwait. Berkeley: University of California Press, 1960.

20 Versuch über die Krankheiten des Kopfes.

21 Untersuchung über die Deutlichkeit der Grundsätze der natürlichen Theologie und der Moral.
E: "The Distinctness of the Principles of Natural Theology and Morals," in 34 E.

22 Rezension von Silberschlags Schrift: Theorie der am 23. Juli 1762 erschienenen Feuerkugel.

23 Nachricht von der Einrichtung seiner Vorlesungen in dem Winterhalbenjahre von 1765–1766.

24 Träume eines Geistersehers, erläutert durch Träume der Metaphysik.

E: *Dreams of a Spirit Seer, and Other Writings.* Trans. with commentary by John Manolesco. New York: Vantage Press, 1969.

25 Von dem ersten Grunde des Unterschiedes der Gegenden im Raume.

E: (1) "On the First Ground of the Distinction of the Regions in Space," in 1 E.

(2) In 17 E.

26 De mundi sensibilis atque intelligibilis forma et principiis.

E: (1) "The Forms and Principles of the Sensible and Intelligible Worlds," in 1 E.

(2) *Kant's Inaugural Dissertation of 1770.* Trans. with an intro. by W. J. Eckoff. New York: AMS Press, 1970.

(3) In 17 E.

27 Rezension von Moscatis Schrift: Von dem körperlichen wesentlichen Unterschiede zwischen der Struktur der Tiere und Menschen.

28 Von den verschiedenen Rassen der Menschen.

29 Aufsätze, das Philantropin betreffend.

30 Kritik der reinen Vernunft.

E: (1) *Critique of Pure Reason.* Trans. Norman Kemp Smith. New York: St. Martin's Press, 1929, 1952.

(2) Same, trans. F. Max Müller. 2d rev. ed., New York: Anchor paperback.

31 Prolegomena zu einer jeden künftigen Metaphysik, die als Wissenschaft wird auftreten können.

E: (1) *Prolegomena to Any Future Metaphysics.* Trans. Lewis W. Beck. New York: Liberal Arts no. 27, 1951.

(2) Same, trans. Peter G. Lucas. New York: Barnes & Noble, 1954.

32 Grundlegung zur Metaphysik der Sitten.

E: (1) *Foundations of the Metaphysics of Morals.* Trans. L. W. Beck, with critical essays edited by R. P. Wolff. Indianapolis: Bobbs-Merrill, 1969; Liberal Arts no. 113; also in 34 E (1).

(2) *The Moral Law, or Kant's Groundwork of the Metaphysic of*

Morals. Trans. H. J. Paton. New York: Barnes & Noble, 1948, 1967; Harper Torchbooks paperback.

(3) *Kant on the Foundation of Morality: A Modern Version of the "Grundlegung."* Trans. with commentary by Brendan E. A. Liddell. Bloomington: Indiana University Press, 1970.

33 Metaphysische Anfangsgründe der Naturwissenschaft.

E: *Metaphysical Foundations of Natural Science.* Trans. with intro. and essay by James Ellington. Liberal Arts no. 108, 1970.

34 Kritik der praktischen Vernunft.

E: *Critique of Practical Reason and Other Writings in Moral Philosophy.* Trans. and edited with intro. by L. W. Beck. Chicago: University of Chicago Press, 1949.

35 Kritik der Urteilskraft.

E: *Critique of Judgment.* Trans. J. H. Bernard. New York: Hafner, 1951.

36 Die Religion innerhalb der Grenzen der bloßen Vernunft.

E: *Religion within the Limits of Reason Alone.* Trans. Theodore M. Greene and Hoyt H. Hudson, with a new essay, "The Ethical Significance," by J. R. Silber. 2d ed. La Salle, Ill.: Open Court, 1960; Harper Torchbooks paperback.

37 Die Metaphysik der Sitten.

E: Part I ("Rechtslehre"), *The Metaphysical Elements of Justice.* Trans. with intro. by John Ladd. Liberal Arts no. 72, 1965.

Part II ("Tugendlehre"), *The Doctrine of Virtue.* Trans. with intro. and notes by Mary Gregor; foreword by H. J. Paton. Harper Torchbooks, 1964; Philadelphia: University of Pennsylvania Press, 1972.

38 Der Streit der Fakultäten.

E: In Hans Reiss, *Kant's Political Writings.* Trans. H. B. Nisbet. Cambridge University Press, 1970.

39 Anthropologie in pragmatischer Hinsicht.

40 Anzeige des Lambert'schen Briefwechsels.

41 Nachricht an Ärzte.

42 Rezension vom Schulz's Versuch einer Anleitung zur Sittenlehre für alle Menschen, ohne Unterschied der Religion, nebst einem Anhange von den Todesstrafen.

43 Idee zu einer allgemeinen Geschichte in weltbürgerlicher Absicht.

E: (1) In *Kant on History,* ed. with intro. by L. W. Beck; trans. L. W. Beck, R. E. Anchor, and Emile Fackenheim. Liberal Arts no. 162, 1963.

INDEX OF PERSONS
OTHER THAN KANT

INDEX OF WORKS BY AUTHORS
OTHER THAN KANT

INDEX OF WORKS BY KANT

Hans Saner studied philosophy, psychology, and Germanic and Romance languages in Lausanne and Basel. Among his philosophical teachers were Karl Jaspers, Hans Barth, Eugen Fink, Karl Löwith, and H. A. Salmony. Dr. Saner is the author of *Karl Jaspers* and has contributed numerous articles to scholarly publications.